WILD PHILLY

WILD

PHILLY

Mike Weilbacher

EXPLORE THE AMAZING NATURE IN AND AROUND PHILADELPHIA

TIMBER PRESS • PORTLAND, OR

Lovingly dedicated to Gari Julius Weilbacher,
the wildest Philadelphian I know and the
keystone species in our family's ecosystem,
and to our daughters, Hannah Zoe and Molly.
I look forward to many more walks with all of them.

Published in 2023 by Timber Press, Inc.,
a subsidiary of Workman Publishing Co., Inc.,
a subsidiary of Hachette Book Group, Inc.
1290 Avenue of the Americas
New York, NY 10104

timberpress.com

Printed in China on paper from responsible sources
Layout by Sarah Crumb, based on a series design by Anna Eshelman
Cover design and illustration by Melissa McFeeters

ISBN 978-1-64326-104-1
A catalog record for this book is available from the Library of Congress.

CONTENTS

INTRODUCTION

A peregrine falcon leaps from its ledge on a Manayunk church steeple and plucks a hapless pigeon out of the sky above the Schuylkill River. A coyote quietly shuffles down Domino Lane only a stone's throw from the garden of radio towers on the city's highest spot. A bald eagle launches itself from a massive nest perched high atop a pine tree, with jumbo jets roaring not far away. A biblical number of toads swarm across Port Royal Avenue on a rainy spring night to partake in an orgy in the abandoned reservoir across the road. A red-tailed hawk nests on a ledge at the Franklin Institute, feasting on squirrels it finds along the Ben Franklin Parkway.

All of this—and more—happens within the city limits of Philadelphia. Surprise! America's sixth largest city is one wild place, blessed with an abundance of nature. Though far better known for Ben Franklin and Betsy Ross, cheesesteaks and hoagies, M. Night Shyamalan and Patti LaBelle, opinionated sports fans and a funny brogue—*wooder ice* and *downa shore*, for two—William Penn's proposed "greene Country Towne" has become exactly that.

This green city is chockablock with an entire rainbow of nature: red foxes, orange monarch butterflies, yellow-bellied sapsuckers, green frogs, great blue herons, purple martins. And every so often, a black bear wanders through the city. And when it does, all hell breaks loose: it's the big story on Action News.

Welcome to *Wild Philly*, a guidebook celebrating the nature of the Philadelphia region. A series of introductory chapters sets the stage for the nature of Philadelphia. We'll explore why William Penn founded the city between two rivers, introduce the ecological and geological forces that define the region, and learn how the Lenape, the region's first people, were themselves active forces in shaping the landscape in surprising ways. We'll learn about the rich history of natural exploration in the area, as John James

▶ A red-tailed hawk alights atop a Philadelphia Museum of Art griffin.

◀ The bald eagle, America's symbol, had once vanished from Wild Philly. Today the species nests in several places in the city.

▶ An abandoned coal-fired power plant along the Delaware River with clear evidence of beavers living nearby.

Audubon started his career in, where else, Audubon, Pennsylvania, and artist Charles Willson Peale invented the diorama in America's first natural history museum, located in Independence Hall. We'll consider threats to Wild Philly, including invasive species and climate change, then meet people working every day to protect and preserve this nature. And this guidebook offers twenty-five ways you can join in this important work, including becoming a citizen scientist.

Next we'll turn to 101 of the coolest wild inhabitants of Philadelphia and its nearby environs, from lowly ferns you can easily identify to that bald eagle nesting in Tinicum Marsh. The list has been carefully curated with the help of naturalists from across the region.

The final section describes twenty-five of the best nature walks you and your family can take in and around Philadelphia to find those 101 species—

▲ Modern Philadelphia, the city between two rivers. As water quality in the Schuylkill River (foreground) has improved, wildlife has returned.

◀ Spring wildflowers bloom at Bowman's Hill Wildflower Preserve in New Hope.

and at the right time of year to walk them. Amble Valley Forge National Historical Park in the early summer to enjoy the mountain laurel in bloom, then catch the goldenrods ablaze at the Pennypack Preserve in the fall. Sit in a cozy century-old Abington cabin with a cup of hot cocoa to watch chickadees and cardinals feed on a snowy morning, then head up to Bowman's Hill Wildflower Preserve in April to catch nature's quickly fleeting flower show.

The book also has a few extra-credit field trips a little farther afield as well. Though there is plenty of nature in Wild Philly, Philadelphians flock by the score to Cape May Point in New Jersey to witness the migration of monarch butterflies, up north to Hawk Mountain to gaze at the uncountable hawks soaring overhead, to the Pine Barrens to watch carnivorous plants snare and eat hapless insects, and to Delaware Bay to search for exhausted red knots, small shorebirds that land along the shoreline to engorge

themselves on horseshoe crab eggs—the bird's migration exquisitely timed to match the crab's. If you are a Philadelphian in love with nature, there's no question you'll want to take these trips.

Two important notes about these trips. First, I defined the Philadelphia region by the relatively standard one often used by both the media and government, as the five counties in southeastern Pennsylvania (Philadelphia, Bucks, Montgomery, Delaware, and Chester) plus the three New Jersey counties across the Delaware River (Camden, Gloucester, and Burlington). With apologies, other areas with remarkable sites and species outside this geographic region were omitted.

In addition, a different author would likely have selected a different mix of twenty-five hikes. A Naturalist Advisory Team of eight biologists, naturalists, and environmental educators from across the region had continuous input into both the 101 species and the twenty-five field trips, and I am deeply indebted to them for their help. Their names are listed in the back of the book. As a naturalist who has walked this region for 40 years, I offered those trips I thought gave you the greatest variety of habitats, the most interesting vistas, and the most diversity of species. If I missed your favorite walk, please accept my apologies immediately.

That said, let's start our adventure!

▲ Walkers enjoy Forbidden Drive in the Wissahickon Valley.

◄ Carnivorous plants like this pitcher plant inhabit cedar bogs in the Pine Barrens.

► Birdwatchers take in the hawk migration at Cape May Point.

WILD PHILLY

Our "Greene Country Towne"

Philadelphia is a city of American firsts: the nation's first hospital, public school, volunteer fire department, printed treatise against slavery, paper mill, and asylum for treating mental illness. The Swedes built America's first log cabins along the Delaware River in the early seventeenth century, and the city's Quakers later built America's first brick houses. A hot-bed of natural history and science, Philadelphia is also the home of America's first natural history museum, botanical garden, zoo, and science institution, the American Philosophical Society.

We're also America's first planned city, the first and only one designed by Quakers. Anchored by the five public squares that are America's first parks, Philly was designed by surveyor Thomas Holme and William Penn himself, whom architecture critic Inga Saffron notes "was, at his core, a real estate developer—among America's first."

But why is Philadelphia located where it is? How did nature fit into Penn's plans, and what was the land like when Penn first sailed up the Delaware on the *Welcome* in October 1682?

Though the land was inhabited by the Lenape for millennia, the colony that would be called Pennsylvania was founded a year earlier, in 1681, when King Charles II gave William Penn a charter for more than 45,000 square miles of land in the New World, settling the king's debts to his father, Sir Admiral William Penn. Wanting a holy experiment where Friends (as the Quakers are known) and others could practice religious freedom—also an American first—Penn originally christened his new holdings Sylvania after its forests. It was King Charles who renamed it Pennsylvania, Penn's Woods, in honor of the elder Penn.

"Always Be Wholesome"

When he founded Philadelphia, William Penn wrote as a key organizing principle for the city that it would be a "greene Country Towne which will never be burnt and always be wholesome." It was less that Penn was a

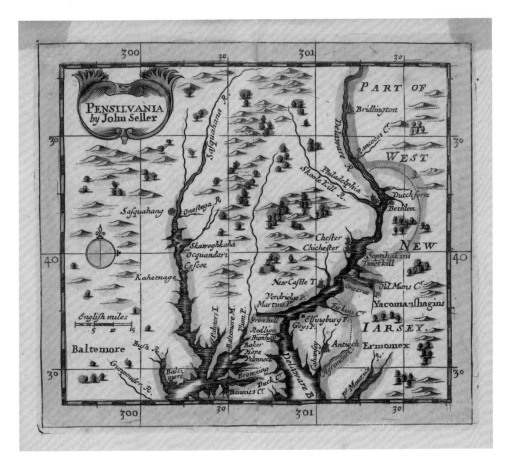

▲ A map of "Pensilvania" in 1690, by British cartographer John Seller. By then, there were already many European place names along the Delaware (Philadelphia, Chester, New Castle), but a strong presence of Native American place names along the Susquehanna River and in "West New Iarsey." Note the spelling of "Skoole Kill" River.

nature-loving visionary with a grand notion of open space and more that he was a smart and surprisingly practical man reacting to two seminal events from his native London: the Great Plague of 1665 and the Great Fire only one year later. The former killed perhaps 100,000 Londoners, some 7600 in its first week alone, and the latter swept through the wooden city, burning more than 400 acres, more than 13,000 homes, and 87 of the city's 109 churches. Then a young man in his twenties, these events would have been seared in Penn's memory.

For Penn, Philadelphia was a chance to right London's wrongs. One significant change from London was that in Philadelphia homes would be spaced far apart on wide boulevards. He was practicing a seventeenth-century form of social distancing to combat both fire and plague. He also advocated for wide lots "so there may be ground on each side for Gardens or Orchards, or feilds [sic]."

In 1681, Penn sent a team of commissioners across the Atlantic to seek out a site for his planned city and negotiate purchases with the Lenape and other settlers. He told his team that the river had to be navigable, and the bank needed to be "high, dry and healthy," not a marshy lowland that would breed diseases like malaria (literally "bad air"). Equally important, low-lying

LANDING OF PENN. DOCK CREEK

sites would prove difficult moorage for ships that needed to load and unload both cargo and immigrants for the city. It should also be open land free of other inhabitants, and if people were living there, perhaps they would agree to trade for land elsewhere.

But when the commissioners arrived and began scouting the new territory, they did not find unsettled land along the river. In fact, Swedes and Finns had been inhabiting what they called New Swedeland for 50 years already. The commissioners' first choice was a settlement called Upland, at the site of today's Chester, but they were unable to purchase that site.

So the commissioners moved upriver, where they found a few hundred farmers, trappers, and traders strung out along both the Delaware and Schuylkill Rivers, the settlements then extending along the Delaware as far as today's Trenton. Among the most attractive sites (spoiler alert) was the narrow neck of land at the junction of the Delaware and the Schuylkill. The rivers were both navigable, at least for small vessels; "the bank was bold and high," said an 1851 biography of Penn, "the air pure and wholesome, the neighboring lands were free from swamp, clay for making into brick was found on the spot, and immense quarries of good stone abounded within a few miles."

The commissioners first purchased 300 riverside acres from the Swedish Swanson brothers in today's Queen Village, where the now-filled Hollander Creek once emptied into the Delaware. Near today's Gloria Dei Church, the Swansons called this site Wicaco, the Lenape name for their former settlement there, an anglicized and shortened corruption of a Lenape phrase roughly meaning "the place of pine trees at the head of a creek." This history

▲ William Penn's arrival in Philadelphia in 1682, as depicted by William L. Bretton in 1833. Penn stands in the center of a smaller boat, as his *Welcome* remained anchored in today's Chester. Note even then the presence of an inn where Dock Creek meets the Delaware River and the watchful Lenape in the foreground.

is captured by the church's address on Swanson Street. Other Swedes ultimately sold (the Swedes pointedly say "surrendered") some 1200 acres for the new city. While not the 10,000 acres Penn originally hoped for, it was a start.

"A Lush American Eden"

"While Penn envisioned Philadelphia as a lush American Eden," wrote Inga Saffron, he also "recognized that the inclusion of open space could help make his urban experiment more appealing to buyers." So with his surveyor Thomas Holme, Penn laid out the city with High Street running between and connecting the two rivers and Broad Street dividing the city vertically. Both streets were more than 100 feet wide, wider than any London boulevard at the time.

With the city in four quadrants, they designed the now-iconic five town squares, one in each quadrant with a fifth in the middle where Broad meets High. Penn had envisioned the city's public buildings lining the center square and facing it, which did not happen.

While the new city's gridded river-to-river map was widely circulated, new settlers had other ideas. "Early development," notes architecture critic and Philadelphia writer Michael J. Lewis, "huddled with near-medieval intensity along the Delaware River, where the city's economic life was based." They were not spreading out as Penn hoped. Tour guide and author Jim Murphy adds that settlers "developed their own system of alleys or cartways," like the frequently visited Elfreth's Alley, America's oldest intact street. "By 1698," Murphy added, "nine lanes ran from Front to Second Street, thwarting Penn's plan and violating his dream of a green country town."

▼ William Penn's iconic layout of the new city, with five squares and generous avenues.

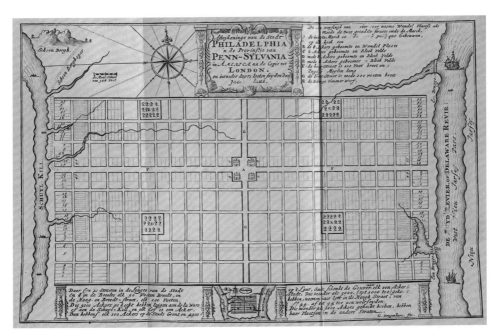

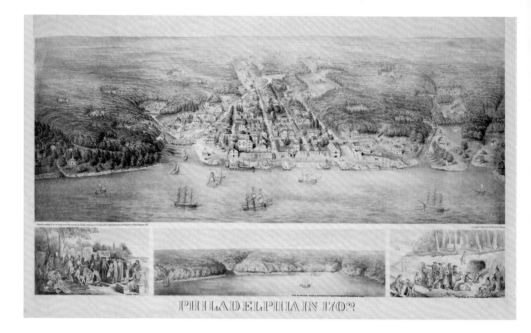

PHILADELPHIA IN 1702

In 1698, more than 15 years into this holy experiment, a young British Quaker named Gabriel Thomas offered in his "Account of the Country of Pensilvania" this assessment of the new city: "Since [its founding], the industrious inhabitants have built a noble and beautiful city . . . which contains above two thousand houses, all inhabited; and mostly stately, and of brick generally three stories high." Commenting further, Thomas seems to sarcastically poke at two professions. "Of Lawyers and Physicians, I shall say nothing," he wrote, "because this countrey [sic] is very peaceable and Healthy; long may it so continue and never have occasion for the Tongue of the one nor the pen of the other, both equally destructive of Men's Estates and Lives." Even then the Philadelphia lawyer was famous.

By 1700, more than 5000 people called Philadelphia home, and the city continued growing, with 13,000 residents in 1740 and 28,500 in 1790. By the end of that century, Philadelphia was not only the American capital, but the most populous city in the new country and the second largest city in the English-speaking world after London.

> ▲ An intriguing 1702 aerial sketch of the growing city shows, among many things, "caves" along the Delaware, an "Indian camp" in South Philly, and Dock Creek, a stream flowing from a "Duck Pond" into the Delaware below Walnut Street. Dock Creek later became a pollution concern for Ben Franklin.

"Few Rivers of America Have More"

In his ship's log of 1634, British Captain Thomas Yong wrote that the Delaware "aboundeth with beavers, otters, and other meaner furs. . . . I think few rivers of America have more . . . the quantity of fowle [sic] is so great as hardly can be believed. Of fish here is plenty, but especially sturgeon." Penn himself noted the sturgeon. When he first sailed up the Delaware in 1682, he wrote of 6-inch oysters in the river "too big to be eaten whole" and large sturgeon that "played in the river all summer."

► A 1777 map of Philadelphia beautifully rendered for the British shows the city still hugging the river, with Passyunk and Moyamensing as separate townships. Note the network of islands where the Delaware and Schuylkill meet, which have since been filled in, and the hills around the "Faire Mount," the area of the Philadelphia Museum of Art.

Writing to the Earl of Arran in 1684, Penn described the animal life of his territory, in the curious archaic spelling of that era: "the food the woods yeild is your Elk, deer, Raccoons, Beaver, Rabbets, Turkey, Phesants, heathbirds [quail?], Pigeons [passenger pigeons] & Partridge [grouse?] innumerably . . . of foul the swan, white & gray & black goose and brands [brants], the best teal I ever eate and the Snipe & curloe [curlew] with the Snow bird are also excellent."

In the same vein, Penn wrote back to England that "the trees of most note are the black walnut, cedar, cypress, chestnut, poplar, gumwood [sweet gum], hickory, sassafras, ash, beech, and oak of divers [sic] sorts, as red, white, and black, Spanish, chestnut, and swamp, the most durable of all; of all of which there is plenty for the use of man." After cataloging the trees, he noted the abundant fruits available for eating: "The fruits that I find in the woods are the white and red mulberry, chestnuts, walnut, plums, strawberries, cranberries, huckleberries, and grapes of divers [sic] sorts."

The importance of trees in the new Penn's Woods is only elevated when you remember the names with which he christened the streets of Philadelphia's Center City: Chestnut, Walnut, Spruce, and Pine. A street he named Sassafras was later used for horse races, so much so that its name was altered to Race.

While nature was abundant around Philadelphia, the new inhabitants impacted that nature with frightening speed. Those beavers that Thomas Yong noted? They were removed from the Philadelphia region by colonists trying to feed the frenzy for beaver-pelt top hats in Europe, disappearing from Philadelphia as early as the end of the seventeenth century—the same century that Yong noted their abundance. Otters, martens, and fishers soon followed. Deer, ubiquitous today, quickly became surprisingly scarce, as did their larger, slower cousins, the elk. All of these mammals were not only hunted by the new colonists, but by the Lenape, who of course always hunted them—sustainably. The difference now was the Lenape began trading skins and meat for European manufactured goods like pots and blankets, accelerating the loss of these mammals.

Of course, large predators are never welcome in any city, so wolves, lynx, cougars, and more were immediately pushed back, along with the innumerable trees that were felled to build and heat the growing metropolis.

"Filth of Various Kinds"

Dock Creek once flowed through the city where today's Dock Street stands— explaining that street's quirky diagonal slice through Penn's tidy grid. The creek was used as an open sewer for industrial effluent from tanneries and slaughterhouses. In 1739, only 58 years into the green country town's holy experiment, a young Ben Franklin petitioned the Pennsylvania General Assembly to remove those polluters who were harming both creek and river (and likely stinking out his Market Street print shop). He wrote in his gazette that the creek was choked with "hair, horns, guts and skins," and that if a fish swam in the creek it would "soon float belly up."

In another publication, residents described Dock Creek as "a Receptacle for the Carcasses of dead Dogs, and other Carrion, and Filth of various kinds, which laying exposed to the Sun and Air putrefy and become extremely offensive and injurious to the Health of the Inhabitants." A visiting Englishman wrote a 1769 travelogue of America and dismissed the Philadelphia stretch of the Delaware as "a mess."

Between 1762 and 1769, an older, wiser Ben Franklin led a committee to regulate water pollution in the city. Not long after the Revolution, Dock Street was covered over, a bandage over a very sore wound. Franklin died in 1790, and his will set aside funds for a pipeline to provide Philadelphians with fresh, clean water; its construction led to the creation of the Philadelphia Water Commission, the forerunner of the Philadelphia Water Department. For his public health advocacy, Franklin has been christened "America's first environmentalist" by many, another feather in his very crowded cap.

▲ Fairmount Water Works was built to supply clean drinking water to the city.

In less than a century, Philadelphia had strayed far from the green country town that would "always be wholesome." Still, city government came up with a wonderful answer that likely would have been approved by Penn himself, one that added some luster to Philadelphia's diminished image. From 1812 to 1815, the Fairmount Water Works was built on the banks of the Schuylkill to supply drinking water to the city, with river water being pumped to the top of the "Faire Mount." Fairmount Dam was also built across the river then, to both direct water to the mill house and prevent saltwater from the tidal Schuylkill reaching the drinking water source.

When commercial development threatened the large estates just upriver from the water works, to protect its drinking water the city government smartly began purchasing these properties, including Lemon Hill in 1843 and the adjoining Sedgeley estate in 1857. Fairmount Park was thus born. Today, counting neighborhood parks, the Philadelphia park system encompasses more than 8000 acres, including what the city calls "watershed parks" along large streams—Wissahickon Valley, Cobbs Creek, and Pennypack Parks—to protect water and happily preserve habitat as well.

A City on the Fall Line

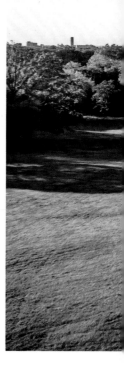

Not only was Philadelphia founded between two rivers, the city straddles two great geological provinces—which is the reason it is located here. The cities of Trenton, Baltimore, and Richmond reflect the same story: they bridge these same two geological worlds.

To get a better understanding of this, let's go back—way back—in time, about 280 million years ago, 60 million years *before* the very first dinosaurs. At that time, the Earth's ever-shifting crustal plates aligned so that all of the present continents slowly crushed into each other to form the supercontinent Pangaea, which literally means "all the land." As today's Europe and Africa crunched against North America, the continents buckled and folded not unlike cars in a head-on, albeit very slow motion, collision. As a result, the Appalachian Mountains were pushed up west of Philadelphia and down the whole length of North America.

Such collisions are still occurring today, notably where Italy is pushing against Europe to form the Alps and where India has been ramming Asia for millennia to build the Himalayas. But this mountain-building event took place so long ago that the Appalachians—once as tall and jagged as the Himalayas—have since become eroded and worn down, with gravity, wind, water, and weather conspiring to slowly smoothen their jagged edges. West of Philadelphia are the hard-rock remnants of the roots of these ancient mountains; east of Philadelphia, New Jersey sits atop soft sediments eroded off of those mountains. Hold those thoughts for a moment.

Consider how different the landscape is as you leave Philadelphia and drive to the Jersey shore. Southern New Jersey, in a huge change from Pennsylvania, is suddenly flat, sandy pinelands, radically different from Philly. And there are few rocks in southern New Jersey. What happened here?

As Pangaea split up, Europe and Africa moved away from North America, opening the Atlantic Ocean—which is still widening today. In fact, the Atlantic is growing at about the rate your fingernails do. And the ocean is a dynamic system that continually changes as well. Essentially, New Jersey's

▲ From Belmont Plateau, as you look down on the Philadelphia skyline, you are standing on the Piedmont and looking into the Atlantic Coastal Plain.

sands were deposited as sediments at the bottom of the post-Pangaea ocean, as there were times when the Atlantic covered southern New Jersey, even coming very close to today's Philadelphia, and times like the Ice Age when land extended much further east.

Welcome to the Atlantic Coastal Plain, a province that begins in Massachusetts and stretches into Florida. It includes most of southern and even central New Jersey and all of Delaware, plus the eastern portions of coastal states from Maryland southward. The land here is typically flat, the soils sandy, and the sediments derived from ocean beds. Much of Philadelphia, including Center City and the Northeast, is located in the Coastal Plain, on this province's western fringe.

At Germantown, Phila. 1870. Mill built 1683, taken down May 1870.

Perched on the Fall Line

Starting just beyond the Philadelphia Museum of Art is the Piedmont, a large and important geological province that slices through Philadelphia's heart. Its name derived from the Italian word meaning "foothill," the Piedmont's rocks are remnants of older and eroded mountain chains that predated the rise of the Appalachians. The Piedmont is made up of low plateaus and hills—neither of which could ever be called mountains. This province begins in central New Jersey and extends south all the way into Alabama.

The eastern edge of the Piedmont is the Fall Line, a dramatic drop-off between the hard rocks of the Piedmont and the soft sediments of the Coastal Plain. The best place to see the Fall Line is by standing at Belmont Plateau, or "the Plat," as high school kids in the area call it, and looking east, Center City beautifully splayed out in front of you. Or drive up Ridge Avenue west from Kelly Drive to head into the Wissahickon neighborhood of Roxborough: you are climbing the Fall Line. Likewise, a drive up Green Lane, the famed wall in Manayunk bike races, is ascending this feature.

The Delaware River seems to parallel the Fall Line for much of its run; so does the New Jersey Turnpike. In fact, have you ever noticed that the turnpike seems to magically delineate the line between snow and rain during many winter storms? Blame the Fall Line again. "While elevations along the Fall Line," writes weather reporter Anthony R. Wood, "may be only a few hundred feet above sea level, those elevations can make dramatic differences in a storm." The air is slightly colder atop the Piedmont than on the Coastal Plain below, and that can make a measurable difference in snowfall depths.

▲ This 1870 watercolor by Augustus Kollner depicts the Roberts Mill built on Wingohocking Creek in 1683 in Germantown, the state's first grist mill.

The Fall Line crosses the Schuylkill River from West Philadelphia into East Falls, creating the Falls of the Schuylkill, a once-famous geological formation that gave the East Falls neighborhood its name. The Lenape called this site Ganshewahanna, which translates as "noisy water."

In 1820, a dam at the Fairmount Water Works was erected across the Schuylkill River to create a source of dependable drinking water for the city. The project raised the height of the river behind the dam, flooding the falls. Nowadays, only a few rocks poking out of the river hint at what the falls once looked like, and most Philadelphians have long forgotten how the East Falls neighborhood earned its name—or how the falls there once roared.

Geology, of course, influences so many things. Water-powered mills were among the region's first industries after colonial settlement. As water tumbled down the Fall Line from one province to another, its velocity turned water wheels across the region, grinding flour, sawing logs, making cloth and paper, and so much more.

Remember that I asked you to hold those thoughts about the Piedmont and the Coastal Plain? Philadelphia sits on the Fall Line, a perfect location for commerce. Think back to the early colonial history of a developing America and the importance of boats in that era. Where rivers like the Schuylkill cross the Fall Line, waterfalls form. Cities develop at these locations because ships reach the inland limit of navigation—and cargo must be off-loaded for land-based transport, which back then involved horses. Philadelphia, Wilmington, Trenton, and Princeton are all sitting on the Fall Line, as are Baltimore, Richmond, Washington, D.C., Raleigh, and Tuscaloosa. While Philadelphia was planned by William Penn, most of these other cities organically evolved where the Piedmont spills into the Coastal Plain, as that was a logical place for ships to meet wagons, and each city provided the infrastructure for the two to meet.

"So Remarkable a Loveliness"

Now let's complicate and amplify the story hidden in the rocks by visiting Philadelphia's most dramatic rock formations in Wissahickon Valley Park, where a walk along the Forbidden Drive reveals a whole new world of steep-sided cliffs and extraordinary views. Writer Edgar Allan Poe, a one-time Philadelphian, once wrote to a friend, "now the Wissahickon is of so remarkable a loveliness that, were it flowing in England, it would be the theme of every bard."

The city's Grand Canyon, the Wissahickon Valley formed from the exact same forces as that western landmark: as the land around it rose from tectonic activity, the stream eroded the rock while staying in its ancient bed, just like the Colorado River scouring down deeper into the Grand Canyon. Wissahickon Creek has been flowing through this valley for about a million years, geologists think.

Sarah West, a retired science teacher who has led dozens of geology walks along Wissahickon Creek, says the valley is "a fascinating place, with some mysterious things about it. For example, it is a backwards creek.

It arises in gently rolling land, and its major headwater is runoff from a parking lot at the Montgomery Mall. It ends in this little mountainous gorge. That's exactly backwards. Most creeks start in mountainous gorges, then flow through gently rolling land, and then maybe some kind of marshy area and out into a bigger body of water. But the Wissahickon doesn't follow that pattern." For Sarah, this is a clear signal that something is different.

The Earth's crust rests on plates that were moving long before Pangaea—and continue moving today. Wissahickon Valley's rock outcrops are the roots of an ancient massive mountainous land more than 500 million years old, formed from rocks laid down at the bottom of an ancient ocean, the Iapetus (who in mythology is the father of Atlantis); this ocean was a precursor of the Atlantic. So Wissahickon rocks are twice as old as that Pangaea collision.

As the Iapetus Ocean closed, a chain of volcanic islands in the ocean were pushed up onto the North American continent, and then buried and folded onto.

"Think of the Mediterranean Sea," West explained, "which is a closing ocean. And whenever you have a closing ocean, you get a mountain range. Land masses like Italy and Sicily are stranded in this closing ocean; Italy is already stuck to Europe." So the Wissahickon's rocks were all formed somewhere else—exact origin unknown—and were left behind when the Iapetus closed.

One of the signature rocks in the valley is schist, a metamorphic rock. You can pick it out very easily, as it's loaded with glittering mica flakes, which erode from the rock to make Wissahickon Valley Park dirt sparkle in sunlight. Schist is also a very soft rock, easily eroded and broken away from the rock face, which is why you see so much of it scattered on the ground as you walk. It formed first as shale, a layered sedimentary rock created from muds settling in shallow waters. When that shale is exposed to intense pressure, heat, and time (lots of time) it changes, metamorphoses, into schist.

Wissahickon schist also typically include garnets, but none of gem quality. Schists often look like chocolate chip cookies, the muddied garnets the chips in the schist cookie. This is a very important rock in Philadelphia, as so many of the area's homes, including the Mount Airy one where Sarah West raised her children, have schist foundations.

Gneiss (a homophone of *nice*), another metamorphic rock typical of the Wissahickon Valley, is the basement rock of the valley. Its signature is fine, narrow bands of alternating colors of rocks. One common gneiss features handsome black and white bands, a second orange and gray. When gneiss was forming deep underground, feldspar minerals flowed like putty, oozing in between layers of schist; when exposed to time, heat, and pressure, the rocks hardened, leaving the darker schists with lighter feldspars in between. The lovely curves, wiggles, and U-turns in the white bands illustrate the remarkable deformations the rock was subjected to deep underground.

There's an especially large outcrop of gneiss just west of the Bell's Mill Road entrance into Wissahickon Valley Park, but on the eastern (opposite) shore. Dubbed "Sarah's Rock" by her friends, as it is West's favorite, she describes her eponymous rock as "probably descended from schist, and

▶ Lincoln Drive slicing through the Wissahickon Valley, Philadelphia's Grand Canyon and the remnants of an ancient mountain system.

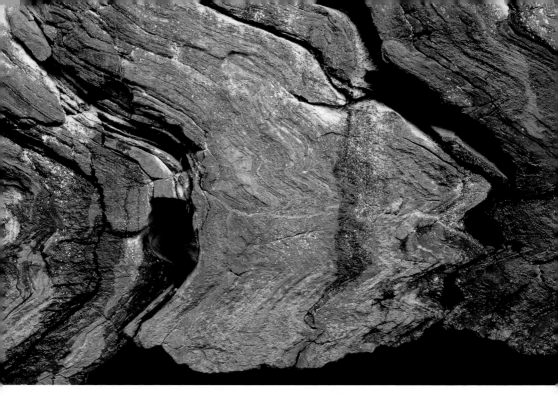

formed 10 miles down, [it] has worked its way to the surface slowly over the last 250,000 years," as the rocks above it were slowly weathered down and eroded away. The pressure 10 miles down is remarkable.

When visiting Wissahickon Valley Park, mixed with all of the above, look for a bright white crystalline rock, looking completely out of place and wonderfully different. This is vein quartz, an intriguing example of chemical sedimentary rock, which forms, Sarah offers, "when very hot silica-rich fluid of water and other liquids flows through cracks in deeply buried schist, later cooling and solidifying underground to make a cast of the crack in which it flowed." While some of this rock is white, more of it is rusty or gray, and, on closer inspection, looks like fused sand grains.

Not far from the Valley Green Inn and just across the creek is Devil's Pool, a site that causes grave concerns among city and park officials as park visitors love to jump off the rock into the plunge pool far below, too many hurting themselves, some even dying after striking rocks. The unusual landscape appears to have resulted from a crack that opened in the rock while it was deep underground, and as Cresheim Creek cut its way through to Wissahickon Creek, the water slowly eroded softer rock layers to form the dramatic gaps and pools.

▲ One of the many dramatic rocks in the Wissahickon Valley.

Fault Lines

Speaking of cracks in bedrock, at the northern end of Wissahickon Creek, just past Northwestern Avenue, is the Huntingdon Valley fault line. Faults are places—like in San Andreas, California—where masses of bedrock slide along large fractures. And when they move, of course, the earth quakes and two different masses of rock may end up opposite each other. On the northeastern side of this fault line, you find sedimentary rock made from settled sand or mud particles, very different from the metamorphic rock in the Wissahickon Valley; the sedimentary rock once covering the Wissahickon's schist and quartzite has eroded away long ago. So while the Huntington Valley fault is no longer active, at some point in the fog of geologic time, rocks shifted, and those on either side of the fault are now discontinuous.

Fault lines often shape the courses of waterways. From its source below Montgomery Mall, Wissahickon Creek flows through Whitemarsh Township's limestones, hits that fault line and harder rock, and suddenly zigs, quickly curving not far from Morris Arboretum's gift shop. It then flows through Chestnut Hill College and abruptly zags near the Cedars House, a cafe in the park—that large Z traced by the steam reminding us of a dramatic geologic event that occurred long ago.

Wissahickon Creek continues flowing downhill through the gneiss valley, eroding these metamorphic rocks, and empties into the Schuylkill River, flowing inexorably over the buried Falls of the Schuylkill, depositing its waters into the Delaware River just below Citizens Bank Park. And all along the way, that water is tracing the unique geological history of Philadelphia, a city perched on the Fall Line.

The Lenape, the First Philadelphians

Kwangomelhenna wuntschi Lennapeuhockink
We greet you from the land of the Lenape

Pennsylvania schoolchildren are still typically taught that the state's history begins in 1681 with William Penn and the naming of this part of what we still call the New World. Of course, the land already had a name: Lenapehoking. And it was hardly new: for 10,000 years or more before William Penn, the Lenape inhabited Lenapehoking.

As that time also marks the end of the Ice Age and the beginning of modern history in Europe, the Lenape earned the meaning of their name, "original people." Among many First Nations, the Lenape hold themselves to be among the oldest tribes.

Living in small towns across the region, the Lenape's territory stretched from Maryland and coastal Delaware through eastern Pennsylvania, included all of New Jersey, and swept north deep into upstate New York. It was the Lenape who famously "sold" the island of Manahatta to the Dutch in 1626 (some 55 years before William Penn was granted Pennsylvania), and the Dutch who built a wall around New Amsterdam to protect themselves from the British and the Lenape. The island, of course, is Manhattan, and Wall Street marks the boundary of that wall.

The Iroquois inhabited the area north of the Lenape territory, and the Susquehannock inhabited the lands to the west of the Lenape, lending their name to that river.

Northern Lenape clans spoke the Munsee dialect; Manahatta is a Munsee word. The southern Lenape of Pennsylvania and southern New Jersey spoke Unami, a Munsee word meaning "people downriver," which they were—from the Munsee. In between the two, a third clan, the Unalachtigo, "people who lived near the ocean," inhabited a swath of land from the Lehigh Valley to the central Jersey shore.

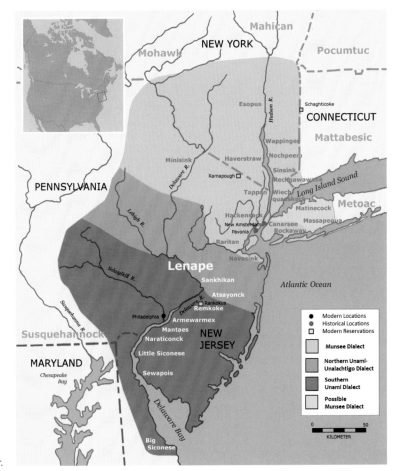

► Map of Lenapehoking. The swath of land inhabited by the Lenape extended from Delaware north into Connecticut and west to the Susquehanna River watershed, with many large settlements along the Delaware River.

Lenapewihittuck

The Delaware River, of course, had a name then as well: Lenapewihittuck. It is appropriate that the Lenape tribal name is embedded in the river's, as the river was the main artery that flowed through Lenapehoking; one writer called it their Main Street. Delaware is a name the British bestowed on the river after their Lord de la Warr, and that name then was appended to Lenape as the British name for the Native Americans who lived along the river.

In addition, many sources routinely identify them as the Lenni Lenape. Adam DePaul, Storykeeper and Council Member of the Lenape Nation of Pennsylvania, notes that "this term is an anglicized grammatical error that basically translates as the 'original people people.'" He acknowledges that although many Lenape identify as either Lenni Lenape or Delaware, "the best word to use when referring to us is simply Lenape."

The Lenape story is long and complicated, involving multiple signed treaties and endless forced movements to other places—the Lehigh Valley, Ohio, Oklahoma, Kansas, Wisconsin, and even Canada. The tragedy of the Lenape story is compounded by their history being incorrectly passed on for centuries and largely written by European colonists. My purpose here is not to share the full arc of the Lenape story—though that needs to be done—but more simply to share the profound impact of the Lenape on Wild Philly.

Most accounts of the Lenape (and actually of most Native Americans) present them as living passively on the land, treading lightly, hunting a few animals here and there, using every part of that animal, having little or no impact on the land. Early American writers thus dubbed the New World "pristine," "untouched," and that most ridiculously and horribly loaded word, "virgin." The "noble savage" myth dehumanizes the Lenape as completely as the "fierce warrior" does. All this mythology still permeates our understanding of First Nations, as we never give them the three dimensions that they deserve. So let's muddy these waters completely.

To start, as Charles C. Mann brilliantly recounts in his seminal *1491: New Revelations of the Americas Before Columbus*, there were far more First People living across the Americas than any historians traditionally estimated, living here far longer than most have estimated, and creating societies far more complex than given credit for. By the time any European chronicler began writing about Native people, their populations were already plummeting from multiple epidemics: smallpox, diphtheria, measles, typhoid fever, whooping cough, and bubonic plague, among others. Even the common cold was brought to the New World from Europe. So almost no European witness ever saw the original thriving Native cultures.

I recently came across this sentence in a blog post, "At the most, there were 8000 Lenape Indians living between Trenton and Wilmington when the European settlers arrived in the area," a statement supported by other writers. Ironically, the writer may be correct, but the inference is that this was always the case, which is just not so. By William Penn's arrival, the Lenape had already been so reduced in numbers that they reluctantly agreed to rearrange and consolidate their clans.

Wigwams and Sachems

The Lenape lived in towns alongside streams across broad swaths of the region, building wooden *wikiwama* (the plural of their word for house, *wikewam*, which morphed into the anglicized *wigwam*) with bark roofs as their homes. One important Lenape site seems to be at the confluence of the Brandywine and Schuylkill Rivers, underneath where today's Wilmington sits; another is in West Philadelphia along the Schuylkill near today's Woodlands Cemetery, a site that might be 6000 years old.

The seventeenth-century Lenape were a democratic and egalitarian people, and each town claimed a territory that was overseen by a *sakima*, a leader and a word that has been translated into *sachem*, a Narragansett word. Sachems consulted not only with a council of male elders, but also the clan grandmothers, a group of the most respected female elders in the community. Though the sachem was male, the society was a matrilineal clan system in which children belonged to the mother's clan and hereditary leadership passed through mothers. There were three main clans, named after the Lenape words for wolf, turtle, and turkey, and Philadelphia-area Lenape were members of the turtle clan.

The Lenape ate an incredibly diverse and remarkably healthy diet of wild foods supplemented with agricultural crops. Women and children gathered leaves, roots, berries, mushrooms, and nuts, eating everything from wild strawberries to cattail roots to chestnuts, a tree that dominated Pennsylvania forests then. Acorns had a central place in the diet too, being ground into flour for bread and mashed into a hot porridge.

► A Lenape settlement of wigwams drawn by Swedish Lutheran minister John Campanius, likely in the 1640s, who lived in New Christina, Delaware, and served as a missionary to the Lenape.

The women and children farmed, growing the Three Sisters of maize, beans, and squash. This highly successful form of agriculture spread across pre-Columbian North America, with maize making its way north from its native South America. The maize stalk served as the pole that the beans climbed up, the bean plants restored nitrogen to the soil, and the squash's large leaves shaded out weeds from growing below them, an effective and highly sustainable system.

Skilled with bow and arrow, Lenape men hunted the many animals that lived here then: deer, elk, bear, raccoon, beaver, rabbit, and turkey. When flocks of passenger pigeons flew or roosted nearby, they caught them in nets woven from hemp. The Lenape used nets and even weirs to fish in the region's rivers and creeks, where they gathered the then-innumerable shad that ran by the millions up the Delaware and the Schuylkill each spring to spawn, providing an abundant feast and marking a critical time in the Lenape calendar. Six-foot sturgeons were harder to catch, so the Lenape crafted spears, using deer-antler tips as the points, to snag this delicacy. Meats and fish were often smoked and dried so they would last longer. Lenape living near rivers and streams collected freshwater mussels and crayfish, and those living near the ocean dined on clams, oysters, and scallops.

It's likely not surprising that many of the region's largest roads were once well-traveled Lenape trade routes. Ridge Avenue, for one, runs down the spine of Northwest Philadelphia, linking Plymouth Meeting to Center City. But it was then the trail that connected the Lenape to the Susquehannock nation in the interior of the state. Its name was Manatawny, a derivation of which is today a small road off Ridge Avenue in Andorra. "A tawney," wrote Deborah Del Collo, an archivist for the Roxborough, Manayunk, and Wissahickon Historical Society, "is an open road," and since *mana* could mean either "raging" or "god," she wonderfully translates Manatawny as "an open road from our creator."

Some of these trails were long and highly connective. "The Allegheny Path," historian Matthew A. Zimmerman wrote, "ran from the future location of Allegheny Avenue in Philadelphia, through Paoli to Harrisburg, across the Susquehanna and into Carlisle," where branches continued west, linking the entire state. "The Perkiomen Path," he continued, "ran from Philadelphia to Norristown, crossed Perkiomen Creek, and extended into Reading, where it joined the Allegheny Path." The Minsi Path ran hundreds of miles, from Chestnut Hill north to Bethlehem, then across the Delaware at today's Port Jervis, New York, and all the way to the Hudson River around today's Kingston. Nowadays, its Pennsylvania reach is the well-traveled Bethlehem Pike.

Southern New Jersey is no different: Route 47, where so many cars pile up on summer weekends, was a Lenape route to the shore. Another major trail traces almost the exact route of today's New Jersey Turnpike, paralleling the Fall Line.

Sadly, these same trade routes allowed diseases to spread like wildfire across the Americas throughout the sixteenth and seventeenth centuries, well before William Penn.

LAP-PA-WIN-SOE.

A DELAWARE CHIEF.

► A 1735 painting of Lenape leader Lappawinsoe, the first Native American to ever sit for a portrait. His forehead tattoos include powerful symbols, two thunderbirds and a snake. While this portrait is widely reprinted, one has to notice a certain melancholy in his appearance.

Fire Ecology

Most importantly, Lenapehoking was never a pristine, untouched, virgin forest. Hardly. The big surprise of modern Lenape scholarship, arrived at from studies of both paleoecology and forest ecology, is that the Lenape practiced a highly skilled and remarkably common form of fire ecology, one actively practiced by many indigenous people across the Americas.

In short, the Lenape routinely burned Lenapehoking. The forest was continuously sculpted by Native hands to create a wide variety of desired benefits. Most importantly, fire favored the growth of oaks, chestnuts, hickories, and walnuts, trees that offered so many other benefits, especially mast, the forester's name for nut production. Blueberry bushes, their fruit so nutritious, also respond to burning, producing more fruit in the year right after a fire.

"Fire enhanced [the Lenape's] production of mast and fruit," says Penn State forest ecologist Marc David Abrams, who has been researching fire ecology for 40 years, "not only to feed themselves, but to feed the animals they were hunting; it was a win-win." More mast meant more deer, turkeys, passenger pigeons, rabbits, and bears, animals the Lenape wanted and needed for food, bones, fur, and feathers.

But the benefits don't stop there. The ash resulting from fire was nutrient-rich, offering many plants the ability to grow healthy and fast. Some of the plants that came back after a burn were medicinal plants with important healing properties. Fire cleared out the underbrush, allowing hunters to cover more land more easily while giving them better sightlines to find and shoot prey. Ticks and other harmful pests overwintering in the undergrowth were also killed in a spring fire, and these fires prevented the buildup of too much brush on the ground, which would lead to major conflagrations.

Of course, these were not the wildfires making headlines in so many climate-challenged places. No. These more modest fires quickly burned off the leaf litter, with the moist soil preventing the fire from completely destroying the soil's upper layers. The fire moved quickly through dry leaf litter, and taller trees kept their branches well above the flames, their thick bark charring but protecting the tree.

Acorns and chestnuts cannot sprout and grow underneath their parents' dense canopy, as they require more sunlight hitting the soil than a dense forest offers. Thus, burning cleared out gaps in the forest for acorns and nuts to sprout and grow. If the Lenape did not burn, the forest would have matured and growing underneath the oak trees would be the late-stage successional trees of maple, beech, birch, and hemlock—fine trees all, but with lower wildlife value and fewer nuts for themselves. So the Lenape kept Lenapehoking forests frozen in mid-succession. Dr. Abrams researched an old-growth forest in West Virginia that was being logged and found burn scars in many of the cut stumps indicating that indigenous people would burn a section of forest every 8 to 10 years or so, a number backed up by research from others in the field.

So Penn's Woods neither belonged to Penn nor was a pristine wilderness. Lenapehoking instead was a highly managed and yet sustainable forest artificially kept at an earlier stage of succession in many areas, propping up the plants the Lenape needed nearby, especially chestnuts and oaks. Among their many qualities, the Lenape were exceptional ecologists continuously molding the land to fit their lifestyle.

▲ In Wissahickon Valley Park, the statue of Teedyuscung looks west to where the Lenape were sent.

About That Statue in the Wissahickon Valley Park

On your walks in Wild Philly, you'll find little evidence of the Lenape aside from so many place names preserving their language (see sidebar). On your walk in the Wissahickon Valley Park (Trip 24), while examining the dramatic geological features, you might also visit a perhaps well-intended statue in the park that perfectly summarizes our sad relationship with the Lenape.

It's a 15-foot-tall marble statue of the Lenape leader Teedyuscung (often spelled with one e as well), and it sits upon a prominent outcrop called Council Rock. Teedyuscung, whose name means "as far as the wood's edge," signed the 1758 treaty agreeing that the Lenape would leave Pennsylvania for good. He tragically died only a few years later when his Lehigh Valley house was deliberately burned down at night with him sleeping inside. In his statue, he's frozen in time staring west—in the direction of where his people were heading. And he is incongruously wearing a feathered headdress more suitable to tribes of the Great Plains, which only indicated the laziness of the artist commissioned to carve him. While it was not intended to be a like-ness of any one Lenape, at the statue's 1902 unveiling ceremony, a speaker dubbed it "Chief Teedyuscung," and the name stuck.

Legend has long held that the Lenape gathered at the statue's site for councils, especially after the signing of that treaty to discuss how they would move out of Lenapehoking. But there has been vigorous disagreement about this, with most scholars dismissing the idea, as the site is too inaccessible, too precarious, and too small all at once, and no Lenape artifacts have ever been found in Wissahickon Valley Park. If this were a site of councils, archaeology would likely back it up.

In the Civil War era, however, Indian Rock Hotel, one of many roadside inns then strung along the then-named Wissahickon Turnpike (today's Forbidden Drive), was thriving at the Rex Avenue bridge—with a view to the stony outcrop. The legend of the council persisted even then, embedded in the name Indian Rock, so the proprietor placed a wooden cutout of an Indian on Council Rock, encouraging his guests to climb up for the view, just as they do today.

The statue of a Lenape orator who was never in the Wissahickon Valley and never wore a headdress, perched on a rock where a council was never held, encapsulates our fractured relationship with the Lenape. The only truthful element of the statue is that he is looking west to where so many of his people ended up, as a large settlement of Lenape still exists in Oklahoma.

But the triumph of the Lenape story is that so many did not obey the treaty (including Teedyuscung), staying in Lenapehoking and, at some risk, fighting prejudice and misguided preconceptions all the time. Even better, there are many Lenape still living—and thriving—in Philadelphia, many more have returned, and there is a long overdue resurgence of interest in their history and language.

Lenape Names

While most Philadelphians know little about the Lenape, their language has been wonderfully preserved in so many of its place names.

Like the Schuylkill River, which of course is a name from the Dutch. But the Lenape called it Manayunk, which is often translated as "watering place" or "the place where we drink," a fitting name for the bar-centric Manayunk neighborhood tucked against the river. But another translation I like more is "roaring waters," named for the river's rock formations and whitewater.

Wissahickon Creek was called, well, Wissahickon, which is typically translated as "catfish stream," but is more correctly translated as, and I love this, "a large catch of catfish found at the mouth of the creek."

Conshohocken translates to "pleasant valley" or sometimes "elegant land." Miquon, a small community alongside Conshohocken that was once its own stand-alone town, is Lenape for "feather." It's also what they called William Penn himself, as he signed treaties with quill pens. His feather pen became an inside-joke Lenape pun on his surname. (Native Americans are also rarely credited with a sense of humor.)

Aramingo is a corruption of *Tumanaraming*, which means "wolf walk," the Lenape name for a stream in Northern Liberties that has been long buried—and the wolves are gone too.

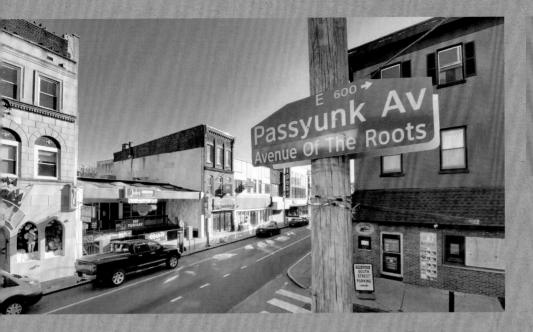

Cinnaminson could either mean "rock island" or "sweet water." Kingsessing is "a place where there is a meadow," and Wyomissing means "land of the flats." Perkiomen? "Where the cranberries grow." Passyunk? "The place between the hills."

Tulpehocken, the name for a creek, a street, and a train station in Germantown, translates as "land of turtles," as the turtle was sacred in Lenape mythology; Lenapehoking was formed from mud brought up by a turtle, all of us now living atop that turtle's back. Nearby Wingohocking, another buried creek system, could either be "crooked water" or "favorite land for planting."

Shackamaxon is usually translated as "place of the council" and marks the large Fishtown-area village where William Penn signed a peace treaty with the Lenape. Penn Treaty Park ostensibly preserves the spot where the Treaty Elm once stood. But the name could equally (more likely?) mean "place of the eels," marking a notable fishing spot.

Down the shore, Manahawakin might translate as "land of good corn" or possibly "fertile land sloping into the water." Love them both.

My personal favorite? Moyamensing. A *Philadelphia* magazine writer noted in 2015 that "nobody's certain of the derivation of this name. ... It either means 'place of judgment' or 'pigeon excrement.'" There's a great story in either choice.

Lastly, many assume that Wawa, the Delaware County town where the dairy and the company was born, is Lenape for Canada goose, the company logo. It does mean goose, but in Ojibwe, an Upper Midwestern tribe. In Lenapehoking, the animal was called *opsuwihele*.

Philadelphia's Forests

There is a wonderful legend that I confess to happily passing on to thousands of children for decades now. The story says that in the time before colonial settlement a squirrel could cross today's Pennsylvania from east to west without ever once touching the ground. The critter would simply scamper from branch to branch high above the ground across the massive old-growth forest of our Edenic state—and might only need help crossing the Susquehanna.

That myth is busted, as Philadelphia would have looked decidedly, well, settled. "We believe that the Philadelphia area," says Penn State forest ecologist Marc David Abrams, "would have had large Lenape villages, agricultural fields, trails, prescribed burning, and even silviculture, the planting of nut trees. Calling it 'wilderness' would have been insulting to the Lenape."

Were there old-growth forests where Philadelphia today stands? "That is a big controversial topic," he answered.

Echoing this notion, author Charles C. Mann writes, "By 1800, the hemisphere was thick with artificial wilderness. If 'forest primeval' means woodland unsullied by the human presence . . . there was much more of it in the nineteenth century than in the seventeenth. The product of demographic calamity, the newly created wilderness was indeed beautiful. But it was built on Indian graves and every bit as much a ruin as the temples of the Maya."

Still, even with this paradigm-altering view, the importance of Pennsylvania's forests in the founding of both city and state is reflected in William Penn's use of *sylvania* in the state's name. The state is considered to have been 90 percent forested in Penn's time. As noted earlier, one of Penn's first letters back to England was a veritable catalog of the trees he found, "of all of which there is plenty for the use of man." Trees, then, meant houses, fuel, furniture, wagons, barrels, and much more, but they also were for exporting back to England.

Between Lenape settlements and tucked into the tapestry of maize fields and mixed oak and chestnut groves were the ancestral Pennsylvania forests.

▲ A stream flowing through a mixed hardwood forest represents the quintessential view of Penn's Woods. While forests still cover 60 percent of the state today, the composition of that forest has changed—and keeps changing.

◄ Old growth hemlocks in Rothrock State Forest in the center of Pennsylvania. Forests like this—with trees this old—were once far more common in Philadelphia than they are today.

41

Likely the deeper into the state and the farther away from the Schuylkill and Delaware Rivers one went, the denser the forest may have become. So what was the original Pennsylvania like? Would you recognize Penn's Woods?

"The Jade Awning"

Ice Age Pennsylvania was a very different forest, composed of cold-adapted trees like fir, spruce, birch, pine, and alder. And people living here then were using stone tools and spears to hunt very different animals, like mastodons and mammoths, Ice Age elephants living here then.

As the climate warmed, the more familiar oak-hickory forest began moving up from the south, replacing the northern forests with trees very similar to those today. But the size of the trees of Lenapehoking require a mind shift. In their four-volume masterwork *Metropolitan Paradise: The Struggle for Nature in the City*, for example, historian David Contosta and landscape architect Carol Franklin wrote about the old-growth forest of this era, less shy in using that term than Abrams. "A significant number of trees in this landscape," they wrote, "were very old and of huge girth and height—experienced as tall straight trunks with branches only very high in the canopy." On a 1743 journey on the Susquehanna River, Philadelphian John Bartram, founder of Bartram's Garden, still operating today as America's first botanical garden, discovered forests so thick "it seems almost as if the sun had never shown on the ground since the creation." His son William, himself a noted explorer-botanist, observed eastern white pines over 230 feet tall that may have been 400 years old and black oaks measuring 30 feet around.

Michael A. Godfrey, writing in *A Sierra Club Naturalist's Guide to the Piedmont*, considers that "the canopy [of trees] claims the direct sunlight completely by filling every gap with a broad-leaved parasol, cantilevered aloft. No part of the jade awning is within 100 feet of the ground. The trees holding it aloft are chestnuts, white oaks, mockernut hickories and tuliptrees. Only around the younger dominants, say those under 200 years, could two lovers link hands. Many are more than four feet in diameter." Some hemlocks in this forest were more than 900 years old, and the American chestnut accounted for perhaps a quarter of the trees in Penn's Woods.

To envision a real slice of old Pennsylvania forest, you might visit Carpenter's Woods in West Mount Airy (Trip 4), one of Wild Philly's oldest forests. Protected as a bird sanctuary in 1921, the site boasts 200-year-old oaks of several species, plus massive tuliptrees (our region's tallest tree), along with beech, black gum, sassafras, and more. It is a bird migration hotspot, a magnet for both migratory birds like warblers and the birdwatchers desperate to find them. While the trees are not (yet) the girth noted above, they are among the oldest in the area, and we only have to wait a few centuries for them to achieve that.

Contosta and Franklin's book also offers a compelling portrait of the pre-Columbian Wissahickon Valley, a vision that likely works across Lenapehoking, with eastern white pines dominating hilltops, chestnuts lining the ridges, the oak-hickory complex growing on plateaus, hemlocks

► Loggers assessing American chestnuts circa 1910. Chestnut trees were not only huge, but common—one out of every four trees in Penn's Woods.

blanketing colder northern and eastern slopes, beeches on the opposite southern slopes, and sycamores, red maples, and ashes in the valley bottoms.

When not subjected to Lenape burning, these healthy forests would boast a full complement of forest layers. Large canopy trees grew far taller than today's much younger second- and third-growth forests. Just below them, the understory was composed of younger trees pushing up to the canopy alongside trees evolved to occupy the understory niche, like dogwood, witch hazel, sassafras, and shadbush. Northern spicebush, mountain laurel, azalea, and blueberry occupied the shrub layer below this, and the forest floor was covered with a herbaceous carpet of wildflowers and ferns.

The profusion of ephemeral spring wildflowers must have been a sight to see, which Contosta and Franklin describe as "as much a show as the riot of colorful leaves in the fall." Today, places like Bowman's Hill Wildflower Preserve in New Hope and the Mt. Cuba Center in Delaware offer hints of this former glory.

The pre-Columbian forest would have been a remarkable sight, but over time at least three profound changes were swept into action in Pennsylvania: the chestnut blight, settlement, and the timber frenzy.

"Almost a Perfect Tree"

According to the American Chestnut Foundation, eastern North America's chestnut trees "were among the largest, tallest, and fastest-growing trees. . . . The wood was rot-resistant, straight-grained, and suitable for furniture, fencing, and building. The nuts fed billions of wildlife, people and their livestock. It was almost a perfect tree."

CHESTNUTTING.— By Winslow Homer. (See Page 691.)

◄ *Chestnutting*, an 1870 engraving, shows foragers awaiting chestnuts dropped from the climber up in the tree. Chestnut gathering was a huge event in the natural year's cycle.

Tragically, dead chestnut trees were first discovered in the Bronx Botanical Garden in 1904. A fungal blight had been accidentally imported from Asia, where that continent's chestnuts had evolved alongside the fungus and were resilient to its impact. The American species, however, encountering this novel threat for the first time ever, simply had no immunity and quickly succumbed. The fungus spread like wildfire, reaching Philadelphia in 1908 and rippling across the northeast. The American Chestnut Foundation calls it, without exaggeration, the "greatest ecological disaster to strike the world's forests in all of history."

Gone now for almost 100 years, it is easy to forget how important the American chestnut was to the forest as a source of food for both humans and animals. In William Penn's letter back to England where he catalogs the important trees, he adds a second sentence: "The fruits that I find in the woods are the white and red mulberry, chestnuts, walnut, plums, strawberries, cranberries, huckleberries, and grapes of divers [sic] sorts." Notice his mention of the chestnut again, as it was both food and wood, and as many as 4 billion trees strong dominating the eastern forest.

"The American chestnut tree survived all adversaries for 40 million years," summarizes the foundation's elegy, "then disappeared within 40."

Dead Stumps and Dry Branches

While the chestnut blight was spreading, Philadelphians and Pennsylvanians were quickly clearing the state's canopy of trees. By the Civil War, millions of acres had been cleared for the state's 128,000 farms, as trees were obstacles to farming and the farmers needed trees to build and heat their homes and cook their food. Loggers cut down the massive pine and hemlock forests of the Susquehanna Valley, floating millions of logs downriver to the sawmills at Lock Haven and Williamsport, the latter serving as the "Lumber Capital of the World" in the 1870s, with more millionaires per capita than anywhere else in the country. (Amazingly, its high school teams are still called the Millionaires.)

On top of this, millions of acres more were cleared to feed the charcoal furnaces of Pennsylvania's new and growing iron industry. Coal mines used billions more board feet to prop up mine walls and ceilings. When railroads rose to prominence, they were using more than 15 percent of the country's timber, as each mile of track required a whopping 2500 railroad ties. In the 1860s, pulpwood began to be used to make paper, and during the Civil War demand skyrocketed for wood to build fortifications, with even more trees tumbling down.

► Perhaps too much of Penn's Woods looked like this at the turn of the twentieth century. Forests have been recovering ever since.

In short, by 1900 Pennsylvania had lost almost two-thirds of its forests, perhaps the state's most precious resource. Compounding this misery, on the barren moonscapes left behind, rains eroded huge amounts of soil into local streams. Adding insult to injury, massive forest fires roared through the dead stumps and dry branches left behind, devastating these forest communities.

In hindsight, it is amazing there are any trees left in Pennsylvania. Demand for wood never slowed, of course. The loggers simply moved south and west.

Red Maple Rising

While Wild Philly's forests contain many tree species that have been here for millennia—tuliptree, beech, oak—the *composition* of Penn's Woods is radically different from the past, which doesn't bode well for the future. Red maples have become far more numerous than they ever were historically, while beeches and oaks have trended in the opposite direction, reducing the nut crop that a diverse assortment of mammals and birds have relied upon for ages.

Remember that the Lenape burned forests to retain the oaks and beeches, which cannot sprout in their own shade. Without this burning, the forest is maturing, leaving these trees behind. Red maples, on the other hand, are shade tolerant and sprout beneath the oaks—striving to take their place in the canopy.

The suppression of fire in a post-Lenape world has been a powerful driver of forest change. "Modern forests are dominated by tree species that are increasingly cool-adapted, shade-tolerant, drought-intolerant pyrophobes," Abrams notes. The last word refers to fire-intolerant "trees that are reduced when exposed to repeated forest burning. Unlike species like oak that are largely promoted by low to moderate forest fires." In short, he offers, the

⊳ A red maple tree blossoms along Cobbs Creek in early spring. Its red flowers are just one reason the tree earned its name, as its leaves turned red in the fall as well.

▽ Bloodroot, an early spring wildflower, growing in West Philadelphia's Morris Park, one of many hopeful signs for the future of the region's forests.

lack of burning in the modern era has led to denser forests filled with trees intolerant of fire. "This change in forest composition," Abrams summarizes, is making eastern forests more vulnerable to future fire and drought."

The remaining trees are suffering from an onslaught of chestnut-like issues. The hemlock woolly adelgid, another imported Asian insect, is killing the hemlocks that graced cooler forests. The emerald ash borer is killing off all North American species of ash trees. The red-spotted lanternfly, which only arrived in the state in 2014, is literally sucking the life out of a wide variety of trees, including, ironically, tree-of-heaven, one of its native host plants and a tree that has been invasive in the United States for more than a century. A fungus has been attacking dogwoods since 1978, and another is challenging red oaks. Meanwhile, invasives like cork trees and Norway maples have invaded the region's forests and are ascendant, a situation we will discuss further in "Threats to Philadelphia's Nature."

Good News

Though the region's forests are troubled, there is some good news. Today, Pennsylvania has improved its tree cover to 60 percent of the state, and the state reports that 2 acres are now planted for every acre harvested, which is a far more sustainable situation. The state itself has protected 4 million acres of forest, but fracking for natural gas threatens many of these, as most Pennsylvanians know far too well. Public lands conservation has been supplemented—maybe even supplanted—by a network of private conservation groups that simply did not exist 100 years ago. The city of Philadelphia, recognizing the importance of trees in fighting climate change, has created the Philly Tree Plan, a 10-year-plan for growing a resilient, environmentally just urban forest. The plan calls for more trees to be planted in currently treeless neighborhoods, aiming at shading about 30 percent of the city.

◄ While even parts of Center City are shaded, like the Ben Franklin Parkway, too much of the city lacks tree cover, especially in low-income neighborhoods. Trees have become a justice issue.

The Animals of Penn's Woods

On any walk in Wild Philly, you are guaranteed to see a bouquet of plants arrayed in front of you: trees of many kinds mixed with shrubs, wildflowers, grasses, ferns, and more. You likely won't see too many animals—except maybe robins, squirrels, chipmunks, and perhaps rabbits and deer, the latter two if you are walking at dusk.

Deer are today the largest mammal in the region, and rodents like squirrels and mice are the most common. Since so many of Wild Philly's mammals are nocturnal, when the night shift takes over at dusk, the forest comes alive with raccoons, skunks, opossums, bats, flying squirrels, even coyotes, all quietly out and about while we're asleep.

The bird life of the region's forests is especially diverse and reveals itself to you if you can learn a few calls by ear. Expect to hear a "chick-a-dee-dee-dee" greet you as you walk, this from a bird that tells you its name. But cardinals, crows, mourning doves, song sparrows, blue jays, and many more are relatively common and typical of almost any walk on the wild side.

Lift a log to peek underneath, and a red-backed salamander or garter snake may greet you, along with an ant colony and maybe a millipede or centipede. Insects are everywhere in the forest, especially the cabbage white butterfly, an invasive pest. In springtime, look for tent caterpillars in cherry trees. In the fall, a wooly bear caterpillar might cross the trail as it seeks out a hibernation spot.

Walk near water, and the animal life multiplies exponentially, with great blue herons spearing fish near sunbathing painted turtles, a green frog hopping into the water with a "plunk!" as you startle it.

Wild Philly's forests, fields, streams, and ponds are filled with animal life of all kinds. Simply slow down to look and listen. Sometimes you need luck and enough walks, but the region's wild animals reveal themselves surprisingly often.

▲ Philadelphia's forests are filled with a rich diversity of animal life.

From a historical perspective, however, the forest has changed dramatically: you won't see a whole range of animals that have been banished from the Delaware Valley and others that have disappeared from the state. Gone from Pennsylvania are wolves, wolverines, moose, lynx, and cougars—though rumors of cougars in the state's northern tier relentlessly troll the internet. Still present elsewhere in the state but long gone from the Philadelphia region are bears, bobcats, elk, pine martens, and fishers. We almost lost turkeys and deer too, but both have rebounded, deer now more numerous than ever.

Two extraordinary animals—both now extinct—are emblematic of humans' tortured relationship with nature and our persistent misunderstanding of ecology. Both are cautionary tales. The first is the passenger pigeon, the second the woodland bison. Yes, the iconic bison once roamed Lenapehoking.

Passenger Pigeons:
A Living Illustration of Abundance

▼ Audubon's illustration of the now-extinct passenger pigeon.

▲ An 1875 magazine illustration shows the passenger pigeon hunting craze at its peak.

Famously prolific, forming flocks that darkened the sky, the passenger pigeon was relentlessly, even manically, hunted by early American settlers. The last passenger pigeon—dubbed Martha after George Washington's spouse—unceremoniously died in 1914 in captivity at the Cincinnati Zoo, where a memorial to the species now stands. "Once the most numerous bird on Earth," the memorial reads, "the passenger pigeon was hunted into extinction."

Artist and naturalist John James Audubon, himself once a Pennsylvanian, watched a flock pass overhead for *three days*, estimating that at times more than 300 million pigeons flew by him every hour. "The air," he wrote, "was literally filled with Pigeons; the light of noon-day was obscured as by an eclipse." John Muir, founder of the Sierra Club, reported, "I have seen flocks streaming south in the fall so large that they were flowing over from horizon to horizon in an almost continuous stream all day long, at the rate of forty or fifty miles an hour, like a mighty river in the sky."

There are stories of passenger pigeons in a feeding frenzy in a mast year, vomiting their stomach contents to continue their gluttonous eating. Others report birds so overstuffed with food they'd fall off a branch and literally explode when they hit the forest floor, a gruesome image.

The passenger pigeon became, as noted by Charles C. Mann in *1491*, "a symbol of the earth's richness." Mann quotes a pigeon enthusiast of the era describing it as "the living, pulsing, throbbing, and picturesque illustration of the abundance of food, prepared by bountiful Nature, in all her supreme ecstasy of redundant production of life and energy."

But passenger pigeons were competitors for the same mast that the Lenape and other First Nations people across the eastern forests coveted.

Mann's extensive research includes reporting from archaeologist Thomas W. Neumann, who specializes in indigenous diets. To his surprise, Neumann has not found many pigeon bones at archeological sites. "They almost aren't there," he told Mann. "It looks like people didn't eat them."

Not that they didn't want to. It's simply that "passenger pigeons were not as numerous before Columbus," believes Neumann. "What happened was that the impact of European contact altered the ecological dynamics in such a way that the passenger pigeon [populations] took off."

So Audubon's three-day flock, a story recounted in hundreds of books over the last 200 years by conservation writers like me as a cautionary tale of what we have lost, was not that at all. Instead, it was an anomaly, an abomination, a post-Lenape blip, a sickly aspect of Neumann's "outbreak population—always a symptom of an extraordinarily disrupted ecological system."

The Iconic Bison

America's largest post–Ice Age animal, the shaggy, horned, humpbacked beast was given the scientific name *Bison bison*. The creature had as many as four subspecies, with the iconic Great Plains version given a third *bison* in its name. Less well known was its cousin, the eastern woodland bison, formally named *Bison bison pennsylvanicus* in honor of the state. The smallest of the four subspecies, it is now extinct, a victim of the same hunting pressure that took out the passenger pigeon. The last herd of eastern bison was hunted in Union County, Pennsylvania, in the winter of 1799–1800, and the last individual was shot in West Virginia in 1825.

There is a curious and nagging thread of disbelief that the subspecies actually existed at all, as it may have always inhabited Pennsylvania in small numbers and there are extraordinarily few (some say no) bones of this beast on record or in collections. Still, Joseph Merritt, in his definitive 1987 *Guide to the Mammals of Pennsylvania*, wrote that "during historic times bison

► The woodland bison on display at the State Museum of Pennsylvania in Harrisburg.

inhabited valleys, foothills, and forests of Pennsylvania. With the arrival of the first European settlers and increasing hunting pressure, the numbers of bison rapidly declined."

▶ The timber wolf has disappeared from the entire East Coast.

Across North America, bison populations have been estimated at biblical numbers, as many as 60 million animals at the highwater mark. Its story parallels the passenger pigeon's: extraordinary numbers, profligate hunting, and a population crash. According to the U.S. Fish and Wildlife Service, by 1884 a measly 325 bison were left, with only 25 in Yellowstone National Park. Thankfully, this story ends differently, as preserves, zoos, and even sympathetic ranchers conspired to save the creature from the pigeon's fate. Today, as many as 500,000 bison roam America.

Still, after First Nations populations collapsed and they were no longer hunting bison, the lid on the animal's population was removed and the numbers boiled over. "The massive, thundering herds were pathological," summarizes Mann, "something that the land had not seen before and was unlikely to see again." Perhaps even the eastern woodland bison gained in numbers too, giving the region's early European settlers a skewed notion of "normal" in Wild Philly.

The bison's hoofed cousin the elk followed a similar path. Elk were relatively rare in Lenapehoking as a result of hunting, with the population then exploding after first contact decimated the Lenape. But this didn't last as elk soon faced hunters on horseback with rifles. Elk were gone from southeastern Pennsylvania by 1800 and from the rest of the state by the 1870s. In 1913, the still-new Pennsylvania Game Commission imported fifty elk from Yellowstone National Park, re-establishing the species in western Pennsylvania, where it has since taken hold.

▶ While reports of Pennsylvania mountain lions linger on the web, the state's Game Commission considers the animal extinct in the state.

Ironically, our image of American wilderness as teeming with giant flocks of passenger pigeons flying over huge herds of bison is just another bubble we need to burst, another canard, another underestimation of the extensive way the Lenape managed Lenapehoking.

▶▶ Bobcats, meanwhile, do live in Penn's Woods.

Killing Carnivores

The first settlers of Pennsylvania pushed the forest back. They removed trees to use the wood for timber and fuel, while clearing the land to remove hiding places for the many large carnivores that inhabited the forest, especially wolves and cougars, but also martens, fishers, and wolverines. John Fanning Watson, a Germantown resident who wrote *Annals of Philadelphia* in 1830, observed that several wolves and a black bear were killed along Wissahickon Creek in 1796. So, big animals were here into the early nineteenth century.

The wolf vanished from the state in the very early 1900s. But which wolf or how many species of wolves were here is surprisingly confusing. In his 1917 pamphlet *Extinct Animals of Pennsylvania*, newspaper publisher and conservationist Ernest Shoemaker reported on three species of wolves in the state: black, gray, and brown. According to Shoemaker, the black wolf—an animal drawn by Audubon in his *Quadrupeds of North America*—was "far the superior of the others" in intelligence, theorizing it was crossbred with

"Native American dogs," which it may have been. Contemporary biologists, however, dismiss separate black species, saying it was the gray wolf (a.k.a. timber wolf, *Canis lupus*) that was driven from Pennsylvania. Today there is no wolf in the eastern United States. But many early settlers in the center of the state always assumed there were three kinds of wolves.

Shoemaker's brown wolf is interesting, as it is the smallest of the group; some think this must have been the coyote. There are two schools of thought here. One thinks that coyotes were southern and western canines kept out of northeastern states like Pennsylvania by the larger, stronger wolf. The other believes that small populations of coyotes must have existed here, but were never numerous owing to competition with wolves and disappeared at roughly the same time.

But Pennsylvania did once have three different wildcats living here: mountain lion, lynx, and bobcat. Today, only the bobcat remains. Biologists estimate some 4000 of them roam the state, though none in the southeastern corner. The mountain lion, once the region's largest cat, is an animal of too many names—panther, puma, cougar, catamount, wildcat—and the mascot of too many schools and colleges. It seems we love them as sports teams, but hate them as neighbors, as Pennsylvania's last mountain lion was killed in 1871 in Berks County. One of the state's last mountain lions is mounted and on display at Penn State University, as the Nittany Lions play football in the shadow of Mount Nittany. There have been no Nittany lions on Mount Nittany in more than a century.

While the Pennsylvania Game Commission doggedly maintains there are neither cougars nor lynx in the state, there have been innumerable reports of both of these secretive animals returning. While many sightings have been investigated, most turn out to have been bobcats—still officially the region's only wildcat.

Wildlife Rebounding

As Pennsylvania's forests were clear-cut and wild animal populations plummeted, some animals vanished from either lack of habitat or overhunting or both. Throughout the twentieth and into the twenty-first century, the state's forests have grown back, but these are very different from the pre-Columbian forests. Still, animals have been rebounding, like the river otter. Once common, the state's otter population was greatly reduced, losing 75 percent of its numbers. But through habitat preservation and smart conservation practices, this species is resurgent.

▼ The fisher, a once-vanished member of the weasel family, has returned to Pennsylvania.

▲ Beavers, one of the first animals to vanish from Wild Philly, are undergoing a resurgence across the region.

◀ Tom Witmer of Philadelphia Parks and Recreation inspects beaver-damaged trees on Cobbs Creek in West Philadelphia.

The otter is not alone. The fisher (like the otter) is a large member of the weasel family. This poorly named cat-sized predator (it doesn't eat fish—its Dutch name *fisse* refers to its pelt) once lived across the state, but it had disappeared by the 1920s, yet another victim of clear-cutting.

As second-growth forests returned in the late twentieth century, fishers returned to other sections of the state—but not yet to Wild Philly. "Today," reports the Game Commission, "fisher populations are well established and increasing throughout southwestern, central and northern regions of the state, and fishers have become established even in some rural and suburban habitats once thought unsuitable for this adaptive forest carnivore." The website LancasterOnline recently ran a headline that screamed "Fierce Fishers Storming Back in Pennsylvania." Even today, we unnecessarily lean on pejorative words for toothsome animals, wielding fear as clickbait.

Also storming back are beavers, those popular semi-aquatic dam-building mammals. While the furbearer disappeared from Pennsylvania in the early 1900s, naturalist Bernard "Billy" Brown holds that beavers vanished from Wild Philly early in colonial settlement, as early as the 1600s, as their fur was wildly coveted for the European craze of felted hats like the top hat. Swedish and French fur trappers were here long before William Penn, sending pelts back to Europe. The Lenape began trading large numbers of beaver, deer, and other pelts to trappers and traders in exchange for European commodities like pots, blankets, and axes. After all, one beaver pelt was worth $4 in 1800, not quite a king's ransom but about $80 in today's value.

Beavers were removed not only from Pennsylvania, but from most of the eastern United States. As forests grew back, the animal rebounded, moving first down the Delaware River and then up the Schuylkill. Today, there are beavers across the entire state. In Wild Philly, they can be seen (if you come at the right time of day) on several of the field trips, including Palmyra Cove Nature Park, the Schuylkill River in Roxborough, Tinicum, and the Black Run Wildlife Refuge, and are thriving elsewhere, like along Cobbs and Tacony Creeks in the city. The beaver has returned.

◄ The fast-flying peregrine falcon now nests in many places in Wild Philly.

One More Lazarus

The peregrine falcon is the world's fastest animal, dive-bombing hapless birds from the sky while reaching astonishing speeds of greater than 200 miles per hour. But the widespread use of the pesticide DDT starting in the 1940s to address mosquito control had an unexpected consequence, causing eggshell thinning among many birds of prey, including the peregrine. When peregrine parents—their nests were historically high up on cliffs, often along rivers—sat on their eggs to incubate them, they inadvertently cracked the shells and killed their own young, a tragic occurrence replicated among bald eagles, pelicans, and so many other birds.

The peregrine's population plummeted almost as fast as its dive, crashing through the 1950s until the eastern subspecies had completely vanished by the mid-1960s, with the bird almost gone across the rest of the country as well. Cornell University began a captive breeding program then, merging other subspecies together in an attempt to recreate the eastern race, and eventually released peregrines back into the wild. That, along with the 1972 ban of DDT, allowed the peregrine falcon to stage a Lazarus-like return.

Today, peregrines nest in many places in Philadelphia, including most river bridges, the City Hall tower, a church steeple in Manayunk, and the 2400 Chestnut apartment building, which smartly uses its famous peregrine residents as marketing for the building.

So this one species is back from the dead—but only after great cost and remarkable effort.

The Coyote

As one last example of wildlife rebounding in Pennsylvania, consider the coyote, perhaps the most surprising of the region's new urban residents. As noted earlier, there is vigorous disagreement on the history of this wild

▲ A coyote in the Dixon Meadow Preserve in Whitemarsh Township.

canine in Pennsylvania. However, if they were here historically, it was always in small numbers, their population decidedly kept in check by wolves.

The Game Commission offers that "pictures dating to the 1930s have appeared over the years in the Pennsylvania Game Commission's magazine, and these animals look like the same coyotes being killed today. The first coyote identified as an animal similar to what we today call the 'eastern coyote' was killed in Tioga County in 1940." Writing from a hunter's perspective, the fact is that while the coyote's history is murky at best, there is no doubt there are coyotes in the city and surrounding regions today.

In fact, coyotes have been heard howling in every county in the state. And even as elusive as they are, coyotes have been spotted in unlikely places. In South Philadelphia in 2018, game wardens captured and put down a coyote that seemed used to being near people, suspecting it had become too comfortable seeking trash as food. Sadly, Philadelphia is overflowing with trash.

▼ A coyote pup emerges from its Valley Forge den.

Biologists guess that coyotes entered northern Pennsylvania from the Catskill Mountains of New York in the 1970s, so the state's highest population then was in the Poconos. Using that as their home base, coyotes spread south and west. By 1990, in less than 20 years, the wily coyote had either conquered for the first time—or conquered again—the Keystone State. I'll let you decide which version of history you like.

Philadelphia: A Natural History Hotspot

When Thomas Jefferson completed the Louisiana Purchase in 1803, greatly expanding the young United States, he tasked his personal secretary Meriwether Lewis with exploring the western lands. Lewis, of course, did what any smart explorer of that era would have done. He came to Philadelphia to learn what to do next.

For the Philadelphia of the late eighteenth and early nineteenth centuries was the Athens of the western world. Not only was it the largest city in the colonies, but also a center for commerce, industry, medicine, science, and even finance, as the Bank of the United States, the country's central bank, was located here. Unlike most American cities then, Philadelphia was paved and lighted, and drinking water flowed through wooden pipes to homes. New York envied its southern neighbor.

So it's no surprise that eighteenth-century Philadelphia was a hotbed of natural history, then widely practiced by intellectuals. Birdwatching, butterfly collecting, rock collecting, botanizing, even egg and nest collecting were *pro forma* practices among the learned elite. Ben Franklin, of course, was busily conducting numerous electrical experiments and, in 1752, flew that kite in a thunderstorm to prove lightning was electricity.

In 1769, David Rittenhouse, born in Rittenhousetown tucked up against Wissahickon Creek, used twenty-two telescopes and money from the colonial government to track the journey of Venus across the face of the sun, a huge event in its day. Rittenhouse used the transit to somehow calculate Earth's distance from the sun—93 million miles—a number that you likely

▼ The Meriwether Lewis historic marker in front of the Academy of Natural Sciences of Drexel University.

▲ Today's Ritten-housetown in Germantown, one of Philadelphia's earliest settlements and the 1732 birthplace of David Rittenhouse.

learned in school some 250 years later. He later became the first American to spot Uranus, taught astronomy at the University of Pennsylvania, and directed the U.S. Mint under George Washington. His acclaim was such that Rittenhouse Square was named in his honor.

The American Philosophical Society, founded in 1743 by Franklin, Rittenhouse, and many others, was the nation's first scientific society. Thomas Jefferson once famously quipped he'd rather attend one of their meetings than spend a week in Paris.

The Bartram Legacy

The region's reputation as a center for natural sciences begins with John Bartram, a third-generation Quaker born in Darby in 1699. After buying some 100 acres in Kingsessing along the Schuylkill in 1728, he began farming. However, he was bitten by the botany bug and "systematically began gathering the most varied collection of North American plants in the world," notes the website of Bartram's Garden, the nonprofit flourishing at his Kingsessing home.

A self-taught naturalist, Bartram established a portion of his property as a garden for plants he thought interesting. Now considered the father of American botany, he quickly adopted Linnaeus's newly introduced taxonomic system for scientific naming. Not surprisingly, he was a good friend of Ben Franklin and a cofounder of the American Philosophical Society. Thomas Jefferson and George Washington are among the many luminaries who visited Bartram's garden. Farming soon took a very back seat to plant

and seed propagation—which grew to be the real family business—and his garden essentially became the New World's first botanical garden.

Franklin introduced Bartram to the Royal Society in London, where he began corresponding with its members. He soon was sending plants and seeds around the world, even to Linnaeus himself. He annually sent "Bartram's boxes," a crate filled with seeds from as many as 100 different plants, plus dried specimens and other intriguing artifacts, to his growing list of European collectors. Bartram's popularity in England even led to him being declared the King's Botanist for North America by none other than the infamous King George III.

Bartram traveled extensively around the colonies to find new plants and wrote books on his travels. American books being rare and still novelties then, he was first published in London; his books were some of the first travelogues of the New World. One described a 1765 expedition to the South with his son William, where they discovered a new and rare species of tree in Georgia. Featuring large fragrant white blooms, William christened it *Franklinia* after their family friend, the only species in its genus. A mysterious tree, the Franklin tree oddly disappeared from the wild in the early 1800s. Today it only exists in a handful of botanical gardens and private collections—one is at Bartram's Garden even today—and each is a descendant of seeds collected by William on a later trip.

William Bartram, an important naturalist, artist, and author in his own right, continued the garden with his brother John Jr. He is especially well known for a wide-ranging botanical trip through the South, the one where he collected Franklin tree seeds. William's 1791 *Travels*, his account of that trip, included many of his drawings of the flora and fauna he encountered. The volume is a landmark work of American natural history, widely read on both

▼ John Bartram, the father of American botany, as drawn by nineteenth-century illustrator Howard Pyle.

▲ John Bartram's Kingsessing home, today the headquarters of a beloved nonprofit institution.

sides of the Atlantic and beloved by both scientists and poets, as Coleridge and Wordsworth both read—and were influenced by—his book and its vivid descriptions. Bartram's *Travels* is still read even today.

John Bartram's great-grandson Thomas Say, born in 1787 on a property adjoining the garden, continued the family tradition in a different direction. He became the father of American entomology, publishing a three-volume masterwork, *American Entomology, or Descriptions of the Insects of North America*, while naming 1000 species of beetles and 400 other kinds of insects. Say's phoebe is named for him, as are many crabs, clams, and snails.

The Philadelphia Museum, an American First

▼ This portrait of Ben Franklin, painted by Charles Willson Peale in 1785, was one of the artist's paintings of American leaders on display in the Philadelphia Museum, the country's first natural history museum.

The Bartram family was not alone in pioneering in the natural sciences as a family affair. Charles Willson Peale, the acclaimed eighteenth-century portrait artist who painted so many founding fathers, was the head of a family of painters, who were aptly named Raphaelle, Rembrandt, Rubens, and Titian. Like most artists of the time, Peale displayed his portraits in his home for prospective clients to see. When asked to paint mastodon fossils from a western expedition, this painting attracted such unusual attention from his callers that Peale began displaying natural history specimens in his home.

In 1784, Peale formalized his collection, dubbing it the Philadelphia Museum—the nation's very first natural history museum—and charging admission. Within 10 years he moved it to the American Philosophical Society's headquarters, where visitors could not only see his famous portraits of Revolutionary heroes, but stuffed natural history specimens, skeletons, and fossils. Visitors walked under an arch formed by the jawbones of a whale into a room dominated by a huge mastodon skeleton, one Peale himself collected in upstate New York, the first mastodon ever assembled in a museum. The museum also boasted a live menagerie, a quixotic collection of disparate animals like monkey, grizzly bear, and what Peale called "the white-headed eagle," as he thought that a much better name for the bald eagle.

In 1802, the growing Philadelphia Museum moved again to the Pennsylvania State House, that era's name for Independence Hall, where it greatly expanded its collection. The science museum occupied the tower and the upper floors of the building. The space was filled with some 200 taxidermied animals in the Quadruped Room, including a massive bison, and the high-ceilinged Long Room displayed Peale's vast collection of more than 700 American birds.

But Peale displayed his birds differently. Arranged by species in the new taxonomic classification system Linnaeus was only then inventing, Peale arranged his creatures in their boxes in lifelike poses in what appeared to be their natural habitat. The scion of a large family of painters, he placed watercolor skies and landscapes behind them. In short, Peale invented the diorama, now the standard of every natural history museum everywhere. He also pioneered the use of arsenic in taxidermied animals to preserve fur and feathers from hungry insects, and painted lifelike eyeballs on the interiors of glass spheres to serve as eyes—again, now all standard practices.

Alexander Wilson

Early in the nineteenth century, William Bartram took under his wing another soon-to-be giant of American ornithology, Alexander Wilson. A taciturn Scottish master weaver who had found teaching jobs in Pennsylvania, Wilson settled not very far from Bartram in Kingsessing. Wilson's reading of Bartram's *Travels* likely influenced his decision to study and collect "all the birds in this part of North America" and to illustrate them in a series of volumes. Self-taught as both illustrator and birdwatcher, Wilson sent many of his drawings to Bartram, who generously corrected and helped identify the animals.

From 1808 to 1814, Wilson published *American Ornithology; or, the Natural History of the Birds of the United States*, a series featuring his full-color

◄ A plate from Wilson's *American Ornithology* showing a variety of birds, including the common yellowthroat (bottom left) and the summer tanager (top left).

▲ Mill Grove today, Audubon's first American home.

illustrations of American birds. Subscribers paid $120—a kingly sum back then—for the 10-volume series, as full-color engraved volumes like this were expensive and time-consuming to create. George Ord, the influential president of the newly founded Academy of Natural Sciences of Philadelphia, this hemisphere's first such institution, championed and financially supported Wilson's work.

Many now consider Alexander Wilson to be the father of American ornithology, as 26 of the 268 species described and illustrated in his volumes were new to science. His name has been affixed to several species of birds, including the impossibly yellow Wilson's warbler and Wilson's storm petrel, the most common bird in the North Atlantic.

Audubon: Colorful and Controversial

Today, Wilson is not a widely recognized ornithologist. That distinction goes to John James Audubon, he of the best-known surname in conservation. Like Wilson, Audubon was an immigrant who decided to draw America's birds *at the exact same time*. But the two were otherwise completely different people: Audubon flamboyant and outgoing, the Scotsman far more introverted. Eventually they collided, matter smashing into antimatter.

Audubon's colorful and controversial life has been recounted in several outstanding biographies, and he deserves the full motion-picture treatment. Born on a Haitian sugar plantation to a French naval officer and his younger chambermaid mistress, Audubon's father left Haiti when afraid of a slave revolt and raised his son in France. Despite the fact that Audubon spoke no English, his father nonetheless sent him to America in 1803, wanting his 18-year-old son to avoid serving in Napoleon's wars.

Luckily, his father was a real estate investor who owned Mill Grove, a 284-acre homestead on the banks of Perkiomen Creek not far from Valley Forge. The land included a lead mine, which the family hoped to develop into a business.

From his earliest days in France, Audubon had an affinity for birds. "I felt an intimacy with them . . . bordering on frenzy [that] must accompany my steps through life." He brought that affinity to America, and his house (like Peale's) immediately became a small natural history museum. His neighbor and later brother-in-law Will Blakewell wrote that "the walls were festooned with all kinds of birds' eggs, carefully blown out and strung on a thread. The chimney-piece was covered with stuffed squirrels, raccoons, and opossums, and the shelves were likewise crowded with specimens, among which were fish, frogs, snakes, lizards, and other reptiles. Besides these stuffed varieties, many paintings were arrayed on the walls, chiefly of birds. He had great skill in stuffing and preserving animals of all sorts."

An avid hiker—he dubbed them "rambles"—Audubon's favorite walk was along the ledge of rocky bluffs above the southern bank of Perkiomen Creek. Richard Rhodes wrote in his *John James Audubon: The Making of an American* that "from the bluff he could observe kingfishers perched above the creek. Often fish hawks [ospreys] appeared and sometimes even a white-headed eagle. On one of his early Perkiomen rambles he found a cave that he began using as a solitary study." This cave became iconic in American ornithology.

Audubon noticed that phoebes were nesting in this cave and leaving after the nesting season was over. Wondering if the birds were loyal to nest sites, in 1804 he attached light threads to the legs of the nestlings—becoming the very first instance of bird banding in the United States.

"I fixed a light silver thread to the leg of each," he wrote, "loose enough not to hurt the part, but so fastened that no exertions of theirs could remove it." The next spring, he discovered two arriving phoebes that still carried silver threads nesting, not in the cave, but in a Mill Grove grain shed nearby.

Audubon drew birds fanatically while studying taxidermy and collection methods. He visited Peale's museum regularly, admired it greatly, and the museum's diorama arrangements likely influenced his plans and thinking. Like all animal artists of the era, Audubon shot specimens for painting—by all accounts he was a fabulous marksman—but grew increasingly frustrated that they would not "pose" for him. He awakened one night with an inspiration and hopped on his horse for a predawn ride into Norristown, well before the city's businesses opened.

Audubon then rushed home with his just-purchased wires of varied thicknesses. He took lengths of soft wood to use as a base and jabbed the wires into the wood so they stood vertically. He ran to the river, shot a kingfisher, and arranged the dead creature on the wooden contraption, the wires piercing the body but holding it up. Audubon then used individual wires to arrange the bird's legs, head, and wings in the positions he wanted and manipulated the animal into a pose where it appeared to be alive. Then, elated, he painted it. This would be how Audubon operated from then on.

▲ An 1826 portrait of John James Audubon.

◀ Audubon's portrait of the wild turkey, the first page of his masterpiece *Birds of America*.

Within a few years, Audubon married his neighbor Lucy Bakewell. His father had to sell the Mill Grove home and lead mine, and, painting all the time, Audubon headed west with his bride to set up a business with his new brother-in-law in Louisville, Kentucky. Ironically, who walked into his store in 1810 but the ornithologist and bird painter Alexander Wilson. They had never met in Philadelphia, but when Wilson decided to head west to paint new species, people recommended he look up Audubon. He arrived in Louisville in a boat he had purchased and christened *The Ornithologist*.

The men ended up birding and collecting, America's two best birders visiting a roost where both whooping and sandhill cranes were nesting alongside each other. Of course, each showed the other his bird paintings, each sizing up not only the other's paintings, but the other's reaction to his work. Wilson was much more impressed with Audubon's work than Audubon was with Wilson's.

Wilson was much further along in his project, actually showing Audubon the first two completed volumes in his series, the second having just been finished. Audubon almost subscribed to the project, picking up his pen to write a check, for how could he not? But his brother-in-law, watching over Audubon's shoulder, said in French that Audubon's paintings were much better. He put down his pen, made an excuse, and snubbed the livid Wilson.

Audubon continued through several careers and adventures, living in many places while his art skills matured. In 1824, he returned to Philadelphia to find a publisher for what he is now calling his *Birds of America*, the magnum opus that established his fame. Surprisingly, there were no takers. Audubon also hoped to secure a membership in the Academy of Natural Sciences. But with George Ord backing Wilson's project, Audubon was denied admission, a rejection he did not take lightly. Wilson's revenge? Perhaps.

Finding no publisher in Philadelphia, Audubon made a bold decision with a huge payoff: he sailed to London with a portfolio of more than 300 drawings. Audubon played up his image of the American woodsman, donning a coonskin cap like Ben Franklin did in Paris 50 years earlier. He wrote, "I have been received here in a manner not to be expected during my highest enthusiastic hopes."

Ultimately, through a lot of hard work, the monumental work was printed, consisting of "435 plates including 497 species!" as he excitedly wrote to a friend a little later. Printed in double-elephant sized folio paper, each page measures a whopping 26 by 39 inches. Audubon estimated the effort had taken 14 years and cost $115,640, an extraordinary sum for that era. Rhodes wrote that this was "a staggering achievement, as if one man had single-handedly financed and built an Egyptian pyramid."

Audubon's work, of course, became iconic, widely recognized and imitated. His prints are still commonly found in homes, antique shops, and the offices of nature geeks across the country. In the library of the Academy of Natural Sciences, the place that denied him membership 200 years ago, a double-elephant folio version of Audubon's work occupies pride of place in the room. Each day its staff lifts its protective Plexiglas cover and turns one page.

This is the Philadelphia that Meriwether Lewis visited in 1803 at President Jefferson's request, the Philadelphia of learned naturalists and scientists. Lewis established connections with the Bartrams, visited the Philadelphia Museum, and learned from Penn professor Benjamin Smith Barton about how to collect plants. He learned about diseases from Benjamin Rush, one of the city's preeminent doctors, and visited Caspar Wistar, founder of the Wistar Institute, to learn about animal and fossil collecting.

On a more mundane note, Lewis also purchased supplies like camping gear, clothing, books, trading goods, food, containers, guns and ammunition, and scientific instruments in the city, as Philadelphia was the best place to do that at the time as well. During and after the journey, Philadelphia scientists played important roles in receiving and cataloguing the expedition's findings.

"After completing the expedition in 1806," wrote historian Luke Willert in the online *Encyclopedia of Greater Philadelphia*, "Lewis returned to Philadelphia and bequeathed many of his western treasures to Peale. Peale then displayed the objects, mostly diplomatic gifts from western Indians, in a special exhibit and painted portraits of both Lewis and Clark that remain on display at Independence National Historical Park."

Where Are They Now?

While Philadelphia has changed dramatically in the last 200 years, many of the people and places mentioned here have lived on. Bartram's Garden, a National Historic Landmark, is owned by the city but successfully run by the Bartram's Garden Association. The Philadelphia Museum, highly successful in its time, moved out of Independence Hall in 1827 to a larger site and established additional museums in New York and Baltimore. But with the passing

▲ Artist and naturalist Charles Willson Peale, inventor of the diorama, founder of America's first museum, and the preeminent portrait painter of his era, created "Self-Portrait" in 1822 when he was 81.

of time and Peale's death, it fell out of favor. The entire collection was purchased by none other than P. T. Barnum, and much of it has tragically been lost to the ravages of time.

But if you go to the Pennsylvania Academy of Fine Arts, that magical building on Broad Street, you'll be greeted by one of Peale's very last paintings. In his magnificent life-sized self-portrait, he holds a curtain aside to tease you with a glimpse of his museum in all its glory—with the mastodon hiding behind the curtain, only its feet showing. It remains my all-time favorite painting in my all-time favorite building.

Audubon, of course, lent his name to the society much later founded in his honor, now one of the country's oldest and most revered conservation groups. His beloved Mill Grove was purchased by Montgomery County and is run by Audubon Mid-Atlantic, which recently refurbished the house and barn and added a stunning new interpretive center with interactive exhibits. And the town that Mill Grove is located in? Why, it's Audubon, Pennsylvania.

In the waning days of his life, Audubon visited Philadelphia one more time. "Passed poor Alexander Wilson's schoolhouse," he wrote in his journal, "and heaved a sigh. Alas, poor Wilson! would that I could once more speak to thee, and listen to thy voice." Then he switched topics: "When I was a youth, the woods stood unmolested here, looking wild and fresh as if just from the Creator's hands. But now hundreds of streets cross them, and thousands of houses and millions of diverse improvements occupy their places. Bartram's Garden is the only place which is unchanged. I walked in the same silent wood I enjoyed on the same spot when first I visited the present owner of it, the descendant of William Bartram, the generous friend of Wilson."

If pre-Civil War Philadelphia was filled with "millions of diverse improvements," what would Audubon say of today's city? This he would recognize: Philadelphia remains a hotbed of natural history.

Threats to Philadelphia's Nature

I'm sitting in the Schuylkill Center's forest in Upper Roxborough, looking out at a bucolic scene of bright green forest in the first blush of spring. Trees are leafing out, while eastern towhees exhort me to "drink your tea!," a common transliteration of their insistent song. Through the trees, I can see three deer gingerly sneaking by, aware I am here.

Then my inner naturalist kicks in, and I snap to attention. I notice that the tree closest to me is an Amur cork with its characteristic spongy bark; an autumn olive vine wraps around the tree. Garlic mustard plants with

▼ Wild Philly's forests are filled with invasive non-native plants.

bright white cross-shaped flowers spring from the ground around the base of the tree, and the flowers are visited by a cabbage white butterfly looking for a place to lay her eggs. A grove of devil's walking sticks pokes up through the forest behind the cork tree.

The bucolic scene suddenly crumbles into a nightmare. Except for the deer and towhee, every one of the creatures noted above is not native to Pennsylvania. None were here in Lenapehoking; none should be present in Penn's Woods. All are crowding out too many native species of too many kinds. And the deer, lacking any predators save cars and more numerous than they ever were historically, are browsing out native plants while leaving too many invasives in their hungry wake.

This scene is replicated at many seemingly natural areas throughout the region. The Schuylkill Center was set aside for environmental education programming in 1965, its forests regenerating during that whole time. What is growing back, however, is a novel ecosystem that has never existed on this planet before, a mishmash of Pennsylvania natives alongside plants and animals either brought here accidentally or on purpose, that, with few biological checks, have overrun the region's landscape.

Complicating this, our climate is changing rapidly. Philadelphia is becoming hotter, wetter, and weirder. Which of the species present in the region's forests today will be able to survive the new climate in 20 or 30 years? Few have any idea—yet.

I reach out and touch the Christmas fern growing nearby, one of the few native species in front of me, an old friend I'm glad to see.

Although the nature of Philadelphia is threatened by numerous problems, we'll focus on five dynamic issues that are literally rearranging the region's physical landscape: deer, invasive non-native species, stormwater, sprawl and development, and climate change.

White-Tailed Deer

Deer were a necessary animal to the Lenape, invaluable for their meat, hides, and even bones and antlers. The Lenape, remember, actively burned forests to foster the acorn- and nut-bearing trees that both they and wildlife needed. The burned areas also created the shrubby edge habitat that deer require—which was great for the Lenape, who kept deer populations artificially higher near their villages.

But even with this active management, deer populations remained low. There remained long stretches of dense forest that deer avoid, and deer were preyed upon by wolves and cougars. Biologists estimate that the population density of white-tailed deer in Lenapehoking was between eight and ten deer per square mile.

As European settlement expanded, the Lenape were forced out and large predators disappeared. The removal of forest habitat also quickened, with the land cleared for farming, milling, firewood, and of course lumber. Although laws regulating the hunting of deer were passed as early as 1721, they were routinely ignored. Consequently, deer populations plummeted. By 1905, estimates the Pennsylvania Game Commission—itself only formed in 1895 to protect this important animal—there were only 1000 deer left in all of Pennsylvania (and only 300,000 in the entire country, an astonishing 1 percent of estimated pre-Columbian levels). Deer were virtually wiped out.

The state's Game Commission began to import deer into the state while passing stronger, better-enforced laws, especially one protecting antler-less deer—does and their young—from being hunted. Logged-out areas rebounded with second-growth forests, the young shoots offering prime deer forage, and deer populations exploded. By 1928, a million deer inhabited the state, a 99,900 percent increase in only 23 years.

Today, scientists estimate Pennsylvania's white-tailed deer population at 1.5 million, as many as 30 deer per square mile, a tripling of its historic density. In some places in suburbia, deer have been measured at 100 per square mile. Suburban and exurban sprawl especially favors deer, as it creates the edge habitat the animals desire: small forested woodlots bordering suburban backyards planted with a smorgasbord of delicious plants. Valley Forge National Historical Park, a beloved but deer-overrun park, was home to fewer than 200 deer in 1985. By 2009, more than 1200 deer lived there alone—more than lived in the entire state in 1905.

While Joe Kosack, author of the book *The History of Pennsylvania Game Commission, 1895–1995*, lauds this comeback as "one of the greatest success stories in the history of wildlife management," many would disagree, especially those worried about the health of forest ecosystems.

▲ Too many deer have heavily browsed the region's forests.

Such explosive growth in one species never happens without ripples throughout an ecosystem and across human communities. By 2000, every single day more than 3000 American cars were colliding with deer, which were also causing billions of dollars in damage to crops and landscaping. White-tailed deer were vacuuming out forest understories, removing important plants, and halting the regeneration of forests. Birds and even insect populations were harmed from the loss of nesting sites and food. Then there is Lyme disease, spread by the deer tick, which uses the deer as one of its hosts.

In the same year Kosack was lauding the deer's success, a survey of a heavily browsed forest in northwestern Pennsylvania revealed a loss of between 59 and 80 percent of its historic shrubs and wildflowers. Hobble-bush, for example, a shrub in the *Viburnum* family that produces red fruits eaten by many wildlife species, had disappeared from this forest plot, later found nearby in small, fragmented populations.

Bowman's Hill Wildflower Preserve in New Hope can only preserve its botanical diversity because of a 100-acre deer fence. The staff only recently discovered that deer would leap over their cattle grate at the preserve's entrance to sneak in. Only with deer finally excluded in 2021 did wild hyacinth blossom, a welcome sight.

White trillium, one of the showiest spring ephemeral flowers, is especially sought after by deer—so much so that biologists can estimate a forest's deer density by examining the browse level of this one flower. Several state

◄ A seedling oak, a too-rare sight in Philadelphia forests.

endangered species, including the showy lady's slipper and yellow fringed orchid, have been slammed by deer, and the critically endangered golden puccoon came *this* close to vanishing from Presque Isle near Erie. A deer control program there allowed the plant to recover.

Deer devour young trees, and a whole generation of Penn's Woods has been unable to grow back. All of the oaks, a keystone tree in Pennsylvania's forest arch, are especially sought after by deer during the winter. The state's oaks are not regenerating. In a study of a central Pennsylvania forest preserve where hunting is not allowed, there were thirty-six times fewer small trees regenerating than in nearby (hunted) state game lands.

The deer shockwave ripples through birds too. With both forest floor and shrub layers cleared out, there are fewer thrushes, flycatchers, vireos, and other birds—even fewer salamanders and toads. As the vegetation keeping in the soil moisture is eaten, the forest floor dries out faster, impacting snail and fungi populations. Few people might have guessed that more deer means fewer snails.

Adding insult to all of this injury, deer often avoid eating invasive non-natives like garlic mustard, Japanese barberry, Eurasian species of honeysuckle, and tree of heaven, favoring the spread of these and other non-natives. In short, overbrowsing by the historically large deer herd results in fewer native species of many kinds coupled with a new dominance by a few unpalatable, often non-native, species. So it may come as no surprise that every nonprofit organization responsible for managing forests for biological diversity engages in deer control programs—or wants to. There is no other rational choice.

Invasive Non-native Species

In 1967, a small sap-sucking insect with an unwieldy name, the woolly adelgid, was first discovered in Pennsylvania. In the last 50-odd years, it has been literally sucking the life out of the massive state tree, the hemlock. While "there are still an estimated 124 million hemlock trees greater than five inches in diameter alive" in the state, notes Ad Crable in the journal of the Chesapeake Bay Foundation, "that's nearly 13 million fewer than in 2004 and the mortality rate has increased fourfold since 1989. In Pennsylvania's Tuscarora State Forest, the Hemlock Natural Area, a 120-acre stand of virgin hemlocks 'untouched by man' is now gone, touched by insects."

Turn over a hemlock branch and look on its underside: that little fuzzy wiggling mass is a group of adelgids. While foresters are racing to save the tree with a variety of remedies, 400-year-old giants are succumbing daily.

For more than 500 years, during what has been named the Columbian exchange, plants and animals have been sent hither and yon. New World potatoes and tomatoes became staples in European cuisine, horses and hogs were brought to America. A New York pharmacist decided Central Park needed every bird mentioned in Shakespeare (really?) and released starlings in the United States, now one of the most numerous birds in the country. A Massachusetts artist imported the gypsy moth into the United States to create a hardy silkworm, and the larvae escaped, going on to defoliate entire forests.

Many introductions were accidental, like the emerald ash borer, another Asian import discovered in Michigan forests in 2002. It has swept through Wild Philly in recent years, killing (or about to kill) just about every ash of all species in the entire region, that tree soon joining the chestnut and hemlock. Or the fungus that causes white-nose syndrome in bats, likely accidentally imported from overseas on the boots of a cave explorer. The fungus has killed millions of bats across North America over the last decade, decimating the little brown bat populations of Wild Philly.

Multiflora rose, now in the United States for decades, has choked out native species and compromises nesting birds. Non-native *Phragmites* reed forms dense stands in waterways that push out native vegetation. Garlic mustard becomes a dominant forest floor plant and a host of the cabbage white butterfly, the non-native insect that is now the region's most common butterfly. Japanese stilt grass forms dense carpets in many forests, crowding out native species.

Introduced carp roil Tinicum Marsh waterways during their mating rituals. The Chinese mantis crowds out its native cousins, while Japanese honeysuckle, Oriental bittersweet, and mile-a-minute vines completely enshroud trees, choking them and stunting their growth.

Morris Arboretum has catalogued 439 species of non-native plants in Pennsylvania, almost 40 percent of the state's flora. And the state has introduced mammals, reptiles, birds, fish, insects, and fungi as well. Often with no natural enemies, these species reproduce rapidly and spread quickly. The one-two punch of deer overbrowsing native plants while leaving non-native ones alone has severely compromised the biological diversity of the region's forests.

◄ The mile-a-minute vine buries native trees and shrubs under an emerald blanket.

Stormwater

Hey, Philadelphia, we finally beat New York City at something! In 2015, the data clearinghouse Climate Central released its study of fifty American cities, tracking the increase in heavy downpours. Using the number of storms in the 1950s with at least 3 inches of rain as its baseline, the group measured downpours in the decade between 2005 and 2014. Philadelphia's increase in downpours was a whopping 360 percent, more than quadruple its 1950s number. New York's growth, by contrast, was a paltry 350 percent. Philly's was the third largest growth of any American city, with only McAllen, Texas (700 percent), and Portland, Maine (400 percent), topping us.

Climate Central's report noted, "Climate models predict that if carbon emissions continue to increase as they have in recent decades, the types

▼ The emerald ash borer, shown here alongside the D-shaped hole from which it emerges, is decimating all species of North American ash trees.

▲ A dense stand of phragmites chokes out native vegetation at Tinicum Marsh.

of downpours that used to happen once every 20 years could occur every 4 to 15 years by 2100. As the number of days with extreme precipitation increases, the risk for intense and damaging floods is also expected to increase throughout much of the country."

This is not a competition we'd like to win, but the region's precipitation is noticeably shifting. Also, in the 1950s the wettest days used to be storms dumping between 2 and 3 inches of precipitation on us. Nowadays, heavy downpours deliver almost 4 inches. Historically, we expected about 41 inches of rain and snow in the region, but some models predict that by 2080 annual precipitation will peak above 51 inches.

This new rain regime has radically altered stream ecology. Sheets of rainwater pour across the region's vast expanses of impervious surfaces—roads, parking lots, rooftops, driveways—immediately into storm drains. This wall of polluted water then floods into streams and rivers, its velocity scouring stream beds, increasing the amount of sediment in the water, and dumping that sediment downstream. Check out the Schuylkill River after a rainy day. That coffee-colored water is a high sediment load delivered from upriver streams—the new norm.

The region's stream beds, once rocky bottomed, are now instead silty and sandy, with sediment covering the rock, filling in the gaps between stones, and changing the invertebrate fauna living there. Whereas trout streams should be home to insects that thrive in clean, clear, cold water, like mayfly and stonefly nymphs and caddisfly larvae, they are instead home to pollution-tolerant species like gnat larvae, and—you'll love this name—rat-tailed maggots. The biological diversity of local streams has been greatly reduced in recent decades, with stoneflies especially all but vanishing from many streams.

Almost 200 species of fish once swam in Pennsylvania's streams. Twenty-eight species have already disappeared, and another 45 species—representing 28 percent of those remaining—are threatened, including the brook trout, the state fish and Pennsylvania's only native trout.

► Flooded neighborhoods are becoming an increasingly common sight in Philadelphia.

On top of this, fast-flowing water erodes stream banks, cutting cliffs in them and pulling trees and sometimes trails down, as you may have noticed along Wissahickon Creek. Nonprofits and governmental agencies that manage streamside parks and preserves are continually bedeviled by stormwater, as fast and fierce water compromises bridges, buildings, benches, and more, greatly increasing the cost of managing these special places not only for fish and other fauna, but for us.

▲ As storm severity increases, streams everywhere, even small ones like Mount Airy's Carpenter's Run, are suffering from eroded banks.

Development and Sprawl

The Delaware Valley has long struggled with suburban sprawl. Although population growth lags in the state (Pennsylvania just lost a congressional seat in the 2020 census), sprawl does not. In 1982, Pennsylvania was losing 100 acres per day to sprawl, and the issue was considered a crisis. After decades of wrestling with this crisis, sprawl tripled, climbing to more than 350 acres daily by 2002.

Ben Moyer, author of the state-funded 2002 report "Pennsylvania's Wildlife and Wild Places," called sprawl "more irreversible than any [change] endured in the past. It is a change that banishes wild things and wild places from its path, that rends apart established communities and neighborhoods, and threatens the diversity of life around us."

"In the three centuries that followed Penn's landing on the Delaware in 1682," Moyer continued, "three million acres of Pennsylvania landscape were converted to urban uses, concentrated in downtown sectors of cities and towns. But in the past two decades (1982–2002) another 1 million acres of woods, fields, marshes, and mountainsides have been irreversibly converted to other uses, creating a new kind of landscape we know as sprawl."

▲ Between 1982 and 2002, 1 million acres of Pennsylvania was developed.

It's not like Americans were flocking to Pennsylvania. At that time, while only four states suffered from worse rates of sprawl, the state ranked forty-eighth in population growth. Essentially, the state's towns and cities were spilling out into the surrounding countryside, businesses moving with them, causing the Brookings Institution to cleverly label this situation "the sprawl of the wild."

And this was 20 years ago. Although small battles have been won, notable landscapes preserved, and Center City finally gaining population, Pennsylvania has long been losing the war against sprawl, which only harms the natural world. The state is still almost 60 percent forests, but those forests have gotten noticeably smaller, with the vast majority less than 5000 acres. The size of forest patches is critical for important animals like bobcats, bears, fishers, barred owls, and goshawks. While none of them live within the Delaware Valley, because the region's forests are too small, these animals are now threatened statewide.

Most of Wild Philly forests are small blocks of privately owned spaces, and few of them can be categorized as "core forest," whereby the forest's interior is more than 300 feet from a road, farm, or tract housing. Much of the region's forest wildlife thrives in that core forest—and struggles in the forest edge. For instance, the wood thrush, the area's most operatic singer, needs a forest patch larger than 100 acres to successfully nest. Wood thrush numbers have declined 1.8 percent annually in the last decades, both in the state and nationally, a number exacerbated by the fact that Pennsylvania is home to 8.5 percent of all American wood thrushes. Today, the bird's population has been halved from its 1960s levels, and it is not alone: ovenbirds, black-throated blue warblers, and scarlet tanagers are also birds requiring core forests whose numbers are in decline.

Roads have made life more difficult for woodland turtles, like the box turtle. These small, slow-moving reptiles are too frequently hit by cars as they cross roads carved into their territory. Smaller forest patches also have a greater amount of edge than do larger forests. Too much edge dries out the forest, making life challenging for salamanders and other moisture-dependent creatures, like the snails mentioned earlier.

In addition, invasive non-native plants use roadways and the disturbed soil of new housing subdivisions as pathways for establishing their kind, meaning that sprawl worsens the invasive species problem. And, of course, sprawl adds impervious cover atop the land, exacerbating the storm-water issue.

Climate Change

Carbon dioxide is a powerful greenhouse gas that holds heat in the Earth's atmosphere. Historically, Wild Philly evolved over millennia in an atmosphere of roughly 280 parts per million (ppm) of carbon dioxide, or only 0.028 per-cent of atmospheric gases. But the burning of fossil fuels has so increased the carbon dioxide concentration that by the summer of 2021 it had risen 50 percent to 419 ppm, a number never seen in the history of humankind.

Pennsylvania is 2.4°F warmer, on average, than it was in 1970. But given that Philadelphia is less forested than the state—and tree cover cools the climate—the city has seen its temperature increase by 3.1°F. No, it's not your imagination, the city *is* hotter. In 1970, for example, there might be only two or three summer days above 95°F. By 2018, however, there were six more days of this high heat annually. One worst-case scenario predicts, unless we act now, Philadelphia will see 104 days of 95°F weather by 2080. That's 3 months—an entire summer—of extreme heat.

By 2050, if we stay on the current path, Climate Central predicts that Philadelphia's temperature will resemble that of Richmond, Virginia, and by 2100, that of Brownsville, Texas, a city on the Mexican border. A warmer region will exacerbate the already struggling native species in Wild Philly's forests. The mix of plants and animals that we find here will change, as northern forest species that are already close to the southern extent of their range slowly decline, even disappear, and southern species move into the warmer north.

A 2019 National Audubon Society study warned of the impact of climate change on many of the region's birds, including the ruffed grouse, the state bird. A deep forest dweller dependent on winter snowfall for its survival, the ruffed grouse is disappearing along with the once-predictable winter snowfall. Others impacted include the brown thrasher, eastern towhee, whip-poor-will, fish crow, field sparrow, pine warbler, scarlet tanager, gos-hawk, and black duck. "Forty percent of Pennsylvania's 227 bird species are vulnerable to climate change," emphasized Greg Goldman, then the execu-tive director of Audubon Pennsylvania.

On the flip side of this coin, the black vulture, a bird of the southern United States, was not found in Philadelphia until the 1990s, and today it is

▲ The scarlet tanager is one of Wild Philly's many songbirds likely impacted by climate change.

◀ The hellbender, an already rare salamander in Wild Philly, is at great risk across the state as streams warm.

remarkably common. Historically, the northernmost portion of the Carolina chickadee's range was southeastern Pennsylvania—it was never found elsewhere in the state. Nowadays, it is moving north and west across the state, where it is pushing out its cousin, the black-capped chickadee.

Of course, it's not just birds that are being impacted. The state amphibian, the hellbender—a great name for the region's largest salamander—is at risk from warming streams. So, too, is the brook trout, the state fish and Pennsylvania's only native trout species. The bog turtle, already an endangered species and New Jersey's state reptile, is a likely loser in a warming climate. On top of all this bad news, a warmer climate likely increases the occurrences of insect outbreaks, and new invasive species will be able to expand their range northward, bringing new diseases with them.

Climate change also exacerbates the stormwater concerns mentioned earlier. In September 2021, Hurricane Ida roared through the region and caused historic flooding, especially along the Schuylkill River, drowning Manayunk, Bridgeport, and many other riverside communities. The storm even spawned tornadoes that ripped through homes around Mullica Hill in Gloucester County, New Jersey. Climate-fueled storms are increasing not only in number, but in intensity as well.

This is why I am sitting in the Schuylkill Center's forest rubbing a Christmas fern for luck. With all of the above—and more—it is remarkable that this fern and all the species described in this book are still with us.

Twenty-Five Ways You Can Help Nature

Although nature is in trouble—not only in Wild Philly, but across our beleaguered planet—there are thousands of people working to improve the state of the environment. This green army of passionate preservationists is dedicated to restoring habitats, saving species, cooling the climate, moving toward zero waste, and so much more. We are in a race against time, and every action helps. Philadelphia is a hotbed of this activity, with a huge network of nonprofits, government agencies, businesses, and just plain great people working 24/7 to preserve nature.

So what can you do to support this work, to buttress populations of local insects, amphibians, reptiles, and songbirds? What concrete actions can each of us take to keep the wildness in Philadelphia and in our local communities doing well? First, anything that conserves water, land, and energy while reducing waste is simply critical. If you own or rent a piece of land of any size, whether in the city, the suburbs, or the exurbs, the goal is to enjoy a yard, patio, or deck in which butterflies are flitting, bees are buzzing, and hummingbirds are hovering. Chipmunks are scouring the ground looking for acorns, while toads take up residence under that rock in the corner. Goldfinches and downy woodpeckers are feasting, while flying squirrels and bats will be visiting in the evenings.

Let's explore twenty-five actions you can take that support the nature we've been meeting in these pages. Here is a ladder with twenty-five steps, moving from incredibly simple to increasingly hard. As you climb the ladder the actions get tougher—but go for it. Perhaps you've already climbed far up the ladder. Great. See how much higher you can climb.

Easy

1. LEARN
The environmental field is cluttered with books telling you what you should do this week to protect the Earth—and this is yet another. But some of them

forget the simplest, easiest, even best thing you can do. Learn. Grow. Read. Find a nature center and go on walks there. Spend more time outdoors, as nature is the best teacher. Sit by a brook or a pond and just watch.

2. LEAVE LEAVES IN CORNERS

Every insect in this part of the world is adapted to survive winter in only one stage of its life cycle: the tiger swallowtail as a chrysalis, the ladybug as a larva, the mosquito as an egg, the yellowjacket as a queen. Every other stage dies. Each fall, insect larvae and pupae burrow into the leaf litter to hibernate and await spring; many eggs are hiding there too.

When we rake, blow, and scrape every leaf off our lawns in the fall, we are accidentally and clumsily killing uncountable numbers of hibernating insects. So be a messy gardener like me: leave the leaves in corners and along strips. Designate "no rake" areas. You'll be supporting the insect life that neighborhood songbirds and toads need to survive. And you'll be increasing the biological diversity of your yard.

I've carried this to extremes in my own yard. While we have a very small front yard that was originally all grass and one small tree, I've slowly removed the grass and transformed it into a small slice of forest—and I leave the leaves alone in the fall. But you're not me: start small and expand as you wish. The bugs will thank you.

3. PILE THOSE ROCKS

Equally easy, imagine creating a small crevice-rich pile of rocks in a corner of your yard. This will become a beacon for a large menagerie of small creatures looking for dark moist places to escape the summer sun: salamanders, toads, centipedes, spiders, millipedes, isopods, even—be brave now!—small (and harmless) snakes.

◄ Bird strike decals
are easy to install
on key windows.

4. INSTALL DECALS ON WINDOWS

The Wildlife Clinic at the Schuylkill Center treats thousands of injured animals. Too many are dazed, sometimes dying birds brought in because a bird flew into a picture window. One estimate places the number of birds killed this way in the United States alone at 1 billion annually.

Many skyscrapers are especially harmful to migrating birds slamming into the glass structures; the National Audubon Society is one of many organizations working hard to address this issue. In our homes, birds sometimes see the landscape reflected in a window and assume they can keep flying in that direction. In the spring, territorial birds sometimes fly at their own reflection in a window to chase the "intruder" away—and smack the glass. If a bird strikes a window in your home, the fixes are numerous and easy. Many nature centers stock window decals that break the spell glass casts on birds. Our center's glassy lobby has windows sporting soft mesh netting to prevent window strikes, which is another solution. Sometimes just moving a bird feeder a little away from a window stops this too.

5. DONATE

The Philadelphia region is blessed with an abundance of nonprofits that strive to preserve Wild Philly in thousands of ways, from small friends groups that have adopted green spaces in the city and across the region to large nonprofits that have protected thousands of acres of open space. Find an environmental organization that appeals to you, one that works in your neighborhood perhaps, or one that addresses a creature you find especially compelling. Doesn't matter how much—just give until it feels good.

▲ A monarch butterfly lays her eggs on the underside of a milkweed leaf.

6. GOT MILKWEED?

Populations of monarch butterflies have declined by 80 percent in only the last 20 years. The causes are numerous—modern farming practices are the lead suspect—but you can help in one key solution: monarch adults lay their eggs on only one plant, milkweed, their host plant. The caterpillars eagerly devour the leaves before metamorphosing into butterflies.

So if you plant milkweed, you'll entice monarchs to lay their eggs there. There are several milkweeds that work well in native plant gardens, including swamp milkweed (*Asclepias incarnata*) and butterflyweed (*Asclepias tuberosa*), the latter my favorite plant.

My own home came with a small strip of common milkweed (*Asclepias syriaca*), a 6-foot giant in the garden that most people remove. Recognizing its value, we've kept it. In some years we've seen upward of thirty chrysalises on the stone wall adjoining the strip. But in 2020, sadly, there were none that we saw.

Still, if you have a garden and haven't yet got milkweed, pull a Nike. Just do it!

A Little Harder

7. VOLUNTEER

Nurturing nature in this time of extreme need is an all-hands-on-deck proposition that requires each of us to pitch in. Happily, many of the same organizations that you might consider donating to also host volunteer programs where you can help with clearing trails, removing invasives, and planting trees and wildflowers.

8. PLANT NATIVE TREES

While Philadelphia boasts yards with massive trees, too many are non-native, even invasive. Too many streets are lined with London plane trees, and too many yards have Norway spruce and Japanese maple. Contrast that with natives. Plant a wild cherry tree near a native oak, and almost 1000 species of just moth and butterfly caterpillars will be raised on those two trees alone. The oak's acorns will feed a host of organisms, and the cherry's flowers are craved by insect pollinators, its berries by hungry birds. So plant a native tree—or many.

▲ Planting native trees is a powerful act that can help to restore the health of Wild Philly's ecosystems.

9. AND LEAVE PUPATION STATIONS UNDER THOSE TREES

Insects use native trees as food sources, with the larval stages of many inhabiting the trees. But when they pupate—when they go into that in-between resting stage—they drop down to the ground and burrow into the leaf litter. Suburban homes in particular typically boast those lifeless circles of root mulch around them. Banish that circle, and plant a variety of shade-loving natives under your tree, even placing a few rocks here and there as well. The insects will drop from the tree, pupate in this more natural-istic setting, and emerge as adults to start the life cycle over again.

10. REMOVE INVASIVE PLANTS

By now, you've caught on that non-native invasive plants are one of the largest threats facing local ecosystems. They proliferate, choke out natives, and provide little to no food value for the rest of creation. So learn to identify the common invasive species in your area, then walk your yard and begin selectively removing some of the invasives there. If you own a large well-established home with a big yard, this is a huge task. But if you bite off small chunks of this over time, you'll be doing nature a huge favor.

11. FEED THE BIRDS

Millions of Americans and many nature centers and parks attract birds
to bird feeders. There are many problems associated with bird feeders,
including the spread of disease and the increase of nuisance animals like
rats among them. But the joy of watching a pair of cardinals feed or hearing
that familiar "chick-a-dee-dee!" in your yard, or, yes, seeing a Cooper's hawk
snatch a mourning dove right off your lawn, for me, outweighs the problems.
Proper cleaning of your feeder and the land underneath it is essential; read
up on this and commit yourself to a cleaning regime.

12. WHILE WARMING THEM IN WINTER

Alongside your bird feeder, place a well-larded suet feeder in your yard to
bring in more nuthatches, chickadees, and woodpeckers. The fatty food
offers fuel to warm them when they need it most.

▼ A goldfinch at
an upside-down
feeder. Squirrels
can't get to the
seeds, but finches
easily can.

◄ A downy
woodpecker visits
a suet feeder.

13. PROVIDE ANIMALS WITH WATER TOO

As all living things need water, even small insects, including a water source
in your yard greatly ratchets up its nature friendliness. Like feeders, water
sources such as bird baths need constant attention and cleaning so as not
to become mosquito breeding grounds. Some enthusiasts even keep heat-
ing coils on their bird baths to allow them to function all winter. Others put
bubblers in their baths to aerate them, keeping down mosquito numbers
while the gurgling sound lures birds in.

◄ House wrens readily adapt to a wide range of backyard nest boxes.

14. AND GIVE THEM HOMES

Hanging a birdhouse is one of the easiest and first things many families do to attract wildlife. Birdhouses are a great way to bring all kinds of songbirds to your home. House wrens, chickadees, robins, even woodpeckers and wood ducks all respond to species-specific houses. Make your own, or visit your nature center gift shop to purchase one that does double duty, serving the birds while supporting the nonprofit. And like the bird feeders, cleaning these out after the season is important.

15. BE GOOD TO BEES

While the plight of the European honey bee (*Apis mellifera*) has received tons of deserved press, native bees—the ones that evolved in Wild Philly— need your help, too. Native pollinators of many species are on the decline, and even city dwellers with small yards or even just terraces can help here too. Beebalm, coneflower, and sunflowers are among the natives they buzz to. Plant these in your garden or in pots on your terrace, and the bees will come.

16. HELP THE HUMMINGBIRDS

One of my great summer pleasures is waiting for a hummingbird to show up at the feeder outside our kitchen window in the morning and feel- ing an intense thrill when it comes. Hummingbirds, those jewel-colored mini-helicopters, are easy to attract to your yard with feeders or the right flowers. Hummingbird feeders are easy to hang—the challenge is making and replacing nectar all summer while keeping the feeder clean and free of ants. If you are committed to that, you are golden. Nectar-making is easy (mix one part sugar with four parts water), but it is an ongoing commitment.

You can also plant the many native plants that hummingbirds love and fly to naturally, like beebalm, cardinal flower, trumpet vine, coral honeysuckle, or beardtongue. These flowers bring them in too, while also feeding many other pollinators, like the hummingbird moth that artfully mimics the bird.

17. REMOVE SOME LAWN

Americans love our lawns, and Philadelphians are no different. University of Delaware entomology professor Doug Tallamy recently studied land use in twenty-two suburban developments. Tallamy discovered that an "astounding" 92 percent of the area that could be landscaped was instead "planted in turfgrass."

Lawns are ecological deserts supporting precious few plants and animals: earthworms, robins, and little else. Studies indicate that some 30 percent of water used in the eastern United States in the summer is dedicated to watering these thirsty deserts, and dense turfgrass is as porous to stormwater as concrete—meaning hardly at all. The Environmental Protection Agency estimates that about half of the fertilizer we dutifully spread on our lawns ends up in our waterways, choking aquatic life with the resulting algal blooms.

Begin switching from lawn to garden, which will help stormwater to percolate underground, essential in assisting the water cycle. You can even grow food where a lawn once was, and it can also save on fossil fuel use as you'll have less lawn that needs to be mowed.

► A hummingbird hovers at a nectar-filled feeder.

18. USE ANIMAL-FRIENDLY LANTERNFLY TRAPS

There's a relatively new public enemy number one in the eastern United States, the dreaded spotted lanternfly from China. While everyone hates the critters, most people do the *exact wrong thing* to control them: placing a coil of duct tape around the tree trunk, sticky side out. While the tape does catch lanternflies, it also works indiscriminately, also catching good insects like ants and bees. Hummingbirds and woodpeckers have gotten caught on these tape traps too and are rarely able to be pulled from the tape alive. Our Wildlife Clinic staff have tried, and it is usually fatal for the bird.

Instead, go to YouTube and the web to search for animal-friendly traps. There's one produced by the Schuylkill Center staff that catches only lanternflies. These traps can be a little complicated to make, but they protect the rest of creation while effectively removing this invasive species.

19. ANSWER THE BAT SIGNAL

Bats are a critical component of local ecosystems, as they devour tons of insects, especially mosquitos. But populations of little brown bats, the region's most common bat, have plummeted as a result of white-nose syndrome. Bat Conservation International is the go-to nonprofit for all information on bats. Visit its website for details on how to help bats, especially for its approved construction plans for bat houses. Help keep this critical creature flying across Wild Philly.

▼ This bat house is loaded with hungry insect hunters.

Hardest

20. GO ORGANIC

I remember driving through a Gladwyne neighborhood years ago, with its large houses on steeply wooded streets. And there, inexplicably, was a gentleman in a business suit standing on a slope with two spray bottles of Roundup in his hands, squirting fiercely at the ground. This backyard Rambo was desperately trying to whack the witch's brew of invasive plants growing in his yard, which was a naturally wooded slope. Ugh.

Herbicides and pesticides rarely kill only one species. In fact, most impact a wide variety of species, even you and your pets. Rat poison, for example, harms the foxes and hawks that prey on the rodent. Bees are especially sensitive to pesticides. So to keep butterflies, bees, and birds with us, go organic. Most lawn care and pest control companies offer green and organic versions of their services. And if you reduce your lawn, you need these services far less.

▲ Cats sadly kill billions of birds annually. For the love of nature, keep your cat indoors.

21. KEEP YOUR CAT INDOORS

While cats make great indoor pets, outdoor cats are hugely problematic. Biologists estimate that outdoor cats kill some 2.4 billion birds annually—a *huge* number—and between 6 and 22 million mammals as well. Because of this, the American Bird Conservancy lists cats as the "number-one direct, human-caused threat to birds in the United States and Canada," and the International Union for Conservation of Nature agrees, naming cats as one of the world's worst invasive species. Worse, cats have directly caused the extinction of sixty-three species of birds, mammals, and reptiles worldwide.

22. ADOPT A SPECIES

Something about the monarch's migration story grabbed my attention and never let go. I've read incessantly about them, written and lectured about them, helped tag them at Cape May, donated to organizations that support them.

What species captivates you? The oak tree? The shad? Find a species that sings to your soul, adopt it, and help make sure we keep this species with us. Imagine if every American, every school kid, every politician adopted a plant or animal. It would be powerful.

23. LOWER YOUR CARBON FOOTPRINT

Climate change is the single largest threat facing humankind and nature alike. Although few of the actions noted above will alleviate that warming, they are squarely aimed at improving local biodiversity. Still, as climate change threatens nature on a massive scale, anything and everything you can do to conserve energy and burn less fossil fuels—from turning off that light switch to trading in your Hummer for an electric car—unconditionally helps nature.

24. TESTIFY

Communities have a number of official and semi-official organizations dedicated to guiding community policy on nature and the environment, from shade tree commissions to environmental advisory boards. Find out who makes these decisions in your own community, then go to a meeting to see what they do. And testify, work to change local laws, or get appointed to one of these groups yourself.

25. ADVOCATE FOR LARGE-SCALE CHANGE

Let's be honest. For people and nature to truly coexist in any way that approaches a sustainable relationship, massive large-scale changes are needed: how we power our communities, how we make and distribute products, how we use water, how we preserve land, how we educate our children—and how we value nature. Any and all advocacy you do on behalf of nature is not just important, at this point it is required. Vote for candidates that treasure nature. March. Protest. Don't forget to celebrate and revel in nature, but none of us can sit out the struggle ahead.

▲ To advocate for a more sustainable world, we must march, protest, and vote.

Citizen Science

As the previous chapters have been demonstrating, the Philadelphia region is unbelievably rich in natural wonders and natural areas awaiting your discovery. The previous chapter outlined twenty-five ways you can help nature, but the bottom line is there are actually only two things for you to do: learn more and then take action.

While the ecological challenges we face seem daunting and the tasks ahead herculean, scientists are still trying to understand many of these challenges, making research crucial. And thanks to widely available technology,

▼ People engaged in citizen science.

anyone in the twenty-first century can marry learning with action to help advance scientific understanding. In short, you can become a citizen scientist.

Darlene Cavalier, the Philadelphia-area coauthor of *The Field Guide to Citizen Science* and founder of the online citizen science portal SciStarter (www.scistarter.org), notes that you might not change the world, "but you can change your corner of it while being part of an effort to change bigger things."

Darlene's book is a wonderful intro to citizen science, and the SciStarter website lists more than 2000 science projects that have more than 110,000 "registered and very active users" studying a wide variety of issues affecting climate, ecology, health, psychology, genetics, and more. Her group has begun partnerships with Girl Scouts and 4-H, and PBS's *SciGirls* has made use of the data. And they are responsive: only moments after my conversation with Darlene, the website included a special link, www.scistarter.org /philly, that aggregates Philadelphia-specific projects. Make sure to visit.

One local citizen science project is PhillyTreeMap (www.opentreemap .org/phillytreemap/map/), a crowdsourced map of the region's tree cover. Thus far, some 60,000 trees have been entered, but the website has also identified 120,000 vacant tree sites ripe for planting. The website notes that the region's trees have provided more than $10 million in ecosystem services, like sequestering 150 million pounds of carbon dioxide while filtering 125 million gallons of stormwater. So create an account on PhillyTreeMap, enter your home's or street's tree(s), and become a citizen scientist, generating real data used by real scientists to solve real problems.

Ant Picnic

What child isn't intrigued by ants, as they beg so many questions. What do ants do underground? How do they follow each other? Where do their ant trails lead? And what do they eat? Everything? Or are they picky?

North Carolina State University sponsors Ant Picnic, a great activity for families with kids or organized groups like Scouts and classrooms. Go to the SciStarter website and search for "Ant Picnic." You'll get instructions for how to become an ant chef, mixing up bait to entice ant customers using, among other things, sugar, salt, pecan cookies, and water.

Once the baits are mixed following their directions, you'll set the baits up in two different locations, one in a green area and one on pavement. Simply wait about an hour—that might be the hard part for some kids!—photograph your experiment, and record how many ants are on each bait in each location. The data students collect contributes to a large and growing database from researchers, who are mostly kids. The university notes that "scientists use this data to explore regional and global trends in ant food preferences so they can learn about more complex things like the environment and climate change."

SciStarter recently listed more than 1800 participants in this citizen science project, from elementary school kids to college students. "This project

► An Ant Picnic is a fun citizen science project in which you bait ants and then observe their behavior.

was so much fun for my Scouts," reported one participant, "and the results were completely surprising. They are already asking to do another project, they loved this one so much."

City Nature Challenge

It started off as a cheeky challenge between rivals San Francisco and Los Angeles. For the first Citizen Science Day in 2016, the two cities' science museums sponsored an eight-day competition to see which city could record the most biological diversity. In the end, more than 20,000 observations were made by more than 1000 people cataloging about 1600 species in each city.

Only one year later the City Nature Challenge went national and the following year international. In 2019, a group of local naturalists, Navin Sasikumar, Robin Irizarry, Tony Croasdale, and Bernard "Billy" Brown, entered Philadelphia into the challenge. By 2020, even in the midst of a pandemic, 244 cities across the planet participated—Tokyo, Zagreb, São Paulo, Moscow, Philadelphia's sister city Wilmington—with 41,000 citizen scientists uploading 815,000 observations of 32,000 species, 1300 of which were rare or endangered.

Participants enroll through the website (www.citynaturechallenge.org), upload the iNaturalist app on their smartphones, and then simply start uploading data during the late April to early May window the challenge operates within. The winning city is announced a few weeks later.

Billy Brown, one of this book's Naturalist Advisory Team members, says, "We hope the [City Nature] Challenge connects Philadelphians to the nature around us, whether we're in a park or on our block. I also hope the city grows to regard all places as habitat for wildlife and all places as sites for biodiversity conservation."

▲ Participants in Philadelphia's City Nature Challenge.

CoCoRaHS: It's Raining Data

Don't let its difficult acronym deter you from one of the most important citizen science projects, the Community Collaborative Rain, Hail, and Snow Network. Pronounced "Co-co-rahs," the project was started in Colorado in 1997 when an unexpected flash flood killed five people near Fort Collins. A state meteorologist began asking residents of Fort Collins for rainfall data, and the numbers showed a surprisingly wide distribution of rainfall across the region during any one storm—pouring over here but very little over there—and CoCoRaHS was born. Today, tens of thousands of volunteers in Canada, the United States, and the Bahamas take measurements from a 4-inch rain gauge every day at the same time (7:00 a.m. is recommended, but variability is allowed), and enter that day's data.

Given that a warming climate is supposed to trigger more rainfall and heavier downpours in Philadelphia, CoCoRaHS can begin to tell climatologists how much heavier the storms are and how much more rainfall the city is getting. Since the city's official rainfall meter is at the Philadelphia International Airport, far from Center City, more rain gauges across the region give us a more finely tuned understanding of weather. To sign up, visit the website (www.cocorahs.org) and follow its prompts, watch the training video, and purchase the recommended rain gauge.

"It must be hard to fathom that precipitation data is so useful and that backyard rain gauges have a place of importance in national and global climate monitoring in the 21st Century," notes the CoCoRaHS website. "But the fact is, it's true. Your rainfall reports—including your reports of zero precipitation—are very valuable and are being used *every day*. When you see forecasts of river stages and flood levels . . . guess what data are helping the forecasters make these forecasts? Yes, timely CoCoRaHS data!"

Here's your chance to become not only a citizen scientist, but a citizen climatologist.

iNaturalist

One of the world's most popular nature apps (and the app of choice for the City Nature Challenge), iNaturalist has recorded more than 70 million observations of plants, animals, and fungi from 1.6 million users, with new data pouring in daily. Even better, iNaturalist can help you identify the plants and animals around you. Simply upload a photo, and the website's "identifiers" help you out, or its automated species identification tool searches its database to either identify the species or give you a limited range of possibilities.

You can run the program from either a laptop or smartphone. People upload their observations and discoveries, contributing to a burgeoning dataset of observations. You can also follow iNaturalist users, search for projects, and seek out certain species you'd like to see.

Although not a citizen science project itself, users have created and contributed to tens of thousands of different science projects by using iNaturalist. For example, many nature centers, preserves, and even cities have performed "bioblitzes," biological surveying events that strive to record all the species found

▲ The iNaturalist app allows you to identify the nature around you.

within a designated area, and iNaturalist is hugely helpful here. So when the National Park Service created a National Parks Bioblitz in 2016, iNaturalist was the natural partner.

The app developer also offers a family-friendly version, Seek, that allows children to participate without having to set up an account. Kids can find things in their neighborhood while earning badges.

Grab your smartphone, set up an account, and go for a walk, taking a million iNaturalist friends along with you as backup.

Journey North

Every spring, thousands of animals migrate north across, over, and around the Americas: birds like warblers and thrushes, butterflies like monarchs and painted ladies, even gray whales. Now you can participate in this extraordinary phenomenon through Journey North, a web-based project sponsored by the University of Wisconsin-Madison's Arboretum. More than 25 years old and used by more than 60,000 participants, it's one of the largest, best-established citizen science programs in the country and great for classroom teachers.

Visit www.journeynorth.com, where the home page gives you an enticing menu of many choices. You can track the migration of monarchs, hummingbirds, gray whales, loons, or swallows or report when the ice melts, when trees leaf out, or when the first frog croaks in your local environs. You can even plant a Journey North Tulip Test Garden that will contribute to a long-term database informing us on how fast our climate is changing.

On a recent dive into the monarch section, a Horsham resident had reported a "single monarch sighted" on April 10, a Pottstown participant saw "a weathered female laying eggs on every little milkweed sprout we have" on April 27, and in Downingtown on May 5 another was seen "flying around the field near the water." Even better, you can play—and share—the time-lapsed Google pins dropping onto the map, creating a wave of migrants washing over the country. That feature alone makes the whole website enticing.

▲ Journey North's website tracks, among many things, the northward migration of monarchs back to the United States.

National Audubon Society's Christmas Bird Count

For much of early American history, hunters engaged in a holiday tradition known as the Christmas side hunt, heading off with their guns to shoot animals. Whoever killed the most birds or mammals won. By the early twentieth century, many conservationists were growing increasingly concerned about the wanton destruction of so many animals, as they saw populations of many in decline.

Enter a giant in ornithological circles, Frank M. Chapman, a curator at the American Museum of Natural History in New York City and an early leader of the new National Audubon Society. In 1900, Chapman proposed a new tradition, that birders head out on Christmas Day to count—not shoot—birds. That year, only twenty-seven birders on twenty-five counts across the country recorded ninety species of birds.

But the idea took root, and from a modest acorn a mighty oak sprouted. The event no longer happens only on Christmas Day, but instead over a range of days within Audubon's established window of time. In 2020–2021, the Christmas Bird Count, now an entrenched and beloved national tradition, saw more than 2400 counts happen across North America, recording an unbelievable 44 million birds. These records have provided critical information to scientists about the state of American birds, allowing us to compare diversity and populations over long periods of time.

There are so many ways to participate in this crowdsourced science event through the many Audubon chapters in the Philadelphia region, including Wyncote Audubon, Valley Forge Audubon, Bucks County Audubon, and Washington Crossing Audubon, the last of which includes a portion of Burlington County. Even nature centers like the Schuylkill Center offer winter bird counts unaffiliated with, but certainly influenced by, Audubon's gift to the birding world, the Christmas Bird Count.

▶ Birders of all ages participate in the National Audubon's famed Christmas Bird Count.

Project Feederwatch

Want to help birds, but perhaps from the comfort of your home? That's easy. Use your backyard bird feeders to conduct citizen science. Actually, you don't even need a feeder; a backyard with plantings, habitat, food, or water that attracts birds is sufficient.

Founded in Canada by Long Point Bird Observatory in the 1970s, Project Feederwatch spread to the United States in the 1980s, when it partnered with Cornell University's Laboratory of Ornithology. By 1987–1988, more than 4000 people had joined the program, and in recent years enrollment was more than 20,000.

The schedule of when you count birds is flexible, and the numbers are entered online. Over the years, the data has shown biologists that cardinals are continuing to expand north into New England and Canada and that evening grosbeaks are contracting as a species. The Cooper's hawk, a bird that hunts other birds, is increasingly common at winter backyard feeders, as ironically the raptor visits feeders to pick off the birds we are trying to feed.

Simply go to www.feederwatch.org and register on the website; there is an entrance fee that supports the project. Once your welcome kit arrives, you are set to go.

Toad Detour

Though something similar to this happens across the world, there's nothing quite like Roxborough's edition. Every spring, likely sometime in March, American toads hibernating in the Schuylkill Center's large forest awaken from their winter slumber intent on one thing: finding water, mating, and laying eggs.

On the evening of one of the first warm rains of early spring, a horde of toads hops across Port Royal Avenue in Upper Roxborough, leaving the center's forest behind to head uphill to an abandoned reservoir that is now one of the city's newest urban parks. Unfortunately, toads have not evolved alongside cars, so they cross the road at sundown during the evening rush hour, where they are immediately flattened by cars.

Enter Toad Detour, one of the Schuylkill Center's citizen science programs. The center's volunteers monitor the program's Facebook page, and if an advance scout puts out notice that the toads are moving, the group—armed with a permit from the city—closes Port Royal Avenue and adjoining Eva Street to traffic. The volunteers usher the toads (and sometimes green frogs too) across the road to the reservoir. During the migration, some males are already clasping a female in a lover's wrestling headlock while the female doggedly tries to cross the road. The lead volunteer counts the number of toads crossing each night, so the Schuylkill Center gets some sense of how toad populations are performing.

▲ A toad crossing Port Royal Avenue in Roxborough.

One of the pleasures of Toad Detour is, after the shift, walking up to the reservoir's edge to listen to the incredibly loud and surprisingly pretty nocturnal chorus of toads trilling, males singing for the privilege of mating with a female.

Six or so weeks later, little toadlets, perfectly formed toads that can fit onto your thumbnail and freshly metamorphosed from tadpoles, leave the reservoir to take up home in the Schuylkill Center's forest. Once again, the volunteers close the roads to allow the impossibly small youngsters to survive this journey.

To give the toads of Wild Philly a hand, check out the Toad Detour Facebook page.

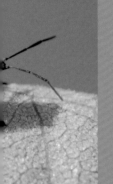

101 SPECIES TO KNOW

Ferns, Fungi, and Lichens

Christmas Fern

Polystichum acrostichoides

The first ferns appeared on our planet some 360 million years ago, 100 million years *before* the earliest dinosaurs. Ferns are so ancient they predate flowers, so stegosauruses might have munched on ferns, but they never ate a flower. In Pennsylvania's geologic history, ferns dominated the dense primeval swamps that were buried underground, the peat slowly cooking to form coal, the state's iconic fossil fuel.

Ferns are still very much with us today, some 10,000 species worldwide, and are easy to spot on your walks in Wild Philly. But ferns are notoriously hard to tell apart, lots of lacy green leaves. For me, a seasoned naturalist who's been leading field trips for 40 years, I know only a handful of ferns by their proper names. (Please don't be disappointed in me.)

Happily, one is very easy to identify and is probably the most common fern in the area.

▲ Christmas fern is one of Wild Philly's most common ferns.

The leaves are evergreen, so on a Christmas morning walk through a forest, you'll see its fronds poking through the forest floor. And if you check out a leaflet, it has a little bulge on the bottom, looking—without stretching the imagination too far—something like a Christmas stocking hanging from a fireplace.

A Worldwide Success

The Christmas fern's genus, *Polystichum*, is very successful and found worldwide. While Christmas fern can form colonies, it more typically grows singly or in twos or threes, the foot-long fronds appearing rather tough and leathery. In the winter, it is not unusual to find flattened fronds on the forest floor, squashed from a snowfall, but doggedly remaining green. One reason Christmas fern is so common in the region is that deer do not seek them out—a great advantage in forests over-browsed by deer.

Ferns create spores, not seeds. Most do so on fertile fronds, specialized fronds carrying structures holding the spores, often on the undersides of the leaflets. In Christmas fern, the fertile leaflets are at the tops of their fronds. Sterile fronds typically encircle taller fertile ones, which are also held more erect. In Wild Philly's Christmas ferns, spores tend to be created between June and October when the conditions are right. Check out frond undersides during summer and fall, looking for brown spots, the sacs that create spores. In the winter, those fertile fronds die away, leaving their sterile evergreen sisters.

Where to See It

Look for Christmas fern on all the forested walks, but these plants are especially abundant along the Ridley Creek Trail and the Valley Creek Trail on the Valley Forge walk.

Lichens

Various species

Growing as splotches or crusts on rocks and trees, the mysterious lichen is very common but entirely misunderstood. Not a plant but confusingly plant-like in many ways, each lichen is a community of an alga, a fungus, and sometimes even yeast packed into one organism. As you likely learned in middle school science, it is a classic example of symbiosis and interdependence, with the algae capturing sunlight energy to produce sugar while the fungus absorbs water and nutrients and gives the lichen structure.

Of great diversity in size and shape, lichens are represented by more than 20,000 species worldwide and 3600 in the United States. They are everywhere! Some 8 percent of our planet's land is covered by lichens, in just about every habitat, including the poles, and at every elevation. And they can be incredibly old; some Antarctic lichens are estimated to be

5000 years old, whereas reindeer lichen, a very common lichen in Wild Philly, might be "only" a century old or so.

Lichens are important colonizers, being among the first living things to grow on bare rock. These pioneers release acids that eat away rock, forming dust that slowly becomes a layer of soil for small plants to anchor themselves into.

Given that lichens grow on rock, scientists long considered them to be among the first life forms to have evolved on land, predating plants and animals. New research indicates, however, that lichens appeared about 250 million years ago, just before the dinosaurs. While that's pretty ancient, the first plants marched onto land some 500 million years ago. So, plants beat lichens onto land by 250 million years, a fact that no one expected, not even the researchers. Which is the beauty of

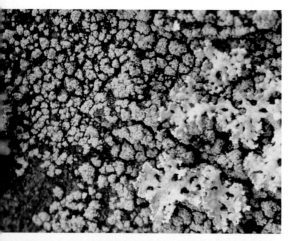

◄ Crustose and foliose lichens grow together on an oak branch.

science—when we ask a question, we may be surprised by the answer we find.

Orange and Gritty

Lichens cover almost the entire rainbow from red, yellow, and orange to blue, brown, and black. And some are remarkably beautiful—if you look closely, which I highly recommend. Crustose lichens appear like crusty patches of gritty paint stuck to a boulder. Foliose lichens look like small leaves glued onto a surface. Fruticose lichens branch out like miniature trees, and gelatinous lichens are simply small blobs.

Not only are they attractive, lichens are also very useful. Hummingbirds and vireos pull foliose lichens off tree bark to incorporate into and camouflage their nests. In northern climes, reindeer lichen is hugely important in the diet of its namesake animal.

Where to See It

Look for lichens on the surfaces of large boulders and old trees, especially on walks along the Wissahickon, Black Run, Ridley Creek, and Pennypack Park. Reindeer lichen is easily found on the Pine Barrens walks at Woodford Cedar Run Wildlife Refuge and Batsto.

▲ Shield lichen is one of the many foliose lichens.

Turkey Tail

Trametes versicolor

Turkey tail is one of the most common mushrooms in North America's woods, growing on fallen logs and tree stumps. Once you see it, the name is obvious. The shelf is composed of concentric circles of many different colors and layers (explaining the species name *versicolor*). Although there are other shelf-like mushrooms, including a false turkey tail, this one always has a white outer edge lining the shelf.

Like all of its fungal kin, the turkey tail we see is only the tip of the mushroom iceberg. The organism has thousands of threads winding through the tree from which it grows, and the bulk of the fungus is actually this almost-invisible network. The only part of almost any fungus we see is the fruiting body, the aboveground part designed to reproduce the species.

▲ It's rare to see one turkey tail growing alone. More typically, you'll see a whole bunch of these mushrooms piled one atop another.

One cannot overstate the importance of those fungal threads, as they perform the necessary ecosystem service of decomposing dead wood. As such, turkey tail, like all fungi, is critical to the healthy functioning of the region's forests, recycling carbon and nutrients from dead trees for new plants and animals to incorporate into their tissues.

Blowing in the Wind

Peek underneath the shelf of a turkey tail, and you'll see a white surface pockmarked with small dots. Millions of the fungus's microscopically small spores are released from tubes that end at these pores. Each spore becomes airborne, thrown to the winds, hoping to land on a surface with the right conditions to start a new fungus.

Turkey tail is a cosmopolitan species, native across North America, then stretching across the northern hemisphere into Europe and Asia. The fungus is deeply embedded in the traditional medicine of many countries: for centuries Chinese herbalists have made tea from it to boost the immune system, and polysaccharides extracted from the fungus are used to treat cancer in Japan.

Where to See It

Everywhere and all year round! Walk through any mature forest anywhere in Wild Philly, and keep your eyes peeled for logs and stumps sporting turkey tails.

Herbaceous Plants

Beebalm

Monarda didyma

This summer bloomer's name says it all: it's balm for the bees. This member of the mint family with impossibly red tubular flowers is a magnet for these pollinators, not to mention butterflies and hummingbirds. Beebalm is found in sunny meadows across the eastern United States. I've bumped into stands that approach 5 feet in height, and the number of insects buzzing on and around it is a delight to witness. Beebalm blooms from mid-summer deep into the fall, becoming an important plant for hummingbirds migrating south and needing nectar to refuel.

The plant has been readily adopted by gardeners of all stripes, so many people know it by its Latin name, *Monarda*. Beebalm has a lavender-colored close relative, *M. fistulosa*, that equally attracts those same pollinators and also has been pulled into native plant gardens. Look for either one on your summer and early fall walks in Wild Philly.

▲ This red-flowered beebalm is attractive to hummingbirds.

Wild Bergamot and Oswego Tea

Another common name for beebalm is Oswego tea, as First Nations people and later settlers steeped the plant's aromatic leaves to drink. Since the tea's flavor reminded early settlers of the bergamot orange used in Earl Grey tea, they christened it wild bergamot.

The plant's aromatic chemicals have also had numerous medicinal uses over time. For example, it's a natural source of the antiseptic compound thymol, the primary active ingredient in today's mouthwashes. Beebalm poultices were used by indigenous Americans to treat infections, sores, and wounds. And while beebalm is balm for the bees, the name actually refers to how the plant was used to treat bee stings. Even better for gardeners, these aromatic compounds tend to deter both rabbits and deer.

Where to See It

In meadows across the region, including at the parking lot of the Valley Forge walk and along the trails at the Crow's Nest Preserve. Beebalm's lavender-colored cousin, *Monarda fistulosa*, grows profusely in the Andorra Meadow and at the Pennypack Ecological Restoration Trust.

Beechdrops

Epifagus virginiana

On the forest floor underneath beech trees, you just might find a modest brown plant, one of the stranger inhabitants of Philadelphia's forests. Its color suggests that it may be a mushroom, but it is in fact a flowering plant.

But it's a strange flower. Unlike most of its kin, beechdrops is unable to photosynthesize, so it has no chlorophyll and is not green. Like we have that vestigial appendix and snakes still have hip bones in their legless skeletons, beechdrops have small scaly leaves—vestiges of an ancestor that photosynthesized and produced chlorophyll.

This herbaceous plant is a parasite, attaching itself to a beech tree's roots and sucking the tree's sap. This lifestyle gives the plant its genus name, as epi is the Greek word for "on" or "about," and *Fagus* is beech's genus name. *Epifagus virginiana* is so unusual, its genus has only this one species. Happily, beechdrops rarely seem to impact the beech tree itself, something most parasites cleverly avoid. You don't want to bite the hand—or the roots—that feed you.

Two Kinds of Flowers

You can find beechdrops' highly variable white-and-purple flowers in bloom from July into October, and they are surprisingly pretty. Unlike the leaves, the flowers actually function. But the flowers are as strange as the plant, with open flowers higher on the plant that are pollinated by visiting insects, combined with closed flowers lower down the stem that apparently self-pollinate. Once a flower is

▲ Beechdrops grow only at the base of beech trees, this parasite's host.

pollinated, it produces very small seeds that disperse in the rain—the seeds cannot travel too far because they need that beech's roots.

Though it may take several years for a beechdrops plant to form aboveground flowers, once it does the plant dies within the same year of blooming on the forest floor. Meanwhile, many smaller beechdrops are busily connecting to the roots below ground.

Where to See It

As you walk Wild Philly, check out the beech trees in any of the region's forests and watch for the plant.

Canada Goldenrod

Solidago canadensis

The brightly lit tiki torches of goldenrod flowers are among autumn's most spectacular sights. While there are many species of goldenrod in the area, including a woodland variety and a seaside species, Canada goldenrod is one of the taller, sturdier plants that predominate in fall meadows. Easily reaching 6 to 8 feet tall, Canada goldenrod has three strong veins running down each leaf. Rough goldenrod (*Solidago rugosa*), a close cousin, is almost as common.

Ecologically, goldenrod flowers are profoundly important. While trout lily and trillium perform the necessary function of feeding pollinating insects awakening from a long winter's nap, goldenrod is the last chance for so many insects to find pollen and nectar in the season soon ending. In turn, many birds come to goldenrod fields to find insects in one easy place.

Monarch butterflies stop here to fuel up for their flight to Mexico, and many other butterflies and moths join them: eastern tailed blues, hummingbird clear-wing moths, and skippers of many kinds. Goldfinches eagerly descend on the ripening seeds, as do sparrows and their kin. Bees, wasps, beetles, and flies are pulled in for nectar and pollen. Crab spiders and praying mantises sit atop the flowers lying in wait for prey, while dragonflies and swallows cruise above, strafing the flying insects. A goldenrod field in full flower in mid-autumn is an ecological gold mine.

When walking along a goldenrod meadow, you might notice funny growths—round swelling—on the stems. These are goldenrod ball galls, made by the peacock fly, which lays her egg in the stem of goldenrod along with chemicals that irritate the plant and cause the swelling. The fly's larva grows up inside the ball, surrounded by plant tissue to feed upon. The larva pupates inside the gall over the winter, with a new fly emerging in the spring. Downy

▲ Bright yellow goldenrod flowers are a signature of autumn in Wild Philly.

woodpeckers have discovered this, and over the winter they peck holes in the galls to eat the helpless pupa.

A Whole Bouquet

As weather becomes chillier in the fall, cold-blooded insects have a harder time feeding, as flying becomes problematic in the frosty air. In the coevolution of flowers and insects, composites like goldenrod made a smart, successful move: each flower is effectively a bouquet unto itself, each "petal" of a composite its own flower with its own nectar pot. Instead of flying from flower to flower, a bumble bee landing on a goldenrod gets clusters of flowers. This saves the bumble bee immense time and energy in foraging for food, and the composite gets pollinated and can make seeds.

Many fall-blooming flowers, like asters, are composites, and asters and goldenrod dominate fall meadows, often side by side. Daisies, Joe-pye-weed, New York ironweed, and even dandelions are among the many successful composites you'll meet in goldenrod fields. In short, a goldenrod field is a necessary stop for your autumn hikes.

Where to See It

On all of the fall walks, look for Canada goldenrod, as it is very common. You can especially find it at Andorra Meadow, Pennypack Ecological Restoration Trust, and Rancocas Nature Center.

Common Cattail

Typha latifolia

A hugely important plant in freshwater wetlands, cattails, with their iconic sausage-shaped flower heads, are one of the easiest plants to identify. Those dark brown cattails atop the plant are densely packed clusters of all-female flowers; it is these that mature into the downy seeds blown everywhere by wind. There are also small male pollen-producing flowers on the fuzzy spike above the cattail. This spike dries up and falls off once the pollen is gone.

Also called bulrush and sometimes punk, the common cattail is unbelievably useful for both people and animals. Many creatures nest in and around cattails, including red-winged blackbirds, marsh wrens, ducks, geese, bitterns, and even fish. Muskrats and beavers munch on its roots and leaves, and many waterfowl and wetlands animals devour its seeds.

▲ Cattails are easy to recognize in freshwater wetlands of Wild Philly.

So Many Uses

This plant, called *awpahi* by the Lenape, had so many uses for First Nations people that it was a veritable supermarket in itself. Here is just a sampling: its starchy root was roasted or ground into meal, its shoots were eaten like asparagus, its pollen became flour for bread, and immature flower spikes were boiled and eaten like corn on the cob. Its roots were pounded and made into poultices to heal wounds and burns, while the flower heads were eaten to relieve diarrhea. The fluff was great tinder for fire-making and stuffed into bedding, and, for the baby, it prevented chafing. The long spear-shaped leaves were woven into wigwam roofs, baskets, rugs, and dolls. The list goes on, and many of these uses were of course adopted by settlers. As recently as World War II, the water-repellent seeds filled life vests.

While the common cattail is still common, it has struggled with competition from a non-native and invasive reed, *Phragmites australis*. The reed has pushed the common cattail out of its wetland habitat and sadly provides far fewer ecosystem services. Still, the species is found across the continental United States, even up into Alaska.

Where to See It

At FDR Park at the pond's edge near parking lot no. 2, plus the John Heinz National Wildlife Refuge at Tinicum.

Common Duckweed

Lemna minor

Floating on top of ponds are the small round bright green leaves of common duckweed. Looking at first glance like algae, common duckweed is not just any flowering plant— it produces the world's smallest flower at only 1 millimeter (4/100ths of an inch) long. The flower has been widely studied, as botanists have tried to figure out where it belongs in the

▲ This mallard duck swims in a pond covered with its namesake, duckweed.

floral family tree. Most now agree it is an arum, like skunk cabbage and Jack-in-the-pulpit, which look nothing like it.

Common duckweed, one of several species of duckweeds inhabiting the United States, has spaces in the leaf's interior that capture air to give the leaf buoyancy, and a waxy cuticle allows it to shed water. A small root-like structure dangling below the leaf looks like a root but is actually a modified stem. This dangling stem is sticky, allowing duckweeds to get stuck to the feet of ducks and other waterfowl, who inadvertently spread the plant to new ponds.

Explosive Growth

The flowers of common duckweed float as well, even forming miniscule seeds. The plant also reproduces by budding, with new leaves popping off its sides and separating to become new clonal individuals. Therefore, duckweed can grow explosively, giving some ponds the appearance of a luxurious green carpet. This makes a great place for frogs to hide, their skin camouflaging against the plant, and the small fry of fish seek shelter underwater just below the leaves of duckweed.

Ducks do feed on duckweed, as do other creatures. The plant is rich in protein, and in Asia it has been widely cultivated and fed to pigs, ducks, and fish. In Thailand, an even smaller duckweed species has been eaten for centuries as *kai-nam*, "eggs of the water."

Surprisingly, this powerful little plant packs a wide array of industrial uses too. For example, duckweed absorbs arsenic and lead, and it has been tested in the bioremediation of hazardous waste sites as well as wastewater treatment plants.

Where to See It

Look for common duckweed in many small ponds across the region. It is guaranteed at the Schuylkill Center's Fire Pond and in the Briar Bush Nature Center's pond as well.

Common Milkweed

Asclepias syriaca

Considered a weed by many people, milkweed is simply an essential plant in the American landscape. It is the host plant of monarch butterflies, and monarch females will only lay eggs on *Asclepias*. Milkweed bugs and milkweed beetles live on the plants as well, and the round clusters of surprisingly beautiful and amazingly scented flowers draw hundreds of different pollinators and nectar feeders, including bees, flies, wasps, and beetles, while predatory insects and spiders scour milkweed in search of prey.

The plant is a chemical powerhouse, hinted at in its genus name, as in Greco-Roman mythology Asclepius was Apollo's son and an expert healer. Among First Nations people, milkweed had numerous uses. Food historian E. Barrie Kavasch, a descendant of the Cherokee, Creek, and Powhatan, writes, "Indians in the east used regional milkweed infusions for respiratory, flu, and heart problems, as well as for ceremonial uses; roots were pounded into poultices to dress wounds and even a baby's navel after childbirth." The Lenape turned its fibrous stems into fishing nets.

Every part of the plant is rich in latex, the milky substance that gives the plant its name. Alkaloids in the latex impart a bitter taste to the plant and to the caterpillars and milkweed bugs that eat it, which offers some protection from birds that try to eat these insects. The Lenape used the sticky latex to remove corns and calluses. More recently, during the rubber shortage of World War II, the United States experimented with using milkweed latex for rubber tires, but scaling up was impractical. But its fluffy seeds were used in the war for life preservers, bedding, and pillows. Speaking of

▲ The flowers of common milkweed have a sweet and intoxicating scent.

fluffy down, that's of course how the seed is dispersed, flying away on tufts of silk. The plant also spreads underground via rhizomes, such that each stand of milkweed is a clonal colony.

Milkweed Deserts

The use of pesticide-resistant, genetically modified corn and soybeans across the Midwest has resulted in milkweed deserts with little or no milkweed in farm fields and hedgerows, and monarch populations have crashed. Many people are aggressively planting *Asclepias* plants, especially butterflyweed (*A. tuberosa*) and swamp milkweed (*A. incarnata*), as both are great home garden plants that support monarchs.

When I moved into my home 30 years ago, I inherited a patch of milkweed in a small strip of land between the driveway and foundation. Recognizing our luck, my family left the milkweed intact. Over the years we have gone through booms and busts with monarchs. In some years, we've raised thirty or more butterflies, while in too many others, none at all. But it's been a joy to host them.

Where to See It

Look for common milkweed in meadows and abandoned lots across the region. You can easily find it in Bartram's Garden's meadow, Crow's Nest Preserve, Pennypack Ecological Restoration Trust, and Andorra Meadow.

Common Yarrow

Achillea millefolium

▲ The flat-topped composite flowers of yarrow bloom from early summer well into autumn.

Common yarrow can be found along the edges of fields and roadsides and in abandoned lots, and it is an extraordinary plant for so many reasons. Yarrow is native across the United States and Canada, as well as Europe and Asia. Cultures on all these continents have an array of medicinal uses for the plant, as attested to by its genus name *Achillea*: the Greek warrior Achilles brought it into battle to heal his soldiers' wounds.

Yarrow blooms as a flat-topped cluster of bright white flowers with yellow centers that many confuse with Queen Anne's lace. But common yarrow is identifiable by its leaves, incredibly beautiful and lacy structures that inspired the species name *millefolium*, or "thousand leaves." This species is a composite, a member of the large Asteraceae family, along with goldenrod and aster. While goldenrods and asters are quintessential fall flowers,

yarrow blooms from early summer deep into the fall. The flower and the leaves are an important food for many pollinators, especially butterflies and moths, so this plant has been adopted by those planting butterfly gardens.

Woundwort, Bloodwort, Stanchwort

Modern studies show that Achilles was right: yarrow possesses two chemicals that coagulate the blood. Used during the Civil War for that purpose, it was called soldier's woundwort, and in Europe it's been known as knight's milfoil, bloodwort, and stanchwort. Yarrow has also been called nosebleed as it has been used medicinally to treat those as well. Used by all First Nations people, the Lenape called it *anshikëmënshi*, crushing its roots to make a tea that treated menstrual cramps. It's even been brewed into beer.

The Brits developed many legends around the plant. For one, if you hold yarrow up to your eyes it might offer you visions of the future. Likewise, if an Irish lass sought a vision of her true love, she'd sew a sprig of yarrow leaves into a square of flannel, place it under her pillow on All Hallows' Eve, the precursor of Halloween, and recite this ditty: "Thou pretty herb of Venus's tree / Thy true name is yarrow / Now who my bosom friend may be / Pray thou tell me tomorrow." Before she awoke, she'd have a vision of whom she was destined to wed.

While there are numerous cultivars of yarrow sold for home gardens in a rainbow of colors, give me the straight-up roadside weed, a plant with a multicultural, circumpolar story.

Where to See It

Look for common yarrow in meadows and roadside everywhere, but it is especially profuse all along the trails at the Crow's Nest Preserve.

Eastern Skunk Cabbage

Symplocarpus foetidus

▲ Skunk cabbage's flowers are on the knob tucked inside the hood.

▲ The leaves of eastern skunk cabbage appear later, as the hood disappears.

Eastern skunk cabbage grows in marshy places where its feet are wet. It is named for its large stinky cabbage-like leaves, with its Latin name proclaiming it fetid. This odor likely discourages herbivores from nibbling on the leaves, which can grow to be 2 feet long. The leaves of skunk cabbage appear in spring, after the plant has flowered.

The stems of skunk cabbage remain buried below the surface, contracting as they grow, effectively pulling the stems deeper into the mud. In effect, eastern skunk cabbage is an upside-down plant, with the stems growing downward, making older plants practically impossible to dig up.

Body Heat

Eastern skunk cabbage is one of my favorite spring wildflowers and the first to bloom—as early as late February. The plant sends up a mottled purple hood that's able to generate its own heat and burn through ice, what botanists call thermogenesis. A knobby orb is nestled in the hood, and those knobs are its flowers.

The flowers reek, giving off a smell akin to rotting flesh, which attracts its pollinators, the flies and bees that scavenge on rotting flesh. They crawl into the hood looking for dead meat and accidentally pollinate the flower—an effective strategy. One of its pollinators is a blowfly with the wonderful species name of *vomitoria*. (Need we say more?) The smell also explains the purple mottling of its hood, common among plants imitating dead flesh.

Measurements of the heat generated by the hood of eastern skunk cabbage indicate temperatures as much as 60°F higher than the air around it. This thermogenesis not only melts the ice, but also helps disseminate the smell. And pollinators are likely to come into the hood seeking the warmth that it generates.

Where to See It

In wet forested areas across the region, but especially at the Bowman's Hill Wildflower Preserve, on its Marsh Marigold Trail; along Valley Forge's Horse-Shoe Trail; at the Schuylkill Center's Ravine Loop; and in Carpenter's Woods.

Jack-in-the-Pulpit

Arisaema triphyllum

Another common, easy-to-recognize spring wildflower is Jack-in-the-pulpit, resembling a minister standing to offer a sermon on the forest floor. This tall slender flower is a cousin of the eastern skunk cabbage, with the same arrangement: a hooded and striped spathe covering a fleshy inflorescence, the spadix. Reverend Jack is clothed not in robes, but in flowers.

The plant is a sequential hermaphrodite. A mature Jack-in-the-pulpit first produces male flowers higher up the spadix and then female flowers lower down, a clever way of preventing self-pollination. Younger, smaller individuals only produce male flowers; only older plants possess the resources required to produce female flowers. While the hooded spathe is often striped purple-brown and green, the brown varies in intensity and color,

▲ Jack-in-the-pulpit is a common spring flower in woodland settings.

115

and sometimes the hood is simply striped in lighter and darker greens.

Trapped!

Like the flower of its cousin, Jack-in-the-pulpit is not trying to attract the attention of butterflies. Hardly. Its pollinators are fungus gnats, tiny flies that lay their eggs on mushrooms that provide food for their larvae.

The flower emits a smell like fungus, which pulls the gnats into the pulpit. The gnats bounce around inside the hood looking for mushrooms, but cannot get out. As a roof covers the opening, they cannot fly straight up, and the sides of the hood are slippery. The gnats continue to fall into the bottom of the spathe, getting coated in more and more pollen and eventually discovering a small exit hole at the spathe's bottom. But a Jack with female flowers does not have that exit hole: the gnats bounce around, stuck inside, perishing in the pulpit after pollinating the flowers—an extreme and unusual strategy for ensuring your flowers are pollinated.

Once pollinated, the flower produces bright red berries that are eaten by a wide array of forest dwellers, including and especially turkeys and wood thrushes.

Where to See It

In most woodlands across the region, but especially, in season, at Bowman's Hill Wildflower Preserve, Carpenter's Woods, and the Schuylkill Center's Wildflower and Ravine Loops.

Jewelweed (Spotted Touch-Me-Not)

Impatiens capensis

▲ The bright tubular flowers of jewelweed provide nectar to hummingbird pollinators.

A tall, colorful, easy-to-find plant, jewelweed—named for the bright orange flowers that dangle like earrings from its branches—thrives in moist areas and is often found in shady places close to streams. The orange flowers bloom from late spring into the fall and are pollinated by bumble bees and hummingbirds. In fact, check out the dots on the orange flower: they are arranged to form a landing strip to guide pollinators in.

This annual species has a close cousin, pale jewelweed (*Impatiens pallida*), that looks just like it, except the flower is yellow and unspotted. The two occasionally grow side by side in their streamside habitats.

Flying Seeds and Silver Leaves

The pollinated flowers ripen into spring-loaded seed pods that snap open when touched—POP!—flinging seeds in all directions when a deer brushes against them. This feature lends the plant another of its common names, touch-me-not. Kids love grabbing fat seed pods in their hands and gently squeezing them to see them explode. Cooler still, those seeds are edible, with a nutty taste.

Here's another task for your young sidekick: grab a jewelweed leaf and submerge it underwater in the stream inevitably nearby. Small hairs on the leaf hold a layer of air that tightly coats the leaf, giving it a silver sheen in the water and yet another name, silverleaf.

If any of your hiking group rubs against poison ivy, the clear liquid flowing from a snapped stem of jewelweed will soothe the itch, something the Lenape have known for thousands of years.

Once you meet this plant, you'll never forget the hummingbird-pollinated, poison-ivy-treating, oxygen-grabbing, seed-popping, nutty-tasting jewelweed.

Where to See It

Look for jewelweed in moist woods, like along the Bartram's Garden River Trail, along Valley Forge's Valley Creek Trail, and at the Briar Bush Nature Center's front door.

Mayapple

Podophyllum peltatum

Mayapple is one of the easiest spring wildflowers to identify, often appearing as a grove of bright green umbrellas carpeting the forest floor, some of them reaching almost a foot tall. That leaf resembles a large bird's foot, and the genus name translates as "foot-leaf."

The plant's underground rhizome sends up one leaf for many years, that leaf photosynthesizing and sending sugars underground to be stored. One year, it is finally large enough and has enough resources to send up *two* leaves—and there you'll find the white round flower dangling between the crotch of the leaves. Look underneath a few of the parasols, and you'll find the flower.

▲ A mayapple plant grows for several years before producing a delicate white flower.

While the plant's name implies a springtime ripening of the flower into fruit, it must have been named by a Southerner. In Wild Philly it's still blooming in May, and the round green apple-like fruit doesn't form until June.

Wildlife Food and Strong Medicine

The mayapple's green fruit is craved by a number of animals, including raccoons and especially eastern box turtles, the main dispersers of the mayapple's seeds. Box turtles devour the fruit and defecate the seed elsewhere, spreading the plant across the forest floor.

Also called American mandrake, the mayapple has numerous medicinal uses, especially among Native Americans. Technically, the entire plant is poisonous, and the chemical in the roots is strong and highly reactive. The Lenape taught early settlers how to use the plant to treat jaundice, constipation, hepatitis, fever, and syphilis and as a purgative, emetic, "liver cleanser," and worm expellant. In modern times, chemicals derived from mayapple have been used to remove warts, and two derivatives are used in chemotherapy.

Where to See It

Mayapple is found in most forests in the region throughout April and May, but especially at the Bowman's Hill Wildflower Preserve, Carpenter's Woods, and the Schuylkill Center's Wildflower Loop and Ravine Loop.

New England Aster

Symphyotrichum novae-angliae

▲ The nectar-rich flowers of New England aster are important to many kinds of insects, but especially bumble bees.

New England aster is a showy autumnal flower that blooms a delightful purple, with a bright yellow center offering pollinators a bull's-eye target. Despite its name, the plant ranges across the eastern United States and is very common in Pennsylvania meadows, often growing alongside goldenrod, its cousin.

Stars of the Show

Aster is Latin for star, named for the stellar flowers. Like goldenrods, asters produce composite flowers and lend the entire composite clan its name, Asteraceae. But while there are many asters, New England's purple-flowered species is a standout.

On a walk, try getting closer to one. The "petal" of an aster is actually a complete flower unto itself, and the central disc of the flower head is composed of smaller tube-shaped flowers as well. Plants with composite flowers densely pack small florets into a compact cluster that, on colder autumn mornings, allow nectar-feeding insects a target-rich environment and more streamlined feeding. So, one aster "flower" is actually a bouquet of flowers—anything to serve their insect pollinators.

New England aster is a nectar-rich plant important for migrating monarchs, not to mention other butterflies, moths, ants, flies, wasps, beetles, and bees, especially bumble bees. The pearl crescent butterfly uses asters as a host plant, the caterpillar munching its leaves.

Once these insects have visited the flowers, the flowers ripen into seeds launched into the sky on small fuzzy parachutes. Look for these on late autumn and early winter walks. Few things capture autumn like this flower blooming alongside goldenrod. Since yellow and purple are complementary colors on the color wheel, it's as if Mother Nature were an artist deliberately choosing her palette.

Where to See It

Look for New England aster growing alongside goldenrod across the region.

Stinging Nettle

Urtica dioica

If you walked Wild Philly, you've likely bumped into stinging nettle—literally. Aptly named, the plant's stinging leaves dangle at just the right height to brush against your shins, causing you to recoil in pain and shock. Like poison ivy, it's a good plant to learn to identify to avoid this unpleasantness.

Growing as an understory plant in wetter environments and in meadows, stinging nettle is a tall plant, from 3 to 7 feet in summer, with strongly toothed and deeply veined leaves that are 1 to 6 inches long. Look for the clusters of tiny greenish flowers that hang from the axils where the leaf meets the stem. Once you see these tassels, you'll remember the plant.

The species name *dioica* means "two houses," a reference to its flowers. The European subspecies, which has been imported and is common in Wild Philly, is dioecious, meaning there are plants with male-only flowers and others with female-only flowers—each sex has its own "house." But the American subspecies is monoecious, meaning each flower contains both male and female parts.

Look closely at the flowers next time you find one. When a plant produces nondescript flowers, it's a signal it's not interested in attracting pollinators. Instead, nettles are wind pollinated—and prolific, with one plant pumping out as many as 20,000 seeds. Several

▲ Although getting poked by stinging nettle is painful, it has long been used as a medicinal plant.

butterflies use nettles as their host plant, including the red admiral and comma butterflies, whose larvae consume the leaves.

A Medicine Cabinet

The plant's sting is an evolutionary adaptation to prevent herbivores from munching on it. Small hollow hairs on the leaves and stem break off at the touch, becoming tiny hypodermic needles that inject the victim with histamine, serotonin, and other chemicals. Julius Caesar's soldiers are said to have swatted themselves with nettles to stay awake during long night watches.

The compounds in stinging nettle are immensely useful in so many surprising ways. The plant is a medicine cabinet by itself, widely adopted by Native Americans and Europeans to treat respiratory ailments, anemia, labor and menstrual pains, and kidney stones. Even today, extracts are sold in health food stores, and the plant has a listing in WebMD.

Stinging nettle's fibrous stems were made into fishing nets by people across the globe for centuries. The edible leaves can be boiled and are rich in vitamins, and modern-day foragers turn them into soup and pesto. Chlorophyll-rich, the leaves are also routinely used to extract the green chemical to use as a dye.

All that in one annoying plant! Isn't nature wonderful?

Where to See It

Common along many trails in the region, stinging nettle can easily be found on the Pennypack Ecological Restoration Trust walk.

Trout Lily

Erythronium americanum

▲ The nodding yellow flowers of trout lily dot the forest floor in early spring.

The incandescent yellow turban-shaped blossoms of trout lily are one of the most recognizable flowers of the region's forests in early spring. Rising only 4 to 6 inches above the soil, the flower is common across a broad swath of the eastern United States. It's named after the brownish gray mottling of the plant's leaves, which resemble a trout's back. And, yes, the plant is one of the many members of the very large lily family.

The bright nodding flowers do attract pollinators, and the seeds produced afterward play a clever trick. In a strategy adopted by a range of plants, the seeds sport little caps called elaiosomes, fleshy structures rich in fats and proteins craved by ants. Worker ants dutifully carry the seeds into their nests to feed the fatty elaiosomes to their larvae. The seeds are then discarded underground, where they grow into plants. Trout lily essentially bribes ants into sowing its seeds.

Incredibly Patient

The trout lily is also a patient species. It quietly produces a single mottled leaf each spring, which photosynthesizes to send starches into its tuber. After 4 to 7 years of growing, the plant has at last stored enough material to produce two leaves, and between the two leaves rises the bright yellow flower. Every trout lily flower you see belongs to a plant that could be a decade old—or more.

Trout lily grows in large colonies, covering, for example, one entire hillside at the Schuylkill Center. Evidence suggest that some colonies may be 200 years old. But while the Schuylkill Center's colony could be old, there are remarkably few flowers in the group: calculations show that only 0.5 percent of the species' plants make flowers. So when you see a trout lily, stop to enjoy its patience, beauty, and age.

Where to See It

Trout lily is widely distributed in mature forests across the region, but deer have sadly scoured out some colonies. Trips 3 to 6 all take you to wildflower hotspots where you can easily find trout lilies.

White Snakeroot

Ageratina altissima

Another member of the large clan of composites, snakeroot's clusters of bright white flowers bloom from early summer deep into the fall, earning it the genus name *Ageratina*, meaning "un-aging." Tolerant of shade, the flower can be found in habitats ranging from disturbed roadsides and powerline cuts to forests and thickets. White snakeroot even volunteers in gardens like mine, though few others welcome it as I do.

The plant can grow up to 3 feet tall; *altissima* translates as "tallest," as this is the tallest member of its genus. Snakeroot's coarsely toothed leaves have long tips at their ends. The abundant white flowers are flat-topped and mature into fuzzy white seeds that are spread widely through wind dispersal.

Milk Sickness and Mrs. Lincoln

I've always assumed the plant must have a snaky root—which it sort of does—but that's not the source of the name. Instead, because the plant is toxic, it was mistakenly thought that a poultice of its roots could cure snakebites. When cows eat the plant, however, the toxin tremetol passes into both meat and milk, and if someone consumes enough it may cause death. Milk sickness, as it was called, is likely what killed Abraham Lincoln's mother,

◄ White snakeroot is a tall plant that blooms from early summer well into autumn.

Nancy. Because there was so much snakeroot growing near newly cleared farms, milk sickness was a huge problem for pioneer settlers. Goats, horses, and sheep also fell victim to the plant's poison.

The toxin was used for its medicinal properties among Native Americans, and the leaves were burned to create a smoke that revived unconscious people. Legend holds that the doctor who finally cracked the mystery of milk sickness was actually tipped off by a Shawnee healer, who of course did not get credit.

Once you know the plant, you'll be surprised by the number of places you'll stumble upon it. Just don't eat it!

Where to See It

Everywhere—in meadows, along trails, on roadsides, and in vacant lots across the city and region—even your own backyard.

White Trillium

Trillium grandiflorum

Of the many ephemeral spring wildflowers that bloom within a small window of time, white trillium is many people's favorite. Its species name *grandiflorum* means "large flower." And it is magnificent, as those 2- or 3-inch petals are among the biggest of the region's spring wildflowers. There are pink and pink-striped variants as well, so you may occasionally stumble upon a pink or pinkish one, but it is still white trillium.

White trilliums often grow in clonal colonies that form a white beacon shining on the forest floor in mid-spring. Bumble bees are one of the pollinators lured to the scentless flowers by that color. Like trout lily, pollinated flowers produce seeds with elaiosomes that are pulled underground by ants, which aids in seed dispersal and planting.

Multiples of Three

The plant's generic name *Trillium* simply translates as "tri-lily." Everything in trillium comes in groups of three or multiples of three: three leaves, three bright white petals, three sepals below the petals supporting them, six pollen-producing anthers topped by three pistils, and three greenish white stigmas atop a six-sided ovary.

You can also tell that it is a member of the lily family, one of the larger families in the

▲ The leaves, petals, and sepals of white trillium all come in groups of three.

botanical world. Examine the leaves and notice the strong parallel veins running their length—one of the signatures of lilies.

Like many of the lilies, white trillium is a preferred food of the white-tailed deer, of which there is no shortage in Penn's Woods. Studies have shown that deer will seek trillium above other plants, which causes problems with its survival in many forests. Deer select the taller trilliums first, leaving shorter ones behind, allowing keen-eyed scientists to estimate deer density by the height of the trilliums. But deer foraging also reduces the plant's ability to photosynthesize and send sugars and starches into the underground root system. So deer browsing also results in shorter trilliums in the forest, if any at all.

Where to See It

In mature forests across the region and especially along the Schuylkill Center's Ravine Loop and at the Bowman's Hill Wildflower Preserve. (There is also a stand of white trillium in the Blue Ridge Mountains of Virginia estimated to number 10 million individuals; it is worth a trip to visit.)

Woody Plants

▲ A beech twig showing the leaves and ripening beechnuts.

▲ The solid gray trunk readily identifies the beech tree.

American Beech

Fagus grandifolia

Beech is a common and important tree in the region's forests, and it is also among the easiest to identify. With smooth gray bark, large beech trunks look like elephant legs stomping in the forest. If you squint your eyes, their roots even appear to be large toes.

Sadly, young lovers long ago discovered that the tree's uniquely smooth bark preserves their initials for decades, so it is too common to see hearts, initials, and years carved into its bark. That's another way to identify the tree, by the carvings, which of course are bad for the tree.

Beechnuts

The tree's seeds, beechnuts stored in spiky triangular hulls, are greedily devoured by a who's who of forest animals: squirrels and chipmunks, of course, but also rabbits, raccoons, foxes, opossums, and birds like wild turkeys and pheasants. Along with acorns, beechnuts were a critical food for passenger pigeons, and when beech-oak forests were cleared the pigeon population crashed. While deer don't prefer beech leaves, they will eat them, and some twenty species of caterpillars use beech as a host plant.

American beech is also one of the climax trees in the region's forests, a signal of a forest nearing the final stage of succession. Shade-tolerant young beech trees are able to grow in the shadows of their parents. The trees grow to be more than 100 feet tall, with an impressive girth around the middle, and can reach more than 200 years old.

Although the beechnuts grow into trees, a beech tree can also send sucker trees up from its roots. If you find an old beech—what some call the mother tree—you will likely find dozens of young beech saplings growing up around it, the entire grouping essentially comprising one superorganism.

The tree's bark allows American beech to be readily identifiable in winter forest. But next time you walk through a forest in the cold season, notice that beech trees often hold old raggedy brown leaves through a large chunk of the winter, allowing this species to be even more easily spotted. And look closely at its uniquely long, skinny, spear- or cigar-shaped buds. American beech gives you innumerable ways to identify it throughout the year.

Where to See It

While every forested walk in this book includes beech trees, Wissahickon Valley Park, Bowman's Hill Wildflower Preserve, and Pennypack Park offer numerous beeches for your pleasure. A large one dominates its spot at Bartram's Garden near the Bartram house.

American Sycamore

Platanus occidentalis

The trunks of American sycamore were once the widest of any tree in a Pennsylvania forest, attaining the width of 12 feet or more. That would have been an impressive sight! Even today, sycamores are striking trees that are easy to spot, as they love to grow alongside streams and their bright white bark, especially at their tops, is diagnostic. Legend holds that when First Nations people were lost, they would climb into trees and look for the white bark in the distance, beckoning. It would invariably bring them to a stream, a source of water and a place to get their bearings.

The sycamore's large toothed leaves are very maple-like in appearance, but bigger, the teeth more jagged, the leaf usually wider than long. The next year's bud hides, cozily tucked into a conical pocket in the leaf's petiole, the small stem that connects leaf to twig. Sycamore seeds are brown fuzzy orbs that dangle from the twigs like Christmas ornaments, even as late as December. Then the balls start falling apart, sending small seeds wafting into the sky on small parachutes.

Parent to a Popular Hybrid

The outer bark of American sycamore cannot stretch, and it peels off in a characteristic

▲ American sycamore has striking jigsaw puzzle bark.

125

jigsaw puzzle pattern to reveal the white below. Its close kin, the London plane tree (*Platanus ×acerifolia*), is widely planted along city and suburban streets throughout the Philadelphia region. Usually the bark of London plane peels to a light green or even yellowish hue, not white, its seed balls hang in clusters of two or three, and the bark peels all the way down the trunk. Another tell: if you find one growing alongside a stream, you've likely got an American sycamore.

Developed in England, London plane is a hybrid of the American and Chinese species of sycamore, *Platanus occidentalis* and *Platanus orientalis*. Literally, East met West in Europe. The first American sycamore was brought to London back in 1636. As the natural range of Chinese sycamore extends from Asia into eastern Europe, it was known in London by then. Once developed, the hybrid quickly took off as an English street tree, as it could almost magically withstand London's smoggy Industrial Revolution air. It remains unclear when the hybridized London version—half of its genes being American—returned to the States.

Now, London planes are ubiquitous in settled areas, and its American kin, the true species, continues to hug the streams in local forests.

Where to See It

Alongside rivers and streams in most Wild Philly forests, American sycamores are especially abundant on the Valley Creek Trail in the Valley Forge walk (there is a massive one behind Washington's Headquarters where the walk begins), along the Schuylkill in the Flat Rock Dam walk, on the Pennypack Park walk, and along Wissahickon Creek in Wissahickon Valley Park.

Black Cherry

Prunus serotina

A mature black cherry tree can be readily identified by its bark, which is covered in what resemble burnt potato chips. When young, the tree's bark is smooth with horizontal lines, looking very much like a black birch, which just might be growing nearby.

A pioneer species, black cherries are one of the first trees to colonize an area. They're also fairly long-lived, lasting more than 100 years as the forest matures around them, then giving way to climax trees like oak and beech. The wood, while valued for furniture, is sadly weak; my staff at the Schuylkill Center spends an outsized amount of time dealing with cracked and fallen black cherry limbs.

Everyone Loves Cherries

The black cherry is a member of the rose family, one of the largest groups in the plant kingdom. The tree produces a long plume of

▲ The bark of mature black cherry trees looks like burnt potato chips.

▲ The long flowers of black cherry attract many pollinators.

▲ The tree's dark red fruit is craved by birds.

five-petaled white flowers. When the flowers open in May, the trees are abuzz with bees, flies, wasps, and more. Once pollinated, the flowers become small blackish red fruits, lending the tree its name. According to one source, these fruits are eaten by thirty-three species of forest critters, including birds and mammals. Black cherry is also the host plant of two butterflies, the eastern tiger swallowtail and red-spotted purple.

The black cherry is also the plant of cough syrup fame. Its inner bark includes a medicinal compound long used in cough syrups and tonics. Scratch a twig and you can smell a distinctive almond odor from this compound, which contains—gulp—cyanide. While livestock have been poisoned by eating too many dried black cherry leaves, the amount historically included in cough treatments is not harmful.

Where to See It

Common in many forests in the region, black cherry is especially abundant at the Briar Bush Nature Center, the Schuylkill Center, and the Pennypack Ecological Restoration Trust.

Black Walnut

Juglans nigra

With its large, perfectly round, and greenish yellow balls dropping onto streets, lawns, and cars in the fall, it's hard to miss the black walnut during nut season. Those nuts are an important wildlife food, as squirrels, chipmunks, and many other animals work very hard to crack them open. The walnut shell we know so well is surrounded by that outer greenish yellow layer, so animals have to work doubly hard to get the nut meat—and they do.

In fact, that covering makes the fruit a perfect sphere, inspiring their Lenape name tùkwim, which simply means "round nut." Like oaks and hickories, walnut production occurs irregularly, with larger crops some years. While black walnut trees only a few years old start producing nuts, large nut crops don't begin until they are about 20 years old. The trees can live for more than a century.

The leaves of black walnut turn yellow in autumn and fall earlier than those of many other nearby trees. It's also oddly one of the last trees to leaf out in the spring.

Oh Pioneer!

The black walnut is native to the eastern United States, and Philadelphia bumps against the northern limit of its range. The tree is far less common in New York and rare in New England. A pioneer species alongside red

▲ Walnut leaves are long compound structures, and the nuts are covered with a green rind.

maple and black cherry, black walnuts grow in younger forests. Their seeds cannot sprout in shade, so they drop out of older forests. Cleverly, the tree's roots produce a noxious chemical that inhibits the germination of other seeds, a trick not unique to walnuts.

When black walnuts hit the ground, you may have noticed discolorations on the pavement. The nut also discolors the hands of anyone trying to crack open the shell. So it's no surprise that the nut and especially its hull have long been used to make dyes, with the color of the dye varying. Early in the year, the dye is yellowish green like the outer shell; as the nut ages, however, the hull darkens, as does the dye, becoming brownish black.

You've likely seen a squirrel crossing a street with a walnut in its mouth, heading off to cache it somewhere for later use in the winter. Happily, squirrels don't use every nut they bury, and the walnut grows into a tree—the squirrel's special way of atoning for all the nuts it has eaten.

Where to See It

Look for squirrels carrying the nuts, a hint as to where the tree grows. In the Andorra Meadow, black walnuts grow interspersed with the meadow wildflowers—look for them above the milkweed. At the Pennypack Environmental Center, a black walnut greets you at its front door, and the Pennypack Ecological Restoration Trust harbors a walnut-filled forest.

Eastern Hemlock

Tsuga canadensis

The Pennsylvania state tree, the eastern hemlock, is an evergreen member of the pine family and one of the region's tallest, most

long-lived trees. The Seneca tree in Cook Forest State Park stands at least 144 feet tall, the tallest measured in the Northeast, and a giant growing in Tionesta in the northwestern corner of the state is pre-Columbian, almost 600 years old.

The tree's name may be confusing, as there is a poisonous flowering plant called hemlock, which killed Socrates. Early settlers thought the tree's crushed needles smelled like poison hemlock, giving it this name, but in fact the tree is not poisonous.

Eastern hemlocks grow in cool, moist forests and are shade tolerant. Look for them especially on the northern slopes of hillsides facing away from the sun, their signature position in Penn's Woods. The tree is easily identified, as its small flat needles attach singly to the twig, unlike its pine cousins whose needles cluster in bunches. Its cones are rounder and daintier than a pine's as well. Turn a branch over, and the underside of the needles will show light-colored stripes, appearing like miniature surfboards.

Troubled Trees

Sadly, the eastern hemlock is in trouble. Big trouble. The hemlock woolly adelgid, a sap-sucking member of the aphid clan, was introduced into the United States from Asia in 1926 and has been wreaking havoc on the tree ever since. While Asian hemlocks are resistant to the pest, the lack of natural predators in the United States has allowed it to run rampant, a too-common story in conservation circles. So if you turn a branch over looking for the stripes, you might instead see little fluffy white balls. These are the adelgids. Today, it's rare to find a healthy grove of hemlocks; most eastern hemlock trees are exhausted from the struggle with the insect and are dead or dying.

While lots of research is being done on both tree and insect, once again conservation is in a race against time. Let's hope conservation—and the hemlock—wins.

Where to See It

The geology walk through Wissahickon Valley Park is one of the outstanding places to see eastern hemlocks growing, in groves on the colder and shadier sides of the ravine.

▲ Hemlocks are easy to identify by their needles, each of which have two white stripes on the underside.

▲ The white fluffy balls are hemlock wooly adelgids, sap-sucking insects that harm eastern hemlock.

Eastern White Pine

Pinus strobus

"There is no finer tree," wrote Henry David Thoreau in his journal of the eastern white pine, originally the tallest tree in a Pennsylvania forest. The British (and later the American) navy chose mast pines that were specially marked and reserved for the Crown to use in British ships. And how many of us grew up watching television in a pine-paneled den? The eastern white pine is so useful that only 1 percent of old-growth pine forests remain in the eastern United States—all the rest were logged.

Today, eastern white pines of 100 feet in height are common, but back in the day 200-foot pines were more typical. In Cook Forest State Park in Pennsylvania's Clarion County, there is a stand of uncut eastern white pines; one, named the Longfellow Pine, is almost 184 feet tall and is regarded as the tallest white pine known today.

Like all pines, the eastern white pine holds its needles in clusters, something that spruces and firs do not do. Each pine has a characteristic number of needles, which in the eastern white pine is five. Although the tree is an evergreen, its needles live about 18 months. So every autumn the eastern white pine sheds its needles from two springs ago in a surprising orange-brown shower.

Tree that Produces Gum

The eastern white pine produces both male and female cones, with the female cones the more familiar one. The smaller, nearly inconspicuous male cones form in the spring, releasing billions of pollen grains into the air, as the tree is wind-pollinated. Yes, pine pollen likely makes you sneeze. The long, conspicuous female cones of eastern white pine produce seeds, which are craved by a large number of animals, including squirrels and many birds.

▲ The Pine Grove at the Schuylkill Center is a stand of eastern white pines.

▲ The eastern white pine's needles and female cones.

The female cones also ooze sap, which gives us the specific name *strobus*, Latin for "tree that produces an odiferous gum." While that gum is annoying to people when pines drip sap onto their cars, it was lifesaving to indigenous and colonial people and had a million uses, of which only a few are offered here. Naturally antibacterial and anti-inflammatory, white pine sap helped treat wounds and burns. When it was taken orally, the sap became a chewing gum with medicinal properties, especially effective for respiratory ailments. Because it is highly flammable, the resin was used in fire starting and torch making. The sticky sap is also a natural glue used to waterproof canoes.

Gum is only one important product of this tree. A new recognition of the importance of pines has come as people rediscover the health benefits of trees and forests. In one extraordinary experiment, a Japanese scientist sprayed a small amount of pinene, the chemical that gives pines its characteristic scent, in a hospital's neonatal ward, allowing newborns who have never been outside to smell its scent. Their blood pressure dropped as the babies chilled out. Turns out we are hardwired to be calmed by pine trees.

And it turns out Thoreau was exactly right.

Where to See It

While not as numerous or as common as it once was, the white pine can be seen on many of the forest walks, including Wissahickon Valley Park and the Pennypack Ecological Restoration Trust. But the Schuylkill Center's Pine Grove is a magical place to enjoy these trees.

Fox Grape

Vitis labrusca

Looking out into a Pennsylvania forest, it's not unusual to see a tangle of thick, shaggy, even ropy vines climbing up, into, and around trees. These fox grape vines sometimes make acrobatic loops as they course through the forest. While there is a witch's brew of invasive vines pestering, even compromising, the region's trees—Oriental bittersweet, mile-a-minute, English ivy—this one belongs in Pennsylvania.

Fox grape is a native of North America and a close cousin in the same genus as the wine grape cultivated in Mesopotamia several millennia ago. It's also presumed to be the vine that Viking explorer Leif Erikson observed when he landed, likely in Newfoundland, around 1000 A.D. and christened it Vinland. In the nineteenth century, a farmer in Concord, Massachusetts, planted 22,000 fox grape plants to experiment with producing a robust American grape and successfully bred what would be deemed the Concord grape in 1849. The region's Vineland, in southern New Jersey, was the home of dentist Thomas Welch, who in 1869 took the Concord grape to make America's first unfermented grape juice, still sold today under that name. So when you meet fox grapes, you're touching the genetic ancestor of the jelly you've been eating in your PB&J seemingly forever.

High Wildlife Value

Fox grapes produce flowers that ripen into purple-blue fruit, which are smaller than those of the Concord grape. Because of the flowers and fruit, the vine has tremendous wildlife value, as it feeds almost the entire forest. Many bees, bumble bees, and other pollinating insects are drawn to the flowers, and a wide variety of birds and mammals feast on the fruit. The Illinois Wildflowers website documents forty-five species of birds eating the fruit, including the now-extinct passenger pigeon, plus thirty moth caterpillars chewing on its leaves, and notes that predatory mammals like

▲ Fox grape can most easily be identified by its twisting wooden stem looping through the forest.

bear, coyote, and fox crave the fruit as well. There's even a host of insects that have specialized on fox grapes, including the grape flea beetle, the grape rootworm, the grape trunk borer, and the light-loving grapevine beetle.

The vine is either named for the fact that foxes love the fruit almost as much as people do or that the ripe grapes have a musky, even foxy, smell—there has been a vigorous dispute over this. William Penn himself wrote in 1683 that "fox grape" was "an established name in American speech." So, the name is deeply embedded in its native soil.

Where to See It

In every forest walk in this book, look for fox grape's characteristic long twisty vines snaking through the forest.

Northern Spicebush

Lindera benzoin

Any healthy forest should appear like an apartment house, with homes found in multiple layers. Some animals inhabit the canopy, the shroud of leaves that cover a forest high up. Below that, understory trees are shorter and often younger, offering leaves at a more modest height. And below even that, a forest should have a shrub layer, woody plants that get only 10 feet tall at most.

It's that lowest layer that has been especially devastated by the state's white-tailed deer, busy herbivores that clear out the shrub layer and vacuum the forest floor, where herbaceous plants should grow cheek-by-jowl.

▲ The mature fruits of northern spicebush are bright red and hard.

Single-Sexed Shrubs

In the spring, before the leaves bud out, look for modest sunny yellow flowers bursting along the branches of northern spicebush. The plant is single-sexed, so this shrub here sports only female flowers while that one over there is all male. You need both sexes in the area for the flowers to become pollinated.

Northern spicebush is an important plant in the region's forests, as it is the host of the spicebush swallowtail, a large metallic black butterfly whose caterpillars require its leaves. (The caterpillars will also eat sassafras, but only these two plants.) Several other butterfly and moth species, including the promethea silkmoth and the eastern tiger swallowtail, also use spicebush as a host plant.

In the fall, the female flowers ripen into bright red but hard berries. Rich in fats, these berries are craved by many birds and are especially important for migrants bulking up for the trip south. And its leaves turn a lovely yellow that almost rivals the flowers themselves.

Where to See It

Easily found on many of the forested walks, northern spicebush is especially common at the Pennypack Environmental Center and the Schuylkill Center.

Forest biodiversity has taken a monstrous hit from the work of deer.

So it's always a pleasure to meet northern spicebush, a modest shrub that stubbornly inhabits the shrub layer of the region's forests, poking into the understory maybe 12 feet up in larger shrubs. You can tell why it is one of the most common shrubs in today's forests by crushing a leaf: you immediately smell a yummy citrus odor. That smell, hinted at in its species name *benzoin*, a Far Eastern spice, is perhaps why deer let it be. This chemical warfare seems to be winning for now.

Poison Ivy

Toxicodendron radicans

Neither tree nor ivy, poison ivy is instead a member of the pistachio family. While most of us know the ditty "leaves of three, let it be," few of us can actually identify poison ivy. For example, wild blackberries, which often grow in tangles alongside poison ivy, sport three leaves too. It behooves all us to know the plant, as the oil in its leaves causes the well-known itchy, blistering rash. In fact, its genus name translates directly to "poison tree."

The plant's three glossy leaflets are highly variable, with leaves on the same plant sporting a maddeningly irregular number of teeth—and sometimes the leaf margins have no teeth at all. The greenish or yellowish flowers (and later berries) grow in clumps from the leaf stems. Poison ivy's growth habit is also highly variable, growing both across the ground and up tree trunks, where it can be readily identified by the hairy roots glued to a tree's bark.

▲ Poison ivy with its leaves and berries.

▲ The leaves of poison ivy are wonderfully colorful in the fall.

While poisonous, 25 percent of us are immune to urushiol, the allergenic oil produced by poison ivy. Still others become even more sensitive to it after an exposure. So be careful. The oil is in the leaves, the stem, the roots—all parts. Never ever burn poison ivy, because the oil goes airborne and into people's eyes, nostrils, and lungs, which can cause a severe allergic reaction and make breathing difficult. Ingesting poison ivy can also be fatal, so watch your children on the trail!

And there's one more wrinkle. As the vine is particularly sensitive to carbon dioxide levels, its toxins have become more powerful as carbon dioxide has risen. With higher concentrations of stronger oils—one study indicates poison ivy's potency has doubled since the 1960s—it's almost as if the plant is mutating into its DC comic book namesake, one of Batman's many foes.

Its Good Qualities

The plant isn't all bad. Poison ivy's modest flowers ripen into waxy white berries that are absolutely devoured by, and even necessary for, migrating songbirds in the autumn. The plant also grows well in sandy soils, so it has been planted to stabilize sand dunes along beaches (and it keeps people off the dunes as well).

And finally, the leaves of poison ivy turn a wide variety of colors in the fall, including orange, red, and even burgundy. The red is hands-down my favorite color in autumn's palette. I love when a tree loses its own leaves to reveal the vine's deep red leaves hugging the trunk.

Where to See It

Common along the forest floor and growing up tree trunks, poison ivy is especially easy to find on the River Trail at Bartram's Garden and along the last stretch of the Forest Loop on the Andorra Meadow walk.

Red Maple

Acer rubrum

The most common maple species in Penn's Woods, the red maple is well named, as it offers red in every season. In the spring, its small, dangling flowers burst red early on, one of the season's first flowers, and its staminate male flowers look like small red spiders clinging to the red twigs. When its seeds ripen, they have a reddish cast to them. Its summertime leaves attach to twigs on red petioles. In autumn, its red blaze is stunning, and in winter the tree's buds remain red. No surprise its species name *rubrum* is Latin for red, the root of "ruby."

Red maple is a versatile tree that you can find in just about any habitat. It ranges from dry conditions to wetlands—one of its nicknames is swamp maple—to everything in between and it grows from lowland valleys up to 3000-foot ridges. This tree also boasts the greatest north–south range of any tree species living entirely in eastern forests, growing from Newfoundland all the way to southern Florida. In fact, the species seems to have expanded its range in post-colonial times, crossing the Mississippi into Missouri and east Texas, places it was not found historically.

The tree was a modest part of the Pennsylvania forest historically. William Penn's letter to England listing the trees found here did not mention red (or any) maple, and there is no Maple Street in Center City.

A Big Winner Nowadays

But red maple has been a big winner in the state's recent forest sweepstakes. One Smithsonian study indicated that red maple has increased its population by 20 percent in recent decades, with a corollary decline in oaks and hickories. The latter trees' seedlings cannot sprout under a densely shaded forest canopy. Without the benefit of the Lenape fire ecology system that favored these trees, they

▲ Red maple offers stunning autumn foliage.

are ecological losers to other shade-tolerant species, like red maple—suddenly a major player in the twenty-first century Philadelphia forest.

Where to See It

While you can find red maples on every forest walk in the book, there is a great stand of them next to the boardwalk along French Creek in the Crow's Nest Preserve. It surrounds you at the beaver dam at the Black Run Preserve, and there are huge multi-trunked beauties at Bowman's Hill Wildflower Preserve and Pennypack on the Delaware Park.

Sassafras

Sassafras albidum

Sassafras is a medium-sized tree that's very common throughout the region and is easily recognizable. Just look for the tree with three different and distinct leaf shapes, which is highly unusual among trees. There are two-lobed leaves that look like a catcher's mitt, three-lobed versions reminiscent of a child's drawing of a ghost, and unlobed elliptical leaves. And these leaves turn a beautiful shade of copper-tinged yellow in the fall.

In addition, the slender trunks of sassafras rarely grow straight. Instead, they seem to wiggle as they climb into the canopy, making them easy to spot, especially in the winter. Finally, the bark is deeply furrowed and an orange-brown color.

▲ Sassafras is one of the few trees whose leaves come in multiple shapes.

Filé Gumbo

Filled with safrole oil, the sassafras tree is fragrant, and folk legend holds that Columbus discovered America by sailing toward its smell. The tree was exported to Europe and in the seventeenth century was second only to tobacco in importance.

Among the Lenape and other tribes across the eastern United States, sassafras was featured in both culinary and medicinal uses. Its leaves were placed atop open wounds, and sassafras teas were used to address many ills. The Choctaw of the Southeast ground its leaves into a powder to form filé, a thickening agent used in Creole cooking, especially gumbo. Root beer traditionally was flavored using the safrole of sassafras. Since safrole oil was found to be mildly carcinogenic in 1960, however, its use in root beer has been replaced.

The spicebush swallowtail, a large, strikingly metallic black butterfly, uses sassafras as one of its two host plants, with northern spicebush being the other.

Where to See It

The ChesLen Preserve and Rancocas Nature Center are two of the best places to see sassafras trees.

Shagbark Hickory

Carya ovata

The Lenape regularly burned Lenapehoking forests to favor the growth of nut trees, especially oaks and hickories. The name hickory retains those indigenous roots, as it is a corruption of *pawcohiccora*, the Powhatan word for the tree's nut meat.

While several different hickories inhabit the region's forests—pignut hickory (*Carya glabra*) and mockernut hickory (*C. tomentosa*), for example—shagbark hickory is far and away the easiest to identify. The bark on older trees peels into splendidly long strips, unique to this tree, as if a bear were trying to pull its bark off. The leaves of hickories are compound, meaning one leaf is comprised of multiple leaflets; in shagbarks the number of leaflets is five.

Of all the hickories, the shagbark's nut meat is the sweetest, widely used by the Lenape and early settlers. In fact, the Lenape included the shagbark hickory's nut milk in their corn cakes and hominy, the latter being another Powhatan word. In addition to squirrels, the nuts are important to animals ranging from chipmunks to bears, and the peeling bark is a great place for hibernating animals from insects to bats to crawl up into and spend the winter.

Long-Lived and Nutty

The tree is so long-lived, reaching more than 350 years in age, that it doesn't start producing nuts until the age of 10 and doesn't drop masses of nuts until age 40. By design, the tree's nut production booms and busts, with abundant years every 3 or 5 years followed by bust years of few, if any, seeds. The boom year overwhelms nut-eaters and allows many of these seeds to survive and become trees.

The wood of shagbark hickory is hard, tough, and long lasting. It was used by the

▲ The peeling bark of a shagbark hickory provides hiding and hibernating places for many animals.

▲ Shagbark hickory nuts on the forest floor offer a nutrient- and protein-rich food for many creatures, including people.

137

Lenape to make bows and by later settlers for axe handles, ploughs, and the axles of wagons. President Andrew Jackson was christened "Old Hickory" after the toughness of its wood, and his tomb in Tennessee is today guarded by shagbarks. We Americans don't eat hickory nuts very much anymore, but we certainly enjoy smoking barbecue meat with its wood.

Where to See It

There is a great shagbark hickory at Bartram's Garden near the historic house, another on the Bowman's Hill Wildflower Preserve walk, and more accompanying the white oak in Chief's Grove in the Crow's Nest Preserve.

Staghorn Sumac

Rhus typhina

▲ Staghorn sumac has long leaves and an upright plume of fuzzy maroon berries.

Staghorn sumac is a shrubby tree of eastern North America that grows in a wide variety of sites, including waste places and abandoned lots. Its 2-foot-long compound leaves turn a brilliant red in the fall, when its maroon staghorn, a long plume of fuzzy berries, becomes an important wildlife food.

This tree is not related to poison sumac (*Toxicodendron vernix*), a close cousin of poison ivy whose leaves are infused with the same oil. Poison sumac shares the same common name with staghorn sumac, but the former has white berries instead of maroon ones. Staghorn sumac has no poison whatsoever.

Mixture Tree

Brett Paddles Upstream, a contributor to the website of the Nanticoke and Lenape Confederation, reports that in Lenapehoking sumac was mixed with tobacco for smoking: "The

Lenape name, *kelelenikanakw*, signifies this with the meaning 'mixture tree.' The Missionaries wrote that a Lenape camp could often be distinguished from others by the aroma of this smoking mixture used in their pipes."

Though vitamin-rich, the fuzzy dry seeds are not a preferred food for animals craving juicy berries. Because the seeds stay on the shrub all winter, they become an important winter emergency food for wildlife like turkey, quail, and almost 300 different songbirds. Deer nibble on both the fruit and stems of staghorn sumac, and it is a preferred tree for bucks to rub their antlers against in their autumn rut.

The staghorn sumac's berries are widely used by foragers to make a pretty good version of an acidic lemonade, rich in many vitamins. Recipes for sumac lemonade abound on the internet—try some.

Where to See It

As you drive through Wild Philly, look for the prominent maroon staghorn fruits adorning the trees in late summer and into the fall. A great stand of it thrives at the ChesLen Preserve's Lenfest Center and another at the Andorra Meadow.

Tuliptree

Liriodendron tulipifera

The tallest hardwood tree in North America, the tuliptree can stretch almost 150 feet into the sky. At 164 feet, a Longwoods Garden specimen is the tallest on record. Before colonial settlement, however, giants standing 200 feet tall were common.

Growing tall and straight, the tuliptree was coveted for ship masts after eastern white pines were logged out. West of the Appalachians, First Nations people used tuliptree for dugout canoes, earning it the name canoewood in the Midwest, and legend holds that Daniel Boone carved a canoe from a sixty-footer. A giant tuliptree that George Washington planted himself was selected as Mount Vernon's official bicentennial tree in 1958.

Tuliptree is an early successional tree, as its seedlings won't sprout and grow under a dense canopy of leaves. In Lenapehoking, the Lenape's fire ecology system favored this tree as well, as openings in the forest floor created by fire could sprout additional seedlings. Tuliptree disappears in a climax forest.

▲ The tuliptree is the tallest tree in a Wild Philly forest.

▲ A tuliptree's flowers earned the tree its name.

A Tree by Any Other Name Would Taste as Sweet

The tree's genus name, *Liriodendron*, translates from the Latin as "lily tree," but it's not a lily. This species is also commonly called tulip poplar, another misnomer, as the tree is not a member of the poplar family but rather the magnolia family. It's not a tulip either, of course, but its April flower is a beautiful yellow cup with bright orange patches at its base that is reminiscent of a tulip—and the large leaf looks something like a child's drawing of a tulip.

The flowers produce nectar that attracts bees, butterflies, and even hummingbirds. When the flowers are finished, they ripen into winged seeds similar to those of maples and ash. In the fall, the leaves turn a stunning yellow, always a cheery sight in an autumn forest. The seeds cling to the tree throughout the winter, fluttering to the forest floor all season. Forest trails are often coated in tuliptree seeds through most of the winter, becoming an important food source for rabbits, squirrels, and seed-eating birds, among others.

The tree is also a very important host plant for the eastern tiger swallowtail, whose caterpillar eats its leaves. A large moth, the tuliptree silkmoth, does the same.

Where to See It

Found on most of the forest walks, there is a wonderfully thick-trunked tuliptree at the start of the Crow's Nest Preserve walk, another mammoth one on the way to the Andorra Meadow, more at the Pennypack Environmental Center, and several beauties line the trails at Bartram's Garden.

White Oak

Quercus alba

Oaks are a large, important group of trees in northern hemisphere forests, so important that the ancient Indo-European word for oak, *deru*, is the source of the word *tree* itself. In the United States, no oak is arguably as important as the white oak, the most massive member of the oak clan, of which there are numerous North American species.

Under the right conditions, white oaks can live for centuries. A West Virginia tree, the famous Mingo Oak—at 200 feet then the tallest white oak in the world—died in 1938 at the ripe age of 582, having burst from its acorn in 1356. In Maryland a 450-year-old great white oak died in 2006, and in northern New Jersey a white oak died in 2017 after surviving a remarkable 600 years, its acorn sprouting well before Columbus sailed west.

One Tree, So Many Uses

Named more for its white wood than its light bark, the white oak was important to both the Lenape and the region's later settlers. As we know, the Lenape burned forests to favor the growth of oaks, using their acorns for porridges and flour, but they also counted on acorns to attract important game like deer, turkey, bear, and even passenger pigeons.

▲ A huge white oak growing in Collingswood is thought to be the state's second-oldest.

◄ You can tell a white oak by the rounded tips of its lobed leaves and the knobby appearance of its acorn caps.

maturity—when they can produce acorns—does not arrive until 20 years of age, but the tree produces few acorns until its fiftieth year.

In *The Nature of Oaks*, University of Delaware professor Doug Tallamy boasted that "oaks support more forms of life and more fascinating interactions than any other tree genus in North America." More than 500 species of moth and butterfly larvae rely on oaks as host plants, a huge number, and their root system is better at absorbing stormwater than that of any other tree. Its wood and especially its roots are best at sequestering carbon too, and these long-lived trees will store carbon for *centuries*. Want to combat climate change? Don't just plant trees, he says, plant oaks.

The settlers in turn used the wood for log cabins, sailing ships, barrels, furniture, building beams, and more. White oak's dense wood, so incredibly strong, essentially built the country.

Many creatures seek out acorns, including blue jays, nuthatches, squirrels, and chipmunks, in addition to those named above. So, very few acorns are able to sprout into oak seedlings in most years, as most are devoured. White oaks, like all oaks (and hickories), produce mast years with a huge number of acorns; it's these years that likely allow some to sprout. The seedling sends a taproot deep into the ground to begin growth. These trees are marathoners, in for the long haul: sexual

Where to See It

White oaks can be found on most of our forest walks. At the Crow's Nest Preserve, an ancient white oak is the center of the Chief's Grove. As you walk the Briar Bush Nature Center's trail from the nature museum to the bird observatory, you turn left at a wonderful white oak.

Annual Cicada

Neotibicen species

Annual cicadas don't get the attention of their more-famous 17-year cousins, who emerge from their long life as underground nymphs to worldwide headlines. Called annual cicadas because the insects emerge every summer, they are not actually annual at all. Each annual cicada takes 3 to 5 years to mature underground. But since their populations are staggered, cicada adults sing every simmer.

The so-called dog days of summer inspired the name for two of the region's annual cicadas. Davis' southeastern dog-day cicada is a singer of the Coastal Plain from New Jersey deep into Louisiana, and its long name differentiates it from its cousin, the dog-day cicada, an insect found west and north of Wild Philly. Other species inhabit the region too, with wonderful names like the lyric cicada and, my favorite, the scissor-grinder.

Members of the order Hemiptera, along with aphids and water striders, cicadas have needle-like mouthparts they use to spear plants, drinking the plant's juices. These handsome insects have chunky bodies, brightly colored eyes, and clear wings marked with colorful veins. Check a cicada out closely next time you find one.

▲ The scissor-grinder is one of several annual cicada species in Wild Philly.

For Calling Out Loud

Two creatures say summer to me: fireflies flashing at night and cicadas screaming their buzz-saw song during the middle of a hot day. It's an amazingly loud song from a 2-inch insect. Like cricket song and firefly flash, the loud buzz is the male's mating call, made with a tympanum, a stretched-skin akin to a drum, vibrating like mad. The sound is intensified by the insect's mostly hollow abdomen.

After mating, female cicadas lay their eggs in and on trees. Upon hatching, the young nymphs, which look something like smaller wingless versions of the adult, crawl into the ground and latch onto a tree root to suck the root's sap. And there they live for several years, slowly maturing, awaiting their time in the sun. When the time arrives, the adults crawl up the tree to shed their skin on the tree's bark—these cast skins are easy to find in the summer—and begin their cicada solos, so many Cyranos poetically calling to their Roxanes.

Later in the summer, it's not surprising to find dead and dying cicadas rattling on the sidewalk, even in their death throes still trying to sing. Fear not, their nymphs have simply gone underground, sucking the juice out of life—or at least trees.

Where to See It

You'll easily hear annual cicadas everywhere in Wild Philly on hot summer days.

Bald-Faced Hornet

Dolichovespula maculata

The phone rings at nature centers across the region every fall, almost without failure. "There's a giant wasp nest outside my kid's bedroom window!" yells the hysterical parent. "What should I do?"

If I get the call, I know right away what they are worried about: the football-sized nest of the bald-faced hornet, an insect named, like the bald eagle, for a bright patch of white on its face. "There's nothing to do," I try to reassure the parent, "the hornets are all dead or dying."

Life Inside the Nest

The bald-faced hornet is a cousin of the yellowjacket and social like its wasp kin. The colony builds a large nest by chewing on wood, masticating the material in its jaws to mush it into pulp. Then, like tiny bricklayers, the wasps build walls and walls of gray paper—you can easily see the different semicircular layers of wood in the pulp—to create the hive, usually

attached to the end of a twig and sometimes surprisingly right above and overhanging a busy road. *This* is the nest cartoon characters get stuck on their heads, as neither honey bees nor yellowjackets build a nest as large as this.

During the summer, between 400 and 700 wasps live here—and fiercely protect the hive, as their smooth stingers allow them to sting repeatedly. But outside that child's bedroom window and hidden by tree leaves, the parent had no idea a large wasp nest existed there (a good thing for the hornets). As winter settles in, the workers and drones slowly die, as does the queen herself. Most of the time, when we finally see the nest standing out among the now-leafless branches, it is empty and devoid of hornets.

New queens raised in that hive, however, have flown to the ground and are tucked beneath a blanket of leaves for a long winter's

▲ A bald-faced hornet has a distinctive white pattern on its face.

▲ A bald-faced hornet colony builds a football-sized nest from masticated wood.

nap. When spring comes, they awaken and crawl out to select new hive locations, never reusing old nests. Each queen begins building her hive, raising the first batch of eggs herself. When the workers mature, they in turn build a bigger nest while the queen goes into full-time egg laying.

Bald-faced hornets are omnivorous wasps, eating fruits and drinking nectar they bring to the hive to share with developing larvae. They also eat a wide variety of other insects and spiders, even raw meat, and chew insects up to feed to the larvae too.

In late summer or early fall, the queen begins to lay eggs for new queens and drones, and even some of the workers lay unfertilized eggs that hatch into drones. When these mature, they fly away to mate, the new queens then picking out their cozy overwintering spots. And the old queen? She might be killed by her workers or, if not, dies in the cold anyway. The new queens awaken in the spring, and begin the circle of life anew.

Where to See It

You'll rarely see a bald-faced hornet. But in the winter, keep your eyes peeled on your walks—and drives—for the gray hive.

Common Eastern Bumble Bee

Bombus impatiens

While the well-known honey bee is not a native North American, the common eastern bumble bee is Wild Philly's most common, most recognizable, and arguably most important native flower pollinator.

Its fuzzy yellow thorax is the key to its success as a pollinator. As the bumble bee collects pollen and nectar to bring back to its underground hive, it brushes that thorax against pollen-laden anthers, with lots of the sticky grains adhering to the body, more than a honey bee carries. As the bee travels its floral route, pollen is transferred from one plant to another. Bumble bees also carry pollen back to the nest in hairy appendages that function almost like baskets on their rear legs, something easy to spot on many of the bees visiting your garden.

Subterranean Nests

You've likely never seen a bumble bee nest, found underground and filled with hundreds of workers. Often built in an abandoned chipmunk or rodent hole, the common eastern bumble bee's nest is not as organized as the honey bee's famous comb. Instead, clusters of eggs are randomly laid within the nest. Bumble bees produce wax to build cells for rearing young and storing honey, a combination of regurgitated pollen and nectar.

The bumble bee colony has a queen and worker bees who care for the eggs and young. The workers come in a variety of sizes, with smaller bees caring for larvae and larger ones foraging outside. There are drones as well, the male bees whose one job is to fertilize a queen if needed.

Bumble bees are able to forage among flowers in colder temperatures than honey bees, so you'll find them outside in October, even November. Still, many a late autumn morning I've found foraging bumble bees desperately clinging to flowers, likely lacking the energy to make it back to the hive at the end of the previous day's work, the combination of hard work and colder weather conspiring to harm them. Typically only the colony's new queen survives the winter, coming out of hibernation in the spring to begin building a new nest, lay new eggs, and start over.

▲ The common eastern bumble bee forages for nectar and pollen well into autumn.

Where to See It

Bumble bees abound in milkweed patches and goldenrod fields, so all the meadows at Crow's Nest Preserve, Andorra Meadow, and Pennypack Ecological Restoration Trust are wonderful places to find them. So is your home— all you need are some nectar-rich flowers.

Crane Fly

Family Tipulidae

You have probably seen what looks like a giant mosquito, resting against your screen door at night as it was drawn to your porch light, or perhaps you've found one bumbling around the walls of your bathroom, helplessly trying to get out. You may have even killed it, assuming it was a mosquito. It wasn't, but instead a completely harmless, nonbiting, and thoroughly interesting insect called the crane fly.

▶ Although the long-legged adult crane fly looks like a giant mosquito, it is harmless.

145

▲ Most larval crane flies live underwater.

Cousins of the mosquito, crane flies have slender bodies and long stilt-like legs that inspired their name. They not only don't bite, they don't eat much, as the adult crane fly lives only a few days, mating and dying in that time. If a crane fly eats, it's likely eating pollen.

An adult female hatches from the pupal stage with mature eggs and mates immediately, if a male is available. She then lays her now-fertilized eggs, depending on the species, in wet soil, in mats of algae, or on the surface of a water body.

Many crane fly larvae are aquatic, long cylindrical maggot-like creatures that inhabit rocky stream beds and eat organic detritus. Some get to be more than 2 inches long, often among the larger invertebrates living in Wild Philly's streams. Because crane fly larvae are not streamlined for fast-moving water, some can inflate a segment toward their tail end like a balloon, wedging it into the substrate to hold on.

Two Wings

The world's approximately 15,000 species of crane flies belong to the order Diptera, the clan of true flies. That name translates as "two wings," which is the order's key characteristic. While most insects have four wings, the second pair in dipterans have evolved into gyroscopic devices for balance, making true flies among the most acrobatic and most highly evolved of all insects. House flies, mosquitoes, gnats, and horse flies are other common true flies. There are 100,000 named true flies, with many to be discovered.

The crane fly has its share of nicknames. Called the Jersey mosquito by many Philadelphians, it's also dubbed the daddy-long-legs too (although that name is typically reserved for a creature we'll meet soon). And someone decided that they must eat mosquitoes, so mosquito hawks and skeeter eaters are other common names. The long larva, in some species found on land, has been called the leatherjacket for its tough outer skin. Gallinipper, gollywhopper, and whammer are additional names for this insect, the last one perhaps the sound of a hand slapping the poor thing. Now we know to let these harmless flies be.

Where to See It

Since their larvae are aquatic, you might find crane flies flying near streams. Or more commonly, you might see one on your porch at night if you leave a light on.

Daddy Longlegs (Harvestman)

Opiliones species

What kid hasn't marveled at a daddy longlegs or, worse, plucked off one of its eight legs? Incredibly common worldwide, its extraordinary legs gave it both of its names, the better known daddy longlegs and the more correct name, harvestman, a nod to the scythe-like appearance of those famous legs. As there are several other invertebrates also called daddy longlegs, most entomologists use the name harvestman instead.

A living fossil that has been around for more than 400 million years—*long* before the dinosaurs—the animal is not a spider at all, even though it possesses the correct number of legs. Instead, this arachnid is more closely aligned with scorpions. Unlike scorpions and

▲ Daddy longlegs are more closely related to scorpions than to spiders, but they have no venom.

spiders, however, the harvestman has no venom and cannot bite you.

Urban Legends

Which brings us to a fake news alert: there is an ancient urban legend that the daddy longlegs is somehow the most venomous animal on earth. In truth, it's one of the *least* poisonous, as it has no venom. And about kids plucking its legs. While the harvestman might survive that abuse, the leg does not grow back—another widely held misconception.

While spiders are carnivores, possessing piercing and hollow fangs for drinking their prey dry, the daddy longlegs chews its food. And given that it's not very fast, it dines on a wide array of material: insects, plant parts, fungi, dead animals, even bird droppings and dung. When pursuing small insects, a daddy longlegs uses its second pair of legs as antennae or walking sticks, tapping the ground ahead of it as it walks.

Most harvestmen reproduce sexually. During mating season, the males of some species of harvestman offer a secretion from their specialized jaws as a nuptial gift, likely to distract the female during copulation. Uniquely among arachnids, daddy longlegs are often good dads. The male of some species guard and clean eggs, sometimes even protecting them from other egg-eating females.

Where to See It

On any walk in Wild Philly from spring throughout the fall, a daddy longlegs may cross your path.

Deer Tick

Ixodes scapularis

One of the most reviled animals in Wild Philly, the deer tick is the smaller cousin of the dog tick, both of which carry several diseases, including and especially Lyme disease. A deer tick is about the size of a sesame seed, whereas a fully fed adult dog tick is about the size of a watermelon seed.

Deer ticks generally live for 2 to 3 years, the adult feeding primarily on deer but also accepting other warm-blooded animals, including us. In the fall, females feed on the blood of a deer for 4 to 5 days, then drop off to hibernate, emerging in the spring to lay their eggs and die. Larvae only the size of the period

▲ Deer ticks must remain attached to a host for 24 hours for Lyme disease to be transmitted.

do not transmit bacteria from blood to tick. Rodents do.

While roughly 30,000 cases of Lyme disease are reported to the Centers for Disease Control each year, one study indicates that almost 500,000 Americans get infected annually. Complicating matters, many ticks carry more than one kind of bacteria, greatly muddying diagnostic waters. The chameleonic disease is highly variable, having a wide range of symptoms. Some of us get that telltale bull's-eye pattern, for example, though not all (like me), and many patients argue with doctors over their diagnosis or lack thereof. Too many people have too many unhappy Lyme stories.

Worse, climate change will only exacerbate Lyme disease. Warmer winters allow more ticks to survive, increasing the odds one of us will contract Lyme in our excursions into nature. There are so many reasons to combat climate change, but disease is high on the list.

on this page then hatch; they must also take a blood meal to grow, so they search for rodents and birds. After this meal, they drop off that host and molt into nymphs as big as poppy seeds that again require a blood meal. Every stage is a mini-Dracula.

Deer Do Not Transmit Lyme Disease

While deer ticks can become infected with the bacteria causing Lyme disease from their host during any of these feedings, they can only transmit it during the second or third feeding and must remain attached to the host for 24 hours for the disease to be transmitted. While deer are routinely blamed, even loathed, for the disease, it turns out that deer

Where to See It

Let's hope you never do! But after any of the walks in this book, we recommend doing a tick check. Odds are that on one of your excursions you will find one. If you do, use tweezers to grasp the tick by the head (not the body) as close to the skin as possible, and lift up. Then clean the wound and your hands well.

Eastern Tent Caterpillar

Malacosoma americanum

One of the most misunderstood signs of spring is the eastern tent caterpillar's large silken nest woven onto the outer edges of a tree's branches, usually around a crotch where branches meet. This is not the dreaded gypsy moth or a webworm. While tent caterpillars do chew a ton of leaves, their impact on the host tree is not permanent—the leaves will simply grow back, as trees have adapted to this insect's foraging for millennia.

The eastern tent caterpillar is the larval stage of a light brown moth. You might notice the tents being built early in the spring, often in crabapples and black cherries, just when buds open on trees, as they are one of the first caterpillars to appear in the spring. The eastern tent caterpillar is a highly social insect, and as many as 300 might share a tent. They spin their large silken structure to face the morning sun, using its orientation to warm

▲ Several hundred eastern tent caterpillars may share the same silken nest.

up, and the tent has numerous pockets and layers that allow them to crawl to whichever layer features the temperature they need at that moment. Just like honey bees and those marching penguins, tent caterpillars also form balls to warm as well, and the cluster's center under a sun-facing section of silk might be 50°F warmer than the cool morning air!

The tent is also a great place to hide from predators, as many cannot get past the sticky silk. But every lock in nature has a key, and cuckoos specialize in feasting on tent caterpillars.

Frass Raining Down

Eastern tent caterpillars are not eating leaves inside their tents. Instead, they venture forth from the tent on foraging forays, spinning silk as they go and leaving a chemical trail that their tent-mates follow. At day's end, they retreat back into the tent. These caterpillars are famous for their fecal pellets, as almost half of what they eat comes out the other end. In a boom year for tent caterpillars, you might hear what sounds like gentle rain in the forest around you. Well, it is rain—a rainfall of frass. You can easily see these pellets in the inside of the nest.

When full-grown, the handsome caterpillar, now 2.5 inches long with lots of hairs and a yellow racing stripe down its back, crawls away from the nest to find a solitary place to meta-morphose. The adult moths emerge in June, and they live for the sole purpose of mating. To accomplish that, the female secretes a pheromone that the large-antennaed male finds irresistible. They mate, she lays eggs, and the adults die—often within 24 hours of emerging. The female has laid her eggs around the twigs of a black cherry or crabapple tree, and those eggs are covered with a substance that hardens into a shellac that protects the egg mass as it overwinters. Then the warmer sun of spring triggers the tiny caterpillars to hatch, greeting the new season with a silky nest.

Where to See It

The best place is a line of black cherries along the Schuylkill Center's Habitat Loop in April and May.

Eastern Tiger Swallowtail

Papilio glaucus

The first European colonist to draw an American insect chose the eastern tiger swallowtail as his subject. John White, governor of the failed Roanoke colony, sent back drawings in 1587 of both the Algonquian Indians of Virginia and several animals, including a swallowtail he labeled "Mamankanois," presumably his transliteration of the local name for the butterfly.

Perhaps the best-known butterfly in Wild Philly aside from the monarch, the eastern tiger swallowtail is the official state butterfly of Delaware, having won a 1999 vote of Diamond State school kids sponsored by the state legislature.

What's not to love? This is the region's biggest butterfly, and its large size and bright yellow tiger stripes makes it a favorite among the growing legion of butterfly gardeners. There are three broods of these insects from spring

▲ The caterpillar of the eastern tiger has false eye spots to scare off predators.

into fall. While each generation only lives a few short months, we get to see eastern tiger swallowtails from April into October.

Only Females Have the Blues

There are other members of the swallowtail clan, named for the swallow-like projections from their hind wings, in the region. While

▲ An adult female eastern tiger swallowtail, with blue in its hind wings.

the other swallowtails are cloaked in various shades of black, the eastern tiger swallowtail alone is this bright. If you're able to examine a tiger closely, you may see a row of blue spots at the bottom of the hind wings; this lets you know it is a female of the species. "Only females have the blues," butterfly watchers winkingly say.

But there is a black version of the eastern tiger swallowtail too, with dark black striping against a paler black background—and these are all females. The pipevine swallowtail, one of its cousins, is poisonous to predators, so it seems black morphs of the eastern tiger swallowtail are mimicking the pipevine to borrow its protective coloring. Two additional swallowtails do this as well, the spicebush and the black.

Like its kin, the insect's mouthparts have evolved into a long, coiled proboscis, essentially a hollow straw for sipping. Butterflies are incapable of eating any solid food whatsoever—they leave that to their young. As they drink nectar from flowers, they perform the important work of pollination.

Tiger swallowtails lay their eggs on members of the magnolia and rose families. In the region's forests, they place their bright green eggs on the undersides of leaves of tuliptrees and wild cherries, among other plants. Hatching on their dinner plate, the caterpillar chews as it grows, going through several stages, where it gets a little bigger each time. Then it transforms into a pupa—the chrysalis—where its insides completely rearrange into an adult butterfly; scientists are still not sure how this radical transformation occurs. If late in the year, it is the pupa that overwinters, with the adult emerging in the spring.

Where to See It

Look for the adults in meadows across the region, but also in forests, as the butterflies emerge from chrysalises up in the trees. If you plant nectar-rich native plants in your own yard, you can enjoy eastern tiger swallowtails at home as well.

Green Darner Dragonfly

Anax junius

Hundreds of species of dragonflies and their cousins, the more delicate damselflies, inhabit the region. But the green darner is one of the easiest to spot, being the largest of them all: 3 inches from head to tail. Look for its striking green head and thorax contrasting, in the male, with a bright blue needle-like abdomen.

Speaking of needles, the *darner* of its name comes from the long association of dragonflies with darning needles; devil's darning needles is a colloquial name for dragonflies on both sides of the Atlantic.

But devilish they are not. In fact, they are remarkably helpful. Dragonflies are insect-

▲ The juvenile stage of dragonflies is an aquatic hunter.

▲ Two adult green darner dragonflies mating, with the more brightly colored male at the top of the photo.

eaters that specialize in hawking, plucking flying insects from midair. Over evolutionary time, their six long bristly legs have been pulled up beneath their mouth to form a basket that the insect uses to scoop up helpless prey in mid-flight.

Their eyes—the largest in the insect world—help as well. These compound eyes have facets that face in virtually every direction, giving the green darner dragonfly an uncanny 360-degree view of the world. They can see their prey up to 40 yards away and can swoop in at 35 miles per hour—quite fast for an insect. Though living fossils that evolved millions of years ago, dragonflies happily snag more highly advanced insects like flies and wasps, giving it another apt nickname, mosquito hawk.

Long-Distance Migrations

Unusual among insects, the green darner dragonfly is migratory, engaged in a wonderfully complicated multi-generational migration. Adults head south in the winter to lay eggs in warm southern ponds, their next-generation young return north, some as early as late April, and the young those dragonflies produce mature and fly south to begin the cycle again. Only the monarch butterfly migrates farther than the darner.

You'll typically find green darner dragonflies near fresh water, as their young are aquatic. Dragonflies lay their eggs in lakes, ponds, and slow-moving sections of streams. It's likely you've seen mating dragonflies and damselflies laying their eggs, as the partners often stay coupled for hours at a time. The young nymphs are carnivores as well; their lower lip is a hinged hook-tipped projectile that, lightning quick, clasps its prey, usually another underwater insect. But green darner nymphs are large enough to eat tadpoles and even small fish.

Where to See It

Visit any pond in the region in the summer and early fall, and chances are good you will see this and other dragonflies and their cousins, damselflies.

Green June Beetle

Cotinis nitida

Esteemed British biologist J. B. S. Haldane was asked long ago what evolution taught him about the creator. "God," he dryly replied, "has an inordinate fondness for beetles." With almost 400,000 species named worldwide, beetles are astonishingly successful, as they make up fully 40 percent of all named insects and about 25 percent of named animals.

Beetles are hard-shelled insects in the order Coleoptera (meaning the "shield-winged"). Part of their success lies in the first pair of wings that long ago evolved into a tough shell, their turtle-like protection from predators. Those wings have also been used by beetles as a blank canvas upon which evolution has painted patterns almost as colorful as those of butterflies.

Take green June beetles, for example, a common insect in Wild Philly. Sometimes also called the green June bug, it is a scarab beetle whose adults typically emerge in June. Their shells are beautiful and of surprising variety, usually a velvety green rimmed in gold, often with a bright metallic sheen, and a metallic green underside as well. Scarab beetles possess distinctive, club-shaped antennae that end with plates called lamellae that can be compressed into a ball or fanned out like leaves for sensing smells.

About an inch long, the green June beetle is native to North America and not to be confused with the smaller Japanese beetle, half its size and an imported pest especially of roses. It's also not to be confused with the May beetle, a brown nocturnal member of the scarab family that is also sometimes confusingly called a June bug too.

Little Jabba the Hutts

As adults, green June beetles feed on fruit, especially overripe or decaying fruit. And

▲ The shell of the adult green June beetle is usually a velvety green rimmed in gold.

unlike many other beetles, this species is diurnal, active during the day. Female June beetles produce a strongly scented milky fluid that attracts males to mate, after which she lays as many as seventy-five eggs underground over a 2-week period.

Two weeks later, the eggs hatch into grubs, white or yellowish critters that stay underground until the following year. You've likely dug up a June beetle larva, a large C-shaped creature that looks like Jabba the Hutt with small legs. It remains as a grub underground for more than 9 months, tunneling and traveling along on its back. While they are mostly eating humus and organic material, tunneling by too many grubs in one area can damage the root systems of plants. When ready to pupate, the grub can be almost 2 inches long.

Moles are especially fond of beetle grubs. If a rainstorm floods a grub's tunnels, forcing it up from underground, a number of mammals and birds will eat it, including skunks and crows. A large blue-winged wasp also special-izes in parasitizing green June beetle grubs. The female wasp stings the grub while under-ground and lays its eggs inside the creature's body, the wasp larvae devouring the beetle from the inside out.

▲ Notice the hover fly's distinctive and large fly eyes.

Where to See It

Perhaps you'll pull the C-shaped grub out of your lawn while weeding or gardening. Other-wise, keep your eyes open for the metallic green adults, which are common and widely distributed.

Hover Fly

Family Syrphidae

You might be drinking a soda outside and a yellow-and-black striped insect hovers above your straw. "Yellowjacket," you might think, and try to squash it or run. But wait! If the eyes are really large and the insect is hovering like a helicopter, it's not a yellowjacket at all, as yellowjackets cannot hover.

Instead, it's a hover fly, effectively using mimicry of stinging insects (fooled you, right?) to protect itself from predators like birds. Attracted to nectar and pollen, the insect is drawn to your sugary treat, and it has no stinger to harm you. Hover flies are common, cosmopolitan members of Diptera, the true fly order, with about 6000 species worldwide in the family Syrphidae.

Hovering is a complex feat of flying, and hover flies have the most flexible wings of any flying insect, flapping at 300 beats per second. They twist their wings by 45 degrees as they flap, giving them an ideal angle of attack throughout the up-and-down strokes. Also appropriately named the flower fly, this insect hovers around flowers to sip nectar, serving as an important pollinator.

The Eyes Have It

Like most true flies, hover flies have unusually large eyes. In some flies, the two eyes almost merge into each other in the middle. The antennae are also smaller than those of bees and wasps. Hover flies typically have larger eyes than wasps and smaller abdomens than yellowjackets, the abdomen often pulsating

as it seems to breathe—all good tells for you to use.

The hover fly not only hovers to feed, but to attract mates. Length and stability of hover-ing are important traits in mate selection: the longer a male continues to hover, the more attractive—and successful—he becomes.

Like all flies, hover flies go through com-plete metamorphosis, with both larval and pupal stages. The hover fly's larva is a maggot, a wormy, legless creature that eats a range of foods. Some prey on insects like aphids, so they are helpful in agricultural and garden settings, whereas others live in the soil or mud, thriving on decaying organic material.

When a yellow-and-black striped insect next hovers over your Coke, check it out carefully—it might be this helpful insect.

Where to See It

Look for hover flies in gardens, meadows, and goldenrod fields across the region.

Labor Day Ant

Lasius neoniger

While the Labor Day ant—named for when its mating swarms are likely seen—is only one of many ant species in Wild Philly, ant expert and noted author Edward O. Wilson called it "one of the most abundant and conspicuous insects" in the Northeast. This ant nests alongside sidewalks and on grassy median strips, lawns, and even farm fields.

A creature of disturbed soils, which urban and suburban areas excel in creating, this small brown ant eats a wide variety of foods, including many other insects, dragging their dead bodies underground to share with nest mates. The Labor Day ant is one of the first of its kind to appear in newly disturbed soil. Their tunneling effectively greatly increases both soil respiration and local biodiversity, as this action encourages other insects to move in, which brings additional plants and animals.

Labor Day ants also farm aphids, a remarkable relationship between two insect species that happens across the ant and aphid worlds. Aphids are tiny sap-sucking insects that excrete a sweet waste product from their abdomen called honeydew, which many other insects love. (You may find your car windshield covered in this aphid poop after you park under a tree in the summer.) Labor Day ants specialize in caring for aphids that feed on roots, protecting the aphids from other insects while raising their ant larvae in special chambers in their nests. When an ant queen leaves a nest to start a new colony, she may even carry an aphid along with her to start a new aphid colony in her new nest.

Labor Day Ants in the News

When a colony is large enough, often in late August or early September, thousands of

▲ The small brown Labor Day ant is a common insect in Wild Philly.

winged males and winged queens ascend into the air at once. "One year," noted Isa Betancourt, entomologist at the Academy of Natural Sciences, "there was a huge emergence of kings and queens in Philadelphia, so much so that it made news. People hosting Labor Day weekend parties were actually upset as the ants were flying through their parties."

Once mated, the drones (kings) die, their work done. The queens chew their own wings off and start working on a new colony underground. "One time while I was doing a live broadcast from the Schuylkill Center," Isa continued, "I found a winged queen and held it in my hand to show everyone on video. It bit its wings off right in my palm—snip! snip!— which was really cool to show everyone." Look for them in the late summer on a sidewalk near you.

Where to See It

Ants are everywhere. While it is challenging to identify ants to species, as one of the most common ants in Wild Philly, an anthill of this species is likely found not every far from your doorstep.

Large Milkweed Bug

Oncopeltus fasciatus

When you stumble upon a milkweed patch, you are in great luck, as so many insects are drawn to the globes of sweet-smelling, nectar-rich pink flowers. For example, the monarch butterfly completely depends on this flower for its livelihood. But more common than monarchs are large milkweed bugs, which routinely form a rugby scrum atop milkweed seed pods and stems, their orange-and-black harlequin costumes lending them their species name, *fasciatus*, Latin for "striped."

That X-shaped marking on the milkweed bug's back, colors crisscrossing, are a giveaway that this is a member of the order Hemiptera, the "half-wings." The top half of the upper wing is hardened, but the bottom half not, a trait shared by all true bugs, as this order is called.

A Hypodermic Mouth

Like other true bugs, this creature's mouth is modified into a hypodermic needle, which it wields to stab a milkweed seed pod and drink

▶ Large milkweed bugs share the orange-and-black coloration of monarchs, warning predators of the toxins within.

the sap. As members of the seed bug clan, large milkweed bugs especially suck from the skin of seed pods, where they congregate in often surprisingly large numbers. If you find a cluster, you can often see several stages of the life cycle right there—adults with their half-wings mixed with juvenile nymphs, often with little black wing buds.

Possessing the same warning colors as the monarch butterfly, the large milkweed bug also stores the plant's noxious latex chemicals in its system, making it taste bad to birds that might want to eat it. So the bright coloring is a warning to predators.

The large milkweed bug also migrates like monarchs, though not as far away. Since the milkweed bug cannot tolerate cold winters, it leaves for southern climes, where it can continue feasting on milkweeds. Several generations later, the bug find its way back to Wild Philly the following summer.

Where to See It

On just about any milkweed patch, you should be able to find this bug. The Crow's Nest Preserve, Andorra Meadow, and Pennypack Ecological Restoration Trust are perfect places to look.

Monarch Butterfly

Danaus plexippus

Not only is the monarch butterfly one of Philadelphia's most recognizable flyers, it wears the Flyers' colors too, bright orange with black stripes. That coupled with its large size makes it easy to spot.

The butterfly's life cycle is justifiably famous as well, as all of Philadelphia's monarchs fly south to secluded mountain valleys northwest of Mexico City, where they are joined by all the monarchs from the Rocky Mountains eastward. This highly endangered, widely reported-on phenomenon is one of nature's most extraordinary stories. More on that in a moment.

Monarchs hatch from small eggs laid only on the undersides of milkweed leaves. Once hatched, caterpillars begin devouring milkweed leaves. The latex-laden milky sap of the plant contains noxious chemicals that monarchs have adapted to include in their body tissues, so the caterpillars taste horrible to birds trying to eat them. Eating milkweed is their secret weapon.

After 2 to 3 weeks as caterpillars, monarchs leave the milkweed plant to search for a secluded place to turn into a chrysalis, and that green-and-gold chrysalis is one of the most beautiful in the butterfly world. They hang as jeweled pendants for almost 2 weeks, the butterfly forming inside. One day before emerging, the outer skin of the chrysalis becomes clear, revealing the dark adult butterfly inside.

Once a mature butterfly, the monarch uses its flexible straw-like proboscis to search for floral nectar, joining other butterflies on a wide range of flowering plants in meadows and gardens.

Methuselahs

Typically, a monarch goes from egg to adult in about 25 days, and the adult only lives a few weeks. In late summer and early fall, however, this all changes. Monarchs that hatch then are the Methuselah generation, living many months. It is this group that flies south to the mountains of Mexico. A treacherous trip, the lucky ones typically reach their winter destination around November 1, the Day of the Dead in Catholic observance, and the monarchs are welcomed back as the returning souls of Aztec warriors. In Mexico, they cling to each other and to fir trees by the millions.

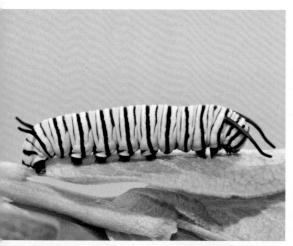

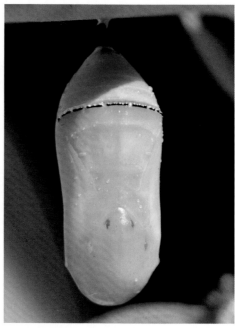

▼ All stages of the monarch are boldly colored, like this caterpillar enjoying a milkweed meal.

▲ The monarch's chrysalis glows emerald green and gold.

◄ The well-known adult monarch is orange and black.

In March, monarchs begin returning north, making it as far as Texas and Oklahoma, where exhausted females lay eggs on the new milkweed plants growing. The next generation continues north further still, but it may take monarchs three or even four generations to get back to their feeding grounds in the north.

This unique migration is highly troubled as monarch populations have plummeted in recent decades. Industrial farming in the Midwest has formed a milkweed desert in that region. While Mexico has established sanctuaries for monarchs there, in some winters monarchs have occupied as few as 2 acres of forest—imagine all of the East Coast's monarchs on 2 acres of fir trees. Some studies indicate that monarch populations have crashed by as much as 90 percent from the late 1990s.

The species is actually found worldwide, and there is even a white-colored version found in Hawaii. West Coast monarchs don't migrate to Mexico, but instead overwinter in a number of places along the California coast. While we may not lose the species, we are in danger of losing this unique phenomenon, an insect flying thousands of miles to migrate with thousands of its kind. This unbelievable event is endangered.

In response, there has been a long-standing but unsuccessful effort to add the monarch butterfly to the endangered species list, and a movement to proclaim it the national insect failed. Conservation groups plant butterfly gardens and monarch way stations, many home gardeners like me plant milkweed, and many schools have adopted monarch curricula and programs as well. Let's hope this works.

Where to See It

In milkweed patches during the summer as they lay eggs and in goldenrod fields in the fall as they fly south. Andorra Meadow, Pennypack on the Delaware Park, and the Rancocas Nature Center are among the best places to find monarchs.

Pennsylvania Firefly

Photuris pensylvanica

What kid doesn't love a firefly—or a lightning bug, as most of us likely called them? And what kid growing up in Wild Philly hasn't caught one in a glass jar to watch it flash its phosphorescent Morse code? A bunch of Upper Darby kids liked fireflies too, so much so that in 1974 they successfully led a campaign to have this one named the official state insect; after all, it's named for our state.

The first flash of a firefly is a wonderful sign that summer is upon us, their fireworks coinciding with the 4th of July. Neither fly nor bug, fireflies are instead beetles, their hard-shelled outer covering characteristic of that large insect order. And their coloration—orange thorax with yellow stripes and big black spot—is warning coloration akin to a yellowjacket's stripes. Fireflies are poisonous to birds.

Their bioluminescence is quite the trick. While many single- and multi-celled creatures glow in the ocean, few besides fireflies do on land. The firefly's abdomen contains a pair of sacs, each loaded with a different enzyme with great names, luciferin and luciferase, the *lucifer* from the Latin meaning "bringing light." When the two combine, the highly efficient chemical reaction produces a lot of light but remarkably little heat.

▲ The Pennsylvania firefly's orange thorax with yellow stripes is warning coloration to birds that it is toxic.

Codebreaker

Those flashing insects flying along your street are all males. In most firefly species, the females, with large abdomens burdened with eggs, are flightless, hiding down in the leaf litter or along tree branches, waiting for a signal. Each firefly species flashes a species-specific code that the female not only recognizes, but answers with her specific response. After mating, the female lays eggs that also glow in the dark, which hatch into larvae nicknamed glow worms that glow in the dark as well.

To complicate this wonderful story, the female of another species in the genus *Photuris* has somehow unlocked the secret code of a *Photuris pensylvanica* firefly. He flashes his question; she flashes the correct response. He alights thinking he has succeeded; she instead devours him, having a guaranteed protein source for her developing eggs. Ah, evolution.

Sadly, fireflies are on the decline across Wild Philly. In addition to the dramatic drop in insect populations worldwide, fireflies may be uniquely susceptible to our use of outdoor lighting, which completely confounds and overwhelms their mating signals—and which seems to be slamming nocturnal insects of many kinds. But citizen scientists are teaming up to send data to Massachusetts Audubon's Firefly Watch to help us understand their story.

I highly recommend you find a good firefly watching spot locally, bring a folding chair and a basket of wine and cheese, and spend an evening toasting this remarkable insect. And as you watch the fireflies, watch their flash patterns. How many different species can you distinguish? And do you see any females answering the call?

Where to See It

The Pennsylvania firefly is another species to look for in the evening on your own street or in a wild place near you.

Six-Spotted Tiger Beetle

Cicindela sexguttata

▲ Although the six-spotted tiger beetle typically has six spots, the number varies.

On many a walk along a sunny, sandy trail, an impossibly bright green beetle has accompanied me, standing on the trail and then leaping forward to land several feet ahead, always advancing as I do. It's the six-spotted tiger beetle, whose metallic emerald green shield is unbelievably shiny and makes this handsome insect easy to identify.

Tiger beetles are a large group within the very large beetle order, with some 2600 species found worldwide, mostly in the tropics and subtropics. Named for their predatory habits, both adult and larval stages devour a wide variety of other arthropods like insects and spiders.

The beetle's species name *sexguttata* simply means "six-spotted," and white spots line the edge of its shield-like wings. But while there are typically six, the number of spots can actually vary from none to eight.

The Cheetahs of the Insect World

Effective predators, tiger beetles are the fastest ground-running insects, which helps them run down their prey. Interestingly, however, they'll sprint quickly toward their target, then suddenly stop and reorient, as if perhaps they move too quickly to visually process the images. An Australian species is the fastest tiger beetle, clocking in at 5.6 miles per hour. While that doesn't seem too quick, it translates to 125 body lengths *per second*!

Tiger beetles also characteristically sport long sickle-shaped mandibles, the jaws insects use to eat their food. The mandibles are white in the adult six-spotted tiger beetle.

Its larva lives in a vertical burrow. When a prey item comes along, the larva pops out like a jack-in-the-box to snare the hapless creature with its own sharp mandibles, dragging it down to the bottom of the burrow to be finished off.

Where to See It

Look for this beetle on all the forested walks in late spring through the summer, especially in sunlit patches. I have seen them on the trails ahead of me at Bowman's Hill Wildflower Preserve, John Heinz National Wildlife Refuge, the Schuylkill Center, and especially at the Rancocas Nature Center.

True Katydid

Pterophylla camellifolia

While fireflies are a signal that summer is here, the song of the katydid—that loud, incessant "kay-ty-did! kay-ty-did!"—is a late July signal that summer is sliding into its rendezvous with fall.

Wild Philly's true katydid, common through the eastern United States, is one of the loudest katydid singers. The males sit high up in trees, especially oaks, fiddling away, rubbing a scraper on one wing over a file on the other, their bowed forewings creating a resonance chamber to amplify the song. When there are many males in one location, they typically form two alternating groups of singers, and the sound can be quite deafening.

Katydids sing deep into the fall, the song's intensity correlating with temperature. I love hearing them around Halloween, when they might manage a slow, slurred, almost cursory "kay-ty," skipping the third syllable altogether. Sometimes it even becomes reduced to a sad,

▲ The katydid is a cousin of grasshoppers and crickets.

slow (one source called it "groaning") "kay." Then you know winter is nigh.

Males of course are singing for female attention, the intensity of the song correlating to the creature's health. To listen, they simply employ their eardrums—oddly located on the joints of their front legs.

The Wing-Leaves

The katydid is a large (2 inches), handsome, bright green insect, a cousin of grasshoppers and crickets. Its outer wings resemble the leaves on which it lives, and the genus name *Pterophylla* translates, appropriately, as "wing-leaf." The veins in their wings even beautifully mimic the venation of a tree leaf.

Katydids rarely, if ever, fly with those wings, typically hopping and crawling instead. When needed, they also sometimes use their long hind legs for jumping. Females are larger than males, as they are carrying eggs, and they also have a long ovipositor at the end of their abdomen for laying eggs on a tree. Leaf-eaters, katydids happily devour the leaves of their host while singing the summer away.

Where to See It

While you will rarely, if ever, see a katydid, you will undoubtedly hear them across Wild Philly, even on your own street. Listen for them.

Water Strider

Family Gerridae

You've likely seen water striders many times on ponds or in calm places on the edges of streams. A ubiquitous aquatic insect, these are true bugs (Hemiptera), their mouth modified into a hypodermic needle that they weld to stab their food and suck it dry.

Water striders are predators that skate across freshwater surfaces in search of insect prey, using the shortened front arms for grabbing and needle-like beak for piercing. The second and third pairs of legs are long and highly modified, the feet containing hairs covered in

▲ Waxy hairs on a water strider's hind legs repel water and allow it to skate across the surface.

a waxy substance. Those hairs repel water, and water striders have the unusual ability to push down on the pond's water tension without breaking through, their long legs helping spread their weight over a large surface area.

Walking on Water

Because water striders perform the miraculous act of walking on water, one common name for them is Jesus bug.

If a water strider is being chased by another predator—there are spiders that walk on water too—they can spray a substance out of their beak, which is pointed back behind them. The soap-like substance breaks the surface tension, effectively ripping the surface in two, and the water strider surfs the rip to quickly escape predation.

If you see a water strider performing its magic act in sunlight in shallow water, check out the shadows it casts on the stream or pond bed below. You'll see large circular shadows around its feet, each shadow circle outlined in bright light. When the strider pushes down on the pond's surface, the water surface bends but does not break, and the sun's rays are reflected away from the foot, creating this unique and beautiful effect.

Where to See It

Look for water striders on any pond or along the edges of streams where the water is still, like Wissahickon, Pennypack, Valley, and Ridley Creeks.

Woolly Bear Caterpillar

Pyrrharctia isabella

Not only does Pennsylvania boast Punxsutawney Phil, a rodent who can forecast the coming of spring, we've got a caterpillar that forecasts the severity of the winter. Or so says the folk legend.

The woolly bear, the caterpillar stage of the isabella tiger moth, is common across North America as far north as the Arctic Circle. It's not unusual to find one crawling across a trail in the autumn on your jaunts through Wild Philly. A chunky, fuzzy creature, the woolly bear wears what looks like a warm winter coat, with a rusty brown middle flanked by two black ends. The legend says that winter's severity is correlated with the amount of black in its fur. Lots of black? Bad winter! Wide brown saddle? Easy winter!

► What kind of winter is this woolly bear predicting?

But fact and science get in the way of a good story, as caterpillars hatching from the same batch of eggs will show a wide variety of stripes. Still, I tell everyone the story when I discover one on a trail, as it is, for me, harmless fun.

Freezing Solid

If you discover a woolly bear caterpillar on a trail, it's walking to find a winter hibernation spot, where it will crawl under leaves, filling its body with the same substance as car antifreeze. Its heart stops beating and the creature essentially freezes solid, thawing out later in the spring. Once it awakens, the caterpillar fairly quickly forms a cocoon and metamorphoses into the isabella tiger moth, itself a handsome dusty yellow insect.

Unlike many other caterpillars, the wooly bear caterpillar is a generalist that feeds on a wide variety of plants. These include farm crops like corn; wildflowers like clover, asters, and sunflowers; and trees like birches, maples, and elms. This means the isabella tiger moth, unlike the monarch, is not dependent on the fate of any one plant.

However, the woolly bear caterpillar is dependent on climate. Although a common insect now, concern is growing over an insect like this that may freeze and thaw multiple times as warming winters produce fluctuating weather patterns. Can it survive multiple thaws? We shall see. In the meantime, enjoy the caterpillar and its folk tale.

Where to See It

There's no one place to guarantee a sighting, but on your walks through Wild Philly's autumn forests, keep your eyes peeled for one crossing the trail.

Yellow Garden Spider

Argiope aurantia

The yellow garden spider is a common spider that's very easy to identify due to its telltale web combined with its bright yellow body. The spider builds a 2-foot-wide circular web in a field or in your garden, one with a unique zigzag pattern down the center. This web has inspired other apt nicknames like the zigzag spider and zipper spider. This spider is active during the day, when it sits in the center of its web, right atop the zigzag with its head pointed down.

The yellow garden spider has surprisingly impacted popular culture. The writer E. B. White noticed one just outside the window of his study, was struck by the zigzag pattern's resemblance to writing, and a plot—and Charlotte the spider—was born.

Like all spiders, this one is venomous, but the venom is mostly harmless to you. The yellow garden spider catches whatever insect flies into its sticky silk, and uses its pincer-like hollow chelicerae—essentially jaw-claw combination mouthparts common to spiders—to inject venom into the insect. The spider then wraps its prey in silk and comes back later to suck it dry, which is pretty much what every spider does.

Why the Zigzag?

Scientists have vigorously debated the spider's characteristic zigzag web pattern, called a stabilimentum. Many spiders spin a similar feature, which originally was thought to stabilize the web, hence the name. But research indicates many other possibilities, including that the yellow garden spider sits atop the structure to seem larger than it is, with the stabilimentum appearing like long legs. Another idea is that birds can see the structure and avoid the web, protecting it from being destroyed.

▲ The yellow garden spider sits on its characteristic zigzag web.

A third says this special silk reflects ultraviolet light, which pollinating insects mistake for an ultraviolet-reflecting flower and fly straight into the web. All theories are still in play.

The female of this species is the 1-inch-long yellow spider. Her mate is only one-third of her size and much duller in coloring. The tiny male may build smaller webs near or even on the female's, then court her by plucking strands of her web in a seductive pattern, all the while ready to drop a safety line if she shows evidence of wanting to eat him. If the female is receptive, he transfers a sperm packet using his pedipalps, specially designed mouthparts that function like small hands, placing the packet inside her body. His job done, the male spider dies soon thereafter—if the female doesn't eat him right after mating. She then lays her eggs, wraps them in silk, and they may overwinter in this cocoon, waiting for spring—just like in *Charlotte's Web*.

"Some pig," wrote Charlotte with her web. "Some spider," we offer back to her.

Where to See It

Look for the yellow garden spider's zigzag web on any summer meadow walk or in a garden in your neighborhood.

Fish

American Shad

Alosa sapidissima

The largest member of the herring family, shad live in the North Atlantic, where they school in great numbers feeding on plankton and shrimp. In the spring, however, like the better-known salmon, shad head upriver to their ancestral hatching grounds to mate and spawn. In colonial times, their migrations up the Delaware, Schuylkill, Brandywine, and other rivers were epic, eagerly awaited, and much anticipated moments in the natural calendar. Think about the stories you've heard of passenger pigeon flocks or bison herds. This was what the shad run was like back in the day.

Among the Lenape names for spring was *mechoammawi gischuch*, "time when the shad return." There were large Lenape fishing stations in many places, including at the mouth of the Brandywine on the Delaware, under today's Wilmington. Shad was such an important fish in colonial times that William Penn himself negotiated for Schuylkill shad fishing rights in the 1680s. In a letter home, Penn noted the fish was "excellent pickled or smoked."

The species name *sapidissima* translates as "very savory," and it is—for those who like it. A rich and oily fish loaded with Omega 3s, shad is boiled, pickled, fried, baked, and famously planked, and some people adore the female's roe. In colonial times when the fish run was huge, pickled shad became an incredibly important source of protein, especially for poor Philadelphians, as everyone had their barrel of shad.

There is a longstanding, intractable, but likely incorrect legend that the springtime shad run saved the starving American militia at Valley Forge during the Revolution in 1778. John McPhee reports in his highly recommended *The Founding Fish* that both Jefferson and Washington ran shad fishing operations in their youth. While the British occupying Philadelphia tried to block shad from passing the city, McPhee could find no reports from that time about the shad's arrival in Valley Forge. He posits the Americans had solved the food shortage before the shad arrived—but the shad were welcome nonetheless.

A Dam Problem

Sexually mature shad enter coastal rivers when the water is sufficiently warm, with Georgia shad running in January and Canada's not until June. Lambertville, New Jersey's twin town across the river from New Hope, has been holding its Shad Festival in late April for decades now. The fish can run far upstream, with Delaware River shad making it almost to New York in Pennsylvania's far northeastern corner.

Spawning fish can lay hundreds of thousands of eggs. Northern shad return to the sea, although southern shad, like salmon, die after spawning. After rolling around on the streambed, the eggs hatch into young fish that head back out to sea in the fall. After 3 to 7 years at sea, the mature fish return to the exact same stream to spawn.

Dams, of course, have blocked their runs up rivers, the first nail in the coffin. Then pollution really hurt the region's shad, as an

▲ American shad has a shimmering green or greenish blue back with silvery sides and a white belly.

oxygen-deficient industrial blight in the Delaware River at Philadelphia blocked them from passing upriver. As we have cleaned waterways and installed fish ladders at places like the Fairmount and Flat Rock Dams, shad have been returning, but sadly not in the numbers seen in the eighteenth and even nineteenth century. Like the bison, they are a shadow of their former selves. But at least they are still with us.

Where to See It
It's always hard to see a fish, but if you visit Lambertville's Shad Festival, you might luck out.

Brook Trout

Salvelinus fontinalis

A handsome animal, the brook trout, a "brookie" to any angler, is the quintessential Pennsylvania stream fish and the official state fish. With a dark greenish brown body, its distinctive feature is a marbled back with light dots along its sides, and red dots outlined in blue are sprinkled around the light dots. The lower fins are reddish with sharp white leading edges, and its belly turns red in mating season as well. Together, these colors and patterns are striking.

While trout are members of the salmon clan, the brook trout is not a true trout, but rather a char, in the same genus as the Arctic char. Like all of these, the brook trout is carnivorous, feasting on the wide array of aquatic creatures one finds in clean streams: caddisflies, stoneflies, mayflies, crayfish, frogs,

167

▲ The colorful brook trout is Pennsylvania's state fish.

salamanders, even unlucky insects that fall into the water.

During the fall mating season, the female uses the violent contortions of her body to dig a shallow depression in the stream bed, the so-called redd. Here she lays as many as 4000 eggs, and multiple males visit to fertilize them externally. The female then covers the eggs with gravel and leaves, never seeing them hatch.

Cold, Clean, Clear Water

A creature of cold, clean, clear water, the brook trout is intolerant of pollution, requiring oxygen-rich water. As farming and cities removed forests from stream banks, the streams became warmer. And as water loaded with pollutants or sediments harmed the fish, brook trout populations began dropping in the nineteenth century, and the species even disappeared from most waterways around eastern cities. The well-known and highly

respected Trout Unlimited was founded in 1959 in large part to save the brook trout.

Nowadays, the fish shares Pennsylvania streams with rainbow and brown trout, though neither is native to Lenapehoking: the rainbow trout is a western fish and the brown trout is Eurasian. Both have been introduced by the state, raised in fish farms for stocking in streams just before fishing season. Competition from these two species has greatly impacted brook trout populations. In an ironic turn, however, brook trout have been introduced out West and in Europe and have become invasive elsewhere, with European brookies giving browns a hard time in their native habitats.

Where to See It

During the spring, many streams are stocked with trout. You can see these fish from spring into summer, but they are usually brown trout. Sadly, brook trout are very hard to see or find.

Brown Bullhead

Ameiurus nebulosus

The brown bullhead shares many features with its catfish kin, including scaleless skin and barbels around the mouth that look like a cat's whiskers, sensitive feelers it wields to find food along a pond or river bottom. Its mouth is positioned toward the bottom of its face to allow for bottom-feeding, its specialty.

The Lenape name for catfish, *wisamèkw*, forms the core of the place name Wissahickon, meaning "catfish stream." And *wisamèkw* translates as "fat fish," as this animal was an important food and symbol for the Lenape—and other indigenous Americans too. Among the Ojibwe, for example, a catfish was one of the animals that rose out of the ocean to form the original six clans.

While multiple species of catfish inhabit the region, the brown bullhead is one of the two that lent its name to the Wissahickon—its cousin the yellow bullhead would have been the other. The brown bullhead is also the state's most widely distributed catfish.

Muddy Waters

The brown bullhead approaches 2 feet in length. Its brownish green body, which gets lighter toward the belly, is speckled with small brown-black spots. This species is found in ponds and the bays of larger lakes while also inhabiting slow-moving sections of streams, where it is "tolerant of very warm water temperatures, high carbon dioxide and low oxygen levels, and levels of pollution that other fish cannot tolerate," notes the Pennsylvania Fish and Boat Commission. The brown bullhead is an omnivore. It dines—usually at night—on the smorgasbord of food along the bottom, anything from algae and other plants to worms, leeches, clams, crayfish, even other fish and their eggs.

Sadly, the fish's population numbers are dwindling, as two introduced species, the channel catfish and the flathead catfish, are outcompeting bullheads. The flatheads are especially worrisome, as noted by Lance Butler, a senior scientist with the Philadelphia Water Department. "Voracious attack predators," he said, "they can grow up to 80 pounds and have bottomless pits for stomachs. We get them in the Schuylkill River, stacked up in our fish ladder all the way up at Flat Rock Dam." You might have seen an angler pull one of them out of the Schuylkill, a remarkable sight but something else the Lenape never saw in Lenapehoking back in the day.

Where to See It

The lakes of FDR Park sport a good population of brown bullheads, and anglers routinely fish there. If you talk to anglers along the Schuylkill or Delaware Rivers, see if any are catching bullheads and take a peek.

▲ The brown bullhead inhabits water bodies with muddy sediment, giving it the nickname mudcat.

Eastern Blacknose Dace

Rhinichthys atratulus

▲ The eastern blacknose dace sports a racing stripe from head to tail.

While most of us use the word *minnow* to mean any generic small fish, the name actually refers to a large family of related species that includes the familiar carp, the biggest minnow. One of this clan, the eastern blacknose dace may be one of the most common fish you've never heard of. This small minnow is an abundant fish in the many rocky streams that flow through the region's landscape, from French Creek to Pennypack Creek.

In the fast-moving world of a stream, the eastern blacknose dace is a very important and surprisingly abundant animal. Only 3 inches long as an adult, the fish sports a bold black racing stripe down its side, which makes it easy to identify—if you can find one. Its species name *atratulus* means "clothed in black," appropriately enough. The common name *dace* derives from the Old French and means "dart," which the fish constantly does as it feeds on the many small invertebrates that inhabit rocky streams, especially insects and crustaceans. This dace also scrapes rocks for algae and diatoms.

Dirty Dancing

Mating occurs in the spring. The male dace stakes out a territory in sandy or gravelly riffles, then dances to attract females into his territory, sometimes attracting more than one female. Each female lays more than 700 eggs, which are then fertilized by the territorial male, and moves on. Neither parent raises the young. When a dace hatches, the fry is only 5 millimeters long or about 1/5th of an inch.

Where to See It

Stand along any of the streams in the region and look for the shadows of fish darting about. It's a good chance you are seeing the eastern blacknose dace.

Amphibians and Reptiles

American Toad

Anaxyrus americanus

In Philadelphia, spring means wildflowers blooming, animals awakening from a long winter's nap, birds returning north. But in Upper Roxborough, spring means the return of an extraordinary phenomenon: the running of the toads.

During the evening of one of the first warm rains of early spring, hundreds of American toads that have been hibernating in the leaf litter of the Schuylkill Center's massive forest crawl out of the ground with one imperative: to mate in the nearest pond. For many, that's the abandoned reservoir on Port Royal Avenue that has become a park, the Upper Roxborough Reservoir Preserve. They hop en masse across the avenue, sometimes during evening rush hour, to get to the standing water. Luckily for the toads, volunteers from the Schuylkill Center's Toad Detour program close the road to help them avoid getting squished by cars during this annual ritual.

The Roxborough story is replicated across the region, as the American toad is one of the most common amphibians in Wild Philly. It's just not as dramatic a migration elsewhere.

▲ A male American toad trills his love song to attract a mate.

▲ American toads mating in a pond, with the smaller male atop the female. Note the string of jelly-like eggs in the water behind her.

The Cycle from Toad to Toadlet

Once the adults reach water, the males trill a lovely loud mating song. Males and females copulate in the shallow water, where the females lay two strings of translucent eggs.

▲ American toad tadpoles consume algae growing in their natal ponds.

When courtship is done, the toads quietly and singly go back into the surrounding forest to take up the adult's life of living in the leaf litter while consuming a variety of small insects, slugs, worms, and crustaceans.

Back in the water, the eggs hatch into tiny black tadpoles, all heads with impossibly small tails. Scraping algae in the water, the tadpoles need 60 days to mature into toadlets, perfectly formed tiny toads that can stand atop your thumbnail. The toadlets leave the pond when their legs and lungs have grown, venturing into the forest. I once saw a horde of toadlets crossing Port Royal Avenue at noon, turning my ride to work into a scene from the Serengeti.

Dry and rather warty, toads create a poison, bufotoxin, that makes them unpalatable to predators. Be careful, as bufotoxin can irritate your eyes and is likely even more harmful to a dog that swallows one. The tadpoles also create toxins, protecting them in that vulnerable stage as well.

Where to See It

The Schuylkill Center's Toad Detour program maintains a Facebook page; check it out and volunteer when the toads are running. You can hear toads singing in spring at the center's ponds in the Upper Roxborough Reservoir Preserve and in the Briar Bush Nature Center's pond.

Common Garter Snake

Thamnophis sirtalis

Easily the most common snake in the Philadelphia region, the common garter snake is native to North America and found across the continent. It can readily be identified by what are usually three parallel yellow lines running down its back atop a widely variable background of black, brown, and even green scales.

Garter snakes are common in part because they are adapted to a variety of habitats: forests, fields, streams, wetlands, marshes, and ponds. The species is often found near water like its cousin, the watersnake. Garter snakes have been found at sea level and in mountains, from southern Florida up to northern Canada.

They're also common because they hunt a wide variety of foods, including frogs and their tadpoles, fish, worms, insects, even small birds and rodents.

Although not poisonous to humans, a garter snake may bite if picked up—it is only defending itself. However, the bite can be toxic to much smaller prey animals, like salamanders and frogs.

An Interesting Sex Life

Garter snakes hibernate through the winter in clusters in subterranean dens. The males wake up first from their winter slumber to be ready. Some males sneakily use a fake female pheromone to lure other males away from the burrow—you'd think they wouldn't be fooled by this, but they are. That faux female then quickly doubles-back to the den to copulate first with females as they emerge.

Given that there are typically more male garter snakes than females, they form mating balls of a dozen or so males surrounding one or two females, a sight that freaks out a lot of people's inner Indiana Jones. The females then hold their fertilized eggs internally to protect them, a practice surprisingly common in fish

and reptiles. After 2 to 3 months, each female gives birth to as many as forty baby snakes.

Where to See It

The garter snake is the likeliest snake you'll find in the region, and it can be seen at any of the walks in this book. But they are most often underneath things like rocks and logs, so sightings are far rarer than the animal itself.

▲ A common garter snake has three yellow lines running down its back.

Common Watersnake

Nerodia sipedon

One of the region's larger—and therefore scarier—snakes, the common watersnake pays the price of being large. While not venomous, the snake is too often killed by people assuming it's a copperhead or cottonmouth. So while it will defend itself by biting if handled, the bite is painful but not deadly. Actually, I've seen the snake described as "aggressive" and even "vicious." Let this snake be.

Its Greek genus name translates as "flowing through," a reference to the snake's aquatic lifestyle. It is typically found along the edges of bodies of water, both ponds and streams, where the watersnake hunts a wide variety of

prey both above and below the water. Smaller, younger snakes tend to eat fish, and older, larger ones switch to frogs, salamanders, even birds and small mammals. They bask in the sun along the edges as well, but quickly dive into the water if they sense you coming. Watersnakes are surprisingly adept swimmers for animals with neither legs nor feet.

Highly variable in skin color, the common watersnake can be anything from reddish brown to black. While it typically has dark crossbands on its neck and dark blotches everywhere else, the snake's skin darkens as it ages, making the pattern more obscure. When

▲ A common watersnake basking in its element near the water.

you encounter a dark black version, identification becomes even tougher, but the aquatic location helps immensely.

The First Snake-tuary

While solitary most of the year, watersnakes are social just before and after hibernation. In one spot along Wissahickon Creek, a cluster of watersnakes annually form large balls on a rock wall near one of the creek's dams. That property's owner, having to stop the park's visitors from clubbing them to death, was inspired to get the city to declare the area a "snake-tuary," his clever turn of phrase and one of the first protected areas for reptiles in the region. It's just remarkable to see so many of them entwined like a ball of yarn.

Larger females mate with smaller males in the spring, anytime from April into June. While most snakes lay leathery-shelled eggs in nests, watersnakes, like garter snakes, are among the few that do not, the female retaining the fertilized eggs inside her to then release live young. This internal retention of the eggs gives the young a higher probability of hatching, as they are fairly well protected inside mom. Once they hatch, however, they are independent, as there is no parental care in snakes. The young start hunting immediately, heading right into the water.

Where to See It

Along Wissahickon Creek just southeast of Valley Green, the "snake-tuary" lies on the Orange Trail at Glen Ford, the historic millowner's house on the eastern bank of the creek, just upstream of the dam. Look for interpretive signs about the watersnake, but of course there's no guarantee you'll see the snakes. A watersnake reliably takes up most summers at the Schuylkill Center's Fire Pond opposite its Visitor Center front door.

Eastern Box Turtle

Terrapene carolina carolina

The medium-sized, orange-blotched eastern box turtle, with its domed shell and slow walk, is one of the most recognizable—and most threatened—reptiles in Wild Philly. Its bottom shell includes a hinge that allows it to pull into its shell and close up like, well, a box, a great defense from predators like foxes. That shell is made of bone and fused to the turtle's rib cage, so those cartoons of turtles walking out of their shells are—no surprise—impossible. The bony shell is covered with keratin, the same protein that makes up our hair and fingernails.

The male's bottom shell includes an indentation allowing him to fit atop the female in mating. Combined with his red eyes—the female's are yellow-brown—it can be surprisingly easy to identify the sex of an adult box turtle, which will likely impress your hiking friends.

The eastern box turtle is a classic omnivore with catholic tastes in food—walking that slowly, you kind of need to be. Its diet includes easy-to-reach, equally slow things like worms and insects of all kinds, snails and slugs, fruit and mushrooms, even dead animals and trash.

The shell of an adult box turtle is about 6 inches long. The scales on the shell grow throughout its life, having annual rings not unlike trees. Eastern box turtles in captivity have lived to be 100; those in the wild likely live shorter lives, but still outlast most other animals described in this book.

Because box turtles are long-lived, they reproduce slowly and it may take a full decade to reach sexual maturity. Then comes the high hurdle—male has to find female—and it's unclear how this happens. Still, the Schuylkill Center's staff has routinely found baby box turtles at the center, so it does happen in Wild Philly.

▲ Can you guess the sex of this eastern box turtle?

Between late spring and midsummer, the female makes a nest in the leaf litter and lays between three and eight eggs per clutch. The leathery eggs are creamy white, oblong, and about an inch long. The female then walks away to let the eggs incubate in the sun. Like other reptiles, temperature—not genes—determines the sex of the young. If eggs are incubated at or below 81°F, the hatchlings will be male; above 82°F, the litter is all female. Understandably, there is great concern for what climate change will do to the sex of baby reptiles.

Tiny Territories

If you find an eastern box turtle—whether adult or baby—please let it be. A box turtle lives in a freakishly small territory that is only about 250 yards from where it was born. It makes a mental map of this home territory. If moved elsewhere, the turtle will work hard to return home, and while it may not be successful, it will doggedly try for years to get back.

If you want to help a box turtle crossing a road, place it on the side to which it was headed. If you place it back where it was, it will simply cross the road again. And please do not adopt a box turtle as a pet; their numbers are crashing in the wild as development chops up the landscape, and biologists are increasingly worried about the fate of this beloved creature.

When you find one in the forest, do say hello, but please let it be.

Where to See It

With no guarantees, one can find a box turtle on just about any of the warm-weather forest walks. But the animal is rare and likely off the trails.

Eastern Milk Snake

Lampropeltis triangulum

▲ Eastern milk snakes are often strikingly colored.

This species is one of the state's most colorful snakes, and the one most widely distributed in North America. The eastern milk snake may also be one of the most confusing, as its highly variable coloration reminds too many people of either copperheads or coral snakes, both of which are poisonous. But the milk snake is not venomous, and the coral snake is found in the Coastal Plain from North Carolina south to Louisiana.

The snake's common name has nothing to do with its appearance, but comes from an old myth that snakes had the ability to milk cows, as they are often found in and around barns. It was never the cows they were after, of course. Savvy farmers would have realized the snakes were simply catching the many rodents attracted there too.

A medium-sized snake that approaches 2 feet in length, the eastern milk snake's most distinctive features include large squarish blotches and lots of banding. The blotches vary in color among browns and reds. The lighter bands, while variable, are often bordered by black lines and with a Y- or even V-shaped blotch behind the head. This variation marks the fact that twenty-four subspecies of *Lampropeltis triangulum* are currently recognized, and the snake's taxonomy will likely be adjusted in the future.

Rattling Away

But while it's not a coral snake, that red, yellow, and black venomous snake does explain the milk snake's colors. Overlapping in range with the coral in the Southeast, the milk snake's skin pattern mimics the coral snake's and affords it protection from animals, which give it a wide berth. On top of this, if you stumble upon a milk snake, it pretends it's a rattlesnake by shaking its tail among dead leaves on the forest floor. Too many milk snakes have left this world from acting out this pretense, too many southern milk snakes have been confused with coral snakes, and too many are confused with copperheads too. It's a wonder there are any here at all.

The eastern milk snake is a constricting snake, wrapping its body around its prey to kill them. It catches small mammals and birds of all kinds, while surprisingly eating other snakes as well. While the garter snake and watersnake are ovoviviparous, retaining their eggs internally, the milk snake is oviparous, laying leathery-shelled eggs in a nest and leaving the young to fend for themselves. The young are more vividly colored than the adults, the blotches usually a brighter red or orange-brown, getting darker and duller with age.

A burrower, the eastern milk snake spends a lot of time underground. When you next lift a log or a stone to see a brightly colored, banded snake staring at you, don't panic. It's just your friendly neighborhood milk snake.

Where to See It

Like all snakes, the eastern milk snake can be a challenge to find, but it is present at most of the sites listed in the field trips.

Green Frog

Lithobates clamitans

You've probably met the green frog many times, likely without knowing it, as it is the most abundant frog in Wild Philly. It can be found sitting alongside ponds, streams, lakes, and even ditches; after spotting you, the frog squawks before jumping into the water.

The green frog is two-tone in color: the head is green but the body is more olive, even brownish. A pair of ridges runs down the length of the frog's body behind its tympanums, the eardrums—ridges its larger, greener cousin, the bullfrog, lacks. Males have eardrums that

▶ The green frog, our most common frog. The male's eardrum is bigger than its eye; the female's is about the same size.

are much larger than their eye, while those of females are about the same size as the eye. Males also sport yellow throats, especially in breeding season, and females tend to be larger than their mates.

Opportunistic carnivores, green frogs will attempt to eat any moving animal large enough to see but small enough to swallow, with their menu changing depending on what's available. They eat both aquatic and flying insects, worms, centipedes, millipedes, tadpoles of other frogs, crayfish, and mollusks, even small snakes and fish. In turn, they are eaten by so many things, including many waterbirds, fish, and snakes. Larger green frogs eat smaller ones, and bullfrogs, the region's largest frog, will eat them too. In one Canadian study, green frog populations quadrupled after bullfrogs disappeared.

Banjo Strings

Its species name *clamitans* is Latin for "loud-calling," a reference to the banjo-string "gunk" that is the male's mating call. Green frogs typically mate in the same body of water they live in, the pair engaging in the coupling common among frogs and toads, where the male externally fertilizes a mass of eggs as the female lays them. A female green frog might lay as many as 7000 eggs in and around submerged vegetation.

Once hatched, the tadpoles are equally opportunistic, eating organic debris, algae, very small crustaceans, and more. In turn, they have more predators to worry about than their parents, including a panoply of predatory aquatic insects like dragonfly nymphs, diving beetles and their larvae, fish, turtles, other frogs, and much more. As Kermit the Frog once complained, "It's not easy being green."

Green frog tadpoles born early in their season might metamorphose into frogs by the fall in time to hibernate for the winter. But those who hatch later in the year will overwinter as tadpoles, transforming in their second year.

On your next walk near a pond, approach the water more slowly. See if you can catch a glimpse of the green frog, usually sitting facing the water, ready to jump, before it— "squawk!"—spots you.

Where to See It

Except in winter, almost every pond in Wild Philly will have green frogs. The Manayunk Canal walk is fairly guaranteed.

Painted Turtle

Chrysemys picta

This species is the most widespread native North American turtle—the only turtle found coast to coast. The painted turtle is named for the bright red and yellow markings on its skin and bottom shell. Its Latin species name *picta* translates as "decorated" or "painted." While its head, neck, and underside are painted, the top of the shell is not, so it often presents itself as a bland blackish brown animal, when in fact it is quite striking.

Lenape legend holds that Lenapehoking rests atop the back of a *taxkwâx*, a turtle. Although the legend doesn't name the species, given that it was Muskrat who dived deep and long to retrieve a ball of mud that became the earth, it seems fitting that the painted turtle might be a candidate for that honor.

The painted turtle is adaptable to a diversity of aquatic environments, so you are equally likely to find it basking along the Schuylkill River or at a small pond at the Schuylkill Center. In fact, this adaptability has been its strong suite—as development and sprawl gobbles up the landscape, the painted turtle has been able to thrive in whatever aquatic habitats are left over.

▲ The painted turtle can be distinguished from the red-eared slider by the yellow streaks behind its eyes.

Its diet is adaptable as well. Like most turtles, the painted turtle is omnivorous, eating a wide variety of plants and animals, from algae and aquatic plants to insects, crustaceans, and whatever fish it can catch. Painted turtle eggs, in turn, are greedily snatched by foxes, raccoons, rodents, even garter snakes, whereas the shell affords the adults protection.

Painted Versus Slider

Like all local reptiles, the painted turtle is a cold-blooded hibernator, and its appearance atop floating logs and rocks in ponds and streams is another welcome sign of spring. You rarely see one painted turtle in the water; more typically there are several lined up on a log or rock. Their hearing is surprisingly good, though, and they'll slip into the water as soon as they hear you coming.

Wild Philly's native turtle also basks alongside the one turtle it is most confused with, the non-native and invasive red-eared slider, the Southern turtle sold forever to kids as pets and indiscriminately released by frustrated parents across the country. The slider, also brilliantly marked, sports red patches behind its ears, which the painted turtle does not have. The painted turtle instead has yellow streaks behind its eyes with red on its underside. There are other differences as well, but this gets you started.

Where to See It

Look for groups of painted turtles on logs and rocks alongside many bodies of water, including the Manayunk Canal and the John Heinz National Wildlife Refuge.

Red-Backed Salamander

Plethodon cinereus

▲ The two kinds of red-backed salamander, the so-called lead-backed and more typical red-backed.

If good things come in small packages, then the red-backed salamander is great. Only a few inches long, it is among the most common amphibians in the region's forests, has one of the widest ranges of any North American salamander, and boasts many highly unusual features.

The red-backed salamander lacks lungs, and oxygen passes directly through its porous skin. These amphibians inhabit tiny territories, moving only a couple of feet daily to hunt the many things they eat, including ants, termites, beetles, snails, and millipedes.

Almost snake-like with tiny legs, the salamander's dark brown body usually sports a red racing stripe down the middle, the species' dominant feature. As a bonus, some come in a different color phase, monotone gray with no stripe, and are given the nickname lead-backed salamander. In Appalachia, where this species first evolved and are more plentiful than even here, there are many more colors and varieties.

An Unusual Lifestyle

The word *amphibian* translates as "both lives," as many live on land as adults while returning to their juvenile aquatic haunts to lay jelly-like eggs. But the red-backed salamander is fully terrestrial, an exception to the rule, and the female lays her eggs in the forest.

When mating season arrives, females crush a prospective mate's feces to determine the health and quality of the output, a clever measure. If he passes muster, mating involves an elaborate courtship, as it does among many amphibians. In this case, it includes a tail-straddle walk, then scratching her skin with special teeth, and finally rubbing secretions from a gland under his chin on those abrasions. Kinky, no?

After mating, the female then lays a clutch of eggs in a moist cavity, typically in a rotting log. While most amphibians lay thousands of eggs and leave, she lays only a small handful, as few as four, as many as a dozen—and stays.

Since the eggs have no shells, the female guards them to keep them moist, while eating very little herself. When the young hatch 2 months later, they remain in this same nest with her for the next few weeks.

Many amphibian enthusiasts roll over forest logs to seek out red- and lead-backed salamanders. If you do, that's fine; just make sure you gently replace the log so as not to dry them out. But I've found them in far simpler places, like under the terracotta pots on my patio where they surprisingly hang out, despite my home being very far from a forest. Maybe your yard has them as well.

Where to See It

The red-backed salamander will be present on almost every forest walk you take, though hiding underground, so you will likely not see any. Be happy knowing they are all around you.

Red-Spotted Newt

Notophthalmus viridescens viridescens

Another fairly common salamander in the eastern United States, the red-spotted newt is aquatic, inhabiting small ponds across the region. Some 3 to 5 inches long, newts are typically olive green above and dull yellow below, with numerous black dots across the body supplemented with a few red dots, each of these delicately outlined in black for sharp contrast. Red-spotted newts are primarily carnivorous, eating a wide array of small animals, including worms, mollusks, insects, other amphibians, and fish and amphibian eggs as well.

Hatched from eggs laid underwater, the newt's tadpole looks like a much smaller version of the adult, except with a wider tail and feathery gills behind its eyes, the latter for underwater breathing. The newt loses these gills when it transforms into an adult.

The Teenage Eft

Unlike most of its amphibian kin, the red-spotted newt has an intermediate migratory stage, the eft—a favorite word of crossword solvers. Something like a teenage newt, the eft is neon orange-red with those same black-and-red spots. Efts leave the pond they hatched in and disperse to find new ponds to conquer and to mix up the gene pool. I've discovered them crossing my path on many walks. Since

▲ An adult red-spotted newt is olive green above and dull yellow below.

▲ The bright orange coloration of the eft stage warns predators that it is toxic.

overland travel is hazardous for the small eft, it is partially protected by toxins in its body that are advertised by that bright warning coloration. In its new pond, the eft metamorphoses into an olive green adult.

Male red-spotted newts can be told from females, as they have more widely keeled tails for seducing females. The male performs a mating dance in which he lures a female by waving his tail, pushing pheromones in her direction. In a final flourish, the male grabs the female with his hind legs while nuzzling her snout. The male then deposits a sperm packet on the pond bottom, and the female walks over and picks it up in her cloaca, the opening for both reproductive and digestive organs, and uses it to fertilize her eggs.

Like most amphibians, red-spotted newt females lay their eggs in the pond and swim off. The young are on their own, as they have been for millennia.

Where to See It

During the summer and fall, look for red-spotted newts in ponds anywhere in Wild Philly, and an eft may surprise you on any autumn forest walk.

Snapping Turtle

Chelydra serpentina

▲ Snapping turtles are huge reptiles that can weigh up to 50 pounds.

The region's largest turtle by far, the snapping turtle is that prehistoric-looking reptile you may have encountered lumbering across a road or glimpsed just below the surface of a pond as it swam by. The turtle's neck is long and nimble, its beak is hooked for grasping prey, and its claws are long and sharp. Both its long tail and the hind edge of its shell bear serrations reminiscent of Godzilla's back. In short, this is a turtle direct from Central Casting.

Males are larger than females, and both grow continuously throughout their lives. Their shells can reach nearly a full foot in length, and big snapping turtles push 50 pounds. They are also long-lived, with an Ontario study finding that some of their subjects may have lived more than a century.

This freshwater animal lives in a wide variety of pond and stream habitats, but generally prefers slow-moving water. Like most turtles, the snapping turtle eats a variety of foods, including plant material like duckweed and algae, and it even scavenges on carrion. But the turtle is also a voracious predator that eats whatever it can catch: fish, frogs, toads, invertebrates like crayfish and insects, even an occasional duck swimming on a pond's surface, which it drags below. Few predators try to capture this hard-shelled creature, but as the female lays its eggs on land (like all aquatic turtles), the eggs are vulnerable to raccoons, skunks, and foxes, among others.

Pugnacious

In the water, a snapping turtle will likely swim away from you if you are wading near it. On land, however, where they feel vulnerable, one herpetologist wrote they become "pugnacious . . . often striking out repeatedly at the collector while forcibly exhaling air from the lungs." Legend says the turtle can snap a broomstick or your finger, but writers have found no verified cases of the latter. Still, if you ever attempt to pick up a snapping turtle, which I don't recommend, grab the shell from the rear above the hind legs—do not grab its tail. If you do try to assist a snapping turtle across a road, place it in the direction it wants to go, and it will likely lumber on.

After mating, the female leaves her aquatic habitat and roams rather far looking for sandy soil to dig a nest and lay her eggs. This is when she is especially vulnerable, and snapping turtles have come to many wildlife rehabilitation centers after being struck by cars while crossing roads.

Like all reptiles, the sex of the eggs is determined not by genetics, but by the temperature of the nest. Those toward the top of the pile, likely warmer, produce females, and those farther down males. Biologists worry about the impact of climate change on reptilian gender. For now, however, snapping turtles are common and of little conservation concern.

Where to See It

Since snapping turtles are typically underwater, they are rarely spotted, though sharp-eye observers sometimes see their triangular nostrils poking out of the pond as they swim. You might start looking for them at the Manayunk Canal.

Birds

American Crow
Corvus brachyrhynchos

Jet black with iridescent feathers, not only are the American crow's feathers solid black, so are its legs and beak. The crow may just be one of the very few birds most Philadelphians can recognize by sight and song, its distinctive black body and raucous "caw" both highly recognizable. In addition, the bird is remarkably common, inhabiting the entire region from urbanized Center City to rural Chester County.

And, wow, are they smart, with some sources comparing them to 7-year-old kids. Crows may be the only nonprimate that makes and uses tools, can solve two-step problems, recognizes people's faces, and can even memorize restaurant schedules to know when staff are visiting the dumpster. Crows have been seen dropping acorns in traffic, then swooping in at a red flight to retrieve their smashed meal, letting the cars do the dirty work.

Crows eat many things, actively hunting small animals like insects, frogs, and mice, while also stealing eggs from nests and scavenging on dead animals and trash. It is not uncommon to see a crow trying to get to a road-killed carcass in traffic. In rural areas, they descend on farm crops, as every schoolkid knows from scarecrows, though ironically crows likely eat more harmful insects and rodents than corn and wheat. A Canadian town once waged a war on what they assumed were crop-eating crows, shooting them on sight; the crows smartly responded by flying high above that town and out of rifle shot.

Loud and Opinionated

That "caw" is only one of many sounds American crows make. Like their cousin the blue jay,

▲ The American crow is cloaked in black from head to toe.

crows are loud and opinionated. When they call, watch them bob their head up and down as they do. Like blue jays, mockingbirds, and only a few others, crows can mimic other birds and sounds.

Monogamous but social, crows form large family groups of up to fifteen individuals of a variety of ages. Offspring from one year will often stay with their parents to help raise the next year's batch.

Crows also mob birds of prey like hawks and owls. If you hear a large contingent of crows calling near your home, they are likely trying to chase a bird of prey away. Very early one twilit morning, hearing a lot of crows worked into a frenzy, I ran into my street just in time to see a great horned owl flying right over me and straight down the road, chased by everyone's favorite plural noun, a murder of crows.

Sadly, American crows were devastated by West Nile virus from 1999 into the early 2000s, with one study indicating as many as 45 percent of crow populations lost in that time. Still, crows are common in Wild Philly and populations have been holding steady recently.

Where to See It

On any of the walks described in this book, or walks around your block, listen for the crow's call.

Bald Eagle

Haliaeetus leucocephalus

"Fly Eagles fly," sing Philadelphia football fans every autumn. But here's the surprise: Philadelphians can spot bald eagles—iconic raptor, symbol of the United States, rare and endangered for so long—across the region, flying down the Delaware, the Schuylkill, even Wissahickon or Pennypack Creeks. While a sighting is not that common, it's also not so rare anymore.

Adult bald eagles are unmistakable—look for long, broad wings on a large dark brown body with contrasting white head and tail; no other large bird has this bicolor appearance. The eagle is, of course, not bald. Rather, that name harkens back to the original meaning of *bald*, someone with white hair, and its specific name *leucocephalus* literally translates as "white headed." The Lenape accented the other end, as their name, *òpalanie*, translates as "white tail feathers."

While bald eagles might hunt for mammals and birds that share their habitat, they subsist mostly on fish, which they snatch from the water with their impressive talons. But they will also frequently feed on dead fish they find, like at dam sites on Lake Nockamixon or the Susquehanna River. Bald eagles steal fish from each other and other animals, scavenging for carrion and even eating garbage. In fact, their feeding habits was one of the reasons Ben Franklin favored the more "noble" turkey as our national symbol.

▲ The finger-like feathers at the wingtips are a distinctive feature of the bald eagle, which does not develop its white head and tail until 5 years of age.

World's Largest Bird Nest

Several pairs of bald eagles nest within the city limits, one at the John Heinz National Wildlife Refuge and another at Fort Mifflin on the Delaware, both in the shadow of the airport. Their nests are massive, not only the largest of any North American bird, but the largest recorded for any animal species; they can measure more than 10 feet deep and 8 feet wide and weigh a full ton. An eagle nest is on display in the Academy of Natural Science's museum in Center City; check it out in the Outside Inn children's area.

Bald eagles take 5 years to reach sexual maturity, and during this time they wear a coat of streaky brown feathers that confuses them with golden eagles, their western cousin. While some occasionally mature more quickly, most bald eagles gain that iconic white helmet at maturity, when they begin seeking mates. Their beaks achieve that stunning golden color at sexual maturity too.

Bald eagles mate for life, the pair returning to the same nest—and adding to it—every spring. If something happens to one of the partners, the mate—whether male or female—will stay at the nest and seek a new partner. The female lays between one and three eggs annually, and the nestlings are ready to try their first flight within 10 to 12 weeks of hatching.

Its call seems out of character with the bird, with the Cornell's Laboratory of Ornithology calling it a "weak sounding whinny." Hollywood producers typically dub in another voice when you see an eagle flying, often swapping in the red-tailed hawk's call and annoying most birders.

We almost lost our national symbol in the 1960s, when bald eagle numbers were greatly reduced due to eggshell thinning. The pesticide DDT moved up the food chain, growing ever more concentrated as it went from insects to the prey animals consumed by bald eagles. DDT caused their eggshells to crack when the parents tried to brood their chicks, leading to use of the pesticide being outlawed in the United States. In recent decades, bald eagle numbers have been on the upswing, and the species is no longer endangered. It's a great conservation success story.

Where to See It

All of the Delaware River walks and Hawk-Watch trips might allow you to see bald eagles. Start by finding the nesting pair at the John Heinz National Wildlife Refuge.

Blue Jay

Cyanocitta cristata

Say "blue jay" in Philadelphia, and most of us still sting from Toronto Blue Jays hitter Joe Carter smashing a ninth-inning Mitch Williams fastball to win the 1993 World Series in six games. Luckily, most of us have forgiven the bird, if not Mitch Williams, some 30 years later.

One of the most recognized songbirds, the blue jay is a character: raucous, insistent, social, and a bully at the bird feeder. A cousin of the crow, its nasal yells are reminiscent of its cousin's "caw." The bird is also a mimic, able to call like a red-tailed hawk to either fool neighboring birds or perhaps warn its kin that a hawk is afoot. Also like crows, blue jays will mob hawks, ganging up to chase them away in a noisy but fun-to-watch show of ire.

While the jay eats a large number of things, including occasional eggs from other birds' nests, most of its diet is insects, but supplemented with acorns, beechnuts, and birch seeds. At bird feeders they especially favor sunflower seeds and peanuts.

Blue jays bury acorns in the ground to hide and protect them; unlike squirrels, though, they can hide an acorn up to a mile away from its mother tree. In *The Nature of Oaks*, Doug

Tallamy estimates that one blue jay can store some 4500 acorns underground annually, quite the feat, but only remembers where 25 percent of them are. According to Tallamy, "The end result is each jay plants somewhere in the neighborhood of 3360 oak trees every year of its 7- to 17-year lifespan! It's no wonder that jays have enabled oaks to move about the earth faster than any other tree species."

Not Really Blue

The odd thing is a blue jay is not really blue. That is, there's no blue pigment in its feathers, unlike a cardinal, which does sport red pigments in its feathers. Blue is a difficult pigment to produce, making it rare in nature. Blue jay feathers include melanin, a brown pigment common in many creatures, even us. Modified cells on the surfaces of its feathers scatter the light striking them, absorbing all colors except blue, which is reflected back to our eyes. It's quite the optical illusion!

While you can see blue jays all year in the area, they do migrate. I've stood in a meadow transfixed at waves of blue jays pouring overhead in small groups of four and five for hours. It seems that jay migration has mystified the experts for years; some remain here all year, while others may be moving throughout their range. Happily, there are still many things to learn about many of the creatures that share our world.

▲ Sunflower seeds are preferred by blue jays at backyard bird feeders.

Where to See It

Blue jays are common and relatively easy to find—and hear—in most forested walks described in this book.

Canada Goose

Brant canadensis

The Canada goose is one of Wild Philly's largest birds, with some reaching nearly 20 pounds. The goose has a distinctive black head and neck, with white cheeks and a white chinstrap. Flocks of Canada geese live near lakes, rivers, and ponds and can often be seen in yards, park lawns, and farm fields. You may have danced around goose poop on your walks. These animals can really pump it out: a fifty-bird flock can generate up to 5000 pounds annually!

Mostly herbivorous, the Canada goose dines on a wide range of aquatic plants, but also grasses and seeds on land and especially farm crops. In fact, migratory geese rely far more on farm fields today for their stopovers than they historically did, to the farmers' chagrin. They especially love corn.

Canada geese mate for life, or until one of the partners dies. Both sexes look alike and both stay near the nest, though the female builds most of the nest herself. When their goslings hatch, they often feed in a line, one parent in front, one at the back. Because lots of animals prey on their eggs and goslings, the parents—as you likely have discovered—are aggressively protective.

▲ More than half of Wild Philly's Canada geese live here year-round.

Seasonal Migration

Once upon a time not too long ago, V-shaped skeins of Canada geese noisily flying north or south were important signals of seasonal change. Amazingly, no Canada geese nested in precolonial Lenapehoking. None. Instead, they all nested up in northern, even subarctic, Canada—hence the name.

Overhunting, however, brought their populations dangerously low in the late nineteenth and early twentieth centuries. So, conservationists began introducing a nonmigratory Midwestern subspecies, the giant Canada goose, into the eastern United States. This subspecies began intermingling with its migratory cousins, and the result is today's mishmash of blended geese: the migratory subspecies still flying overhead in those Vs, passing over their nonmigratory kin nesting here year-round. Back in the day, 90 percent of the region's Canada geese migrated, whereas today only 40 percent do. Most stay here all year, as you likely have discovered on your walks.

And their populations have exploded. Estimates suggest there were 1 million Canada geese in North America in 1970, a number that had increased sevenfold by 2020. The Pennsylvania Game Commission's website states that as a result of its actions to restore the bird, today's "goose population rivals the comebacks of the wild turkey and white-tailed deer." I'm not sure everyone is as proud of this achievement as the game commission is.

Studies have indicated that nonmigratory mixed-subspecies Canada geese might suddenly become migratory again, with one important trigger being destruction of the nest by predators. About 44 percent of Pennsylvania geese that switch from being nonmigratory to migratory have lost their nest; a female nesting on a golf course in Blue Bell may suddenly fly to the Arctic Circle—if her nest is destroyed.

So while some geese are here year-round, others migrate overhead, flying more than 2000 feet high and covering as many as 1500 miles in a single day. It's still a sign of the change in seasons.

Where to See It

Along just about any body of water, but especially in the Wissahickon Valley, at Pennypack on the Delaware, Palmyra Cove Nature Park, and the Manayunk Canal.

Carolina Chickadee

Poecile carolinensis

▲ Carolina chickadees nest in tree holes.

"Chick-a-dee-dee-dee." One of the most common birds in the region's forests, this year-round resident thankfully sings its name, allowing you to readily find it. Not shy, the Carolina chickadee will often hang at the end of tree branches in full view, making it easier still to see. The combination of small size, black cap and bib, bright white cheeks, and song make the chickadee one of the first birds local birders learn.

The Carolina chickadee is also a crowd favorite. While it's not fair to anthropomorphize animals, I'll go out on my own limb to say that chickadees have a distinct personality that people find enjoyable. Like blue jays, they are the extroverts of Wild Philly.

Actually, that "chick-a-dee-dee" sound is its alarm call, warning its flock that you are in their forest, and the number of "dee" notes signals the kind of predator afoot. You likely have also heard their song without knowing it, a surprisingly plaintive four-note "fee-bee-fee-bay."

The acrobatic behavior of hanging from the ends of branches is their feeding strategy. In the summer, chickadees forage for insects and spiders, gleaning whatever adults, larvae, pupae, and eggs they find tucked into nooks and crevices in the branches. In the winter, they supplement their insect and spider diet with fat-rich seeds like sunflowers. They will visit bird feeders in winter; if you put suet out, chickadees will be among the first to partake.

Social Distancing

In winter, chickadees form small territorial flocks, establishing a pecking order within the group. They'll also establish their individual body space, needing as much as 5 feet between themselves and another chickadee; get too close, and the dominant bird complains. A winter chickadee flock will also forage with other birds like nuthatches and woodpeckers. As all find food in slightly different places (chickadees on branches, nuthatches in trunk crevices, woodpeckers inside the trunk), they are not directly competing for food, and the other birds come to depend on that chickadee alarm call. In spring, the higher-ranking chickadees will nest in that territory, the others dispersing out.

Carolina chickadees nest in tree holes, either naturally occurring ones or old woodpecker holes, and will also respond to the appropriate nesting box. The female typically sleeps in the nest, her mate sleeping nearby on a tree branch. The female lays between three and ten brown-splotched eggs, each barely an inch long.

Audubon himself named this bird while he was in South Carolina. Its close cousin, the black-capped chickadee, a stouter species, lives just north of the region, starting around Allentown. Though the two species evolved more than 2 million years ago, the two hybridize where they overlap. In places like Reading you might see the hybrid, while in the Poconos it's the black-capped. Carolina and black-capped chickadees sing slightly different versions of the "fee-bee" song, and hybrids have been heard singing one, the other, and even mixed versions. In Philly, we typically see Carolinas, though there are winters where black-capped chickadees are pushed south and both end up at our feeders, giving birders more to argue over.

Where to See It

In any and every forested walk in this book, but especially in those sites with bird feeding stations, like the Pennypack Environmental Center and Briar Bush Nature Center.

▲ The Carolina wren is a southern species that is becoming more common in Wild Philly.

Carolina Wren

Thryothorus ludovicianus

Pound for pound the region's loudest bird, this 5-inch songster booms a long three-part song that most field guides translate as "Tea kettle! Tea kettle! Tea kettle!" But the song is highly variable, and I swear I've heard it yell, "Cheeseburger! Cheeseburger! Cheeseburger!" No matter what the song, it is insistent, and you're far more likely to hear the song than see the bird.

The Carolina wren is a common bird that lives here year-round, one of several species of wrens including the house wren in the summer and the winter wren in winter. But, as its name suggests, the Carolina wren is another southern bird that has been expanding its range northward in the last century, more common here now than ever before. Tough winters tend to set back its numbers, but they seem to bounce back quickly.

Lying Low

When you do see a Carolina wren, look for russet feathers, buffy sides, a white throat, a bold white stripe above the eye, and a down-curved beak. You're also highly likely to find one low to the ground, as they thrive in tangled vegetation common in forest edges, abandoned city lots, and the corners of suburban yards, furtively hopping within that tangle and making a low flight to the next. Carolina wrens primarily feast on insects and spiders of all kinds and will come to backyard feeders in the winter for suet.

The birds mate for life and typically nest in abandoned woodpecker holes. But Carolina wren nests have been found in tin cans, mailboxes, houseplants dangling on porches, abandoned bald-faced hornet nests, shoes, even pockets of an old coat! The male may construct the female several nests to show his building prowess, and when she chooses a site, they finish it together, incorporating both natural and unnatural materials into the nest: leaves, grasses, feathers, snake skins, plastic litter, shreds of paper, pieces of string, and more.

So listen for the "Cheeseburger!" song. Or, as some books suggest, "Germany, Germany, Germany!" Or "Richelieu, Richelieu, Richelieu!" No matter what the Carolina wren sings, it's loud.

Where to See It

Common across the region, the Carolina wren is likely heard not far from your home or in any of the forest walks of Wild Philly.

Double-Crested Cormorant

Phalacrocorax auritus

The double-crested cormorant is a very social aquatic bird. These dark-colored cormorants are easily seen on the Delaware and Schuylkill Rivers, but especially congregate around the Fairmount Water Works.

Primarily fish-eaters, double-crested cormorants can be seen swimming on rivers, then disappearing as they dive underwater. They use their webbed feet and hooked beaks to chase and catch fish of just about any kind; some 250 species of fish have been found in their gut.

When not diving, cormorants are likely resting. Because they do not have the waterproof

▲ Before a cormorant takes off from the water, it stretches its neck in the direction it intends to fly.

▲ A close-up of the double-crested cormorant's face shows it is surprisingly handsome.

feathers of ducks and geese, cormorants—and this is their giveaway—spread their wings out for the feathers to dry. It would seem that not having that oil on their feathers hampers the birds' ability to swim underwater, but instead this lack seems to assist them in diving deeper than ducks.

Both Sexes Are Crested

The double-crested cormorant is named for a pair of tufts that appear on adult birds in breeding plumage. The tufts can be white, black, or both colors, and both sexes have them. Like blue jays and crows, cormorants are not sexually dimorphic: the two sexes look alike. So, both sexes also have orange skin around their cheeks and chin, which becomes more colorful during the spring.

If two male cormorants are competing for a nest site, they will face off, opening their mouths to display their blue throats, all the while shaking, hissing, and stretching out their necks. The male uses this same very sexy blue maw to show off to a female when she inspects his choice of nest site.

The double-crested cormorant is one of many species whose populations plummeted when DDT caused eggshell thinning, like peregrine falcons, bald eagles, and pelicans, among others. Happily, since the pesticide was banned in the United States in 1972, their numbers have been increasing.

Where to See It

There is one guaranteed spot to find cormorants: at the Fairmount Water Works just above the dam. In fact, they are easy to see drying out their wings here as you drive by on West River Drive or the Expressway. Look for them on the Schuylkill at Bartram's Garden and on the Delaware at the Palmyra Cove Nature Park and Pennypack on the Delaware walks.

Downy Woodpecker

Dryobates pubescens

Several woodpeckers can be found in the region's forests, including the yellow-shafted flicker, red-bellied woodpecker, and hairy woodpecker. But the downy woodpecker is the first you are likely to meet, as it is the most common, especially in suburban areas. This species is also the likeliest woodpecker to visit a winter bird feeder and is especially partial to high-fat peanuts, sunflower seeds, and suet.

Both its common and Latin names derive from the white downy feathers along the white stripe on its back. A handsome black-and-white checkered animal, the downy woodpecker is sexually dimorphic, with the male sporting a bright red spot on the back of its head, the only clue to gender.

The region's smallest woodpecker as well, the bird is only the size of a sparrow. The downy woodpecker eats mostly insects it gleans from the bark and branches of trees, while drilling at dead trees to uncover boring insects it spears with a long, barbed tongue. A year-round resident of Wild Philly, it will also form winter flocks with chickadees, nuthatches, and titmice, all of similar size and all essentially serving as lookouts for each other.

When you hear a woodpecker drumming, sometimes against the side of your house too early in the morning, it's not feeding. When foraging, they are usually quietly pecking away at a trunk. Drumming is advertising for mates. While they do have a weak song, downy woodpeckers drum against hollow trees to advertise for mates and to show that they have a good nest site picked out.

A Keystone Species

Like all woodpeckers, downy woodpeckers create hollow nests in trees that are accessed through perfectly round openings about the

▲ Only the male downy woodpecker has a red spot on the back of the head.

size of a ping-pong ball. That's where they raise their young. Those woodpecker cavities, used by the same bird repeatedly, also later become incredibly precious resources in the forest, as they are reused by cavity-nesting birds and owls of all kinds. That's why some consider woodpeckers a keystone species—a species without which an ecosystem would be dramatically different—their nests become important to other living things as well.

If you attract a downy woodpecker to your feeder or visit them in the wild, odds are you will soon stumble across the hairy woodpecker, which looks remarkably like the downy. This one, also named for the quality of feathers in that white back stripe, is not closely related at all. The hairy woodpecker is bigger, more robin-sized, and its beak more robust; National Audubon's website labels it a "railroad spike" of a beak. The closeness in appearance seems to be a case of convergent evolution, perhaps the smaller downy woodpecker evolving to emulate the larger species, as that must bestow some mysterious adaptive advantage to it.

Rarely, if you are lucky, you will come across the largest of the local woodpeckers, a crow-sized, red-crested wonder named the pileated woodpecker. If you do, especially if you see it feeding, watch closely: its jackhammer beak gouges huge holes in dead trees, chips flying in all directions as the bird seeks carpenter ants. And if you hear its territorial "wuk-wuk-wuk-wuk" call, you'll also see why this was the model for Woody Woodpecker of classic cartoon fame.

Where to See It

Look for the downy woodpecker in any and every forested walk in this book, but especially at those sites that have bird feeding stations, like the Pennypack Environmental Center, Briar Bush Nature Center, and the Schuylkill Center's bird blind. If you place a suet feeder in your yard during the winter, you are guaranteed downies.

Great Blue Heron

Ardea herodias

Standing at 4 feet tall, the great blue heron, Wild Philly's tallest bird, is a striking sight. And if you are lucky enough to see one fly, it's an amazing sight. With a 6-foot wingspan, the heron's ungainly flight is just what a pterodactyl must have looked like. I once spotted one flying low over the Schuylkill Expressway—not what you'd expect when stuck in traffic.

More typically, you find great blue herons and their cousins, other herons and egrets, wading in bodies of water across the region, stalking the fish that comprise the lion's share of their diet. They occasionally also spear frogs and even small mammals. The birds walk slowly or stand stoically still in a yoga pose, the beak suddenly flashing for their catch. Imagine your surprise if you were a koi pond owner and found a great blue heron wading in your water feature, picking off your valuable pets. It happens more often than you might think.

Striking Mating Plumage

The feathers of the great blue heron are striking as well, and the color ramps up during the mating season. Though more slate-gray than blue, there are colorful surprises across the body. Look for russet thighs and black and white streaking along its throat. Its bright white head is bisected by a black stripe above the eye that leads to a long black plume. Both its chest and lower back sport long white plumes during the mating season. The bird's plumage was once highly sought after for hats. Happily, that fad has long faded and the great blue heron is now protected.

Great blue herons usually breed in colonies called rookeries, clusters of large stick-filled nests high in trees, the gangly herons somehow perching in branches. Rookeries can be seen in places like Amico Island in the Delaware River in Burlington County and at Chester County's King Ranch. Adult herons usually return to the colony in early spring to set up shop again. Males arrive first to select a nest, calling to entice arriving females.

Where to See It

Look for great blue herons at the John Heinz National Wildlife Refuge, the Manayunk Canal, and the Palmyra Cove Nature Park.

▲ The great blue heron has an impressive 6-foot wingspan.

Great Horned Owl

Bubo virginianus

▲ The great horned owl has large yellow eyes and pupils that open widely in the dark, giving this nocturnal hunter excellent night vision.

While there are many different owls living in the area, the great horned owl is the largest and the one that makes the classic "hoot" sound. It is also the region's most versatile owl, living in city, suburbs, and rural country. The owls are mostly night hunters, but they have occasionally been seen hunting during the day as well.

Great horned owls boast a diverse diet. While they eat mostly birds and mammals, especially rabbits, they've been found feasting on hawks, crows, insects, fish, reptiles, feral cats, and carrion. And great horned owls are infamous for hunting skunks, as they have an exceptionally poor sense of smell. Biologists looking for them have sometimes found their nests by the overpowering stench of skunk; in one instance, the remains of almost sixty skunks were discovered in a single nest.

Everything about the creature screams hunter: large eyes adapted for grabbing every ray of moonlight, eyes facing forward for binocular vision, incredibly sharp talons, a hooked beak for tearing flesh, and special feathers with soft edges for silent swooping flight. Those so-called great horns are neither horns nor ears, but instead simply tufts of feathers. The great horned owl does have exceptional hearing that allows it to pinpoint an animal's location by sound. Like those of all birds, though, the ears are holes on the side of the skull underneath the feathers, and the owl's beautiful disc of facial feathers steers sound toward the ears.

Early Nesters

This species might also be the earliest bird to lay its eggs in Wild Philly. Great horned owls

195

court mates—with a lot of hooting—in the fall. The females select mates by early winter and may be sitting on a clutch of eggs sometime in February. Given that the owls typically reuse squirrel and hawk nests high up in trees, these adults are incubating eggs even in the middle of fierce winter ice storms. Why go to this extreme? Biologists speculate that this gives their young a leg up when spring arrives, offering a head start on both their prey and other raptors.

Actual sightings of owls are rare, as they are active at night and their feathers blend in remarkably well with their tree roosts during the day. But one great way to find them is to pay attention to crows. If you find a murder of crows angrily gathering around a tree, odds are good they are mobbing either a hawk or an owl.

Where to See It

A nonreleasable great horned owl is on display at the Woodford Cedar Run Wildlife Refuge. While you are unlikely to see a great horned owl on your walks, many organizations in the region sponsor nighttime owl prowls. Try one out.

Northern Cardinal

Cardinalis cardinalis

The bright red northern cardinal is among America's most popular songbirds. It is the state bird of seven states, the mascot of many sports teams, and on more Christmas cards than any animal except the reindeer. The cardinal is also easy to find at just about any Philadelphia yard—if that yard has a feeder and especially if that feeder offers sunflower seeds.

Named for the red robes worn by Catholic cardinals, the male is bright red. The female cardinal, however, is cloaked in warm orange-brown with red highlights. Both sexes have black swaths encircling orange beaks. Even in the winter, it is not unusual to see pairs of cardinals together visiting feeders.

▲ The male northern cardinal is the more brightly colored sex.

▲ But don't underestimate the beauty of the female northern cardinal.

One of the Few Female Singers

The female northern cardinal is also one of the few female songbirds that sings. A friend and I tracked down a singing cardinal in West Laurel Hill Cemetery one spring morning to find it was a female. According to Cornell's Laboratory of Ornithology, "a mated pair shares song phrases, but the female may sing a longer and slightly more complex song than the male."

Primarily ground feeders, northern cardinals eat mostly seeds, as evidenced by that conical seed-crushing beak. They also supplement this diet with small amounts of insects, even drinking sap oozing from sapsucker holes in tree trunks. Like most seed-eaters, young nestlings are fed a protein-rich diet of insects before they leave the nest.

Northern cardinals are surprisingly territorial, singing high up in trees to be seen. The male's high, metallic song attracts females and warns other males to give the singer some space. Social media is filled with videos of cardinals attacking windows and car mirrors. Persistent in defending their territory, the males see the reflection as another bird and doggedly attempt to kick out the intruder. These attacks usually stop once spring hormonal levels ebb.

Where to See It

Look for cardinals in any and every forested walk in this book, especially at those sites that have bird feeding stations, like the Pennypack Environmental Center, Briar Bush Nature Center, and the Schuylkill Center's bird blind.

Peregrine Falcon

Falco peregrinus

Almost 150 feet above Manayunk's sidewalk, six of us crowded into a tiny space at the top of the St. John the Baptist Church steeple, the tallest stone steeple rising above that neighborhood. We had climbed a series of increasingly narrower, ricketier stairs and ladders to get there. But we were thrilled, for we were on a sacred mission: to band peregrine falcon hatchlings.

Peregrines today nest atop that church steeple, and in several other places in the region, like the City Hall tower. The peregrine falcon is the world's fastest animal. Naturally nesting on cliffs, the raptor preys most often on birds, swooping upon them in hunting dives that top 200 miles per hour and smashing into the helpless birds from above. Just as amazing, the peregrine falcon has the fastest visual processing speed of any animal known thus far; its eyesight is incredibly powerful.

▲ The peregrine falcon has huge eyes, a steel-gray back, and light barred undersides.

About the size of a crow, the female is much larger than the male. Both sexes have steel-gray backs, white undersides with black barring, darkened cowls over their heads, and what appear to be black tear-shaped mustaches on their cheeks. Peregrines are one of the most widespread birds of prey on the

▲ An adult peregrine on Philadelphia's City Hall.

planet, with nineteen subspecies spanning the globe from Alaska to Australia.

Slammed by DDT

The peregrine falcon is an endangered species in Pennsylvania, one that had disappeared from the eastern United States by the 1960s. But it has been brought back, Lazarus-like, from the dead.

Peregrines and other birds of prey experienced rapid population declines as use of the pesticide DDT became widespread. DDT was used to kill insects that were in turn eaten by the falcon's prey, and with each step up the food chain, the pesticide became more concentrated. It was absorbed in the falcon's tissues and caused their eggshells to thin, with the eggs tragically cracking when parents incubated them. After DDT was banned in the United States in 1972, populations rebounded, and an intensive captive breeding program reintroduced peregrines to the East Coast.

Sadly, in late 2019 the male from the St. John the Baptist Church nest was found dead nearby, his legs severed, some guess as the result of trying to chase away a drone. But the female stayed, successfully attracting a new male to the site so the nest could continue. Like all peregrine falcons, this new pair will mate for life.

Manayunk's falcons have been there since 2011, each year raising three or four young. We bird lovers must offer big thanks to the church for its patience with their famous avian guests. It's not uncommon to walk up to the church's large ornate front doors while stepping over severed bird heads that have fallen from fourteen stories up. Sounds really gross, but it is actually pretty cool.

Where to See It

The Peregrines over Manayunk trip takes you to visit the peregrines at St. John's. But the falcons can also be seen nesting atop City Hall's tower and at several bridges in the region: Ben Franklin, Walt Whitman, and Girard Point. Also, the Cape May Point and Hawk Mountain Sanctuary bonus trips routinely count migrating peregrines passing overhead.

Red-Eyed Vireo

Vireo olivaceus

▲ The red-eyed vireo may be the most abundant of woodland songbirds across Pennsylvania.

The red-eyed vireo is most common bird you've never heard of. But if you have ever walked through a summertime forest anywhere in Wild Philly, you've heard this bird—and heard it, and heard it, and heard it.

The size of a warbler and usually gleaning insects high up in the treetops, the red-eyed vireo sings incessantly. The bird holds an ongoing monologue of usually three-noted sounds, some rising, some falling, as if it were asking and answering its own questions: "How are you? I am fine. Doing well. Pretty good. Are you sure?"

While I have heard thousands of vireos sing, I can count on only one hand the number of times I have actually seen the red eye—and the first time made me scream with delight. If you can see the red eye, you'll also catch the two black stripes sandwiching a white one, slicing right through the red eye.

I Am Green!

The name *vireo* is Latin for "I am green," which the bird's body feathers are . . . sort of. Its species name *olivaceus* only drives home that point in case you missed it the first time.

Aside from hummingbirds, the red-eyed vireo builds one of the smallest nests, a petite cup that dangles from the crotch of a high tree branch, held together with fibers and spider silk. These nests are even harder to find than the vireo's eye.

The red-eye may be the most prominent member of a clan of songbirds, others of which drive even expert birders batty. Consider the red-eye your gateway into the vireo kingdom. If you've heard one, challenge yourself to see the eye. If you've never heard of this bird, you've got your next assignment.

Where to See It

While you are unlikely to see a red-eyed vireo, as the small bird stays high up, you are very likely to hear it on any late spring or early summer walk in mature forests. Search for the song on the web, listen to it a few times, then see how many times this bird accompanies you on your walks.

Red-Tailed Hawk

Buteo jamaicensis

This raptor is the most common hawk not just in Wild Philly, but across North America. If you've ever seen a hawk circling above you, chances are it was a red-tail. I've seen them perched alongside the Schuylkill Expressway, the Pennsylvania Turnpike, and many lesser roads, clearly waiting for a roadside wood-chuck or other rodent to show up. If you drive through farm country, you'll likely see one perched on a pole or in a tree alongside a farm field.

And you've heard them too. Their call is not only common, but has been dubbed into television shows and movies to swap out for the bald eagle's weak call. Red-tailed hawks apparently sound more like eagles than eagles do! I've also looked for noisy red-tails low in a tree and was amused to discover it was just a cheeky blue jay imitating one.

▲ The red-tailed hawk is the most common North American hawk.

Red Tail, Brown Belt

That red tail can make identifying the bird easy for you, although the cinnamon red can be hard to pick out on gray days and the tail is hard to see on a perched bird. In that case, I rely on the streaky belt of brown feathers across its pale underside, which is often easy to pick out. The hawk's colors are famously variable, ranging from a deep chocolate brown, especially out west, to one almost white, but all versions have a variation on the red(dish) tail.

The red-tailed hawk has adapted to just about every type of habitat across the entire continent—desert, prairie, forest—and eats a wide variety of foods, including mice, rabbits, squirrels, snakes, and birds like pheasants. The bird hunts using its remarkable eyesight, being able to pick out a mouse from 100 feet in the air. Small prey items are carried back to its perch to be eaten, while larger animals are first eaten on the ground before then being carried back for finishing off.

When courting, red-tails perform an aerial show, spiraling up in wide circles, the male suddenly diving steeply only to shoot straight up again. After several of these swooping loops, he might seem to be landing atop her, extending his talons to touch her. They often grab one another with those razor-sharp talons and plummet groundward before breaking off. It looks violent, but it works. The mating couple typically nest near the tops of large trees, both to view their surroundings and to support their 6-foot-wide and 3-foot-tall stick-constructed nest, which is used over multiple years.

Philadelphia's red-tails are likely year-round residents, although the species is seen migrat-ing over Hawk Mountain in the fall. Because Canadian red-tails fly south for a few months in winter, their Philadelphia cousins share their habitat for this brief time.

Where to See It

Nonreleasable red-tailed hawks are on display in outdoor cages at the Briar Bush Nature Center and Woodford Cedar Run Wildlife Refuge.

Wild ones are routinely counted at Militia Hill, Cape May, and Hawk Mountain. Also, all year on any of this book's trips, they may be seen soaring and circling overhead.

Ring-Billed Gulls

Larus delawarensis

While you expect to see gulls of all kinds at the Jersey Shore, you may be surprised to find them in and around Philadelphia, at the Fairmount Water Works, for example, or Penn's Landing or a shopping center parking lot. But, in fact, its species name refers to the Delaware River. This is a Philly bird.

One of America's most abundant gulls, the ring-billed gull's most readily identifiable trait is that black ring encircling its yellow beak. This field mark allows you to tell it from other gulls, especially the also-common herring gull, whose beak sports a bright orange spot. In both cases, nestling gulls use their parent's beak marks as targets to peck at when begging for food.

Fish and Fries

Nesting in Canada and the upper Midwest, ring-billed gulls arrive in the region by summer. They are strong flyers that can move as fast as 40 miles per hour, and they use the wind to great advantage, soaring when needed and hovering in place if they wish.

Down at the Jersey Shore, they compete with herring, laughing, and greater black-backed gulls for similar foods, this foursome comprising the lion's share of gulls you'd see at the beach. Gulls eat a wide variety of foods, from dead fish floating ashore to fries stolen off your plate. As they have readily adapted to scavenging for food, they have become abundant at landfills, parking lots, and shopping center dumpsters. These highly social birds also steal food from each other, which often sets off a chain reaction among nearby gulls.

While young birds are the size of their parents, their plumage is darker and browner than the gray-and-white parents. It takes 2 years for a ring-billed gull to sexually mature, molting as it goes and getting increasingly white as it ages. As all gulls age similarly, telling juvenile ring-billed gulls from young herring gulls is hard for even veteran birders.

Ring-billed gulls suffered at the beginning of the twentieth century from loss of habitat and being hunted for their feathers. The Migratory Bird Act helped them (and many other birds), and now they are wonderfully abundant—even in a parking lot outside the Home Depot.

Where to See It

Look for ring-billed gulls on any summer beach, but also at the Fairmount Water Works and along the Delaware River.

▲ The ring-billed gull's name refers to the black ring encircling its beak.

Ruby-Throated Hummingbird

Archilochus colubris

By far the region's smallest bird, there are very few things a ruby-throated hummingbird can be mistaken for, except a moth or maybe a bumble bee. While the American Southwest is graced with many species of hummingbirds—the calliope, the magnificent, the violet-crowned—the entire East Coast has only one. So, if you see a hummingbird here, you've got the ruby-throat.

Only the males have that beautiful iridescent patch of red on their chins. The patch often appears dark until the sun strikes it just so—and then you gasp at the sight. While a female's throat is white, both sexes wear a stunning coat of emerald feathers that sparkle in the sun, rubies and emeralds on one tiny bird.

Nectar feeders like butterflies, ruby-throated hummingbirds visit red and orange tubular flowers like beebalm, trumpet vine, cardinal flower, jewelweed, coral honeysuckle, and many others. Their population has increased over the last few decades, likely from people like me who put out hummingbird feeders for them. They'll feed on insects and spiders too, even picking insects off spider webs, catching them in midair, or plucking them off tree bark if the bugs are stuck on sap.

Avian Helicopters

Ruby-throated hummingbirds beat their wings in a figure-eight pattern at 53 flaps per second, a remarkable speed that allows them to hover in front of flowers, a trick few other birds can pull off. In courtship, the male flies in a long looping U pattern to attract a female's attention, supplementing that display by sharp horizontal movements back and forth. After mating, the female ruby-throat builds the

▲ The ruby-throat is Wild Philly's only hummingbird.

tiniest nest imaginable, only 2 inches across, hidden on the outside by lichens and moss and held together with spider webs. Then she lays unimaginably tiny eggs that measure only ½ inch across.

The species migrates south in winter to follow the flowers, heading to Central America. The birds bulk up before they go, as they typically make the giant leap over the Gulf of Mexico in one nighttime flight.

It's fairly easy to join the hummingbird feeding club. I cook my own nectar (using four parts water to one part sugar), don't dye it red, and clean the feeder every weekend, as the sugar water will definitely mildew if left out in the summer sun too long. I make a quart batch that's stored in the refrigerator for a few weeks. It's a bit of work, but seeing a hummer at your feeder drinking nectar you made is well worth the effort.

Where to See It

Unless you have a feeder, the ruby-throated hummingbird is a tough bird to spot on most days. You need a meadow or garden filled with hummingbird flowers like beebalm and plenty of patience.

Song Sparrow
Melospiza melodia

▲ The song sparrow can be identified by the large brown spot in the center of its chest.

There are many species of sparrows, small brown seed-eating songbirds often seen low to the ground. But the song sparrow is one of the most common, easiest to distinguish, and, for me, one of the most special. Growing up, this bird's melodious song was the one I most associated with spring—long before I knew any bird's name.

Amazingly, there are twenty-five subspecies of song sparrows across North America, from the Aleutian Islands to one on an isolated Mexican plateau. The song sparrow is a russet brown bird with lots of streaks, especially down the chest, and gray and brown stripes across the head. One key identifier is the large spot in the center of its chest. I always wait for the sparrow to turn its chest toward me to reveal the spot.

On a bird walk, you'll likely find song sparrows in and around hedgerows, often on the ground, even walking on the trail ahead of you. Seed-eaters all year long, they supplement their summer diet with fruits and insects of all kinds. In the winter, they've come to my bird feeders at home, typically hopping along the ground nibbling on seeds knocked out of the feeder by other birds or squirrels.

The Melodious Sparrow

This species' song is so noteworthy (pardon the pun) that both its common name and its Latin species name, *melodia*, refer to its lovely song. Just for kicks, pull up the bird's song on one tab of your computer and Beethoven's Fifth on another. Play the first four notes of one, then the first four notes of the other. Any similarities? After the sparrow's opening notes, the song becomes complex and varied, but always includes a long happy trill.

The males learn their songs from neighboring adults and incorporate elements of those songs into their own. Wonderfully, studies show that female sparrows are attracted to males who are not only the best singers but the best *learners*.

Where to See It

Look for song sparrows in any and every forested walk in this book, especially at those sites that have bird feeding stations, like the Briar Bush Nature Center and Pennypack Environmental Center.

Tree Swallow

Tachycineta bicolor

A fast-flying insect-eater, the tree swallow's bright blue-green iridescent upper body and contrasting white belly—note the species name, *bicolor*—are easy to spot. Plus swallows are often seen in large groups and are like little circus acrobats in flight. In fact, their unpronounceable genus name is Greek for "moving quickly."

Look for the bird's V-shaped tail, the signature of the swallow family. There are very few things you might confuse the tree swallow with, except other swallows. Barn swallows also have blue backs, but with orange bellies instead.

A very common bird, the tree swallow is readily seen in two places: wetlands, where large numbers of them flit above the water, and fields, where you're likely to see fewer of them at once. Tree swallows are cavity-nesters that formerly only nested in abandoned woodpecker holes, the numbers of which are declining along with the region's older forests. But given they are equally happy nesting in boxes, even ones placed for other species, they are readily spotted in these as well. At many preserves, bluebird boxes have been readily claimed by tree swallows, and they'll take over wood duck boxes too.

▲ The tree swallow is a common bird in wetland and field habitats.

this diet with calcium-rich foods like shells, fish bones, and cast-off crayfish skins; they've even been spotted grabbing occasional berries off bushes.

Ranging across most of North America, the tree swallow migrates south for the winter, as flying insects vanish in the region's cold and dry winters. The birds fly—often in great flocks—to the extreme Southeast (including Florida) and Southwest (including Arizona), plus Mexico and the Caribbean Islands. They are also the first swallows to return north, so tree swallows are another sign of spring—and of climate change, as the average date of their egg laying now occurs 9 days earlier than it did in the 1960s.

Winging It

These aerial hunters spend their day on the wing, catching flying insects in midair, snatching dragonflies and damselflies, bees and beetles, moths and mayflies. During the breeding season, tree swallows will supplement

Where to See It

My go-to spot for tree swallows is the John Heinz National Wildlife Refuge, and the walk there guarantees you huge numbers of swallows. But look for them above all rivers and meadows.

Turkey Vulture

Cathartes aura

▲ The featherless face of the turkey vulture helps keep the bird clean after a meal of carrion.

Soaring overhead on 6-foot wings, one of the region's largest birds, the turkey vulture is surprisingly common. You've likely seen dozens of them flying overhead without knowing it. The turkey vulture flies with its wings held high in a large V, wobbling as it circles on rising currents of warm air, the two-toned wings comprised of dark outer covert feathers offset by contrasting grayish wing feathers.

Nature's trash collector, this bird fills the necessary role of helping dispose of carrion, a tough job that someone has to do. While flying above, it scans the ground below with its keen eyesight. The turkey vulture is also able to smell decaying flesh from remarkable distances—the olfactory portion of its brain is huge.

But turkey vultures are clean animals as well—you have to be if your life's work is sticking your head into the bodies of dead animals. So, unlike bald eagles, these birds are truly bald: their head is featherless, which allows them to more easily and quickly clean

their head. The head's skin is red, giving it the "turkey" look of its name.

The First Line of Defense

While turkey vultures feast on dead animals, the carrion has to be relatively freshly dead—not too decomposed, please. If threatened, their primary method of defense is projectile vomiting, throwing up the partially digested decaying carrion in their stomach. First, that stuff reeks. Second, if it hits you in the eyes, that acid burns. The life lesson here is to stay away from vulture nests.

In Wild Philly, a second species, the black vulture, has been expanding its more southern range and often can be seen roosting with turkey vultures. This is another of a long list of southern birds moving north in recent decades, which some suspect is a signal of a warming climate. The black vulture is smaller, more compact, and with a black head and broader one-tone wings. Because the black vulture has a weak sense of smell, it often follows the turkey vulture to food, which the latter often shares.

On the April evening I wrote this text, a pair of turkey vultures swooped low over me above at, of all places, an Acme parking lot on Montgomery Avenue in Penn Valley. I stopped dead in my tracks and watched them fly to a large tree, where both awkwardly landed for only a moment. Then the vultures both took off, locked talons for a brief moment, and flew on, very low. I think I just saw vulture foreplay, a new sight for me after 40 years of birdwatching. All these years later, nature still surprises.

Where to See It

Look for turkey vultures soaring above the city in many places, but a special concentration seems to be in Upper Roxborough around those radio and television antennas. In fact, both black and turkey vultures can be found there together—see if you can tell the difference.

Wood Duck

Aix sponsa

▲ The wood duck drake is remarkably colored.

Easily the king of American ducks for its astonishing looks, the wood duck drake is, for me, the most beautiful North American animal. It has a metallic dark green hood, orange beak, bright red eyes, white stripes through the face, burgundy chest—even its beige sides glow. Seeing one fly straight down Wissahickon Creek at Valley Green in late March is just breathtaking.

You'll almost always find wood ducks around water as their breeding habitat includes creeks, wooded swamps, lakes, and ponds. Like the ubiquitous mallard, the wood duck is a dabbling duck, feeding butt-up and tipping its head underwater to reach what it can; it doesn't dive underwater like some other ducks. And like just about all ducks, the male has nothing to do with child rearing. After mating, the drabber female is on her own.

Look Out Below!

Unlike all other local ducks, the wood duck nests high up in cavities in trees, laying as many as fifteen eggs in a down-lined nest. The female even has special claws on her feet, also unique to her kind, for helping her hang onto the edge of that tree canopy. When her young hatch, they are precocious from the start. Only one day after hatching, they jump out of the nest, with mom on the ground quacking to egg them on. After jumping, they either splash in the water below, or, more likely, bounce and roll across the forest floor after a multistory drop. The ducklings never return to that nest, instead now staying near water. If you'd like a smile, find an online video of wood duck ducklings jumping; it is worth viewing. While they stay near mom at first for security, they soon swim and feed completely on their own.

Happily, the wood duck is another conservation success story. The drake's plumage was so coveted and its forest habitats so logged out that their numbers plummeted by the late nineteenth century, and the species had all but vanished by the first years of the twentieth. But as organizations like National Audubon rose to advocate for birds, a migratory bird treaty was signed in 1916, and people began putting up specially designed nest boxes, their numbers rebounded. Even better, in a wonderful confluence, as beaver populations expanded to create more and additional wetlands, wood ducks have been the beneficiary of the beaver's handiwork.

Where to See It

One of the best places to see wood ducks is along Wissahickon Creek in and around Valley Green in late March and early April, when drakes are pairing with mates and the drakes are in full breeding plumage.

Wood Thrush

Hylocichla mustelina

The throaty flute-like song of the wood thrush always stops me in my tracks the first time I hear it each spring. "Ethereal" is one descriptor you'll encounter when reading about thrush song, as the bird can whistle two notes simultaneously, harmonizing with itself to produce the ringing that is so entrancing. It sings at both sunrise and sunset, making the wood thrush one of the first—and last—birds you will hear that day.

This species is considered the best singer of all songbirds, and no less an observer than Henry David Thoreau agreed. "The thrush alone declares the immortal wealth and vigor that is in the forest," he wrote. "Whenever a man hears it, he is young, and Nature is in her spring. It is a new world and a free country, and the gates of heaven are not shut against him." Doesn't that alone make you want to go hear one?

The bird itself is strikingly handsome. A close relative of robins and about the same size, many websites describe it as being "potbellied," which is cute, but its bright white breast dappled with large round spots is gorgeous. Careful when trying to identify this bird, though, as it has several thrush kin with similar spotting.

An Indicator of Forest Health

A creature of the interior forest and an important indicator of forest health, the wood thrush has become a symbol of the vanishing American songbird. One study estimated that its population in eastern North America has declined 62 percent since 1966. Forest fragmentation is often cited as a chief reason for the species' decline, as it requires more

▲ The bright white breast of the wood thrush is dappled with large round spots.

than small suburban woodlots and fragmented forests offer fewer places to escape predators.

The brown-headed cowbird, a parasite that lays its eggs in other birds' nests, will stay out of deep forest interiors. But it can easily find thrushes in smaller forests and lay its eggs in the nest, with its larger nestling outcompeting smaller baby thrushes for parental attention—even kicking the baby thrushes out of the nest.

The wood thrush is also a victim of being migratory. While North American forests are fragmenting, Central and South American forests—its winter home—are disappearing.

So, like many birds, the wood thrush is being hit at both ends of its migration.

But the first time I hear one in April, I stop and savor the sound—the gates of heaven have just opened.

Where to See It

You're more likely to hear a wood thrush than to see one. Listen for its song in some of the walks in larger forests in this book. But you'll never know where you hear one; when you do, see if you can track it down—you might get lucky.

Wood-Warblers

Various species

In April and May, birders across the region flock to birding hotspots like John Heinz National Wildlife Refuge and Carpenter's Woods in West Mount Airy in search of the bird world's Holy Grail: a glimpse of migrating wood-warblers. Every spring, several dozen species of impossibly colored and incredibly small songbirds pass through Philadelphia from their overwintering grounds in the Caribbean or even Tierra del Fuego, heading north to nesting grounds in the Adirondacks or Canada. The window of opportunity for finding them is so small.

Most are annoyingly high up in trees, so much so that a morning spent looking for them

▲ The yellow warbler is one of the few warbler species that nests in Wild Philly.

▲ The black-throated blue warbler sings a relaxed, buzzy "I am so la-zee."

▲ The prothonotary warbler has impossibly yellow feathers.

▲ Its bandit mask sets apart the common yellowthroat.

gives one a bad case of "warbler's neck." Wood-warblers are insectivores, and many can be seen working the trees, gleaning insects from twigs and leaves.

One of the most common members of the clan is the yellow-rumped warbler. Cloaked in blue-gray with white wing bars, the yellow-rumped has splashes of yellow on its cap, chest, and, yes, the rump, which is very helpful as it flies away from you and shows that yellow triangle. And if you're standing in a crowd of birders when it does, you'll likely hear someone call out, "butter butt!"—its wonderful nickname—and all binoculars snap in that direction.

While named wood-warblers, these birds more buzz than warble, and sharp birders with good ears can help you tease them out. The ovenbird's scolding "teacher! teacher! teacher!" is a classic song, as is the yellow warbler's "sweet, sweet, sweet, it's so sweet" and the common yellowthroat's "witchety." The blackpoll warbler's song is a great imitation of a rusty wheel squeaking.

And, wow, are they pretty: the fierce orange of the Blackburnian warbler, the unique blue of the black-throated blue warbler, the bright yellow belly with contrasting black necklace of the Canada warbler, the red-orange cutouts in the black wings of the American redstart. And Crayola needs to produce a yellow-orange called prothonotary warbler. It's the males of these species who are knockouts. The females, as tends to happen among many birds, are far less colorful—making both spotting and identifying them challenging.

Warbler Season

Wood-warblers migrate through Wild Philly in a relatively consistent pattern. Pine warblers, for example, arrive early in the season, yellow-rumped warblers in the middle in the largest wave, and blackpoll warblers much later, around Memorial Day. The John Heinz National Wildlife Refuge at Tinicum, one of our trips, hosts an annual warbler weekend in early May, with trips leaving almost hourly; there you have a great shot at seeing the full panoply of migrating wood-warblers, including early-season stragglers and late-season pioneers. I highly recommend it and may be accompanying you on one of the walks.

While most are migrating north, a few wood-warblers do nest in Wild Philly, including the ovenbird, which builds an oven-shaped leafy mound on the ground as its nest. The common yellowthroat and yellow warbler are two of the region's more common resident warblers. The Louisiana waterthrush nests here too, but is harder to spot.

Those dozens of species of migratory warblers lose their dramatic spring colors by their fall flights south, and are cloaked in coats that are mere shadows of their former selves. That's the even bigger challenge of warblers—identifying male and especially females of all these species in October.

But in the spring, you deserve a good case of warbler neck. Few sights are as rewarding as a clear view of, say, a northern parula warbler, an astonishing mosaic of blue-gray, bright yellow, and chestnut.

Where to See It

To find migrating warblers, go to any forest in the spring. But Carpenter's Woods in Mount Airy or the John Heinz National Wildlife Refuge at Tinicum in late April or early May are highly recommended hotspots. In the fall, the Cape May trip is highly recommended; while hawks are soaring overhead, warblers are often found in the bushes and trees near the HawkWatch platform.

Mammals

American Beaver

Castor canadensis

▲ A beaver chomps away at the John Heinz National Wildlife Refuge.

North America's largest rodent, the American beaver was once one of the country's most common animals, with scientists estimating that as many as 400 million beavers inhabited Lenapehoking. But the Lenape began trapping beavers to sell to New World traders for sending back to Europe, where the classic felt hat was made with beaver fur, and colonists quickly joined the fur trade. By the time of Swedish settlement in the mid-1600s, the beaver was already rare, and it vanished from the region soon thereafter. For the next 300 years, there were no beavers in the Philadelphia region.

Like the peregrine falcon and bald eagle, the beaver is a conservation success story. In the 1990s, the Pennsylvania Game Commission began introducing western beavers into wilder places in Pennsylvania, like the Poconos, and each generation spread a little further out, using the Delaware River as their highway. Today, you can find urban beavers on the Delaware and Schuylkill River waterfronts; along the Manayunk Canal; at the John Heinz National Wildlife Refuge; in Tacony, Pennypack, Cobbs, and Wissahickon Creeks; and in the Black Run Preserve in Evesham. In short, the beaver has returned.

Chiseled Evidence

Many people are surprised to walk along, say, the Schuylkill River Trail in Manayunk near the Flat Rock Dam and see clear evidence of beavers—trees gnawed by their toothy chisels. While some do build the classic beaver lodge

▲ Beavers use their five-fingered hands to manipulate branches as they eat the inner bark.

▲ A beaver dam (foreground) and lodges at the Black Run Preserve.

(notably at Black Run and Palmyra Cove), most urban beavers do not, instead inhabiting places where they live in dens dug out of the embankments.

Unlike what Saturday morning cartoons may have taught you, beavers don't eat trees per se. Instead, they topple large trees so they can bring branches back to their lodge or dam for building supplies or to eat, as their food is the inner bark of the branches they cut down. You may even find beaver sticks, gnawed-on barkless sections of branches that a beaver ate like we do corn on the cob, using its five-fingered hands to hold the stick.

Active all year long even in the winter, beavers are especially active at night and will slap their tail against the water to warn their nearsighted peers of approaching danger, which may be you. That slap—one thing the cartoons got right—is unbelievably loud.

Where to See It

Beaver lodges are easily found at the Black Run Refuge, Palmyra Cove Nature Park, and the John Heinz National Wildlife Refuge, while the animals live along the Manayunk Canal, where their handiwork is easy to spot.

Coyote

Canis latrans

Most Philadelphians would be surprised to learn that coyotes inhabit the city. While not as common as raccoons, foxes, and opossums, they are hardly rare. Also surprising is the fact that they are one of the region's newer residents. Coyotes were likely not original inhabitants of Lenapehoking, as wolves and cougars kept them away for centuries until those predators disappeared from the state in the 1800s.

But the coyote is a wily survivor. The Pennsylvania Game Commission reports that the wolf's smaller cousin entered the state from the Catskills in the 1960s and has been spreading across the state ever since, establishing residence in Philadelphia around 1990.

A tad larger than a German shepherd, its pointed ears, long narrow snout, bushy tail, and often buffy fur easily identify this canine as a coyote. The animal's success is in no small

▲ The coyote has pointy ears, a bushy tail, and buff-colored fur.

part due to its diverse diet, and coyotes will happily devour rodents and rabbits, frogs and snakes, fruits and berries, roadkill and garbage, and much more.

The Wily Coyote Is Just That

Also surprising is how elusive coyotes are, especially for an animal of their size. While they live near the Schuylkill Center (tracks and droppings are often seen), there have been only two or three occasional sightings by staff in the last several years—and no one here has heard them yipping at night yet. But a roadkill coyote was found a few years back on Ridge Avenue, Roxborough's busiest street, so one never knows where they will turn up.

And yes, while there have been breathless reports on local news stations around the country of coyotes eating people's pets, those events are rare, especially if dogs are kept leashed on walks in natural areas, which should be done anyway.

Biologists have long fiercely debated the genetic history of the East Coast coyote. Studies indicate the region's version contains a healthy mix of dog and wolf genes, leading some to label it the "coy-wolf," others to propose a new species separate from the western coyote, and still others to disagree vehemently with the other two. Science is working it all out.

Coyotes have stirred our passion, anger, and curiosity for centuries, as do all large meat-eaters living in close proximity to people. But while the wolf was brought to the edge of extinction, the coyote has thrived, has expanded range, and is naturalized in Wild Philly. Perhaps that deserves a little respect.

Where to See It

While there are no guarantees with this master of stealth, there have been coyote sightings across the city and region, most of them unexpected and often in the evening when these nocturnal creatures are most active.

Eastern Chipmunk

Tamias striatus

One of the most common and most popular forest animals with kids, the chipmunk is a close cousin of squirrels and woodchucks. Although sometimes said to be named for its loud chipping call, its name instead is derived from the Ojibwe word *ajidamoo*, meaning "one who descends trees headlong."

Its species name *striata* points to the lines—striations—down its back, one of its signature traits. Look for five black stripes and two white ones along the chipmunk's back, plus white stripes on the face above and below its eyes.

▲ The chipmunk uses its greatly expandable cheeks to carry food back to the nest to be stored.

Carnivorous Chipmunks?

Chipmunks eat similar plant material to their squirrel cousins, including acorns and other tree nuts, seeds of all kinds, and small fruits and berries. But that is supplemented with an array of many other foods: mushrooms, insects, bird eggs, snails, and even young mice. Surprise! Chipmunks are occasionally carnivorous.

They live in underground dens with an extensive tunnel system that includes several entrances. These serve as escape hatches from the wide array of animals wanting to eat them, including foxes, snakes, hawks, and owls. It's in these dens that females give birth to the young and that all chipmunks sleep for the winter.

Chipmunks spend the fall stockpiling food underground, stuffing their famous cheeks to haul back to the burrow for caching. While some sources say that chipmunks hibernate, it's not exactly true. Their metabolism slows down greatly and they sleep for long periods of time, but unlike true hibernators who are inactive all winter (such as bats and snakes), chipmunks wake up multiple times during the winter to snack on their caches—and then fall back asleep.

Where to See It

On any forested walk in this book, in any wood-lot near you, and possibly even on your street.

Eastern Striped Skunk

Mephitis negra

At a Blue Bell swim club our family belonged to years ago, we stayed late one summer evening to barbecue with friends. As dusk settled across the picnic grove, we were treated to a wonderfully unnerving sight. In the twilight, a dozen eastern striped skunks waddled out of the shadows, descending on the grove in their search for people's leftovers. Not wanting to experience the animal's famed defense, we quietly watched for a few minutes, transfixed, and then beat a slow retreat.

▲ The skunk's striking black-and-white coloration signals a nocturnal animal.

The word *skunk* is derived from Native American languages, as many northeastern peoples used similar words for them: the Lenape *škakw*, the Abenaki *segankw*, and so on. Given its dramatic coloring and odor, the animal features prominently in many legends, including a Winnebago myth where the white stripe is all that remains of a beautiful woman's long white hair, her transformation punishment for snubbing a powerful spirit.

While urban and suburban skunks will scavenge for trash, in the wild they more likely feed on insects like ants, termites, beetles, grubs, crickets, and caterpillars, their front paws sporting long claws for ripping open rotting logs. They also eat honey bees, cleverly scratching at a hive's entrance to entice a guard bee to come out and inspect the noise. The skunk swats the bee, devours it, and scratches again, repeating this process for hours.

Members of the weasel family, skunks supplement insects by occasionally preying upon other animals, especially rodents, and they are fond of eggs as well. In season, fruits and berries are eaten too. This omnivory and love for trash is one of the reasons skunks have adapted to city life, being found in Philadelphia's urban center.

Skunked by Owls

The foul-smelling spray is produced by a pair of glands bookending the anus, and a skunk can spray at targets 12 feet away. As you can imagine, the noxious sulfur-infused smell works well in warding off foxes, especially when that fox is sprayed in the face, as the acidic spray is blinding.

But that noxious spray works less well against a great horned owl, who swoops silently down on an unsuspecting skunk from above, the spray missing the owl when it shoots out. Owls have no sense of smell anyway, so they just carry the skunks back to their nests to devour or feed to their chicks. Biologists often find great horned owl nests when they come upon a rancid skunky odor around the base of a large tree—telltale evidence of an owl higher up.

The skunk is a nocturnal creature with terrible eyesight but keen senses of smell and touch. The black-and-white fur signals a nocturnal animal, as colors are hard to see at night, and the stripe breaks the body's shape up, making it a challenge for a predator to know where the animal's outlines are. This is a surprisingly effective device used by many other animals.

Skunks dig dens (or reuse other animal dens) and overwinter in them as well, with one male in a den with several females. Not true hibernators, they slow down dramatically but emerge a few times each winter to find food. In the spring, a male skunk will guard the harem of females in his den, fathering skunks with many females.

Sadly, skunks are a major concern for rabies exposure, second only to raccoons.

Be wary around them. If you see one outside during the day, however, that is not as unusual as it seems; unlike in bats, this is not a signal that the animal is rabid. If a skunk is in your trash can, of course never try to lift it out—tip the can gently away from you and step back. The jury is out on the effectiveness of a tomato soup bath for eliminating the spray's smell, something widely believed by many people. Instead, experts recommend a solution mixing hydrogen peroxide, baking soda, and detergent.

Where to See It

As it is a nocturnal creature, you are highly unlikely to see a skunk on any of your walks, though on your walks about, they will be inhabiting most of the forests you visit.

Gray Squirrel

Sciurus carolinensis

Wherever you are reading this in Wild Philly, a gray squirrel is likely not far from you. With a name derived from the Greek words meaning "shadow tail," this member of the rodent family is ubiquitous, familiar, and remarkably adaptable. Walk into a forest for a hike, odds are a gray squirrel will be the first forest critter you see. Walk a tree-lined street in the city, and again, it's likely the first native mammal you meet.

Few critters except Canada geese and deer raise the ire of Philadelphians more than squirrels, especially for people who maintain bird feeders. There really is no such thing as a squirrel-proof feeder, as squirrels are persistent and gymnastic, and many unlucky homeowners have had to call wildlife control companies to remove squirrels from their attics.

Still, give the gray squirrel its due: it is an essential animal in regenerating forests. When fall comes, squirrels famously bury caches of

▲ Gray squirrels build leafy nests high up in the trees.

food like nuts and acorns, with a single squirrel burying several thousand caches. When they feel like another animal is watching them, they even *pretend* to bury the acorn, but hold it in their throat instead. After burying the pretend acorn, they sneak off elsewhere to hide the real one.

Squirrels do remember where many of the caches are and can smell them—and other squirrel's caches— even under some snow.

But industrious squirrels bury more acorns and seeds than they dig up, and many forgotten and unused caches sprout in the forest, having been planted by squirrels. Contemplate their gardening ability on your next forest walk— many of the trees you see have been planted by squirrels (and blue jays, too).

Surprisingly, gray squirrels are omnivores, eating nuts, seeds, leaves, twigs, fungi, and berries, of course, but also eggs, insects, even small animals like baby birds and young snakes. The gray squirrel is also, like the chipmunk, among the few mammals that can descend a tree head-first, rotating its feet so that hind claws point backward to better grip the bark.

Dreying On

High up in the trees, gray squirrels build leafy nests called dreys, round clumps of leaves easy to see in the winter. They use these dreys to escape both hot summer heat and winter's freezing cold. I observed a gray squirrel building one in a pine tree in my backyard in November, tucking dead leaves into a tangle of vines on the trunk to create its winter home. Squirrels can also nest inside cavities in trunks—and in your attic.

Squirrels are prolific. They breed twice annually, giving birth to as many as eight kits each time. They are easily the most numerous animals brought to the Wildlife Clinic at the Schuylkill Center, comprising 40 percent of the clinic's patients annually. Wind sometimes blows babies out of nests, and fallen trees are found to have nests inside.

In fact, gray squirrels have become something of an anecdotal barometer for climate change at the clinic. Squirrels now give birth later into the year than they once did (November), and start sooner than they once did (February) as well.

Where to See It

Everywhere and anywhere—your street, your yard, any one of these walks, even tightrope-walking the electric lines on your street.

Little Brown Bat

Myotis lucifugus

Years ago, watching a Phillies game at the long-gone Veterans Stadium, my eyes wandered off the field, pulled by movement in the floodlights above me. While all kinds of bugs were swirling in the light—a tornado of moths, flies, and beetles—what caught my eye were bats zipping through the insect cloud. The action was way more compelling than that on the field. I was transfixed by their balletic moves.

While nine different species of bats inhabit Pennsylvania, these were little brown bats, far and away the region's most common species and incredibly effective insectivores. Here's a reason to love bats: each bat consumes as many as 1200 insects every hour they are hunting, many of those being mosquitoes, and a nursing mother might double her weight in only one night. A Wisconsin study of genetic material in bat guano (their poop) found that almost three-quarters of it was mosquito DNA. Like dragonflies, these are mosquito hawks.

Fleeing Light

The species name *lucifugus* translates as "fleeing light," a perfect name for this nocturnal hunter. Emerging from their daytime roosts in nooks and crevices in trees and, yes, behind the shutters or in the attics of older houses, little brown bats likely head first for a drink of water, skimming along the water's surface. For those bats at the Phillies game, the Schuylkill was handily right next door, as were the lakes at FDR Park.

▲ The vast bulk of a little brown bat's diet is mosquitoes.

Videos have captured bats eating in slow motion, and you would enjoy watching one. Bats are elegant gymnasts, swatting a moth in midflight, for example, with first one wing, then the other, then using the tail webbing like a catcher's mitt. They twist, turn, swoop, flip, and dive to grab that meal.

In the summer, colonial females live in nurseries of between 10 and 1000 bats; the males roost elsewhere solitarily. As autumn comes, bats enter their mating phase. The little brown bat is promiscuous, so males and females mate in the fall as often as they can. The females store the sperm over the winter, giving birth to only one baby early the next summer.

In late fall, little brown bats move to winter hibernation sites in places like caves and mine shafts, using the same sites year after year. At one time, these sites were impressive: one winter den held more than 183,000 bats. The little brown is a true hibernator, sleeping through the winter, eating nothing, its respiration and heartbeat dropping, its body temperature close to matching that of the cave itself. The bat slowly burns its body fat, losing a substantial portion of its mass.

Sadly, I've not seen a bat fly through Phillies floodlights in a while. Little brown bats have been decimated by white-nose syndrome, caused by an exotic fungus introduced to bat populations. The fungus produces a white growth on the animal's face and wings that arouses the bat from its hibernation, and bats awakened in this manner often cannot get back asleep, burn off their body fat too quickly, and perish. Biologists estimate that 99 percent of little brown bat populations have disappeared, with entire winter colonies vanishing.

Worse still, windmills on ridge lines, while a greener form of energy, slice through bat populations as well, especially migratory bats. On top of all this, scientists suspect that pesticides may be impacting bats too. In an effort to preserve bats, there is a movement to install bat boxes across the region. Lots of nature center gift shops sell bat boxes for you to take home and help buttress populations of this beleaguered animal.

Where to See It

Once upon a time not too long ago, one could stand in a twilit field alongside a forest and expect to see bats cruising the night sky, the still-blue sky silhouetting the animal. In recent years, however, any sighting of a bat is cause for celebration. But try your luck at one of the forests mentioned here.

Raccoon

Procyon lotor

▲ The raccoon is known for its nimble and active front paws.

With its mask and striped tail, the raccoon is both one of the most recognizable and most popular of the region's mammals. A New World creature, the raccoon is also among the most adaptable, inhabiting the entire Wild Philly region, living not only in forests and woodlots, but abandoned homes and vacant lots. Spotting a raccoon in West Philly is as likely as spying one in Bucks County farmland.

The name raccoon is derived from the Powhatan *aroughcun*, a word recorded by Jamestown founder John Smith that translates (roughly) as "one who rubs, scrubs, and scratches with its hands," describing one of the raccoon's most famous actions: the washing of food. Thousands of miles away, the Aztecs in Mexico called the raccoon *mapachtli*, or "one who takes everything in its hands." Cultures as disparate as Germans, Japanese, and Israelis all give the raccoon names that translate as "wash-bears." Even the species name *lotor* is Latin for "washer."

Raccoons actively work with their nimble front paws, and their sense of touch is their paramount sense. Though famous for washing their food, I have to break your heart here: scientists have not observed raccoons doing this in the wild. Instead, they often hunt alongside streams and ponds—it's very easy to find their pawprints in the mud alongside forest streams—pulling small creatures out of the water, often turning them over and inspecting them. It turns out that water softens their paw's tissues, heightening that sense of touch. This behavior was misunderstood as washing.

World's Most Omnivorous Animal

Samuel I. Zeveloff, author of *Raccoons: A Natural History*, calls them "one of the world's most omnivorous animals." Raccoons split their diet almost evenly among plant materials, invertebrates, and vertebrates. They'll happily raid a bird's nest for eggs, grab a crayfish from a stream, munch on blackberries in a forest, and for dessert, raid your trash.

Excellent climbers, raccoons typically live and nest in tree hollows and rock crevices, but have been spotted using burrows dug by other mammals, dense undergrowth, and even crotches in tree branches. Females give birth to between two and five kits in their nest in the spring, each weighing only 2 ounces; the male is not involved in rearing the young. The family usually splits up in the fall, though sometimes first-year young stay with mom through the winter. Male offspring wander farther afield to new territories than the females.

While the raccoon is among the many nocturnal mammals hereabouts, it is not unusual to see one out during the day. This is not automatically a sign of rabies. That said, raccoons are highly prone to rabies, and you must always avoid and sidestep raccoons—and never feed them.

Raccoons have become unpopular in some quarters of Philadelphia, as many neighborhoods have abandoned houses now home to them. In fact, they've even become a hot-button issue in some City Council races. Though adored by most preschoolers, like deer and squirrels, the raccoon is now reviled in much of the city for being a garbage-eating rabies machine. Sigh.

Where to See It

You likely don't have to go too far to find a raccoon. On the day I wrote this, a raccoon climbed down the pine tree in my neighbor's backyard, and I have seen them popping out of storm drains on my street (and both were during daylight hours). They live in every forest mentioned here.

Red Fox

Vulpes vulpes

No matter where you live in Wild Philly, whether urban North Philadelphia, suburban Cherry Hill, or exurban Exton, a red fox doesn't live far from you. Highly adaptable and the most common wild dog in the region, the red fox ranges across the entire northern hemisphere, from North America into Asia, Europe, even North Africa. There are forty-five subspecies worldwide.

Foxes have a long association with people, living in and around human settlements forever. In fact, the word *fox* has Proto-Indo-European roots, an ancient language about 8000 years old; the name refers to the bushy tail, one of the fox's best-known features. In the New World, the Ojibwe of the Great Lakes call the fox *waagosh*, a name that suggests the onomatopoeic up-and-down bouncing of its tail.

Foxes specialize in hunting a wide variety of small animals like rodents, rabbits, squirrels, crayfish, even large insects like grasshoppers. They'll eat eggs and small birds too, even carrion. Skunks and porcupines evolved their special protections as primarily a defense against foxes. But they are omnivores, supplementing this meat with fruits of all kinds, like blueberries, blackberries, raspberries, even acorns and grass seeds. Opportunistic, red foxes will continue to hunt even after they are full, storing extra food under leaves, snow, or dirt.

While they have a good sense of smell, sight and hearing are more important. I once

▲ The red fox mostly uses its eyes and pointy ears to locate prey.

watched a red fox stalking something in the snow, its large ears pointed forward, small satellite dishes pinpointing sound. It suddenly jumped almost straight in the air and came down fast and hard in the snow, pulling out a hapless rodent that had been tunneling below. One Soviet study indicated foxes can hear a mouse squeaking at about a football field away.

Marking Territory

I love a good snowfall at the Schuylkill Center mostly because I know I'll see a fox track. A red fox typically walks through a forest like it knows exactly where it's going—the tracks straight-lined and evenly spaced. We also find fox droppings in the forest, the scat looking like gray twisted rope, except in berry season, when it is loaded with seeds.

But red foxes have also left their scat purposefully at our nature center's front walkway, a reminder that they are here too. Like your dog, they urinate to mark territory or mark a food cache. Foxes have about a dozen urination stances to project their urine in different directions as needed.

Foxes mate in the winter, the vixen denning right after mating, even creating an extra den to use if needed. Almost 2 months after mating, she'll give birth to between one and ten kits. The male brings her food while she is caring for the kits, which start playing outside the den when only a month old. In addition to nursing them, the mother feeds them regurgitated food at first, but soon brings live prey for the kits to toy with and maybe eat. Play helps the kits develop their hunting skills.

Though mostly nocturnal, Schuylkill Center staff often sees foxes out and about during the day. And we often see mangy foxes in the region's woods, the animals suffering from a burrowing parasitic mite that makes their fur fall away. We receive many calls from people wanting us to do something, but sadly, there is nothing we can do but let nature heal.

Where to See It

While common and everywhere, spotting a red fox is not terribly common. Be outdoors a lot and maybe you will get lucky.

Virginia Opossum

Didelphis virginiana

▲ When an opossum feels threatened, before playing dead it will try to look threatening by hissing and baring its sharp teeth.

Widely spread across the region and the city, the Virginia opossum is one unique animal. Australia is famed for its many marsupials, pouched animals like kangaroos and Tasmanian devils, but the opossum is North America's only one and does indeed carry its young in a pouch.

Most baby opossums are born between February and June, blind, hairless, and only the size of a jellybean. They crawl into mom's pouch, grab onto one of her thirteen teats for the next 2 months, and grow quickly. When finally big enough for the great outdoors, they climb onto mom's back, riding there for another few months.

A living fossil, opossum-like mammals were contemporaries of *Tyrannosaurus*. At the same time, the opossum is relatively new to the continent, as it was a South American animal that began expanding its range into North America only about 800,000 years ago (recent in evolutionary time).

The Lenape likely did not know the opossum, as it had only reached Maryland by colonial times. In fact, its scientific name *virginiana* points to its southern roots. The English name is a corruption of the Powhatan name for the creature, which translates to "white dog," a reference to its light-colored face. Since European colonization, the opossum has continued its relentless march north and is now past New England and across northeastern Canada.

An omnivore, the opossum is not discriminating. It eats fruits like raspberries and apples, nuts like acorns and beechnuts, insects like grasshoppers and beetles, small animals like snakes and rodents, eggs from nests, and more. In cities, opossums take seed from bird feeders, dog or cat food left outside, and garbage in trash cans, often having a harder time climbing out than climbing in. In farm country, they even feast on produce growing in fields. Notoriously slow and cumbersome in running, their love of carrion becomes problematic when they dine on roadkill—and get hit themselves.

Opposable Thumb, Prehensile Tail

Opossums live in trees, and an opposable thumb on their hind feet and a prehensile tail helps in climbing. That tail is naked, so many people mistakenly assume the creature is a very large rat, which of course it is not.

They do play 'possum, pretending to be dead. Before that, however, the animal will first attempt to look threatening: hissing, snapping, baring its teeth, raising its fur to look larger. This tends to freak us out when one is discovered in a trash can. Fear not, it is a ploy, as the animal is remarkably docile (just tip the can over away from you, and let it mosey away). But if that play-acting doesn't work, the opossum turns to plan B: it lies limply on its side, tongue hanging out of its open mouth, even breath rate dropping. For added drama, it may also defecate a putrid green substance that literally stinks of death.

The animal plays a central role in Southern cuisine, as an opossum recipe appeared in early editions of *The Joy of Cooking* (for parboiled opossum). I'm betting most Philadelphians will stick to cheesesteaks.

Where to See It

A nocturnal animal, you need luck to see one. Sadly I've spotted more road-killed opossums than I have seen live ones.

White-Tailed Deer

Odocoileus virginianus

▲ More white-tailed deer live in Wild Philly today than ever in history.

White-tailed deer—we love 'em and hate 'em. The white-tailed deer is Pennsylvania's official state animal. The opening day of deer hunting season in Pennsylvania was for decades the largest single-day sporting event in the country. Across wide swaths of the state, it was a holiday with schools and businesses closing. Easily the largest animal in Wild Philly, the deer is common as well. While its fate has been discussed in the chapter on threats to the forest, allow me to simply share here its natural history.

The deer is named for the white tail that it raises as a flag as it runs away, an alarm signal to other deer, especially fawns. The creature is fast, having been clocked at almost 50 miles per hour. The genus name *Odocoileus* translates as "hollow tooth," and the deer wields those teeth to eat many different plants, even poison ivy. Its diet raises the hackles of many home gardeners in deer country.

Active all year, even in winter, white-tailed deer shed their reddish brown summer coat for a duller gray-brown winter one, the crinkled hairs of the winter fur creating a thicker, warmer pelt than in summer.

In the Rut

White-tailed deer seem especially skittish during the fall, when they head into the rutting season. The male bucks scrape the ground, hence the "rut," and urinate on themselves, the urine mixing with pheromones in glands on their legs to trickle into the rut to form an irresistible muddy elixir that does find intoxicating. By winter's onset, just about every doe is pregnant.

Fawns are born in spring, usually one or two per doe. They are odorless to help the young avoid predators, and the mother stays away at first so her scent does not accidentally rub off.

In 1928, when Felix Salter's novel *Bambi* was first written, white-tailed deer were rare in Pennsylvania, on extinction's doorstep from overhunting and habitat removal. To restore deer, the Pennsylvania Game Commission imported some from other states. With predators like mountain lions removed and second-growth forests regenerated, more deer live in Wild Philly today than ever in history, leading to massive complications. But it is another conservation success story.

Where to See It

Be watchful as you walk through forests any time of the year. You may spot the deer's white flag being raised as it avoids you.

Woodchuck (Groundhog)

Marmota monax

One of the region's bigger rodents, the groundhog is the only animal to have a holiday named for it. On February 2, all eyes turn to Pennsylvania to see what Punxsutawney Phil, the world's most famous groundhog, prognosticates that year. Around that same day, people watch that Bill Murray movie, ironically, over and over again.

Of course the animals don't chuck (or even eat) wood. Sources instead indicate First Nations roots for the name. One opinion claims it is from the New England Algonquian name for the animal, *wuchak*, as heard by settlers. Another holds that the Algonquian name was actually *monack*, from which we derived its species name *monax*, which means, appropriately, "digger."

That is what woodchucks do—they dig underground burrows with their powerful limbs and specially designed claws. Their

dens have multiple entrances, long tunnels (some approaching 20 feet long), and side galleries. One woodchuck can displace almost 400 pounds of dirt from its den. Here is where it sleeps, eats, reproduces, raises its young, and runs to for safety when a hawk or fox approaches, often alerting others with a squeal that gives it still another nickname, whistlepig.

A Long Winter Nap

For me, seeing a woodchuck out of its burrow and lumbering around is one of my favorite signs of spring. These animals are true hibernators, vanishing into their winter dens around Halloween. Their body temperature and heart and breathing rates all fall dramatically, and they may lose as much as half of their body weight. Males awaken first and sometimes scout out female dens, maybe as early as

▲ The woodchuck is a large ground squirrel with gray to brownish red fur and a dark tail.

February 2, then head back into their own den—one possible source of the choice of this animal as the region's winter forecaster.

Primarily an herbivore eating grasses and plants of all kinds, the woodchuck eats an occasional insect as well. As autumn approaches, its metabolism slows and its feeding greatly increases, allowing the creature to bulk up significantly and store fat for the critical months ahead.

Where to See It

Surprisingly, one of the most common places I've seen woodchucks is along the Pennsylvania Turnpike, common along the grassy sides of that highway. Check it out.

FIELD TRIPS

SPRING

SUMMER

FALL

WINTER

ANYTIME

FOUR BONUS TRIPS

Tamaqua

28

78 Allentown

476

22

Reading New Hope

3

Pottstown TRENTON

12 422 611 95

King of Prussia 276

8 Bensalem

76

Coatesville PHILADELPHIA 16

30 19 295 Mount Holly

11 Camden

1 206

1 21

Wilmington

95 27

95 40 Hammonton

Vineland

Atlantic City

26

Cape May

29

Although nature is all around us in Wild Philly—and we are an integral part of nature—there are extraordinary places to visit in the region to see the best that nature has to offer. The Philadelphia region is blessed with an abundance of parks, preserves, nature centers, and refuges, and the Naturalist Advisory Team and I have worked to assemble the top twenty-five trips you might take.

Even better, these trips are arranged by season, so you'll know where and when to go to see mountain laurel blooming, frogs mating, peregrines nesting, and hawks migrating. The first twenty-five trips are located in the Delaware Valley. While we could have filled the book with several hundred more trips—and apologies if we missed your favorite—*Wild Philly* offers a great cross section of the best spots with diverse habitats at the right time of year.

We've also added four bonus trips, outside of the region but ones many Philadelphians flock to: Delaware Bay when mating horseshoe crabs and migrating shorebirds collide, the Pine Barrens with its unique ecology and carnivorous plants, and two hotspots for hawk migration, Hawk Mountain to the north and Cape May to the south.

We hope you'll dog-ear this book, crack its spine, and get it mud-splattered as you get to know Wild Philly.

Getting the Most from Your Wild Philly Adventures

In general, as you plan for your Wild Philly adventures, it's a good idea to pay attention to weather forecasts. You don't want to be too far afield in a blizzard, a thunderstorm, or dangerous heat. And it's also always best to walk with a buddy. The company is great, and, if a problem arises, two heads are better than one.

START WITH TRIP 25

"There's no place like home," goes a famous movie line, and it's true. Get to know Wild Philly by walking your own street and neighborhood.

CHOOSE YOUR FIRST TRIPS

The field trips are keyed to the seasons. Decide which trips to take first by reading that season's offerings, and see which ones call to you.

Remember that time of day matters too. While several of the trips take you to places where beavers are active, you'll only see them early in the morning or perhaps at dusk. Want to hear toads singing? Great, but that's an evening jaunt. Want to walk a tidal Delaware? Absolutely, but check the tide schedule and plan to be there at low tide.

Any of these walks can be done any time of year. So, while you might visit the Briar Bush Nature Center in the winter to use its bird observatory, return in the spring as migrating warblers visit the observatory's gurgling water feature as well. We suggest the John Heinz National Wildlife Refuge as a great spring trip, but the site offers rich nature experiences 365 days of the year.

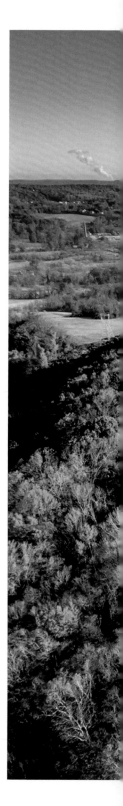

The magnificent 1300-acre ChesLen Preserve on a frosty November morning, one of the many places you'll explore in Wild Philly.

PREP YOUR PACK

As you head out for a day trip, here are some essentials to bring along. For your safety:

- **Smartphone or cell phone** in case of emergencies.

- **First aid kit,** which could be as simple as a few bandages, some tweezers, and a tube of antibiotic ointment, or with more specialized items you might need, like antihistamine, an EpiPen for allergic reactions, or an inhaler.

For your comfort:

- **Water, snacks, and extra clothing,** no matter the time of year.

- **Sunscreen, hat, and insect repellent** in the hotter months (which now start earlier and end later).

- **Extra shoes,** if needed, or **water shoes** to take advantage of wet sites.

For nature spotting:

- **Binoculars,** which are great for more than birds. I've identified tall trees by peering into their high branches looking at leaf shapes.

- **Hand lens or magnifier,** which allows you to see especially flowers up close. You can also hold the magnifier in front of your smartphone's camera to score close-up photos of tiny things.

- **Camera,** whether a smartphone or an actual camera, to record your finds. You can post photos to social media or use an app like iNaturalist or eBird to participate in citizen science and get experts to help you with identification. Start using the hashtag #WildPhilly so we can see your posts.

- **Field guides** like this one. There are great and easy-to-use guides for birds, wildflowers, trees, and more. Try some out.

- **Maps** are incredibly helpful. We hope the maps here are sufficient, but before you visit any site it's a good idea to also go to its website to download a map. The site's own mapping will be more detailed and up-to-date than what we offer here.

- **Field notebook,** so you can start writing your own observations, lists of species, sketches, musings, and more.

Tick Prevention

Deer ticks are unfortunately too common and Lyme disease too prevalent in Wild Philly. To protect yourself, you'll need to be vigilant and take these five easy-to-do precautions.

1. Wear long pants, closed-toe shoes, and socks—no matter how hot. These are necessary to protect your feet and legs. Light-colored clothing will allow you to spot a tick before it gets to your skin.

2. Before your walk, tuck your pant legs into your socks, and spray socks and shoes with repellent. It's not fashionable, but it is totally necessary. Spray repellent on your arms as well. Some people always wear long-sleeved shirts in ticky places, and there is now clothing with repellent actually baked into the fabric.

3. When you get home after a walk, remove your clothing and wash it immediately—and separately.

4. Shower and perform your own visual tick inspection. If you find one, use tweezers to grasp the tick by the head (not the body) as close to the skin as possible, and lift up. Then clean the wound and your hands well.

5. Remember, the tick needs to be actively sucking your blood for 24 hours for you to contract Lyme disease. Use that window wisely.

Hiking in Uncertain Times

Wild Philly was written during the COVID-19 pandemic, which, as you well know, upended the entire world, including the nonprofits that run many of the parks and preserves you'll visit here. We assume that as you read this book the organizations are all operating normally, but this might not be the case. So the hours of operation, the ability to visit indoor museum exhibits, the need for masks, the presence of any staff at these sites—these all may change depending on the course of the pandemic or any new concern that arises in its place. It is always good practice to visit their websites or call the centers to understand how the state of current events may alter their—and your—plans.

Since all of these field trips are outside in fresh air with lots of opportunities for social distancing, do take advantage of these walks to combat crisis fatigue as well. Time in nature alleviates stress, so take advantage of nature's healing powers.

Black Run Preserve

In a timeless rite of early spring, frogs and toads come out of hibernation and head to bodies of water to mate, the males singing impossibly loudly to attract egg-laden females. Black Run Preserve, a marsh complex in Evesham Township, is a great place to witness this delightful phenomenon. You'll need to be there at dusk to catch the action, which is when the preserve's beavers are active as well.

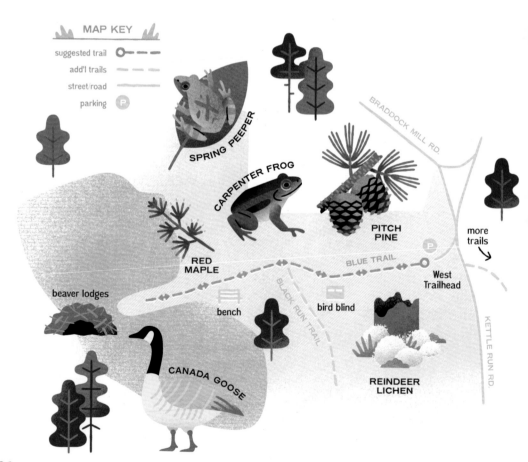

MAP KEY

suggested trail
add'l trails
street/road
parking

SPRING PEEPER

CARPENTER FROG

PITCH PINE

RED MAPLE

BLUE TRAIL

BRADDOCK MILL RD.

more trails

West Trailhead

KETTLE RUN RD.

beaver lodges

bench

bird blind

BLACK RUN TRAIL

CANADA GOOSE

REINDEER LICHEN

▲ The preserve's Blue Trail takes you between these two beaver ponds.

Wild Philly's twenty-five field trips are timed to the seasons. The first walk of the new spring season, when the world awakens and almost anything seems possible, needs to be a visit to see and hear mating frogs. It's almost impossible to describe the cacophony of a frog pond in springtime, when frogs of multiple species gather.

One of the best places to witness this event is an out-of-the-way refuge in Evesham Township, New Jersey, the hidden gem of the Black Run Preserve. This 1300-acre marshland complex on the eastern edge of Wild Philly and the western edge of the Pine Barrens is an extraordinary and unique ecosystem that we will meet in two additional trips, the Woodford Cedar Run Wildlife Refuge (Trip 21) and the intensive New Jersey Pine Barrens adventure (Trip 27). In addition, the Black Run, named for the dark-colored water typical of Pine Barrens streams, is part of the Southwest Branch of Rancocas Creek, a stream we will visit in Trip 16 at the Rancocas Nature Center.

WHERE: West Trailhead, Kettle Run Road, Evesham, NJ 08053

ADMISSION: Free; open daily from dawn to dusk.

PARKING: There is parking, but the lot is fairly small.

DIFFICULTY, DISTANCE, ACCESS: The recommended walk is an easy 1-mile hike on trails that are flat but not ADA-accessible.

FACILITIES: There is no visitor center here, but a portable toilet is located across Kettle Road at the East Trailhead.

BEST TIME: A visit in early April at dusk offers a singular opportunity to witness the spectacle of frog song.

SPECIAL NOTES: Bikes and dogs on leashes are allowed on these trails.

The preserve is not accessible via mass transit.

Once a cranberry bog extensively harvested for fruit production, the Black Run Preserve has now been reclaimed by nature. The forest is recovering, beavers have moved in to rearrange the site's hydrology, and ducks, geese, and other waterbirds are living here as well.

Plan to arrive before dark to become familiar with the site; you might even bring dinner and a flashlight with you. (Please note: while the park's signage indicates it is open dawn to dusk, I've spent many evenings there with no concerns.) Located on Kettle Run Road, the preserve—owned by the township but benefiting from the extensive involvement of a friends group— has two trailheads, East and West Trailheads, on opposite sides of the road. Park in the West Trailhead's modest parking lot in the relatively rugged area set aside for this. If you need a portable toilet, it is across the street at the other trailhead.

The moment you leave your car, you know this is a different place. In the flat, sandy Coastal Plain, the forests are pines and oaks, with red maples and sassafras here too. Look for American hollies here as well, a tree you rarely see in Pennsylvania. The shrub layer is dominated by members of the heath family, including mountain laurel and blueberry, the latter common in the Pine Barrens and a critical component of the Lenape diet in Lenapehoking.

Past the kiosk, the site's Blue Trail is a straight dead-end shot blazed with blue diamonds. As you walk, look along the ground also for reindeer lichens, that blue-gray organism—part alga, part fungus—eaten by reindeer in northern ecosystems. There are other lichens here as well; keep an eye out for them.

Beavers Everywhere

The Black Run Trail, blazed in black squares, soon heads left, but continue straight. A sign references a nature trail on the right, but the beavers have rearranged the trails and flooded that portion, making that trail impassible. Props to the friends group for accommodating the animals' ongoing engineering.

Closer to the marsh, look for a sign on your left interpreting the site's cranberry history. It's hard to imagine this was once an intensive cranberry operation. Behind that sign is a bench, which will later be a great place to listen to the frog chorus.

The trail ends with a delightful vista, a thumb of high land threading between two bogs, the one on the left with lots of open water, the one on the right quickly growing into a red maple forest. Straight ahead, look for two beaver lodges, the classic mounds constructed of sticks. In fact, look carefully to the right of the lodges, where there is an extensive beaver dam built on the right side of the thumb that created the lake on the left.

Are the beavers active? As dusk settles in, you might learn. But a large and noisy group of Canada geese were in the lake the night I visited, raising their own ruckus. And a large group of great blue herons flew directly over me—perhaps on their way to a nearby roost site—something I have never seen in all my years of birdwatching.

▲ Beavers have constructed several lodges within the Black Run Preserve.

If you carefully examine the trees around you, you should notice a lot of red maple. This tree is an early bloomer, and by early April red maple should have many red spider-shaped flowers dangling from its twigs. Its bright red flowers are just one of several reasons this tree earned its name.

The Frog Chorus

On the evening I visited, two different species of frogs were loudly stating their intentions. The first and most vocal was the spring peeper, a tiny tree frog that quietly lives in the forest during most of the year, catching insects from its perch in the trees. In the spring, the frogs awaken from their underground hibernation and hop into ponds like these, the males shouting a high-pitched "peep!" The spring peeper is an impossibly small light brown frog with an X-shaped mark on its back, a mark that lent it the Latin name *Pseudacris crucifer*, the species name a reference to the cross.

The second is the carpenter frog, named for its male song, a call reminiscent of a carpenter hammering nails: "Pa-tunk! Pa-tunk!" The females respond with a chirping noise. This species is a medium-sized, brown or bronze-colored frog with four light brown stripes down its back.

It's especially wonderful to revel in a frog pond like this when you remember the plight of amphibians worldwide. These creatures—with their very sensitive skins—are in trouble and in a steep decline as a group. Hearing these frogs calling by the thousands is all the more gratifying.

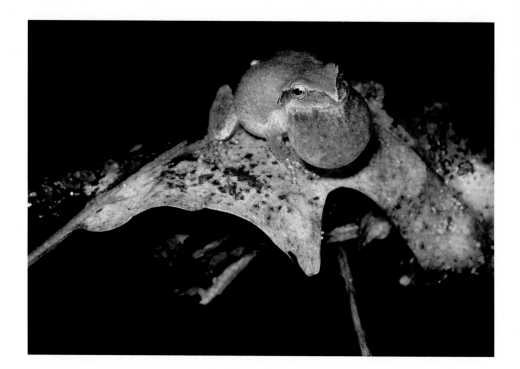

If you have time, the Black Trail we skipped before takes you to another section of this same wetland complex, also with lots of beaver-chewed trees around you. Consider exploring.

And come back again, as a walk at Black Run Preserve in the summer yields numerous flowers in bloom, including white pond lily and yellow spatterdock in the pond, plus blueberries ripe for the picking.

▲ A male spring peeper serenades for mates.

Schuylkill Center for Environmental Education

The city's first nature center, the Schuylkill Center is one of the best places in Wild Philly to witness ephemeral spring wildflowers in a natural setting. Depending on the week you go, its Ravine Loop explodes with a profusion of bloodroot, trout lily, trillium, bluebells, mayapple, and Jack-in-the-pulpit, among others.

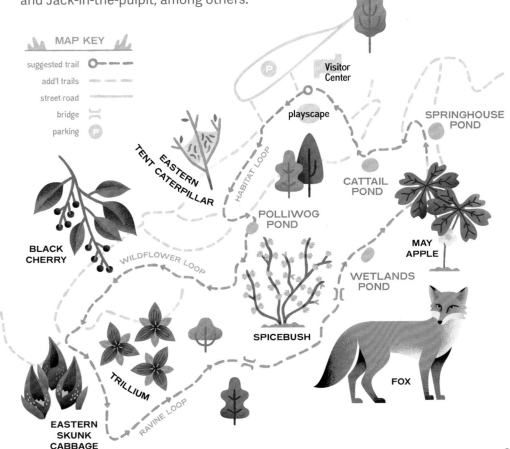

MAP KEY

suggested trail	○-----
add'l trails	-----
street/road	———
bridge	)(
parking	Ⓟ

Visitor Center

playscape

SPRINGHOUSE POND

EASTERN TENT CATERPILLAR

HABITAT LOOP

CATTAIL POND

BLACK CHERRY

WILDFLOWER LOOP

POLLIWOG POND

MAY APPLE

WETLANDS POND

SPICEBUSH

TRILLIUM

FOX

EASTERN SKUNK CABBAGE

RAVINE LOOP

WHERE: 8480 Hagys Mill Road, Philadelphia, PA 19128

ADMISSION: Free; trails open daily from dawn to dusk; the Visitor Center is open from 9:00 a.m. to 5:00 p.m. Monday through Saturday.

PARKING: There is plenty of parking in the Visitor Center's lot and satellite parking on Hagys Mill Road, where visitors can park and walk in.

DIFFICULTY, DISTANCE, ACCESS: The recommended loop is 1.5 miles long, downhill at the start but uphill at the end; its length and terrain can be challenging for very young and elderly walkers. While the Visitor Center is fully accessible and its Widener Trail is a paved nature trail designed for wheelchair use, the Wildflower Loop and Ravine Loop trails are not ADA-accessible.

FACILITIES: The Visitor Center includes restrooms, snacks for sale in the gift shop, a nature museum, art gallery, and nature playscape.

BEST TIME: While peak wildflower season is between April 15 and May 15, the trails offer new delights all year long.

SPECIAL NOTES: Dogs and bikes are not allowed on the trails.

SEPTA's Bus 9 travels from Center City to Ridge Avenue, but it is a hike from the bus stop. You'll get off at Port Royal Avenue, walk a mile to the Hagys Mill Road entrance, and then a half mile down the driveway.

"You belong among the wildflowers," sang Tom Petty, "you belong somewhere you feel free." And in the one-month window between April 15 and May 15, you belong on the Schuylkill Center's Ravine Loop. If you've got a good wildflower field guide, bring it along. Otherwise, just enjoy the flower show. Maybe bring binoculars too, as many birds will accompany you.

Founded in 1965, the Schuylkill Center for Environmental Education pioneered environmental education in Philadelphia, the first to train the area's teachers. Today, it offers a wide slate of education programs for both children and adults. It also houses the state's first nature-based preschool and an ambitious environmental art program, while running one of the few wildlife rehabilitation clinics in the region. You'll also be in the city's largest fully protected open space.

On the map, look for three intersecting loops on the southeastern side of the Visitor Center: the Habitat Loop, the Wildflower Loop, and the Ravine Loop. From the parking lot, walk to the rear of the center's building and turn right onto the Habitat Loop as it skirts the front of the kid-friendly Nature Playscape. Head downhill through a meadow, looking for birds on the forest edge. At meadow's end, turn left onto the Ravine Loop and immediately on your right enter the gate into a fenced area.

Polliwog Pond

Here's where the Wildflower Loop begins. Stop by Polliwog Pond, which, if there has been good rainfall, may be filled with either toad eggs or tiny tadpoles. Walk past the pond into the forest, and find an interpretive sign that introduces spring wildflowers. Just past the sign and where the trail turns right, there is a big stand of blue cohosh, a plant with tons of medicinal uses among First Nations people. Though named for its blue berries, there is a decidedly blue-green blush to its leaves, and its flowers are an indistinct yellowish green.

In that same area, you'll also find shooting stars, Jacob's ladders, white baneberry (also called doll's eyes because of its eerie eye-like berries), Virginia bluebells, violets, and more. There's even Dutchman's breeches, a small,

▲ The Ravine Loop at the Schuylkill Center offers both wildflowers in spring and a shady forest canopy later in the summer.

delicate white flower, a cousin of bleeding heart, the flower of which looks like a cartoonish version of Dutch bloomers.

And then there's mayapple, its umbrella-shaped leaf growing in profusion along this loop. Blooming in mid-May, the flower tucked underneath the umbrella matures into an apple-like fruit in June, one that box turtles especially crave.

After a few hundred yards, you'll come to rugged rock stairs. Head down those, watching for several different violets, the common blue violet plus species that bloom yellow and white.

First Flower of Spring

When you come to the gate that marks the end of the deer fencing, pass through to the Ravine Loop, being careful to lock the gate behind you. Turn left and head downhill. As you walk, look especially on your left for a small flower with almost grass-like leaves, a white blossom with fine lilac-colored lines painted through its petals. Called spring beauty, it loves this stretch of trail.

If it is a rainy spring, a seep of water might travel alongside the trail. Turn left at the stream, and after a grate in the trail, on the left is a great stand of skunk cabbage. The first flower of spring, skunk cabbage blooms in late February. Its purple mottled hood melts the ice as it grows, and the flower is a knobby bulb tucked inside the hood. Later, once the flowers are done, the plant's large cabbage-like leaves emerge and grow several feet tall. See if you can smell its skunky odor.

Philly's Best Wildflower Trail

▲ Virginia bluebells in bloom.

Look down the Ravine Loop: this stretch in front of you is the heart of the best wildflower trail in the city and one of the best in the region unprotected from deer. Walk slowly, as on either side of the trail you will find many flowers that change in the months of March, April, and May.

Look for bloodroot in late March and early April; red trillium, Virginia bluebells, and trout lily in early to mid-April; and white trillium and wild blue phlox in early to mid-May. Solomon's seal, wild geraniums, giant chickweed, and wild columbine all grow here too. The trilliums are delightfully confusing, as there are two species, white and red, but with pinkish versions of white and whitish versions of red mixed in.

When you come to the bridge, the wildflower show is sadly over, so savor them while you are there. Cross the bridge and continue down the Ravine Loop, listening for birds and enjoying the trees. You'll cross a second bridge, pass both Wetlands Pond (where wood ducks are often seen) and Spring-house Pond, leaving the latter by the gate to the left of the springhouse. Walk up the stairs, turn left (you are still on Ravine Loop), and you'll come to Cattail Pond. Check out who lives here.

Just beyond this last pond, turn into Jubilee Grove, a site marked by a sculpture donated in honor of the center's 50th anniversary. Head uphill and you are back at the playscape and the rear of the Visitor Center.

And then come back in 2 weeks, when different flowers will be in bloom.

TRIP 3 NEW HOPE, PA

Bowman's Hill Wildflower Preserve

Home to about 800 of the 2000 native plant species living in Pennsylvania, Bowman's Hill Wildflower Preserve is an oasis of what forests looked like centuries ago. Its stunning floral diversity only exists because of a 100-acre fence keeping deer at bay. In April and May, this is one of the must-see places for spring ephemeral wildflowers, including yellow lady's slipper, a rare and stunning orchid.

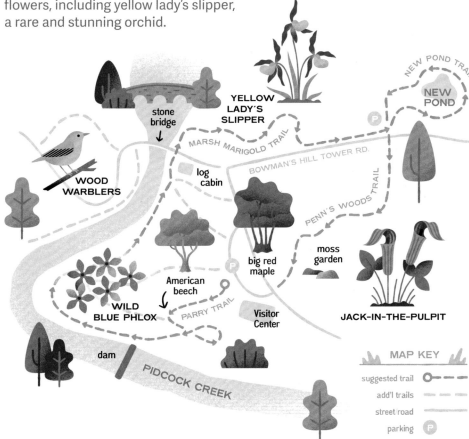

YELLOW LADY'S SLIPPER

stone bridge

WOOD WARBLERS

MARSH MARIGOLD TRAIL

NEW POND TRAIL

NEW POND

BOWMAN'S HILL TOWER RD.

log cabin

PENN'S WOODS TRAIL

big red maple

moss garden

American beech

WILD BLUE PHLOX

PARRY TRAIL

Visitor Center

JACK-IN-THE-PULPIT

dam

PIDCOCK CREEK

MAP KEY

suggested trail ⊙----
add'l trails ----
street road ——
parking Ⓟ

243

▲ A trail at Bowman's Hill offers a blanket of wildflowers across the forest floor.

WHERE: 1635 River Road, New Hope, PA 18938

ADMISSION: Free to members, and $10 for adults, $7 for seniors, students, and military, $5 children (ages 5–14); April–June open daily from 9:00 a.m. to 5:00 p.m., other months open 10:00 a.m. to 4:00 p.m. and closed on Tuesdays.

PARKING: There is plenty of on-site parking, though it may get a little tight during wildflower season.

DIFFICULTY, DISTANCE, ACCESS: The preserve features a total of 4.5 miles of trails of varied length over different terrain; the recommended walk is a fairly easy 1-mile path, with only a few modest hills. Strollers and wheelchairs can travel easily on the paved main pedestrian road and the path around the pond. Most of the rest of the trails can best accommodate strollers with all-terrain type wheels. The main floor of the Visitor Center, the restrooms, and the parking lot are accessible to all.

FACILITIES: Restrooms are available at the Visitor Center, with benches generously distributed throughout the preserve. Don't miss its delightful gift shop.

BEST TIME: Throughout the April and May wildflower season, but the many plants growing here offer plenty of interest the rest of the year as well.

SPECIAL NOTES: The preserve closes at 5:00 p.m. and the last ticketed entry is at 4:00 p.m., so come early in the day. The preserve grows and sells more than 150 species of native plants in their Native Plant Nursery; make sure to take some native plants home.

SEPTA offers both bus and train service to New Hope, and you can then take a ride service to the site.

If it's true that "the earth laughs in flowers," as Ralph Waldo Emerson wrote, then at Bowman's Hill Wildflower Preserve the earth is guffawing. At once a forest, arboretum, and museum with its collection outdoors, it formed in the 1930s to preserve the state's plant wealth—a prescient decision, as this was before deer became so threateningly numerous. Today, it's a pleasure to walk among so many wildflowers, and it could make you weep for what we have lost elsewhere.

Bowman's Hill Wildflower Preserve is surrounded by a deer fence, which allows the flowers to grow in an astonishing profusion. Though the preserve boasts several miles of trails, we're recommending an easy 1-mile walk that begins and ends at the Visitor Center. The staff will give you a trail map to take along with you, but the trails are well-marked, so it's hard to get lost.

Right at the Visitor Center's front door, look for the demonstration garden of columbine, wood poppy, and wild blue phlox. Enjoy that for a few moments, then go for your walk. Head through the parking lot toward the nursery greenhouses, and look for the entrance to the Mary K. Parry Trail on your left. Named for one of the site's founders, the Parry Trail heads downhill through a beautiful beech and tulip-tree forest.

▲ Red trillium, also known as wake-robin, blooms in early spring.

An Infinity of Wildflowers

Turn left at a large beech tree into a loop trail shaped like an infinity sign. Walk that loop to get lost in a rainbow explosion of wood poppies, Jacob's ladders, Virginia bluebells, mayapples, wild geraniums, and Jack-in-the-pulpits. Abundant insect life should accompany you on your walk. On my May walk, bumble bees were cavorting in the bluebells while an impossibly green six-spotted tiger beetle hopped on the trail only a few paces ahead of me.

As you leave the infinity loop, turn back onto the Parry Trail and immediately look for the trillium growing around you. Bowman's Hill has many examples of this notable three-leaved and three-petaled wildflower, including red, yellow, and white species, but you'll also find pinkish versions of the white trillium and whitish versions of the red. Don't sweat the species: just enjoy the flowers. Nearby you'll easily find more: spring beauty, false Solomon's seal, twinleaf, and bloodroot.

As the Parry Trail ends, turn right at the millrace—the arrows point you in the right direction—go past the dam, and look for the Azalea Trail uphill to your right. Here, you'll be greeted by wild blue phlox and Christmas fern. Look up into the canopy to see the stand of hemlocks wrestling with the invasive woolly adelgid insect that has compromised the tree.

A Regenerating Forest

Look along the forest floor here as you walk as well. You'll easily find, because of the fence, a too-rare sight: tree seedlings and saplings growing around you. Forest regeneration doesn't happen enough in forests stressed by deer overbrowsing.

As the trail ends, if you're there at the right time, a pink azalea is appropriately in full bloom on its namesake trail. The Azalea Trail ends at a log cabin built in 1933, the gatehouse of the original preserve. It's made of American chestnut logs from trees that died then from the chestnut blight. Turn left at the cabin and follow the stairs downhill along the Cabin Trail. Cross the old road into the Marsh Marigold Trail, and get ready to be amazed.

The Marsh Marigold Trail begins and ends on the road, but along its way winds through a low-lying wet area crowded with skunk cabbage and marsh marigold, a wonderfully bright yellow native plant. There is an invasive flower, lesser celandine, that people confuse with marsh marigold and that carpets many areas in Wild Philly. Here is the native wildflower in all its glory, with no celandine in sight.

Yellow Lady's Slipper

Make sure to ask the staff where you can find the yellow lady's slipper, as you don't want to miss this moccasin-shaped rarity. Orchids as a group have been double-whammied by first deer and then avid collectors stealing them.

◄ Yellow lady's slipper, a rare orchid, blooms each spring at the preserve.

You'll find more phlox and trillium too, but look for yellow trillium mixed in, a very different kind of trillium than you've yet seen. Among the now-familiar wood poppies and mayapples, don't miss the trout lilies, foamflowers, and columbines.

As you leave the Marsh Marigold Trail and come to the road, there's a great shagbark hickory on your right guarding the uphill entrance of the trail. Stop and admire its shaggy bark, a perfect hiding place for a moth to catch a long winter's nap.

Turn left on the road, head uphill, and turn left onto the New Pond Trail, making a quick circle around the pond, where a whole new world of dragonflies, green frogs, and painted turtles awaits. After this, cross the street into the Penn's Woods Trail, and look for the wonderfully weird carpeting of moss along the trail. There's one last tree to watch for: a quadruple-trunked red maple, one of the biggest of this species I've seen, on the right as the trail ends near the Visitor Center.

Much more than flowers and trees inhabit Bowman's Hill. On my walk, ovenbirds and wood thrushes were calling their distinctive songs, and a very loud woodpecker drummed to advertise his nest site. In May, many warbler-craving birders come to the preserve as well—join that flock. And perhaps return another day to hike some of the more ambitious trails.

TRIP 4 PHILADELPHIA, PA

Carpenter's Woods

Philadelphia's first bird sanctuary, Carpenter's Woods is a hotspot for woodland birds. The site is legendary among the region's many birders as a must-see in April and May for the colorful—and elusive—wood-warblers and other migrants passing through the region.

MAP KEY

- suggested trail
- add'l trails
- street/road
- parking

MAY APPLE

GREAT HORNED OWL

TULIPTREE

WAYNE AVE.

GREENE ST.

N. MT. PLEASANT RD.

GREENE ST. TRAIL

S. MT. PLEASANT RD.

WOOD THRUSH

CARPENTER'S RUN

MOFFETT TRAIL

SPRING TRAIL

JADA'S TRAIL

W. SEDGWICK ST.

WISSAHICKON AVE.

WAYNE TRAIL

ELLET TRAIL

pair of giant oaks

JACK-IN-THE-PULPIT

WAYNE AVE.

CHIPMUNK

WHERE: 7049 Greene Street, Philadelphia, PA 19119

ADMISSION: Free; open daily from dawn to dusk.

PARKING: There is plenty of parking on most streets surrounding the park.

DIFFICULTY, DISTANCE, ACCESS: The recommended walk is three-quarters of a mile over easily walkable trails that crisscross the site with only occasional but gentle slopes. Not accessible throughout, with steps at many of the entrances and rubblestone-surfaced pathways, which present a challenge for strollers and wheelchairs.

FACILITIES: None.

BEST TIME: Throughout April and May, many migrating birds, especially wood-warblers, can be found in the trees. Return in September and October to see these same migrants heading south in their winter coats.

SPECIAL NOTES: Lots of dog walkers come here, with dogs on and off leash, so be prepared.

SEPTA's Bus 53 stops at the Wayne Avenue entrance to the park.

"This is a corner of heaven here," wrote Gerald Stern in his poem "In Carpenter's Woods." Not many natural areas get such treatment, but Mount Airy's famed Carpenter's Woods did, and deservedly so, as birders also wax poetic about the forest, themselves drawn magnetically to the site each spring. Be sure to bring your binoculars and field guide.

Part of Fairmount Park, Carpenter's Woods was set aside as a bird preserve in the 1920s, and the Friends of Carpenter's Woods assists the city in managing the spot today. The National Audubon Society has declared it an Important Bird Area, as 120 species of birds have been spied visiting the site in May alone. The friends group's checklist, compiled by Naturalist Advisory Team member Keith Russell, records 158 species as having been seen here or nearby in Wissahickon Valley between 1970 and 2009. Rarities that nest here include Acadian flycatchers and pileated woodpeckers.

Before you go, visit the Friends of Carpenter's Woods' website to find and print a map of the park. While the trails are all named, there are no signs on the trails themselves. Still, it's hard to get too lost.

Carpenter's Woods is surrounded by city streets and has many entrances. But as a recommended first walk, park along W. Sedgwick Street at the foot of Wayne Avenue. As you approach the park entrance, stop for a moment and listen, as many birds can easily be seen and heard at the site's edge. On the early morning I visited, a red-eyed vireo sang its three-note monologue to my right while a wood thrush performed its organ-pipe solo to my left. I can't think of a better pair of birds to greet you as you begin a walk.

Flames of the Forest

Enter the park and you're on the Wayne Trail, which bisects the width of the forest. At the large crossroads, continue straight ahead, watching for wildflowers around you and noting the trees as well, as there are some large ones here, and continue listening, as so much of birdwatching is actually bird-hearing. Head straight over the hump and downhill to where the trail ends at a meadow and a fence. This forest-meadow edge gives you the possibility of seeing more birds.

▲ An ovenbird, a ground-nesting warbler, is one of the many birds found in Carpenter's Woods.

On my walk, for example, there was a notable warbler call with a sharp note at the end, almost an exclamation mark. Binoculars up, I found several American redstarts flitting among the trees along the meadow's edge—and the sun was in the right position to illuminate them. Nicknamed "flames of the forest," redstarts are striking, their black bodies sporting orange cutouts in wings and tail, an orange swoop where each wing meets its chest. This species is just one of many migrating warblers you may see here.

After watching the meadow, head right (north) up the Moffett Trail, where large tuliptrees and oaks abut the trail in many locations and wild geraniums and skunk cabbage grow along the forest floor. As the Spring Trail heads off and uphill on the right, stay straight. The Moffett Trail soon ends in a Y; take the right fork up the Greene Street Trail to its namesake street—along this path are some of the largest tuliptrees of them all, themselves worth seeing.

At Greene Street, turn back around, retrace your steps, and head left along the Spring Trail, looping back in the direction you came, but making a right at Jada's Trail and another right at Ellet Trail, which brings you back to the intersection of the Wayne Trail. Turn left to head back to the entrance.

Or, if you'd like to keep searching a little longer, continue straight along the Ellet Trail, make a left on the Grove Trail, and loop back to the Wayne Trail, as the Grove Trail ends at the Wayne Avenue entrance as well.

Teacher! Teacher! Teacher!

On my May walk, I met another birder and asked her what she was looking at. "Black-and-white warblers," she answered. I glanced in the direction of her binoculars. Sure enough, a small bi-colored bird was walking around a tuliptree's trunk, the characteristic colors and walk of this warbler. (On your own walk, don't hesitate to ask birders what they are seeing.) That day I also heard several ovenbirds, a ground-nesting warbler with an insistent "teacher! teacher! teacher!" call.

For extra credit, continue birding along the thumb-shaped extension of the park wrapped by Mt. Pleasant Road. This edge offers more sparrows, woodpeckers, wrens, and, if you're lucky, a hawk or vulture.

Saving the Woods

Carpenter's Woods seems to interrupt Wayne Avenue. The city's original plans would have had that road cut through the site, with its stream buried underground and Mt. Pleasant Road built over the stream, obliterating this area. But the City Parks Association wisely advocated for the preservation of streams like this across the city, and Carpenter's Woods was successfully saved in 1912.

The site's name recalls when the forest was part of the vast estate of George Carpenter, who owned 500 acres here by the mid-1800s. He met acclaimed naturalist Thomas Nuttall, became passionate about nature, and built a natural history museum on his Germantown estate, one visited by Audubon himself.

In the early 1920s, Caroline Moffett, principal of nearby Henry School for more than 30 years, worked with her students to have the woods declared a bird sanctuary. For many years her students staged an annual bird pageant in the forest, the students dressed in elaborate bird costumes, which the parents gathered to watch. The trail you walked honors her.

Today, Carpenter's Woods is one of the region's most beloved birding stops, a necessary trip in Wild Philly.

TRIP 5 — PHILADELPHIA, PA

John Heinz National Wildlife Refuge at Tinicum

America's first urban wildlife refuge, this site preserves 1200 acres of the largest remaining freshwater tidal marsh in Pennsylvania. Its diversity of habitats attracts more birds than just about any other site in Wild Philly, plus mammals, reptiles, amphibians, fish, insects, and more. Several endangered species call the refuge home as well.

MAP KEY

- suggested trail
- add'l trails
- street road
- parking Ⓟ

LINDBERG BLVD.

DARBY CREEK

Visitor Center

BIG BOARDWALK LOOP TRAIL

WOOD WARBLERS

OSPREY

observation tower

WETLAND

Tinicum Marsh boardwalk

PAINTED TURTLE

TIDAL MARSH

trails continue

RED-WINGED BLACKBIRD

COMMON CATTAIL

WETLAND LOOP TRAIL

95

It was like a scene from a movie. Yellow irises lined the water in front of me. A pair of great egrets were hunting, stalking fish in ankle-deep water, with a green heron frozen in its Zen stance, ready to stab a fish. A pair of mute swans swam further back, their cygnets splashing like toddlers in a kiddie pool. Above all of this, two ospreys soared overhead. Then I turned around, and—whoa!—a bald eagle was cruising by. All around me, cottonwood seeds were drifting down like snowfall, lending the scene the look of a Hallmark Christmas special. It was breathtaking, but it was just a typical May morning at Tinicum.

One of the region's most beloved natural areas, Tinicum is also one of the most used. On my walk, I was accompanied by bikers, runners, families out for a Sunday stroll, lovers holding hands, and anglers looking for a good catch. And birders, of course, many with some of the largest cameras and scopes you'll ever see. Most are there to catch warblers before they slide through the too-short migration window and are gone. Make sure to take advantage of these birders' eyes and expertise.

With 1200 acres of greenspace, the John Heinz National Wildlife Refuge is an emerald beacon calling migrating birds out of the Atlantic Flyway, a major pathway up the coast for migratory birds coming from Central and South America. This area is a necessary stopover for not just warblers, but thrushes, vireos, swallows, ducks, geese, and so many shorebirds, and its forest is home to the full complement of woodland birds.

Tinicum: Islands of the Marsh

As you walk, consider the historic importance of this site. Once a smaller portion of a vast 6000-acre marsh complex where the Schuylkill and Delaware Rivers met, Tinicum preserves its original Lenape name, Tennakon Minquas, or "islands of the marsh." This marshland was very important to the Lenape, who depended on its natural bounty for everything from wild rice and cattails to beaver pelts. This vast expanse also hid the mouth of the Schuylkill, which seventeenth-century Dutch trappers, legend

WHERE: 8601 Lindbergh Boulevard, Philadelphia, PA 19153

ADMISSION: Free; open daily from dawn to dusk.

PARKING: There is plenty of parking in the visitor parking lot.

DIFFICULTY, DISTANCE, ACCESS: The refuge boasts 10 miles of flat and easily walkable trails on solid ground, allowing you to pick the length of your walk. While there is a paved nature trail, the site's trails are generally well-compacted and perfect for bikes, strollers, and wheelchairs, though getting on and off some of the boardwalks may be challenging for the latter.

FACILITIES: The site includes a Visitor Center with restrooms, exhibits, gift shop, and more, with composting toilets strategically located throughout the refuge.

BEST TIME: Throughout April and May, many migrating birds, especially warblers, are readily found at the refuge, especially in its Warbler Woods. But with nesting bald eagles, soaring ospreys, herons and egrets silently stalking their prey, and turtles piled atop each other, there is just no bad time to walk here.

SPECIAL NOTES: Lots of dog walkers are here, but people seem good with leash requirements.

The refuge is a 1-mile walk from SEPTA's Eastwick train station.

▲ A broad trail at the popular John Heinz National Wildlife Refuge.

says, couldn't find. In their frustration, they named it "hidden river," the translation of Schuylkill.

Those early colonists, however, misunderstanding the ecological necessity of marshes began immediately draining and filling them to provide farmland. As the Philadelphia region grew, the marshes quickly shrank. By the 1950s, the marsh complex had dwindled to only 200 acres, a mere shadow of its former self.

You *Can* Fight City Hall

In 1953, birders fought to save the site from being used for dumping dredge spoils from a Schuylkill River project. The Delaware Valley Ornithological Club won, and the city set aside the 145-acre Tinicum Wildlife Preserve. In 1969, Tinicum was again threatened, as I-95 was to be routed through the marsh, with a landfill burying another portion. Committed conservationists fought yet again, remarkably won again, and in 1972 Congress set the land aside as a national wildlife refuge. In 1991, Tinicum was renamed in honor of Senator John Heinz, who had just perished in a tragic plane accident. Today, the site has actually grown to 1200 acres, which is almost a miracle. While Tinicum is important ecologically as the remnant of a once-vast marsh complex, it is also important as a birthplace of the environmental movement in Philadelphia.

A Birder's Paradise

Depending on how ambitious you feel, arrive as early in the morning as you'd like. In April and May serious birders park outside the gate at dawn and walk in if it isn't yet open. When I arrived at 8:30, the lot was almost completely full.

From the parking lot, head to the Visitor Center (if it is open) to get oriented. As you walk toward the main trail, turn left and head into Warbler Woods, joining the throng of birders in search of the remarkable jewels found flying there. On my walk, a prothonotary warbler greeted me even before I got to Warbler Woods, such a rare and welcoming yellow sight. In the woods, I got a great view of a yellow-rumped warbler and found a black-throated blue warbler, with my favorite blue. Black-and-white, yellow, and blackpoll warblers—this last one making one of the longest journeys of any songbird—rounded out the ones I saw, though other birders in the woods had seen many more.

After Warbler Woods, you've got a decision to make. I elected to do the full Wetland Loop Trail, so by morning's end I had walked 4 miles in 4 hours, saw forty species of birds, and scored more than 10,000 steps. You don't have to be as ambitious.

Instead, you can check out the Big Boardwalk Loop Trail, which cuts across the emergent wetland, where you'll be immersed in red-winged blackbirds and tree swallows. That boardwalk also gets you close to basking turtles, where you can test yourself to see if you can tease out the very common painted turtle, the endangered red-bellied turtle, and the invasive red-eared slider from each other. All three may be piled along the same log, and interpretive signage is there to guide you.

Whichever direction you walk, I highly recommend you include the Tinicum Marsh Boardwalk, which juts out into this preserved tidal marsh and gives you a 180-degree view, a remarkable glimpse of what the wetland complex might have been like back in the day.

In mid-May bald eagles nest on what they now call Eagle Island not far from the boardwalk. Keep your eyes peeled for one of them cruising overhead. The beavers are also active on that side of the refuge as well, so you have many reasons to get to that corner. Another reason to come in mid-May is that swans, Canada geese, and wood ducks all have babies with them, and I saw killdeer nesting on the mud flats near Eagle Island.

As I was leaving, one of the last birds I heard singing was a yellow warbler. "Sweet, sweet, sweet, it's so sweet," he sang. He's right. It was.

▾ A series of overlooks on the boardwalk allow visitors to see the refuge's emergent wetland up close.

▲ One of the refuge's many red-winged blackbirds sings from its perch.

TRIP 6 BALA CYNWYD & PHILADELPHIA, PA

Peregrines over Manayunk

Walk over the Schuylkill River's first pedestrian-only bridge in the second week of June and you'll be able watch peregrine fledglings learn how to fly from their parents. You'll also be immersed in Philadelphia's early Industrial Era history.

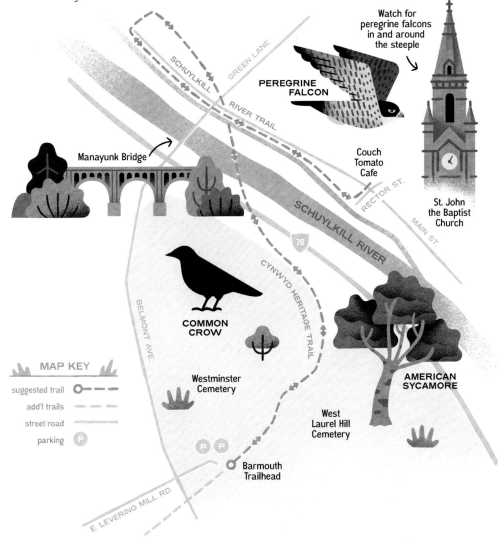

Watch for peregrine falcons in and around the steeple

PEREGRINE FALCON

SCHUYLKILL

GREEN LANE

RIVER TRAIL

Manayunk Bridge

Couch Tomato Cafe

RECTOR ST.

St. John the Baptist Church

SCHUYLKILL RIVER

MAIN ST

76

CYNWYD HERITAGE TRAIL

COMMON CROW

BELMONT AVE.

Westminster Cemetery

AMERICAN SYCAMORE

West Laurel Hill Cemetery

MAP KEY

suggested trail   O‑‑‑‑‑

add'l trails   ‑‑‑‑‑

street/road

parking   P

P   P

Barmouth Trailhead

E. LEVERING MILL RD.

255

WHERE: Cynwyd Heritage Trail's Barmouth Trailhead, bottom of E. Levering Mill Road, Bala Cynwyd, PA 19004

ADMISSION: Free; open daily from dawn to dusk.

PARKING: There is a modest amount of parking in the trailhead's small parking lot.

DIFFICULTY, DISTANCE, ACCESS: This walk is almost 4 miles round trip, with lots of chances for resting and observing. The Cynwyd Heritage Trail portion is flat and has a good asphalt surface, and even the parallel gravel trail is compact. But accessibility into Manayunk and the St. John the Baptist Church steeple along the towpath and surface roads is problematic.

FACILITIES: None.

BEST TIME: While the peregrines are nesting at the St. John the Baptist Church steeple from April into late May, the best time to visit is in early June when that year's fledglings are leaving the nest and learning to fly.

SPECIAL NOTES: The Cynwyd Heritage Trail, the starting place of this walk, begins at the Cynwyd Station, the terminus of SEPTA's Cynwyd Line. Service was suspended in April 2020, and it is unclear if and when service will return.

For the last decade, the once-endangered peregrine falcon, the world's fastest animal, has been nesting inside the top of the St. John the Baptist Church steeple in the Manayunk neighborhood of Philadelphia. Birdwatchers gather at the foot of the steeple and nearby to check up on the raptors, their mating, and their young. There's even a wonderful tradition of birders gathering during the second week of June at Couch Tomato Cafe, the pizzeria on Rector Street, to watch the fledglings learn to fly.

This walk takes advantage of the peregrines, but kicks it up a notch. Since 2015, the Manayunk Bridge, that classic arched bridge that soars over Main Street and is the neighborhood's symbol, has been open to walkers, runners, and bikers, affording you not only unique views of the peregrines, but of the Schuylkill River, and, of course, the expressway that took the river's name.

My recommended trip is to walk the Cynwyd Heritage Trail, the rail trail carved out of the bed of the old Pennsylvania Railroad tracks (now known as SEPTA's Cynwyd Line). This extraordinary multi-use trail is widely loved by locals but deserving to be known by everyone. The trail connects to the Manayunk Bridge and crosses the Schuylkill River, where you can walk onto the Manayunk Canal Towpath, another popular walking trail, which brings you to Rector Street and the peregrines. It's 4 miles round trip. Do any portion you wish, or simply walk the towpath to the peregrines. But don't miss the Manayunk Bridge.

Cynwyd Heritage Trail

Park at the bottom of E. Levering Mill Road in the Cynwyd Heritage Trail's parking lot. You're at the Barmouth Trailhead, named for the old railroad stop from long ago, and in front of you is West Laurel Hill Cemetery, a Victorian landmark. You'll head left, toward the Schuylkill River and Manayunk. The trail gives you options of asphalt or gravel, and one spur wanders off to the left to parallel an old stream and then comes back to the main branch. So, make your best Robert Frost decision here.

While you are not in wilderness or even a forest, I'm always happily surprised at the numbers and kinds of birds I see and hear here, including bright orange orioles. About a half mile down the trail, look for historic

▲ The Manayunk Bridge, now a pedestrian-only bridge, crosses both The Schuylkill River and the expressway while affording unique views of Manayunk and peregrines.

markers noting Clegg's Mill, one of many mills in and around this stretch of the Schuylkill River. This site, reclaimed by nature—a recurring theme in this book—was once the heart of a highly industrialized landscape churning out lumber, cotton, and flour for the growing city.

Eagle's Eye View of the Schuylkill

As you round a curve, you'll see the Manayunk skyline—St. John's is the tallest gray stone steeple in the neighborhood. As you walk onto the bridge, check out the Schuylkill River. On one walk, a Canada goose flew from the river, up and over the bridge, and dove down the other side, coming within only a few feet of startled walkers. But you rarely get a vista of the river quite as high and quite as close as this. Enjoy it.

The Cynwyd Heritage Trail ends on High Street in Manayunk. Head straight ahead on High Street, walking downhill until the street dead-ends onto Leverington Street, and turn left. Remember that you parked on East Levering Mill Road in Bala Cynwyd? The Levering clan was a huge and successful milling family, owning extensive properties and several mills and businesses on both sides of the river. "Leverington," of course, is shorthand for "Levering Town," the original name of this section of Roxborough-Manayunk.

Cross Main Street in front of a brick building on the corner, and, just past the brick building, head down through some bollards onto the Manayunk Canal Towpath, which here doubles as the Schuylkill River Trail. Turn left on the towpath, and head underneath the Green Lane bridge. On your right is Venice Island, with the river beyond the island. This island and the surrounding land was once chock-a-block with water-powered mills like Levering's.

As you walk the towpath, watch for turtles. Every branch or log sticking out of the water typically has multiple turtles basking on it.

The Peregrines

You'll soon be in the center of Manayunk, where the trail parallels Main Street; you'll be passing the rear facades of many of Manayunk's storied restaurants. Leave the towpath trail by turning left on Rector Street, then cross Main Street and walk to the Couch Tomato Cafe. Are birdwatchers there?

If you have binoculars, look at the tallest windows high up the steeple, the ones facing the Schuylkill River. Notice a whitewash of guano cascading down the steeple's stone, clear evidence that birds are nesting there. If you're lucky, you'll see a parent or a fledgling sitting on the ledge, on one of the finials, or even atop the gold cross.

Peregrines are loyal lifelong mates, returning to the same site year after year. In the last decade, some fifteen young peregrines have left this steeple to set up their own nests elsewhere. The original peregrine female who established this nest is still here. After her mate died in 2019, she successfully attracted a new one and the nest continued.

▲ The peregrine mother high on the St. John the Baptist Church steeple while one of her fledglings carefully approaches the ledge.

The peregrines return to the steeple in late December. In March, they mate repeatedly atop the church roof or on nearby structures, and soon thereafter she disappears into the steeple window to lay her eggs. In late May and early June, the fledglings appear at the window and on the ledge. "They start flapping their wings like crazy while they are on the ledge outside the nest box," Judy Stepenaskie, a Roxborough resident who avidly watches and photographs the birds, has observed. "Finally, they can flap enough to take little hops along the ledge. Then they take the leap with their first flight. For the next week or so, they take little flights, struggling with the landings."

To teach them how to hunt, the parents first bring pieces of meat to the young. Then the parents demonstrate dropping and catching food, with the young observing the parents. Finally, they drop food for the young to pursue. These first flights are the most nerve wracking.

Enjoy the peregrines, talk to other birders, take advantage of Manayunk, and walk back to your car the way you came.

TRIP 7 PHILADELPHIA, PA

Bartram's Garden

Nestled between the Schuylkill River and the Kingsessing neighborhood, Bartram's Garden preserves rare and unusual botanical specimens, like the Franklin tree and North America's oldest ginkgo tree. Its river walk reminds us that the Schuylkill, like its larger cousin the Delaware, is a tidal river. The site's wonderful meadow caps off the experience.

public dock & community boathouse

HARLEY AVE.

Welcome Center

gingko

urban meadow

COMMON MILKWEED

RIVER TRAIL

historic house

yellowwood

JEWELWEED

SCHUYLKILL RIVER

Franklin tree

boardwalk

COTTONTAIL RABBIT

cider press

PAWPAW

notched rock

MAP KEY

suggested trail

add'l trails

street/road

parking

259

WHERE: 5400 Lindbergh Blvd., Philadelphia, PA 19143

ADMISSION: Free; open daily from dawn until dusk; the Welcome Center and public restrooms are open daily from 9:00 a.m. to 4:00 p.m.

PARKING: Free parking is available along the oval at the end of the driveway; on special large-event weekends there is a $5 parking fee.

DIFFICULTY, DISTANCE, ACCESS: The recommended walk is only two-thirds of a mile, so it should be easy for anyone. While the Bartram house area is easily accessible on paved trails, as is much of the garden, the walk along the river is not ADA-accessible. The Bartram's Mile, a slice of the Schuylkill River Trail, is fully paved and easily accessible to all.

FACILITIES: The Welcome Center has water and restrooms, and its gift shop has snacks and cold drinks available.

BEST TIME: June allows you to see the Franklin tree in flower, a rare treat. Spring into summer gives you the parade of flowers blooming in the gardens, and summer into fall gives you the full meadow experience.

SPECIAL NOTES: Leashed dogs are allowed on the trails outside of the historic home area.

To reach the garden by mass transit, take SEPTA's Trolley 36, which stops at the Bartram's Garden driveway at 54th Street and Lindbergh Boulevard.

This walk is wonderful for anyone interested in the history of Philadelphia, as the Bartram story (detailed earlier) is central in the city's role as a hotbed of science and nature. While this is one of the easier walks in terms of terrain and distance, the walk packs so much into its two-thirds of a mile, and there are many ways you can expand the experience.

Begin at the Welcome Center, where you'll get your map and orientation. Make sure to ask what's in bloom during the time you are visiting. After reading the interpretive signage placed in the center's courtyard, use your map to navigate the complex of buildings.

John Bartram, a self-taught naturalist and botanist, began building the house in 1728, working on it for the next 40 years. In America's first botanical garden, Bartram assembled what was then the country's most diverse collection of plants, many of which are—almost 300 years later—still on display. The collection was widely used as a reference by contemporaries like Washington and Jefferson, and Bartram sold and traded seeds across America and England.

Franklinia in Full Flower

After paying homage to the main house and nearby structures, I made a beeline for three trees in the garden: America's first and oldest ginkgo, planted in 1785; an aging yellowwood, another of the garden's oldest; and the garden's signature tree, the Franklin tree, a plant of great mystery.

John Bartram and his son William collected the Franklin tree, new to science, and named it *Franklinia* after their friend Ben. With a fragrant and showy white flower, they first discovered it on a Georgia collecting trip in 1765. William brought seeds back from a subsequent 1777 trip, and the plant then, weirdly, vanished in the wild. All existing *Franklinia* today—including those here—are descendants of these collected seeds.

If you visit the garden in June, you can be among the few who have seen *Franklinia* in bloom, as one cannot see this in the wild. Adding to the mystery, the tree blooms later than just about every other tree. Enjoy!

▲ The trails in the historic garden area envelop visitors in greenery.

◄ The rare *Franklinia* tree in bloom.

The garden also includes medicinal plants inspired by Lenape lore; a bog garden of carnivorous plants like Venus flytraps; a row of pawpaws, the North American tree with the largest fruit; and a collection of southern plants like bottlebrush buckeye and camellia. Wander the pathways in the garden, reading both the site's signage and map to inform your choices. A fish pond, recreated to resemble Bartram's, includes native aquatic flowering plants and some turtles. Substantial trees grace the garden, including massive tuliptrees and willow oaks. Take your time here.

The Tidal Schuylkill

When ready, head downhill to the Schuylkill River, turning to the right to find the beginning of the River Trail, one of the few trails you can walk that reminds us that the Schuylkill is a tidal river. Your first landmark on the walk is the notched rock, a large chunk of bedrock jutting from the river's edge that has been a prominent landmark for hundreds of years, a place to tie boats, and a boundary marker for land sales since seventeenth-century Swedish settlers.

Don't forget to look out at the river scenery itself. On one of my walks, a great blue heron flew by, Canada geese honked noisily, a red-tailed hawk was mobbed by red-winged blackbirds, and swallows cruised the river snatching flying insects. It was quite the tableau, all in the shadows of the oil refineries across the river; the juxtaposition between the two banks is jarring.

Walk upriver (left) to find the cider press carved into bedrock by John Bartram himself—it's pretty amazing, especially for younger visitors. Continue walking along the trail, enjoying the riverine forest of sweet and black gum, silver maple, river birch, and even bald cypress. Jewelweed lines the trail, a great antidote to the poison ivy growing nearby on trees.

The trail soon takes you to the community boathouse, where people gather to fish and kayak. Pause here for a few moments, and don't miss the new perspective on Center City's skyline.

A Restored Meadow

You'll quickly notice a large meadow on your left and uphill a 17-acre restoration on what was once a concrete factory. Great clumps of milkweed of several species, including the orange butterflyweed, attract many pollinators during late spring and early summer, including the increasingly endangered monarch—perhaps you will spy one. Black-eyed Susan, daisy fleabane, and vetch are also among the many wildflowers found here. The walk through the meadow is likely buggy—but remember that is a good and necessary thing. In fact, I did a long loop within the meadow to make sure I didn't miss any cool insects. As you walk up the meadow's grassy trail, you're back at the oval where, if you traveled by car, you likely parked.

Bartram's Garden anchors one end of the Schuylkill River Trail, which will soon extend from here all the way to Valley Forge and beyond. In addition, an unused railroad bridge upriver is being repurposed into a pedestrian connection to bring you to the River Trail's much-used Center City section on the opposite side of the river. Until it is finished, you can walk upriver and visit the bridge to chart its progress; downriver, in the opposite direction, you can walk the paved trail to a restored tidal wetland and, beyond that, a plaza that formally ends the Schuylkill River Trail.

Not far from Bartram's Garden is The Woodlands, the preserved historic home of William Hamilton, a Bartram contemporary who also collected plants; it was Hamilton who collected the first ginkgoes, sending one to Bartram. The Woodlands is also a historic cemetery where the likes of painter Thomas Eakins are interred. Consider checking that out as well.

▼ Bartram's meadow offers views of Center City's skyline.

TRIP 8 KING OF PRUSSIA, PA

Valley Forge National Historical Park

Valley Forge preserves not only an iconic historical site, but an important trout stream, Valley Creek. The site also has a surprisingly rich natural setting, including an oak forest on the flanks of Mount Misery ablaze in mountain laurel, the state flower.

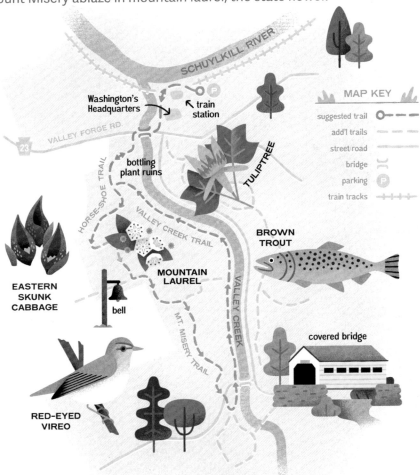

SCHUYLKILL RIVER

Washington's Headquarters

↖ train station

VALLEY FORGE RD.

bottling plant ruins

HORSE-SHOE TRAIL

VALLEY CREEK TRAIL

TULIPTREE

BROWN TROUT

MOUNTAIN LAUREL

VALLEY CREEK

MT. MISERY TRAIL

EASTERN SKUNK CABBAGE

bell

covered bridge

RED-EYED VIREO

MAP KEY

suggested trail
add'l trails
street/road
bridge
parking
train tracks

WHERE: Washington's Headquarters, Valley Forge National Historical Park, Route 23 and Valley Creek Road, King of Prussia, PA 19406

ADMISSION: Free; trails are open from dawn to dusk, but parking areas close within 2 hours of sunset.

PARKING: There is plenty of parking in the site's generous parking lot.

DIFFICULTY, DISTANCE, ACCESS: The recommended walk is a little more than 2.5 miles, but this can be shortened—or lengthened—as you wish. Washington's Headquarters area is wheelchair- and stroller-accessible, but the Mount Misery Trail is not, being moderately steep on rocky trails. The end of the walk along the Valley Creek Trail, however, is flat and easily walkable and this trail by itself is recommended.

FACILITIES: Valley Forge has a central Visitor Center with complete facilities and introductory exhibits; it is open daily from 9:00 a.m. to 5:00 p.m. and until 6:00 p.m. in the summer. There are additional public restrooms throughout the park, including at Washington's Headquarters.

BEST TIME: A walk in late May to early June gives you wonderful views of mountain laurel in bloom.

SPECIAL NOTES: Dogs are allowed but must be leashed. Bikes are allowed on the Valley Creek Trail, but not on the Mount Misery or Horse-Shoe Bend Trails.

SEPTA's Bus 125 stops at the Visitor Center, and free park shuttles take you to Washington's Headquarters.

While most Philadelphians have likely walked among Valley Forge's historical monuments, too few have enjoyed its natural history. The park boasts 26 miles of trails over 3500 acres, and this walk weaves together portions of several trails to experience a rarity in southeastern Pennsylvania—a forest with mountain laurel, the state flower, in full bloom.

Start at Washington's Headquarters off Route 23, and park in the lot provided. Check out the meadow surrounding the parking area, with its wildflowers attracting many pollinators. Walk past the restrooms toward the restored train station, noticing the old Reading Railroad tracks to your right and the Schuylkill River remarkably close below that. The railroad was built in 1911 to bring visitors to the park from the city, and the station today houses exhibits on Washington's Headquarters.

Walk down the stairs at the end of the platform to stand at Isaac Potts' 1770 home, used by General Washington during the winter of 1777–1778, when as many as 20,000 soldiers of the Continental Army camped throughout the area. The house also marks the edge of the small enclave of Valley Forge, a gathering of homes and mills on Valley Creek located at its junction with the Schuylkill and built around a nearby iron forge. The house faces Valley Creek and Potts' long-gone gristmill. Explore these buildings as you wish

Next, cross Route 23 and look for a bronze plaque marking the Horse-Shoe Trail, a well-used trail that starts here and continues almost to Harrisburg. Marked by yellow blazes, the trail travels along the sidewalk to the west, leaving the national park.

As you cross the stream on the Horse-Shoe Trail, peer down. In Washington's time, there would have been a dam here forming a large lake behind it and providing a reliable source of water for mills and forges. After you cross the stream, the trail turns left on the gravel Owen Road, and the yellow blaze can be followed on trees, backs of signs, and rocks.

▲ Mountain laurel, Pennsylvania's state flower, blooms profusely along the trail.

The Legend of Mount Misery

After a park kiosk, the Horse-Shoe Trail begins to climb Mount Misery, at 577 feet above sea level a fairly tall peak in southeastern Pennsylvania. Legend holds that it was named when a pair of settlers were lost here, fearing for their lives. The climb is good exercise.

Only one-tenth of a mile up the trail at an intersection, stay straight on what is both the Valley Creek Trail and the Horse-Shoe Trail (the dash appears on maps but it is confusingly dropped on park signs). Then, after you pass alongside a wet area, the Valley Creek Trail heads off to the left; continue walking uphill on the Horse-Shoe Trail. After another half-mile, look for an old broken stone dam in the stream, one hint of an old settlement in this area. Soon, along this heavily rubbled trail, watch for the haunting ruins of the Colonial Springs water bottling plant, ruins worth peeking into. Here, Civil War hero Benjamin Franklin Fisher, whose house was on the opposite side of the trail (a portion of a stone foundation is still evident), leased land to the Colonial Springs Company to bottle and sell the water. After his death, his heirs sold the site to Charles Elmer Hires of root beer fame; Hires never made soda here, but instead continued to sell bottled water under the Purock label.

After the ruin, the trail makes a hard left and continues uphill on Mount Misery. You are suddenly in a completely different forest, one dominated by oaks of many kinds, a shrub layer of mountain laurel, and the forest floor covered in ferns. It is a beautiful stretch of forest.

If you are visiting in May or June, the mountain laurel will be in bloom. Found on mountainsides like this, mountain laurel possesses evergreen leaves on twisty trunks. But the light pink or white flowers are extraordinary, hexagonal in shape (itself unusual), with spring-loaded stamens bent back and held in tension by the petals—see if you can observe this. When an insect lands on a flower, that tension is released, and pollen is catapulted forcefully onto the insect, each one a little Emeril yelling "bam!" as it covers a bug in pollen.

Come to a place where the Horse-Shoe Trail makes a hard right and continues its journey west. While you're heading straight ahead, look for—and feel free to ring— the bell thoughtfully provided by the trail's volunteer caretakers, the Horse-Shoe Trail Conservancy.

Here you'll switch to the white-blazed Mount Misery Trail through the oak-mountain laurel forest, and come to a covered bridge and great views of Valley Creek.

▲ The Valley Creek Trail includes a historic dam that once powered the creek's mills, which once included the forge, located near this dam.

A Tale of Two Knoxes

As you come downhill off Mount Misery, the forest opens up and invasive plants take over: multiflora rose, wineberry, and Japanese stiltgrass. Emerge back into civilization and Yellow Springs Road. Cross the road, turn left on the sidewalk, and walk toward the covered bridge.

Called the Knox Bridge, it is likely named for Senator Philander C. Knox, Teddy Roosevelt's attorney general and Pennsylvania senator, who lived on a large property on the western side of the bridge. But others assume it is named for General Henry Knox, who directed Valley Forge's artillery, became the first U.S. Secretary of War, and for whom Fort Knox was named. Incredibly, he lived in a farmhouse east of the bridge. Two famous Knoxes lived alongside this bridge in different eras on bookending properties.

Cross the road at the bridge, and dip into the trail alongside the creek. This is Valley Creek, famous among freshwater anglers and designated an "exceptional value" stream, the Department of Environmental Protection's highest level. It's also a Class A wild trout fishery, as a self-sustaining population of brown trout lives here. Valley Creek slices between two hills, the Mount Misery you just walked, and Mount Joy across the stream. The legend holds that those same lost settlers who experienced misery one day climbed the next hill in the morning to find their encampment below and dubbed that one "Joy."

As you walk the Valley Creek Trail, notice jewelweed and Christmas fern lining the trail on your left, tuliptrees guarding the stream on your right. Listen for birds; many can be found here.

You'll also find an old mill dam here as well. The old iron forge—the Valley Forge—was once here. A highly industrial region during the Revolution, Mount Misery has changed, evolving into a delightful oak forest covering the hillside above a stream of exceptional quality, which gives us great joy.

TRIP 9 PALMYRA, NJ

Palmyra Cove Nature Park

A remnant of the tidal wetlands that once flanked the Delaware River, Palmyra Cove Nature Park is a 250-acre oasis of green in urbanized New Jersey. While its unique walk along the Delaware shoreline at low tide is draw enough, the site also includes a tidal cove, home to beavers, herons, and minks, among others.

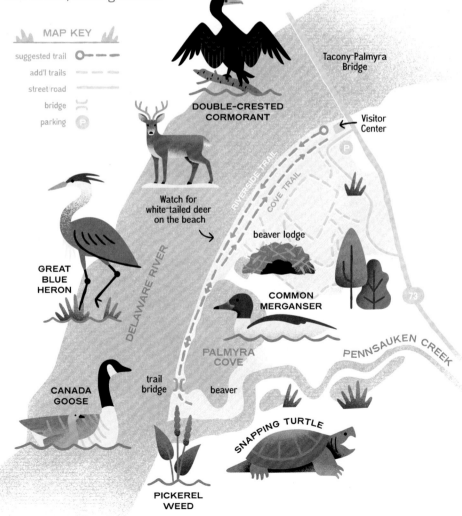

MAP KEY

suggested trail ⊙- - -
add'l trails - - - -
street/road - - - -
bridge ⌣⌣
parking Ⓟ

DOUBLE-CRESTED CORMORANT

Tacony-Palmyra Bridge

← Visitor Center

RIVERSIDE TRAIL

COVE TRAIL

Watch for white-tailed deer on the beach

beaver lodge

GREAT BLUE HERON

DELAWARE RIVER

COMMON MERGANSER

73

PALMYRA COVE

PENNSAUKEN CREEK

CANADA GOOSE

trail bridge

beaver

SNAPPING TURTLE

PICKEREL WEED

WHERE: 1335 Route 73 South, Palmyra, NJ 08065

ADMISSION: Free; open from dawn to dusk.

PARKING: There is plenty of parking in the site's generous parking lot.

DIFFICULTY, DISTANCE, ACCESS: The recommended walk is 3 miles, but this can be altered as you wish. While the Cove Trail and many others on the site are easily walkable and flat, with a surface compact enough for strollers and wheelchairs, the recommended walk along the riverfront on shifting sands is not friendly to either. The Cove Trail, however, is highly recommended.

FACILITIES: Its visitor center, the Institute for Earth Observations, has restrooms, picnic tables, and benches. It is open daily from 9:00 a.m. to 4:00 p.m. (except on major holidays) and opens at 10:00 a.m. on weekends.

BEST TIME: While any time of year is great, go at low tide, which allows you to walk the Riverside Trail, essentially its beach. In early spring, migrating birds can be found along the park's stretch of river and land. In late spring, many species of birds are nesting there as well, establishing territories and singing. In summer, its expanse of pickerel weed is in full bloom.

SPECIAL NOTES: No dogs or bikes are allowed here.

New Jersey Transit Bus 419 stops at Market and Broad Streets in Palmyra. Walk 1 mile north on Market Street, heading toward the river, and look for Temple Boulevard coming in on your right. Where they meet, look for a service road to the right of Temple Boulevard, which goes under the bridge and to the Visitor Center's front door.

Three hundred years ago, a vast expanse of tidal wetlands lined the Delaware River, forming a critical habitat for a diverse array of creatures, including plants, invertebrates, fish, amphibians, birds, and mammals, many not found elsewhere. Here's where cattails thrived, minks and otters swam, beavers built lodges, and ospreys and bald eagles nested. These habitats were also the sponges that soaked up excessive stormwater in large flooding events.

But as Philadelphia and its suburbs developed, this wildly underappreciated habitat was among the first to disappear, filled in with dredge spoils as the river was widened and deepened for navigation. It's this habitat we will especially miss when climate change fuels a rising river and causes increasingly intense storms. We'll want the wetland's ability to mop up these messes.

Which makes the Palmyra Cove Nature Park even more special. Here you find Canada geese nesting on the shoreline, with ducks, cormorants, and mergansers in the river and red-winged blackbirds in the cove. Beavers have built lodges in multiple sites, while herons and egrets quietly stalk their prey. Frogs and turtles abound. Peregrine falcons nest on this bridge as well (the center's website has a live nesting cam).

Gritty Wild Philly

And like its twin across the river, Pennypack on the Delaware Park, Palmyra Cove encapsulates so much of gritty Wild Philly. Starting just below the Tacony-Palmyra Bridge, the site is built on dredge spoils, with pipes for dredging still jutting into the Delaware, and its beaver pond was once a sand mine. A landfill is the site's next-door neighbor, and it's bordered by busy Route 73. To its east is the densely settled town of Palmyra and to its south the equally dense Pennsauken.

To get the tidal Delaware experience, come here at low tide, which exposes a sandy beach along the river. Look for the scenic overlook platform to the left of the Visitor Center and

▲ As the Delaware River reaches low tide at Palmyra Cove, a sandy beach is exposed.

admire the view. To its left, find a handwritten sign that points you to the Riverside Trail, which is only available at low tide. Walk to the beach, and head southwest toward Center City.

You'll easily notice the high-tide line, marked by an astonishing array of natural and artificial debris, from stems of dead reeds to every fast-food wrapper known. Look for the several species of freshwater clam and mussel shells that wash ashore as well; freshwater mollusks are among the most endangered species of all.

In the sand, look for deer and goose tracks. Find the long row of silver maples that line the beach, handsome trees with deeply lobed leaves with silvery undersides. Some of them have been undercut by the tides and are in varying states of toppling—several are defiantly lying on their sides and doggedly sending up sprouts, not giving up.

Animals Galore

On one June early-morning walk, I passed numerous groups of nesting Canada geese, many with goslings. Some of the geese stayed on the beach as I tiptoed behind them. In addition, at least three deer were separately walking along on the beach—deer on a beach is an unexpected treat.

Cormorants and mergansers were swimming and diving for fish, while above them swallows strafed the river for emerging insects. Further along, a dead and eviscerated muskrat met its end on the beach—and I even found two locations where raccoons had dug up turtle nests to eat the eggs, shriveled eggshells and raccoon droppings telling this story.

After 1 mile, you'll come to where the Riverside Trail and its parallel inland cousin, the Cove Trail, meet. Here a walking bridge overlooks Palmyra Cove, a tidal wetlands with an expanse of aquatic plants like pickerel weed and pond lily. Head onto the bridge, looking for the beaver lodge across the cove, its dome poking through the marsh plants.

▲ Palmyra Cove is a wildlife-rich tidal wetland.

If you have time, the Cove Trail continues on the other side of the bridge, turning left, and including two scenic overlooks, the second much closer to the beaver lodge. In either event, the Cove Trail ends here. Simply retrace your steps, but this time staying right after the bridge to take the Cove Trail back; there is a third scenic overlook here, my favorite. Halfway back, look for the intersection with the Perimeter Trail—turn right on this trail to visit the Beaver Pond, which was the old sand mine.

Nature has an extraordinary capacity for healing and survival. As I left, a painted turtle was rummaging through a pollinator garden planted by volunteers in the park's entrance driveway, likely scoping out nesting sites. I crossed my fingers that those raccoons won't find this nest.

TRIP 10 · PHILADELPHIA, PA

Pennypack on the Delaware Park

A remnant of the tidal wetlands that once flanked the Delaware River, Pennypack on the Delaware has amazing biodiversity across its 65 acres. This park in the Holmesburg neighborhood is home to ducks, cormorants, eagles, nesting songbirds, butterflies in the milkweed patch, and, at dusk or dawn, beavers.

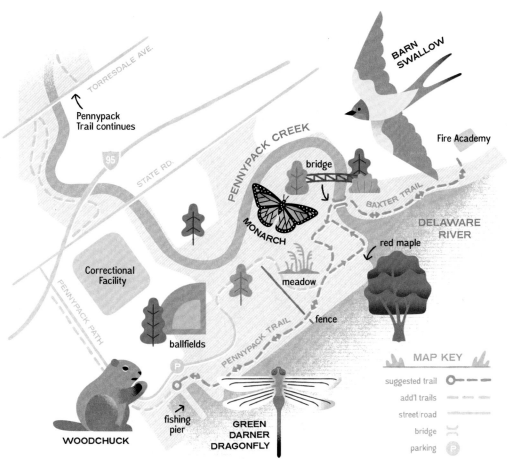

MAP KEY

suggested trail	○‑ ‑ ‑
add'l trails	‑ ‑ ‑
street/road	───
bridge	⋈
parking	P

Pennypack on the Delaware Park, just like its sister greenspace across the water, Palmyra Cove Nature Park, is an oasis of nature shoehorned into an urban streetscape. Tucked between a correctional facility and the Fire Academy, bordered by two shooting ranges, not far from a sewage treatment plant, and with the hum of I-95 always in your ear, a surprising diversity of wildlife awaits you, not to mention great vistas into the Delaware River.

And like Palmyra Cove, Pennypack on the Delaware preserves another remnant of the vast tidal wetlands that once lined the mighty Delaware. Our walk starts on the Pennypack Trail, an important section of the regional Circuit Trail network, and connects to Pennypack Park (Trip 20) and ultimately the Pennypack Ecological Restoration Trust (Trip 17). Those sites are upstream and behind you; for now, we're heading along the Delaware River.

▲ Pennypack on the Delaware Park is home to many shorebirds, like cormorants, herons, and egrets.

Scan the River

But first, I typically head right to the river, making a beeline to the grass-covered, well-used fishing pier found at the beginning of the park. I always scan the river for interesting birds, hoping a bald eagle makes an appearance. If it's low tide, I scan the banks with my binoculars for shorebirds that might be probing the mud with their beaks.

Then simply walk upriver on the Pennypack Trail, keeping eyes and ears peeled for interesting sights and sounds. On one walk in early June, as I rounded a bend, a yellow-shafted flicker—a gorgeous member of the woodpecker clan—was sitting in the trail on the asphalt, likely sunning itself to burn off parasites like lice, while a woodchuck ambled along right behind it. Warbling vireos, nondescript gray birds with beautiful throaty songs, accompanied me for a long stretch. A red-shouldered hawk soared overhead, being chased by an indignant kingbird. A large number of uncommon birds—Baltimore orioles, red-winged blackbirds, fish crows, common yellow-throats, and indigo buntings—sang along the walk as well.

After a half-mile, the trail enters a chain-link-fenced area with a gate that carries an interesting contrast in signs. "Important Bird Area," proclaims one from National Audubon, juxtaposed with its neighbor, "Warning: Live Gunfire Area Ahead." There are two shooting ranges along this stretch, but both are well hidden by berms and thick fencing. You're safe.

Immediately inside the fence, veer right onto a dirt trail that hugs the river, affording you wonderful views of the Delaware and more possible sightings of ducks, geese, cormorants, and even herons and egrets.

Pennypack Creek

The dirt trail soon jogs left where Pennypack Creek, an important stream that drains so much of Northeast Philly, meets the Delaware River, forming a small inlet. Follow the curve and you'll pop out onto the edge of a large milkweed field, where on that same June walk I delighted in spotting that year's

FIELD TRIP 10

WHERE: 7801 State Road, Philadelphia, PA 19136

ADMISSION: Free; open daily from dawn to dusk.

PARKING: There is plenty of parking in the site's long stretch of parking lots.

DIFFICULTY, DISTANCE, ACCESS: The recommended walk is 3 miles, but this can be adjusted as you wish. An easily walkable trail that makes a large loop, those with strollers or wheelchairs can stay on the ADA-accessible paved trail, which is level the whole way. Others can veer off to a gravel trail closer to the river.

FACILITIES: There are no restrooms, but plenty of picnic tables, pavilions, and park benches with great river views.

BEST TIME: While any time of year is great, always go at low tide, as that is when you might see elusive shorebirds not easily spotted elsewhere in the city. In early spring, migrating birds can be found along the park's stretch of river and land. In late spring, many species of birds are nesting there as well, establishing territories and singing.

SPECIAL NOTES: SEPTA's West Trenton Line stops at the Holmesburg Junction on Rhawn Street, an easy walk on Pennypack Path. SEPTA Buses 84 and 70 stop at the Curran-Fromhold Correctional Facility adjoining the park.

first monarch butterflies, those stunning orange-and-black migrators. Turning right, the trail enters the forest and quickly jogs left again. At this sharp turn, look right: the tree closest to the river's edge is a huge multi-stemmed red maple, among the largest of that species I've seen in Philadelphia.

Soon the dirt trail reunites with the asphalt one and continues following the creek, coming to a footbridge. On the far side of the bridge, look down to the right, the river's side of the bridge. There is an old beaver lodge right below the bridge, the beaver-chewed sticks unmistakable but not looking fresh. Beavers are crepuscular animals, so you've got to be here near dawn or dusk to see if the lodge is still active.

The bridge is where Pennypack Trail ends and Baxter Trail begins. If you turn back now and head back to the parking lot, you'll have walked a full 2 miles. But I like to follow the Baxter Trail for a bit and come to the Fire Academy, where new firefighters hone their skills; the brick tower they set aflame has barn swallows darting in and out of the structure. The Baxter Trail ends at Pennypack Street at the entrance of the academy.

Here's where the walk ends, and you turn around and head back to the starting point. This adds a mile to the walk, giving you a 3-mile hike for the day, not to mention tons of nature—and the rare vision of a tidal Delaware.

TRIP 11 `COATESVILLE, PA`

ChesLen Preserve

At almost 1300 acres, the sweeping ChesLen Preserve offers forests, meadows, wetlands, great trails, classic Chester County farmland vistas, a children's play area, and even a bit of history connected to the Mason-Dixon line. But it also preserves one of the rarest habitats in Wild Philly: a serpentine barrens, with unusual and endangered plants.

WHERE: Lenfest Center, 1199 Cannery Road, Coatesville, PA 19320

ADMISSION: Free; open dawn to dusk on Fridays through Wednesdays, closed on Thursdays.

PARKING: There is plenty of parking at the Lenfest Center's generous lots.

DIFFICULTY, DISTANCE, ACCESS: The recommended walk is relatively flat and 1.75 miles, but can be easily combined with other hikes elsewhere on the preserve. The trails are not ADA-accessible.

FACILITIES: The preserve operates the Lenfest Center, located about a mile from this walk, which offers occasional programming and includes restrooms that are open daily from dawn to dusk.

BEST TIME: While any time of year is great, a July walk gives you abundant wildflowers in full bloom in the barrens.

SPECIAL NOTES: Dogs are allowed, but they must be leashed. Bikes are not welcome on the trails.

Located deep in Chester County, the preserve is not easily accessible by mass transit.

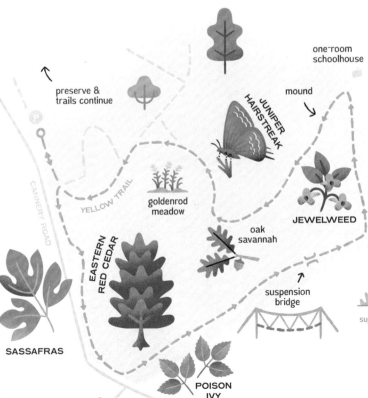

one-room schoolhouse

preserve & trails continue

mound

JUNIPER HAIRSTREAK

YELLOW TRAIL

goldenrod meadow

JEWELWEED

CANNERY ROAD

EASTERN RED CEDAR

oak savannah

SASSAFRAS

suspension bridge

POISON IVY

KELSALL ROAD

MAP KEY

suggested trail ⊙– – –
add'l trails – – –
street road ——
bridge)(
parking ℗

In the geology of Wild Philly, serpentine, a soft and greenish rock named for its serpent-like color, is an ancient but common rock. It is among the oldest rocks in the region, threading through the Wissahickon Valley, among other places. But at a number of sites along the Pennsylvania-Maryland border, broad serpentine outcrops lie at or near the surface. Rich in metals, serpentine creates thin soils dubbed "serpentine barrens," as they are bad for farming. No wonder: the rocks leach high concentrations of iron, chromium, nickel, and cobalt, all toxic to many plant species, and serpentine soils have low amounts of calcium, nitrogen, phosphorus, and potassium. Together, this is a farmer's nightmare.

Happily, however, a number of rare and unusual wildflowers have evolved to grow in these habitats, unique plants not found elsewhere. There are also several species of insects that rely on these specially adapted plants, so serpentine barrens is a rare habitat supporting unusual species. Please do not disturb any plants, animals, or rock here at the preserve.

ChesLen Preserve, owned by the nonprofit Natural Lands, includes several habitats in its 1300 acres, including forests, a bird-rich wetlands, farm fields, and a wonderful serpentine barrens, which the organization is actively preserving and enhancing through the use of prescribed burning and plantings.

To find the barrens, head first to the Lenfest Center in the middle of the property on Cannery Road. Named for Philadelphia philanthropists Gerry and Marguerite Lenfest, who underwrote the facility's costs, stop in to pick up a map of the preserve. Trail maps can also be downloaded from the Natural Lands website, and it offers a free app as well. Visit the center's wonderful native plant garden at its doorstep; it is a knockout loved by insects. Near the center is a nature play area that's great for the young explorers with you.

Serpentine Barrens

The serpentine barrens is located at the extreme southeastern tip of the preserve. From the Lenfest Center, drive down Cannery Road and park at a small stone parking lot lined with boulders. An adjacent stone springhouse is your landmark that you are in the right place. Walk south on the preserve's Yellow Trail and stay straight onto the Gray Trail at the first intersection. Continue for a third of a mile and turn left onto an unmarked path into the woods near the intersection of Kelsall Road. This is your ticket to serpentine.

As you walk in, you'll quickly notice sassafras and poison ivy around you; admire both but be careful with the latter. Also look for holes on either side of the trail. "Those were dug as corundum mines," Sean Quinn, the preserve's manager, told me. "The mineral has a hardness of 9 on the Mohs scale, harder than most things except diamonds." Commonly used as an abrasive, corundum was common in everything from sandpaper and emery boards to large tools used to machine metals.

You'll also notice many eastern red cedars around you, an evergreen tree with blue, berry-like cones. This is a tree we don't see much in Wild Philly, one indicator of a different place. Red cedar is a pioneer species, often one of the

▲ The ChesLen Preserve includes a very rare ecosystem, a serpentine barrens. The nutrient-poor rocks support many unusual plants, many of them small and low-growing and not found elsewhere in Wild Philly.

first trees to grow, and it does well in poor soils—hence its presence here. (Though named cedar, it is more technically a juniper; its European cousin gave us gin.)

The barrens is home to several unusual butterflies and moths, including the juniper hairstreak, an olive-colored beauty that uses the cedars as its host plant. Hairstreaks are named for the thin hair-like projections off the rear of the wings, which some even wiggle like insect antennae—confusing birds into trying to bite the back of the wing thinking it is the head.

Walking on an Ancient Sea Floor

As you walk, look for outcroppings of rock around you, especially in the trail, and notice the greenish-gray character of the rock. This is serpentine. "It's thought," said Sean, "that the serpentine rock at ChesLen is an ancient sea floor, metamorphosed when pushed under the continental shelf, but it is difficult to be completely sure." Familiar schist is here as well, but with a twist. Sean has found some of the largest mica flakes in the region, like shiny sheets of metallic paper several inches wide, formed as the schist cooled slowly during its metamorphosis.

Look also for charred trees and trunks, evidence of Natural Lands' use of fire to "knock back woody plants and invasives like autumn olive," Sean explained. "It looks like the surface of the moon here after a fire, but blacker." Some sections we walked through were burnt only months before, and it was lushly green. "It's a relatively low-intensity fire," he continued, "low and slow like brisket," he said with a smile.

Since this is a barrens, look for low, small flowers growing around you, like whorled milkweed, the fourth species of this important plant we have found in Wild Philly, the other three being common and swamp milkweeds, plus butterflyweed, all members of the genus *Asclepias*. You may also spot a small rosette of deeply-lobed leaves hugging the rock, sending up a stem with tiny white cross-shaped flowers. This is sand cress (*Arabidopsis lyrata*), a plant with a circumpolar distribution—it is found across North America, Europe, and Asia, typically in places like this with thin soils.

▲ The staff at the ChesLen Preserve use low-intensity fires to maintain the preserve's unique ecosystem.

Rare Wildflowers

Many of the unusual serpentine barrens plants have wonderful common names: long-haired panicgrass, Bicknell's hoary rockrose, and round-leaf fameflower. The last one, a pink beauty, is imperiled in Pennsylvania, with only fifteen populations found in the entire state, including here.

About three-quarters of a mile into the walk, you'll cross a suspension bridge over a small stream, like something from an old movie set (if you have kids with you, you may need to spend some time here). As you cross the stream, look on your left at the opposite bank; there is a great layer of serpentine slicing through the Wissahickon schist. See if you can find the grayish green rock.

After the bridge, you are in an oak savannah, oak trees surrounded by open fields and meadows. Kept open by prescribed burning, this is the kind of landscape the Lenape were after as they managed the forest for oaks and other nut trees, plus the game animals attracted by oak acorns.

The unmarked trail will soon turn left and become the Gray Trail. (But notice the old one-room schoolhouse on your right, now a private home, outside of the preserve.) Walk the Gray Trail, and on the right look for a treeless mound ahead; as you pass the mound, on its back side is a trail to its top. Take this side spur to stand atop the mound and notice all the small flowering plants on the serpentine hill, adapted for the nutrient-poor conditions. Back on the trail, you'll cross another bridge with jewelweed all around you, and come up on the other side of the oak savannah.

The Gray Trail meanders along the barrens and turns right where you will cross a bridge and head uphill over several water-bars. At the top of the hill, turn left at the intersection and rejoin the Yellow Trail to return to your car. To your right are ruins of an old stone barn, and on your left is a beautiful goldenrod meadow.

If you have extra time, the preserve's northern extreme offers a parking area that allows you to walk to the Star Gazer's Stone. This was placed in 1764 by British surveyors Charles Mason and Jeremiah Dixon to settle a long-running, often violent dispute between Pennsylvania and Maryland over the location of the border. The surveying of the Mason-Dixon line is considered one of the great scientific achievements of its time, and this critical stone anchored their work. The house where Mason and Dixon stayed during this time still stands near the well-interpreted stone.

▼ Round-leaved fameflower is one of the rare plants growing in the serpentine barrens.

TRIP 12 ELVERSON, PA

Crow's Nest Preserve

Crow's Nest Preserve is the gateway to the Hopewell Big Woods, the largest expanse of forest in southeastern Pennsylvania. The preserve features milkweed-rich meadows that support a large population of butterflies and rare wildflowers like cardinal flower and Canada lily. In Chief's Grove, a massive white oak is said to mark the grave of a Lenape elder.

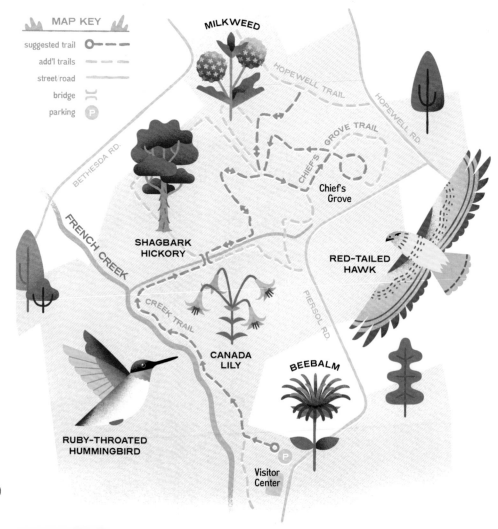

MAP KEY

suggested trail	⊙– – –
add'l trails	– – –
street/road	———
bridge	)(
parking	Ⓟ

MILKWEED

HOPEWELL TRAIL

HOPEWELL RD.

CHIEF'S GROVE TRAIL

Chief's Grove

BETHESDA RD.

FRENCH CREEK

SHAGBARK HICKORY

RED-TAILED HAWK

CREEK TRAIL

PIERSOL RD.

CANADA LILY

BEEBALM

RUBY-THROATED HUMMINGBIRD

Visitor Center

▲ The staff actively manages the meadows at Crow's Nest Preserve through mowing and prescribed burning.

One of the great joys of a summer's day is walking through a meadow, the flowers in full bloom, the butterflies, bees, bumble bees, wasps, hover flies, and other flies flitting around and flirting with the flowers. One of the best butterfly meadows in all of Wild Philly is at Crow's Nest Preserve in Elverson, where you can easily find three species of milkweeds in bloom, not to mention yarrow, daisy fleabane, black-eyed Susan, and evening primrose.

In late June and early July, expect to find a wealth of butterflies: swallowtails, fritillaries, blues, sulphurs, skippers, and, of course, the crown prince of butterflies, the monarch, the region's highly endangered migrator. On a recent June walk I counted at least six monarchs—this after a year when I may have only seen two. With the extensive stands of milkweeds located at the Crow's Nest Preserve, seeing so many was intensely gratifying.

Hopewell Big Woods

Crow's Nest Preserve, in the far corner of Chester County, is 712 acres of protected open space within the Hopewell Big Woods, a sprawling 73,000-acre stretch of forest that is the largest protected unbroken forest in southeastern Pennsylvania. Dan Barringer, the preserve's manager, notes that Hopewell Big Woods "is home to hundreds of plant and bird species and unique forest and wetland communities." French Creek State Park, Hopewell Furnace National Historic Park, and state gameland all surround Crow's Nest.

WHERE: 201 Piersol Road, Elverson, PA 19520

ADMISSION: Free; open daily from dawn to dusk.

PARKING: There is plenty of parking in the site's parking lot.

DIFFICULTY, DISTANCE, ACCESS: The recommended walk is 2.5 miles, but can be adjusted as you wish. While there are gentle rolling hills throughout the preserve, this walk is fairly flat along well-defined trails with occasional wet spots. The trails are not ADA-accessible, and both wheelchairs and strollers would struggle here.

FACILITIES: The site includes a Visitor Center that offers some programming, but the center is open "by appointment or chance." The restrooms are open from dawn to dusk.

BEST TIME: While any time of year is great, a June or July walk gives you abundant butterfly meadows with three species of milkweed that attract monarchs like magnets.

SPECIAL NOTES: Dogs are allowed, but they must be leashed. Horses are allowed on specially marked trails, although trailers are not permitted in the parking lot. Bikes are not welcome on the trails.

Located in the far corner of Chester County, the preserve is not easily accessible by mass transit.

The area's wildlife is amazing: bobcats supposedly have been seen in the Hopewell Big Woods. More credibly, coyote, mink, beaver, and otter live here, and the birdlife is equally rich.

When you visit, park in the designated parking lot on Piersol Road and look for the welcome kiosk with its trail maps—make sure to grab one. (Trail maps can also be downloaded from the Natural Lands website, and they offer a free app as well.) Milkweed greets you along the rim of the parking lot, so look for butterflies immediately.

You'll be walking north on the Creek Trail, but if you head south for just a little, you'll find the Visitor Center and its restrooms, if needed. On the way, check out the trees on your left.

▲ Canada lily plants can be more than 4 feet tall and bear many dark-spotted flowers.

There is a massive tuliptree, a so-called wolf tree that is much bigger than the others in the area, between the parking lot and the Visitor Center. In the nineteenth century, this site would have looked very different, denuded from both the farms and the industrial furnaces nearby. This tuliptree may have been left standing as a place the farmer could use to find some shade. The term *wolf tree* originated with nineteenth-century foresters who believed that these massive trees were taking up too much space and sunlight. The old trees were often removed from the landscape, similar to the wolves that were being killed for consuming too many forest resources.

▲ The Chief's Grove, said to be the resting site of a Lenape elder, is centered on a large white oak.

Head back to the parking lot and take the Creek Trail (look for yellow arrows in circular medallions on trees) north, through the first butterfly meadow, which was a hayfield 25 years ago. The nonprofit Natural Lands actively manages these meadows through mowing and prescribed burning, keeping the meadow from becoming forest. See what other wildflowers you can find here, like yarrow and black-eyed Susan.

The trail heads into a wet forest that parallels—and is occasionally flooded by—French Creek, an "exceptional value" stream that flows through much of the Hopewell Big Woods. Metallic-winged damselflies accompany you here. In this wet stretch, begin looking for Canada lily with its classic Turk's-cap flowers. While usually yellow, the red form is what blooms here. Cardinal flowers may be here as well, their intense red impossible to miss and irresistible to hummingbirds.

Chief's Grove

A half mile after the parking lot, the Creek Trail turns right on the Chief's Grove Trail, but it retains the yellow medallions. The trail soon makes a left over a small bridge—look for a shagbark hickory at the turn—then a quick turn right again at the fields. Natural Lands leases these fields to a farmer for hay and feed corn, giving you a taste of what this nineteenth-century landscape might have looked like.

Walk toward the Chief's Grove, in the middle of which stands a white oak, where legend says a Lenape elder was buried long ago. "We aren't sure of the exact origin of the name," Dan Barringer says. "People with ties to Lenape history and culture have visited the location and suggested it may be the burial location of an elder or a healer, chosen long ago perhaps for the stately white oak that dominates it." The oak is still here, with hickories, sassafras, and ash surrounding it. There is a bench as well; sit for a moment to pay your respects to the elder and enjoy the vista, noting especially Hopewell Furnace's forested ridge on the horizon in front of you.

One more assignment: after you leave the Chief's Grove, look for the purple-blazed Hopewell Trail, which ultimately connects to Hopewell Furnace National Historic Park. You'll only need to go a quarter of a mile down this trail to walk through the site's best milkweed meadows. Look for the tall, pink-flowered common milkweed (and smell a globe of flowers—the scent is intoxicating), plus its cousin butterflyweed. A third species of milkweed, swamp milkweed, is here as well, blooming a deeper pink, almost red, with leaves that are narrower and sharper than those of common milkweed. With all this milkweed, you will undoubtedly find butterflies and bumble bees—and, of course, more monarchs.

Goldenrod grows in these meadows, but this will not flower for a few months. Make a mental note to return in the fall, as goldenrod will be the last chance for all of these pollinators to get nectar and pollen before winter settles in. It's also an important way station for monarchs migrating south to Mexico.

▲ In the fall, Crow's Nest Preserve offers a colorful view of Hopewell Furnace's hills.

TRIP 13 PHILADELPHIA, PA

FDR Park

Like New York City's Central Park, FDR Park was designed by members of the acclaimed Olmsted family. There's more nature than one expects on the park's lakes and along its trails, enjoyed by one of the most diverse groups of park users in the city. FDR Park was the site of the nation's sesquicentennial celebration in 1926, making it a perfect spot for an Independence Day walk.

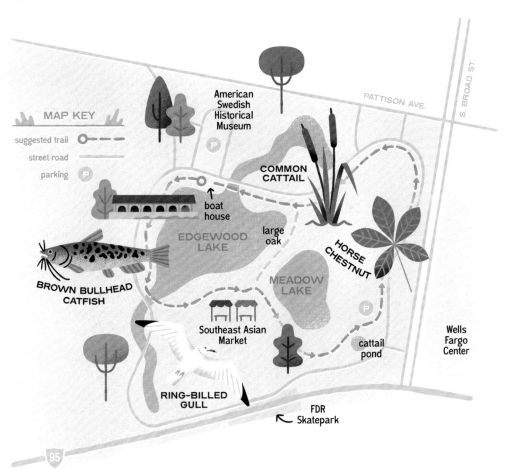

MAP KEY

suggested trail

street/road

parking

American Swedish Historical Museum

PATTISON AVE.

S. BROAD ST.

COMMON CATTAIL

boat house

EDGEWOOD LAKE

large oak

HORSE CHESTNUT

BROWN BULLHEAD CATFISH

MEADOW LAKE

Wells Fargo Center

Southeast Asian Market

cattail pond

RING-BILLED GULL

FDR Skatepark

95

WHERE: 1500 Pattison Ave., Philadelphia, PA 19145

ADMISSION: Free; open from 6:00 a.m. to 9:00 p.m. from April through October and 6:00 a.m. to 6:00 p.m. the rest of the year.

PARKING: There is plenty of parking in the many parking lots.

DIFFICULTY, DISTANCE, ACCESS: The recommended 1-mile walk is mostly a flat sidewalk, perfect for wheelchairs and strollers.

FACILITIES: There are public restrooms, plus portable toilets throughout the park.

BEST TIME: While any time of year is great, an Independence Day walk gives you an extraordinary view of both the city's diversity and our diverse ways of celebrating our independence.

SPECIAL NOTES: Leashed dogs and bikes are welcome on the trails.

Located across Broad Street from the stadiums, FDR Park is easily accessible via mass transit, as both the Broad Street subway and Bus 17 stop at Broad and Pattison.

▲ The sidewalks through FDR Park function as a wonderful nature walk.

With Broad Street and the stadiums on one side and I-95 and the Navy Yard on another, the 348-acre park is well used and well loved by South Philly's many residents. Called The Lakes by locals, visitors come here to walk, bike, fish, barbecue, play soccer and tennis, skateboard, and so much more. Come early before all the picnickers arrive, and do make sure the Phillies are playing an away game, as it's tough to get here through stadium traffic.

FDR Park's lakes and trails are home to lots of nature. Large oaks line the trails and side-walks, not to mention red maples, sweet gum, ginkgoes, even dawn redwoods. Cattails surround the lakes and provide cover to waterbirds of many kinds, especially during migration, when this becomes an important stopover.

The park's lakes are reminiscent of the area's history, as they roughly trace the path of Hollander Creek, a stream that connected the Delaware and Schuylkill Rivers along this route. In the Delaware River just below here was League Island, which vanished under improvements like I-95 and the Navy Yard. The park was originally called League Island Park.

Like the John Heinz National Wildlife Refuge only 4 miles downriver, the land originally consisted of wetlands and marshes, part of the thousands of acres of wetlands that once hid the mouth of the Schuylkill River. Starting in the 1700s, these marshes were slowly drained and filled to support first agriculture and then residential development.

▲ The Boat House was constructed in the 1920s to mark the nation's Sesquicentennial.

The Only Olmsted Park in Philly

The Olmsted Brothers, sons of famed landscape architect Frederick Law Olmsted, designed League Island Park in 1913. Thirteen years later, the park was chosen as the site for the nation's Sesquicentennial, the 150th anniversary of the Declaration of Independence. The classically columned Band Stand and its nearby Boat House, not to mention the American Swedish Historical Museum, were all erected for that event.

Begin your walk at the American Swedish Historical Museum by parking in its generous lot or walking here from the Broad Street bus stop or train station. A row of tall cucumber magnolias guards the museum just inside its fence. On the eastern side, a series of impressive trees stand as well, including dawn redwood, a native of China and a cousin of sequoias, and pond cypress, native to the American Southeast and a deciduous evergreen. Near these is a very large red maple tree; look for its three-lobed leaves and reddish leaf petioles.

Walk toward the underused Boat House to get a view of Edgewood Lake. Look for ducks and other birds on and near the water. Walk the sidewalk trail that circles the lake, heading west to start. As the path bends around the lake, look for cattails and duckweed on the left while admiring the large trees on the right. Oaks of many kinds, more red maples, sweet gum, a few beeches and river birches, and more are here, some reaching impressive sizes.

As you curve around the back of the lake, on weekends you might find a Cambodian food market offering freshly grilled meats, fried street food, mango and papaya salads, desserts, and more. The trail bends to the right to skirt the Richie Ashburn ballfields. On my July 4th walk, several organized soccer games were underway, with their own pop-up barbecues lining the sidewalks there. After the soccer fields, look to the right; under I-95, skateboarders have built themselves a skatepark, which draws a whole different slice of Philadelphia.

Walk across the front of the old park maintenance buildings, one of which has a thriving cattail pond near it, and curve left on the sidewalk trail to head north and parallel Broad Street. After Picnic Area 21, near the tennis courts, your walk is shaded by a grove of impressive horse chestnuts, a tree with wide, beautifully palmate leaves and characteristic chestnut-like fruit.

Curve once more with the sidewalk trail to head west, and the trees become sweet gums, with telltale star-shaped leaves. You're on the edge of Meadow Lake, with a cluster of cattails being threatened by the menacing and invasive phragmites behind them. You'll pass a playground, and on the left is a bridge with an old trail that heads between Edgewood and Meadow Lakes. Head down this trail for a moment—check out the water on both sides of the bridge for any birds; lots of duckweed grows here too. But only a few yards down on the right is one of the largest, most impressive black oaks I've seen in all of Wild Philly. Do introduce yourself.

▲ The Band Stand at FDR Park is an area landmark.

▲ With its green space near the Delaware River, a surprising number of shorebirds and migratory birds can be found at FDR Park, inducing this spotted sandpiper on the edge of one of the lakes.

Return to the sidewalk, turn left and end the walk at the Band Stand. On its left near the lake edge I spotted a large hole, clearly the den of someone like a groundhog or fox, a reminder that many animals have adapted to cities.

A Climate-Resilient Park

I walked through FDR Park after a few days of rain, and there were puddles throughout the park. As climate change kicks in, the Delaware is rising and threatening this park. Given its high usage, the underinvestment in it over time, and the river's rising tides, the city and the Fairmount Park Conservancy have teamed up to develop a "resilient" master plan that balances "nature, water, and play." Many participants in the planning process called for more nature in the park. So, as the plan evolves, for example, a nature trail will be created between the lakes, and the old golf course has already been retired in favor of a meadow. As you return, you can watch the vision unfold.

The nation's official Sesquicentennial opened here in 1926. As the hundredth anniversary of that event is approaching, some have lobbied for a large event here in 2026. We'll see, but a July 4th walk in this urban oasis showcases the wonderful diversity of the people of Philadelphia, a great way to celebrate America's birthday.

TRIP 14 PHILADELPHIA, PA

Andorra Meadow at Wissahickon Valley Park

Perched on Philly's northwestern edge, Andorra Meadow is one of the city's best butterfly meadows, with abundant milkweed, beebalm, sunflowers, and grasses, along with swallowtails, skippers, monarchs, and pollinating insects galore. The nearby forest includes maples, walnuts, tuliptrees, and the recently perished Great Beech, once the state champion, perhaps even the oldest European beech in the city.

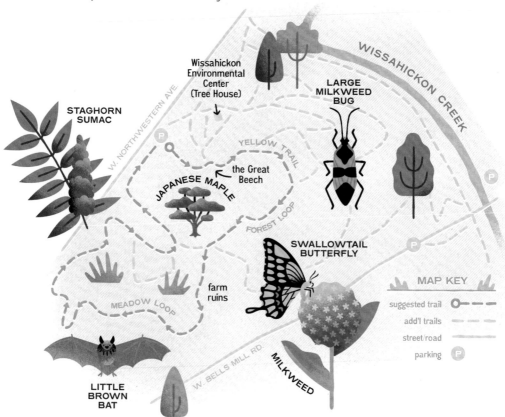

▲ The Andorra Meadow includes a wide variety of grasses and wildflowers.

"Just living isn't enough," poet-philosopher Kahlil Gibran wrote about butterflies. "One must have freedom, sunshine, and a little flower." One of the great pleasures of nature in summer is a butterfly meadow, where freedom, sunshine, and flowers are all plentiful. One of the best meadows in Wild Philly is the 33-acre Andorra Meadow, part of the Andorra Natural Area in the far corner of Wissahickon Valley Park.

Andorra Meadow features large groups of common milkweed and smaller amounts of butterflyweed, the daintier, fireball orange member of the milkweed clan. With milkweeds in abundance, you know what that means: a high likelihood of monarchs, as milkweed is the species' only host plant.

Andorra Meadow is alongside an interesting forest, a former tree nursery that operated from the 1880s until 1961, at its peak the largest tree nursery on the East Coast. With that history, it's not surprising that non-native trees like Japanese maple, blue spruce, Korean evodia, and European beech can be seen along this walk.

In addition, the site boasts the Wissahickon Environmental Center, one of three city environmental centers in public parks. Nicknamed the Tree House, as a tree once grew through its porch roof, the center is a favorite of parents with young children.

WHERE: 300 W. Northwestern Avenue, Philadelphia, PA 19118
ADMISSION: Free; Wissahickon Environmental Center is open Monday through Friday from 8:00 a.m. to 4:00 p.m. and during public programming, but the building is locked when staff are on the trails.
PARKING: Park in Parking Lot 1 on Northwestern Avenue off Ridge Avenue or Parking Lot 3 on Northwestern Avenue off Germantown Avenue.
DIFFICULTY, DISTANCE, ACCESS: The recommended walk is almost 2 miles but can be combined with other hikes elsewhere in the park. The trails are not ADA-accessible.
FACILITIES: The Center offers seasonal programming throughout the year. Composting toilets are located at Parking Lot 2.
BEST TIME: While any time of year is great, a July walk gives you abundant meadow wildflowers in full bloom, along with their insect pollinators.
SPECIAL NOTES: Dogs are allowed on the trails, but they must be leashed, and horses are welcome. Bikes are not allowed.

SEPTA's Bus 27 stops at Ridge and Northwestern Avenues. Walkers, even cyclists, can head down Northwestern Avenue (you'll pass Andorra Meadow on the right) and enter the park from the parking lot on the right. The center is also accessible by the L Bus (to Plymouth Meeting), which stops at Rogers and Germantown Avenue. From there, walk down Northwestern Avenue past Bruno's restaurant on the right and Northwestern Stables on the left, to Forbidden Drive, then up the center's driveway.

The Great Beech

This walk starts at Parking Lot 1. After you arrive, look for the kiosk where you can get oriented, and head into the forest on the red-blazed Forest Loop. While there are trail markers at key intersections, the trails can be confusing and not all trails are marked. Use your map as you walk.

▲ The Wissahickon Environmental Center is widely known as the Tree House.

After only a few hundred feet, look for a sign pointing to the Great Beech and the Yellow Trail. Make a right and pay your respects to the Great Beech. Planted in the Civil War era, the beloved European beech (*Fagus sylvatica*) has been featured in innumerable family photos and selfies. Sadly, the tree died in 2021 from a combination of disease, old age, carvings, and land use. When alive, it was the state champion of its species, boasting a circumference of more than 21 feet and a height of more than 102 feet, making it Philadelphia's third largest tree. Though more than 150 years old, it might have lived much longer. The park staff intends to allow the tree to remain standing for the time being and is encouraging another growing from its roots to become the next Great Beech.

Stay on the Yellow Trail, walk around a huge fallen cucumber magnolia, and look for a bench in the woods on your right. There is a monstrous tulip-tree just beyond that bench worth visiting.

When the Yellow Trail ends at the red-blazed Forest Loop, make a right and walk a quarter mile through an extraordinary American beech forest, the many smooth trunks carved to mark too many teenage relationships (sigh). At a crossroads intersection, you'll be faced with multiple choices; look for the purple-blazed Meadow Loop that veers left, your ticket to butterflies. Take that.

Milkweed and *Monarda*

You'll emerge from the treeline into Andorra Meadow. Look for large clusters of tall, pink-flowered common milkweed. Not only the host plant of monarchs, the nectar-filled flowers are irresistible to bumble bees, honey bees, and so many other pollinators. The 101 Species section featured not only milkweed, but beebalm, *Monarda*, which comes in two colors; this meadow features abundant groups of the lavender-flowered *Monarda fistulosa*. Other flowers here include members of the sunflower clan (*Helianthus* species), daisy fleabane, and St. Johnswort, not to mention many kinds of grasses.

▲ Butterflyweed is a member of the milkweed clan and a butterfly magnet.

As you walk, watch especially for monarchs and see if you can observe any laying eggs on the undersides of milkweed leaves. Other butterflies likely present include swallowtails, cabbage whites, sulphurs, blues, and several species of skippers. Bees, flies, wasps, and moths are likely here as well, and perhaps spiders and praying mantises stalking their prey.

The meadow is actually more savannah, with many large trees sprinkled across the landscape. Many are black walnuts, with their long compound leaves. See if you can spot any walnut fruits forming high up in the branches. As you head toward the back of Andorra Meadow, you'll find a generous stand of staghorn sumacs with their characteristic antler-shaped red fruits.

The entire Meadow Loop is 1 mile. In its last stretch is where I saw significant numbers of butterflyweed, another native milkweed. Near its end is a second, smaller loop, the Meadow Observation Loop in the interior of the Meadow Loop—feel free to linger in the meadow a moment more. The Meadow Loop ultimately ends at the Forest Loop. Head left—careful, the trail here has abundant poison ivy on both sides—and walk through a Japanese maple forest, a new experience for Wild Philly, as you return to the parking lot.

A City Nature Challenge blogger reported recently that almost 250 species of living things have been recorded at Andorra Meadow, including 32 species of birds, 124 species of plants, and 60 species of insects and arachnids. How many did you see or hear in your time in the meadow?

Cedars House Cafe, a historic home that once belonged to the nursery and now has been converted to a beloved cafe, is only a short walk downhill from the Wissahickon Environmental Center. Perhaps stop in for snacks or lunch as you relish the memory of your freedom in a field of sunshine and flowers.

Manayunk Canal Towpath

This path features superb views of the Schuylkill River and Flat Rock Dam, not to mention haunting historic relics including the nation's oldest train station and parts of the Schuylkill River navigation system. Nature abounds here, including cormorants, mallards, Canada geese, turtles, great blue herons, and evidence of beavers.

MAP KEY

suggested trail ○- - -
street/road
parking Ⓟ

parking along Shawmont

Shawmont Station

NIXON ST.

SHAWMONT AVE.

76

SCHUYLKILL RIVER

pumping station ruins

rock outcrop

AMERICAN SYCAMORE

DOUBLE-CRESTED CORMORANT

Flat Rock Dam

Lock 68 & Canal Sluice House

GREEN FROG

MANAYUNK CANAL

UMBRIA ST.

Venice Island

Fountain St. steps

GREAT BLUE HERON

CANADA GOOSE

▲ Shawmont Station is the oldest train station still standing in the United States.

You'll discover both human and natural history on this riverside jaunt. At the bottom of Shawmont Avenue in Upper Roxborough, a small community of homes lies tucked between the Schuylkill River and the Schuylkill River Trail. Park along either side of Shawmont Avenue, and walk downhill toward the river. Make a left on Nixon Street and cross the train tracks at the Shawmont Station.

Looking distinctly unloved as I write this, Shawmont Station is the country's oldest surviving train station, built in 1834 by the Philadelphia, Germantown and Norristown Railroad, the city's first rail company. The building was used for 160 years until it was retired in the 1990s. SEPTA has received funding to stabilize the building, but its future remains unclear.

Head downhill to the Schuylkill River Trail on a remnant of a cobblestone street, wind left onto the trail, and immediately on your right is a vista of the Schuylkill River. Do visit the river, and watch for other such opportunities along the walk. Look also for massive sycamores growing around you, their feet happily wet in the river's floodplain.

WHERE: Intersection of Shawmont Avenue and Nixon Street, Philadelphia, PA 19128

ADMISSION: Free; open daily from dawn to dusk.

PARKING: Parking is available on both sides of Shawmont Avenue, but as this is a popular parking place for people accessing the Schuylkill River Trail, finding a spot can be difficult.

DIFFICULTY, DISTANCE, ACCESS: The recommended walk is a relatively flat 3-mile loop. The trails are not ADA-accessible.

FACILITIES: None.

BEST TIME: A summer walk allows you to cool off in a riverside forest.

SPECIAL NOTES: Dogs are allowed, but they must be leashed.

SEPTA's Bus 62 and the Manayunk/Norristown Line Regional Rail (the Ivy Ridge station) both stop on Umbria Street. From there, walk one long block to Fountain Street, and turn right to walk down the Fountain Street Steps. At the storage facility, head left and downhill, then right to join the Schuylkill River Trail. As you read this walk's description, note that you'll be walking it backwards.

Historic Station, Dams, and Ruins

You should see evidence of stonework nearby: stone steps, columns, walls. Here stood the Roxborough Pumping Station, a huge waterworks completed in 1868. Immense coal-fired turbines pulled water out of the river, and enormous pipes pushed it uphill to a reservoir located behind what is now Shawmont School. Unused since the 1960s, the extraordinary structure was demolished in 2011. As seen elsewhere, the power of nature to reclaim what was once a virtually treeless industrial landscape is extraordinary.

Continue down the trail, where you'll pass under a large outcropping of metamorphic rock overgrown with ferns, mosses, and lichens. If you are a geocacher, stop for the cache that Fairmount Water Works has placed nearby.

Past the rock is the Flat Rock Dam, finished in 1818 as part of a 108-mile system of thirty-two dams to make the Schuylkill navigable, especially for boats from northern coal country. The Manayunk Canal starts here and flows 2 miles through Manayunk; it forms Venice Island, the aptly named land between canal and river.

As you walk the trail, there is a low spot between the trail and canal that frequently floods. When dry, it is fun to explore, and you'll see well-trodden paths winding through it. Silver maple is dominant here; look for the tree's deeply cut, silver-sided leaves.

Lock 68

Additional historic ruins covered in graffiti soon greet you. Look for a complicated structure with a series of arched tunnels through which water would have passed. These are the sluices for Lock 68 of the Schuylkill Navigation System, and machinery in the sluice house once controlled the canal's depth to help all the mills along the canal, not to mention the boats that navigated through it. "The Manayunk Canal," said Sandy Sorlien, a Philadelphia Water contractor who is publishing a book on the system, "is the only canal section of the entire Navigation System that has intact lock chambers at both ends.

▲ The Schuylkill River Trail along the Manayunk Towpath, with the Fairmount Dam in the background.

▲ The graffitied Lock 68 as it appeared in 2021.

Lock 68 is easy to see from the trail, even though its wooden gates are long gone."

The locktender's house, now demolished, stood here for a long time; veteran hikers might remember it. Captain Winfield Scott Guiles was the locktender at Lock 68 for more than 60 years, and his wife, a Lenape woman, renowned as the Manayunk Healer, used herbal medicine to treat locals.

Though the water in the canal flows slowly, the city has an ambitious plan to restore its flow while preserving these ruins. "Since the canal empties into the river at Lock Street," Sandy explained, "not far above one of the city's drinking water intakes, dredging the canal and building a new sluice house will mean cleaner source water for Philadelphia." When this project happens, the site will change dramatically while offering great ecological benefits for the canal, where fish have died from a lack of oxygen.

A few hundred yards beyond the sluice house, as the trail heads over a bridge, beaver-chewed stumps line another low-lying floodplain, marking another site where beavers have staged their comeback. Unlike other sites, however, there is no lodge; the beavers live in the banks of the canal and river.

Walking on, look for waterfowl like egrets, herons, and ducks with ducklings and painted turtles stacked on top of each other, their beautiful yellow-striped necks serving as their signature feature. In the summer, this is a great wildflower site, with sunflowers, jewelweed, ironweed, and the showy pink or white blossoms of swamp mallow, a wild hibiscus. There's also the invasive purple loosestrife, a problematic, albeit beautiful, plant.

The Two Manayunks

Smokestacks appear behind the canal along this section too, belonging to a paper mill that closed in 2017. Opposite this on your left, look for new apartment buildings recently erected with stairs leading to the Schuylkill River Trail—the trail now an amenity for home buyers. This is the two Manayunks, the industrial nineteenth-century mill town metamorphosing into a twenty-first-century residential neighborhood. Whereas the river once delivered coal and lumber to Philly, today it delivers recreation and solace.

After a trailside mural on a retaining wall, this walk ends at Fountain Street. Make a left at the trail entrance there and head up to enjoy the Fountain Street Steps, a beloved place in the community. A great stand of sumacs will greet you.

As with many of these walks, you have a choice: turn around and return or head up the Fountain Street Steps toward Umbria Street, where there is a taproom in front of you and a bakery down the block. All choices are winners.

TRIP 16 WESTAMPTON, NJ

Rancocas Nature Center

Only a mile from the busy I-295, an Atlantic Coastal Plain forest along the tidal Rancocas Creek features some of the oldest hollies in New Jersey. Its diverse habitats include goldenrod fields for migrating monarchs and other pollinators. A large meadow is reclaiming the site formerly leased to the Powhatan Nation, and the walk highlights the country's troubled history with Indigenous Americans.

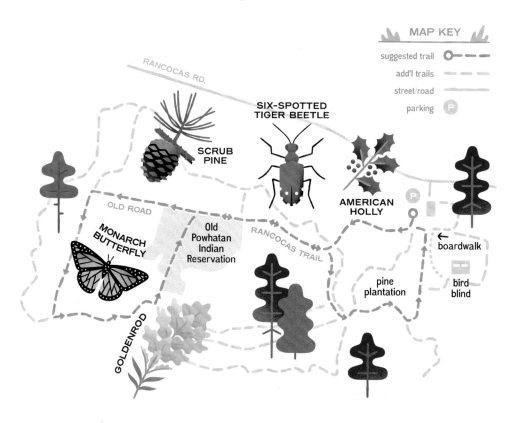

MAP KEY

suggested trail
add'l trails
street/road
parking

RANCOCAS RD.

SIX-SPOTTED TIGER BEETLE

SCRUB PINE

OLD ROAD

MONARCH BUTTERFLY

Old Powhatan Indian Reservation

RANCOCAS TRAIL

AMERICAN HOLLY

boardwalk

pine plantation

bird blind

GOLDENROD

▲ A pollinator garden graces the front of the Rancocas Nature Center.

The Atlantic Coastal Plain, that long, flat stretch of land between the Piedmont and the ocean, provides a radically different habitat from what Philadelphians on the Pennsylvania side are used to. There, forests of beech and tuliptree are the norm. But on the Coastal Plain, the forests are composed of a dizzying array of oaks, including white, red, and black oak, plus pines, hollies, and the versatile red maple, as common on the Coastal Plain as it is in the Piedmont. The herb and shrub layers are different too, with catbriers and shrubby members of the blueberry family.

The Rancocas Nature Center, situated on 210 acres of Rancocas State Park, has 3 miles of hiking trails through diverse Coastal Plain meadows, forest, and wetlands. Opening its doors in 1977, the nature center is located in a nineteenth-century farmhouse, where you'll find indoor exhibits paired with outdoor features like a dragonfly and frog pond and children's sensory play area. It's a great place for young kids.

WHERE: 794 Rancocas Road, Westampton, NJ 08060

ADMISSION: Free, but with a suggested donation of $2 per person; open daily from dawn to dusk.

PARKING: There is plenty of parking in the center's parking lot.

DIFFICULTY, DISTANCE, ACCESS: The recommended walk is about 2 miles, on trails that are relatively flat but not ADA-accessible.

FACILITIES: The Rancocas Nature Center is open to the public on Tuesdays, Thursdays, and Saturdays from 12:00 p.m. to 4:00 p.m. The Visitor Center features a classroom, gift shop, museum exhibits of natural and local history, including live animal exhibits. Restrooms are available, and there is an outdoor picnic area, children's garden, and butterfly enclosure.

BEST TIME: While any time of year is great, an early autumn walk gives you red maples turning colors and monarchs feeding on goldenrods as they head south for the winter, with great views of Rancocas Creek.

SPECIAL NOTES: The site is not accessible via mass transit, and neither dogs nor bikes are allowed on the trails.

The nature center is located on the North Branch of Rancocas Creek, whose headwaters originate almost 30 miles east, near Fort Dix in the fabled New Jersey Pine Barrens. A Lenape word sometimes written as *Rankokus*, the name was given to a large clan of Lenape settling in a village at today's Delran, and the name was then applied to the creek.

Park in the lot and visit the Rancocas Nature Center, if open. There is a very old, wizened red maple between the parking lot and the farmhouse that is worthy of checking out—it is losing its branches, but the trunk is substantial. If the nature center is not open, walk past the farmhouse toward the kiosk to the left of an old white barn. A map is there for you to examine, and one is also available on the center's website.

Hollies and Sassafras

The trail in front of the barn heads into the forest, and ends. Make a left on the Yellow Trail, and not far in turn right to continue on the trail. Notice the forest around you. Can you find the hollies? They will not be turning color, but sassafras offers gorgeous oranges and bronzes, while the leaves of red maples can be bright pale yellow, orange, brilliant scarlet, or even maroon. There are a large number of oaks and hickories here as well, the hickories yellowing while the oaks become brown. And if you find poison ivy, it could turn any of several colors, including a stunningly deep red

Turn left and walk the small meadow loop. The fall wildflowers blooming here include asters, goldenrods, and more. Can you see any monarchs stopping here to rest on their way to Mexico?

Back on the Yellow Trail, turn left, and walk through the forest. Notice the sandy soil and how close to the surface the water table is—the site is incredibly well-watered, with small creeks, vernal ponds, and wet spots. Look for skunk cabbage in the low spots. After the second bridge, the Yellow Trail ends on the white-blazed Rancocas Trail. Turn right here.

The Rancocas Trail becomes thin in places, and you'll likely need to step over some downed trees, but the path is straight and forward. In this stretch, on a July walk I enjoyed the company of many tiger beetles, always jumping ahead of me on the trail.

You'll emerge into a large expanse of meadow, with young pines especially on your right. Check out the pines, and see if you can find the clusters of two short, twisted needles. This is *Pinus virginiana*, which goes by several common names, including scrub pine, Virginia pine, and, appropriately, Jersey pine.

Powhatan Reservation Land

Walk straight ahead for a bit, and you'll come to what seem to be abandoned roads. Herein likes a story. For nearly 30 years starting in 1982, this large expanse was the Rankokus Reservation, home to members of the Powhatan Nation, formally recognized by the New Jersey state government in 1980. They opened a museum and a model village (with a live bison!), held

► The nature center's Blue Trail takes you across a swamp walkway.

twice-yearly powwows enjoyed by thousands of people for decades, and provided social services to the Native community. The relationship sadly soured and ended abruptly in 2010, and nature has been quickly reclaiming the land. You'll find evidence of the reservation in the roads you'll walk here, plus remains of structures and even large spotlights inexplicably standing in the meadow; they once lit the evening powwows.

In the meadow are an abundance of wildflowers, including goldenrod, one of the most important fall wildflowers because it provides sustenance to so many insects in the last months before winter. Look especially for monarchs here as well. On a summer walk, uncountable dragonflies were on the hunt along these trails. Make a loop on the old reservation roads, turning left three times to walk a 1-mile-wide circle, watching for butterflies and birds as you go.

Stay alert—you'll come back to the dirt trail with the young scrub pines, which can be easy to miss. Turn right and head back toward the nature center. This time, for variety, do not turn left to head back on the Yellow Trail, but stay on the white-blazed Rancocas Trail, which heads downhill into the forest alongside a small creek. There is a wonderful hump in the forest with trails atop and alongside—take whichever one you prefer, as they quickly meet up.

You'll turn left onto a bridge to meet the Blue Trail; make a right and head through an old pine plantation—notice how the trees are planted in straight rows. You'll then come to a boardwalk through a swampy area, showing you again how well-watered this site is.

Close to the nature center, there is a bird blind on the right, where you may see cardinals, titmice, even blue jays. You'll soon emerge at a monarch butterfly way station; see if monarchs are here as well.

There are other trails on the property for you to enjoy, and consider returning here on a March evening to listen to the chorus of spring peepers singing in the vernal pools. Check out the Rancocas Nature Center's programming as well.

Pennypack Ecological Restoration Trust

Featuring one of the most astonishing views in Wild Philly, this walk takes you through meadows teeming with many types of wildflowers, butterflies, swallows, and dragonflies, as well as goldenrod stands in full bloom. You'll also meet a Chinese chestnut and American elm, trees with important stories.

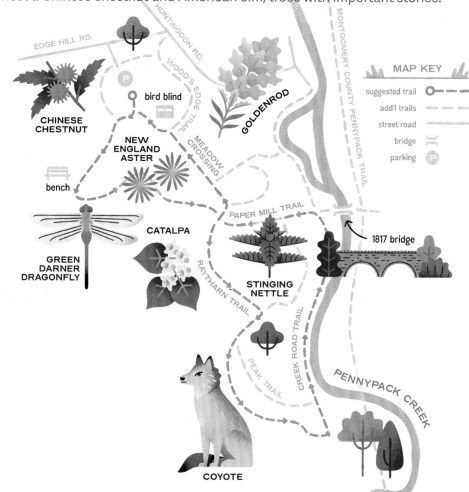

EDGE HILL RD.

HUNTINGDON RD.

WOOD'S EDGE TRAIL

MONTGOMERY COUNTY PENNYPACK TRAIL

MAP KEY

suggested trail ⊶
add'l trails
street/road
bridge
parking Ⓟ

Ⓟ

bird blind

CHINESE CHESTNUT

GOLDENROD

NEW ENGLAND ASTER

MEADOW CROSSING

bench

GREEN DARNER DRAGONFLY

CATALPA

PAPER MILL TRAIL

RAYTHARN TRAIL

STINGING NETTLE

1817 bridge

CREEK ROAD TRAIL

PEAK TRAIL

PENNYPACK CREEK

COYOTE

"There's something about this place that's a bit more peaceful than most," said Mike, a walker who stopped me on the trail to chat. "I've lived all over, and this is my favorite park."

I completely understand. We were standing on the crest of a meadow in the center of the Pennypack Ecological Restoration Trust's 800-acre preserve. Its wide panoramic vista offers one of Wild Philly's best views, grasslands framed by forests with the Bryn Athyn Cathedral in the distance. Add in meadow flowers and butterflies by the dozens, and you've got a must-see location.

The nonprofit Pennypack Ecological Restoration Trust has been stewarding this corner of Wild Philly for decades, quietly preserving critical habitat in the region's northern suburbs. With meadows, a run of Pennypack Creek and its floodplain, forests, and a marsh, the site's mix of habitats and variety of trails offers wonderful opportunities for nature exploration.

▲ The majestic view of the Bryn Athyn Cathedral from the top of the hill in the Raytharn Farm meadow.

Begin your walk at the main parking lot on Edge Hill Road, where both the trust offices and Visitor Center are located. Your first surprise immediately awaits.

A Chinese Chestnut

Large trees grow across the parking area, like large eastern white pines lining the driveway and a copper beech, a burgundy-leaved cultivar of the European beech and the largest tree in that area. One could spend a fine morning simply botanizing in the parking lot.

But notice the large tree on the edge of the lot, the one closest to the Visitor Center. The nut's burred covering is a giveaway. It's a Chinese chestnut, planted long before the trust owned this site. Here is the culprit of the chestnut blight that was described in the chapter on Philadelphia's forests. The Chinese chestnut coevolved with the fungus that attacked American chestnuts. As Americans imported exotic trees to plant in our gardens, the blight came along—and took down four billion chestnut trees. The Chinese chestnut, immune to the fungus, stands as a reminder of the story.

A trail kiosk is located near the chestnut, where you can grab a trail map. Walk to the right of and around the Visitor Center. There are flower gardens here, so see what's in bloom and what pollinators are visiting.

Stairs head downhill into the preserve, swallowing you in an oak forest. As the trail dead-ends, make a right on Wood's Edge Trail. Don't miss the pond on your left, with a viewing deck. You'll be walking through a grove of black walnuts and hardy catalpas; both are difficult to miss, the former with green-hulled round fruits and the latter with giant heart-shaped leaves. Black walnuts accompany you across this entire walk—there seem to be more walnuts at the Pennypack Ecological Restoration Trust than just about anywhere else I've seen in Wild Philly.

▲ Pennypack's trails pass benches strategically placed under monumental trees.

The View

Walk over a boardwalk, and make a left at a crossroads at a large sign welcoming you to Raytharn Farm, the large meadow you're about to enter. You'll emerge from the forest into one of the region's largest grasslands, a rare and wonderful sight. Enjoy the amazing views and the walk.

Here are many kinds of grasses with wildflowers mixed in. Swallows and dragonflies swoop overhead, both looking for flying insects. Crickets abound, so listen for them. A bench is placed at the top of the meadow's hill, with the majestic view sprawling in front of you. Sit for a moment to enjoy this unique landscape.

When you push on, follow the Raytharn Trail as it dips and rises again. Look for milkweeds growing in clusters; in autumn their seed pods should be ripe and opening. The meadow ends at a tree line; turn right to stay on the Raytharn Trail. Cross the Paper Mill Trail to another bench alongside a massive catalpa and walnut tree. Continue down the Raytharn Trail with a line of black cherry and walnut trees on your left. The Management Trail comes in on the left, but stay right to continue on Raytharn, which heads uphill and turns left at another huge tree, this one a black oak.

Goldenrod at Last!

You'll enter the third meadow in the sequence, this one filled with beebalm and more. On one walk I saw a pair of black swallowtails flirting in the flowers, while a cottontail rabbit nibbled on clover. As you head downhill, on your left is a great goldenrod stand, one of autumn's most important plants. Look for the blooms, and see if you can find honey bees, bumble bees, wasps, and flies, among others enjoying the flower.

The Raytharn Trail ends at a parking area where you turn left and head down stairs, turning left again to find the bed of the old Creek Road, now a trail alongside Pennypack Creek. The old road is suffering from erosion issues, so watch your step.

▼ Pennypack Creek as it flows through the trust's preserve.

On your right, take advantage of good views of the creek, but on your left, look for the Peak Trail, which skirts a rocky knob locals call The Peak. This

area holds some of what the Pennypack Ecological Restoration Trust calls "old-growth forest," the oldest trees being oaks "that sprouted from acorns around 1760." Walk up the Peak Trail, pause halfway up to admire this forest, and head back onto the Creek Road Trail.

Crossroads Marsh

The forest opens into a floodplain once dominated by ash trees, which the emerald ash borer has killed, now a gruesome scene. On your right is an 1817 dam, the second oldest in the entire county, which once connected to a paper mill. There is a great view of Pennypack Creek here: walk over the bridge and pause where you can best see the flowing water.

If you face upstream, the first tree on your left is an American elm, a tree that once graced the Main Streets of many American towns. Devastated by Dutch elm disease, most trees disappeared from the region's landscape by the 1970s. Every so often, one happens upon relic American elms that survive into young adulthood, but ultimately perish from this disease. Pay your respects to this one.

From the bridge, walk back to the Creek Road Trail, and cross to the Paper Mill Trail, the bed of an ancient road to a long-gone mill. On your right is Crossroads Marsh, a shallow wetland created by the trust more than 40 years ago, now with an active beaver population. There are benches here for wildlife viewing.

Continue uphill, this trail ending at a T with the Raytharn Trail you walked earlier. Make a right, but quickly stay straight on the Meadow Crossing, a trail that crosses the fourth meadow, this one another goldenrod hotspot. Walk slowly along this stretch, searching for monarchs and more.

Meadow Crossing ends at a T as well; turn left and then take a quick right, heading uphill through spruce trees. This trail ends at a bird blind, where you might find woodland birds like chickadees and downy woodpeckers. The blind is near the trust's offices, close to the parking lot where we started.

Butterflies and Blooms

On two walks at the Pennypack Ecological Restoration Trust, I found many flowers in bloom: butter-and-eggs, black-eyed Susan, goldenrod, white wood aster, phlox, cardinal flower, beebalm, milkweed, dogbane, daisy fleabane, butterflyweed, several sunflowers, purple coneflower, mountain mint, New York ironweed, Queen Anne's lace, yarrow, thoroughworts, asters, wild senna, and jewelweed. And these flowers attracted a raft of pollinators. Just my butterfly list includes monarch, eastern tiger swallowtail (both yellow and black morphs), black swallowtail, common sulphur, cloudless sulphur, cabbage white, comma, eastern tailed blue, summer azure, and red-spotted purple.

Three miles later, you might agree with Mike and consider this your favorite park as well.

TRIP 18 FORT WASHINGTON, PA

Militia Hill at Fort Washington State Park

One of Wild Philly's most wonderful spectacles is the migration of hawks, eagles, and falcons in the fall. These magnificent birds seemingly pour over the landscape, floating in the wind. Militia Hill offers a hawk-watching platform to witness the flight, and it connects to the Wissahickon Trail along that stream, offering a great walk too.

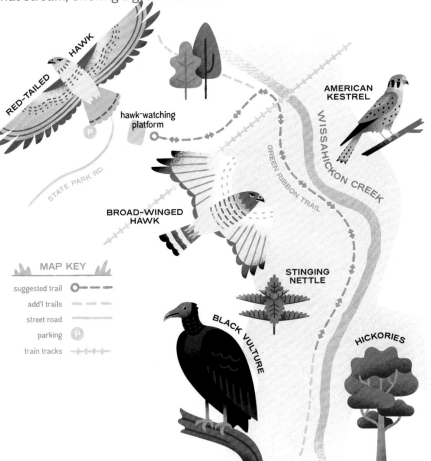

RED-TAILED HAWK

hawk-watching platform

STATE PARK RD.

AMERICAN KESTREL

WISSAHICKON CREEK

GREEN RIBBON TRAIL

BROAD-WINGED HAWK

STINGING NETTLE

BLACK VULTURE

HICKORIES

MAP KEY

suggested trail	○- - -
add'l trails	- - -
street/road	
parking	Ⓟ
train tracks	+++++

WHERE: 449 Militia Hill Rd, Fort Washington, PA 19034
ADMISSION: Free; open daily from dawn to dusk; day use areas are open from 8:00 a.m. to sunset.
PARKING: The site offers plenty of parking near the hawk-watching platform.
DIFFICULTY, DISTANCE, ACCESS: The recommended walk is a relatively flat 2-mile loop along the stream, with some hills to start and finish. While the trail is not ADA-accessible, the hawk-watching platform happily is.
FACILITIES: There are public restrooms near the parking lot, with water and picnic areas.
BEST TIME: A walk along Wissahickon Creek works any time of year, but to catch migrating hawks, fall is unquestionably the best time to visit.
SPECIAL NOTES: Dogs are allowed, but they must be leashed.

SEPTA's Bus 94 traverses Bethlehem Pike; exit at the Farmar Road stop and walk north on Bethlehem Pike to Skippack Pike, veering left on that road, and left again on Militia Hill Road into the state park. The Lansdale/Doylestown Line of the regional rail system stops at Fort Washington Station. From there, it is a 1.5-mile walk south on Bethlehem Pike to Skippack Pike.

On September 19, 2020, the birding gods smiled upon the Militia Hill hawk-watching platform in Fort Washington State Park, only a few miles above the Chestnut Hill section of Philadelphia. Powered by a cold front and clear skies, migrating birds of prey streamed over the ridge that day, with volunteers counting an astonishing 4871 broad-winged hawks soaring above the platform that single day on their southbound migration. They were joined by seventeen bald eagles, twenty-three sharp-shinned hawks, five Cooper's hawks, two ospreys, and more during one of the site's biggest raptor days in years.

Revolutionary War soldiers held this high ground in a temporary fort in 1777 under George Washington's command. The 500-acre Fort Washington State Park, located just below the busy Pennsylvania Turnpike, is enjoyed by thousands of users, including hikers, bikers, dog walkers, even fans of disc golf. The fort is long gone, but its site is interpreted in another section of the park. Park maps are located in kiosks at the parking areas.

All Sixteen Raptors

The hawk-watching platform is easily found near parking lot #5 in the Militia Hill Day Use Area, off Militia Hill Road. Staffed by volunteers from Wyncote Audubon, the site is a great place to view raptors during the migration. In fact, all sixteen species of raptors to be seen in southeastern Pennsylvania have been observed here, everything from sparrow-size kestrels to massive bald eagles.

The site's volunteers are exceptionally helpful and generous with both time and information. The platform has a wheelchair-accessible ramp to allow anyone to see the raptors, and high-quality interpretive signs ring the platform. In addition, there is a bird-feeding station alongside the platform, so you can easily see chickadees, titmice, cardinals, sparrows, woodpeckers, mourning doves, and blue jays, among others. A flock of pine siskins had left the feeders moments before I showed up, and only a few days before a migrating hummingbird was seen refueling at the bright red feeder set aside for them.

▲ The hawk-
watching platform
at Militia Hill.

A butterfly garden even grows alongside the feeders. On the October day I visited—and scored a merlin flying overhead—two monarchs were refueling in the non-native butterflybush before continuing their migration to Mexico. In a poor year for monarch sightings, this was immensely gratifying.

The Green Ribbon Trail

If you'd like to go on a walk too, head downhill from the platform away from the parking lot and follow the well-traveled trail. Make first a left onto the gravel trail, then you'll come to a T-intersection with the Green Ribbon Trail, a paved multi-use trail that follows Wissahickon Creek for many miles.

You can head left (north) to Ambler or right (south) toward Chestnut Hill, the latter being my recommendation. You'll enjoy lots of views of the creek while walking through a bottomland filled with sycamores, box elders, and hickories. There's some poison ivy there as well, notable as it turns an amazing series of colors in the fall, from yellow to purple to everything in between.

Catching a Cold Front

Raptors migrate at different times in the fall, with broad-winged hawks coming early and golden eagles late. As you might with Hawk Mountain Sanctuary (Trip 28) or Cape May Point State Park (Trip 29), watch the weather as fiercely as a hawk. Then, on that mid-September day when a cold front passes through, bringing crisp northern air that gives those birds the tailwind they crave, call in sick (your secret is safe with me) and get to Militia Hill—and maybe score 4871 broad-winged hawks.

TRIP 19 MEDIA, PA

Ridley Creek State Park

Ridley Creek State Park boasts one of the most beautiful walks in Wild Philly, with picturesque Ridley Creek's big boulders artfully arranged in the streambed and white-barked sycamores hugging its banks. Toss a dazzling diversity of habitats and plant life into the mix, stir in a forest cloaked in autumn splendor, and you have a recipe for a delicious walk.

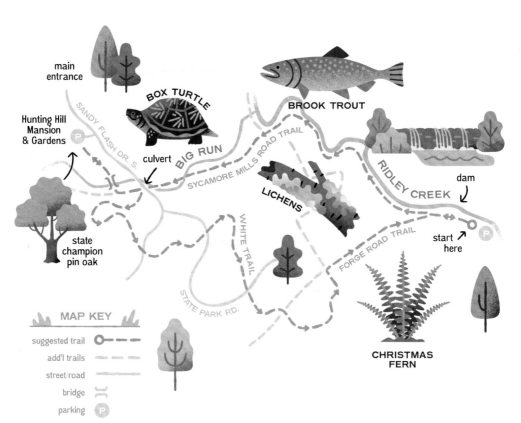

main entrance

Hunting Hill Mansion & Gardens

SANDY FLASH DR. S

BOX TURTLE

culvert

BIG RUN

SYCAMORE MILLS ROAD TRAIL

BROOK TROUT

RIDLEY CREEK

dam

state champion pin oak

LICHENS

WHITE TRAIL

FORGE ROAD TRAIL

start here

STATE PARK RD.

CHRISTMAS FERN

MAP KEY

suggested trail ◦ – – –
add'l trails – – –
street/road
bridge
parking ℗

▲ Ridley Creek flows through a woodland in the state park.

Ridley Creek slices through more than 20 miles of Delaware County, emptying into an industrialized section of the Delaware River between the city of Chester and Eddystone, sliding between a racetrack and a trucking facility. This walk is that area's antithesis, as the stretch of Ridley Creek that flows through this state park is breathtakingly gorgeous, a must-see for nature lovers. And that beauty is kicked up several notches when the forest cloaks itself in autumn splendor.

Ridley Creek State Park's 2600-acre sweep of landscape includes creek and forest, numerous historic buildings and ruins, a colonial plantation, playgrounds and picnic areas, even a stable where you can rent horses. On the perfect October day I visited, anglers lined the creek hoping to catch state-stocked rainbow trout, while caterers set up chairs at the historic park headquarters for a wedding. A whole lot of sardines are packed into this park's tin can.

At the same time, when a park ranger saw my binoculars, he went out of his way to beamingly tell me where purple finches had just

WHERE: Ridley Creek Trail, 509 Barren Road, Media, PA 19063

ADMISSION: Free; open daily from dawn to dusk.

PARKING: The walk starts at one of the smaller parking areas in the park, but you should be able to find a spot.

DIFFICULTY, DISTANCE, ACCESS: Depending on your choices, the walk is between 3 and 5 miles long, with moderately hilly terrain. The trails are not ADA-accessible.

FACILITIES: While restrooms are located at several locations in the park, there are none at the parking area.

BEST TIME: Come at the height of autumn's colors, from mid-October to early November.

SPECIAL NOTES: Leashed dogs are allowed, and bike riders enjoy many of the trails.

The park is not accessible by mass transit.

been spotted only hours earlier. So, while the park can be crowded and there are so many users, it's massive enough to accommodate all of this.

The park is headquartered in Hunting Hill, a picturesque 1915 mansion, and many visitors start there. But I recommend beginning in the park's far southeastern corner where Bishop Hollow, Ridley Creek, Barren, and Chapel Hill Roads all intersect. Two small parking areas straddle Ridley Creek. Park at either one and walk into the well-marked entrance. Grab a map at the kiosk.

Sycamore Mills

You'll find yourself transported to a 300-year-old mill town, first called Bishop Hollow and then Sycamore Mills. Though both sawmill and gristmill are gone, many of the town's buildings are still there, with people living in the historic homes in a state park. Read the interpretive signage, and find the flat space where the waterwheel-powered mill once was the center of a small town.

Walk up the trail that used to be the main road into the town, Sycamore Mills Road Trail, a multi-use trail you'll share with bikers, joggers, walkers, and families. (That is one downside of this walk—you could be joined by more people than you might wish. One solution is to visit at an off-peak time.) At the V-intersection with the Forge Road Trail, a second old cartway absorbed by the park, veer right to hug the creek.

Only a few hundred yards up the trail you'll find the dam that created the race that once sent water to the mill. Linger for a few moments at the gorgeous waterfall flowing over the dam, a favorite vista for the park's many photographers. On just this small stretch of park from the parking area to the dam, you'll find many of the trees written about in the 101 Species section: big sycamores with their splotchy jigsaw puzzle bark, smooth-as-elephant-skin beech trees, red maples, tuliptrees, and oaks. Many of the trees are helpfully labeled with descriptive signage. Christmas ferns dominate the slope on your left as you walk along the creek.

Along the creek, notice lots of boulders in and around the stream, and look for white convoluted bands in some. This is gneiss, an ancient metamorphic rock created a full 1 billion years ago, with pressure from plate tectonics slowly contorting the flat rock layers into crazy swirls and spirals.

You'll stay on this trail for almost 2 miles, but there are multiple benches and picnic tables for resting and refueling. Bring your lunch, maybe even a good book to enjoy.

State Champion Pin Oak

Almost 1.5 miles on this road, you'll pass through a culvert, coming to a bridge on your right over a small stream, the ironically named Big Run. Turn right on that bridge, and immediately veer left on a smaller gravel pathway that takes you uphill to a parking area near the mansion headquarters. Here, turn left and walk uphill to find the house. Facing the mansion, on its left flank you'll find a stunningly large pin oak tree, the state champion. That's another lure of Ridley Creek: there are many such large trees here as well.

▲ The trails at Ridley Creek State Park amble through forest with many different species of trees.

You've got three options for getting back to Sycamore Mills. First, head back downhill to the T-intersection of the bridge over Big Run, turn left and return the way you came. Second, turn right on Sycamore Mills Road Trail, follow it until it ends at Forge Road Trail, and follow this for another 2 miles to make a large sweeping circle back to Sycamore Mills where you started. Finally, check your map and follow the well-blazed White Trail through the interior of the park, leaving behind the bikers and runners; hike the White Trail until it crosses the Forge Road Trail the *second* time, and follow the multi-use trail downhill to your car.

On your drive home, consider checking out the Springton Reservoir off Gradyville Road just a mile or two away. The forested reservoir is resplendent in autumn colors as well. Or if you use West Chester Pike to drive here, consider how Ridley Creek State Park might have looked if this land had not been protected—and be thrilled it was.

Pennypack Park

The "green heart of the Northeast," the park preserves Pennypack Creek, one of the city's major stream systems, and includes the Pennypack Environmental Center. This streamside walk takes you through a maturing forest with some of the region's biggest sycamores and tuliptrees. A butterfly meadow adds interest at the halfway point, and there's history around every corner.

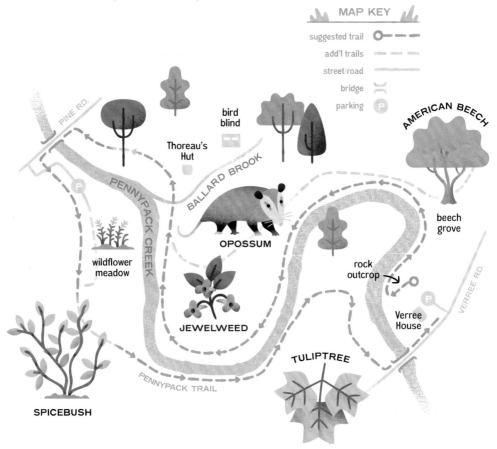

MAP KEY

suggested trail
add'l trails
street/road
bridge
parking

PINE RD.

bird blind

Thoreau's Hut

BALLARD BROOK

AMERICAN BEECH

beech grove

PENNYPACK CREEK

OPOSSUM

wildflower meadow

rock outcrop

VERREE RD.

JEWELWEED

Verree House

TULIPTREE

PENNYPACK TRAIL

SPICEBUSH

WHERE: Pennypack
Environmental Center,
8600 Verree Road,
Philadelphia, PA 19115
ADMISSION: Free; trail open
daily from dawn to dusk; the
Pennypack Environmental
Center is open from 8:00
a.m. to 4:00 p.m. on Monday
through Friday.
PARKING: There is plenty
of parking in front of the
center off Verree Road.
**DIFFICULTY, DISTANCE,
ACCESS:** The recommended
walk is a relatively flat
2-mile loop, which can be
easily extended in several
directions. On the first half
of the walk, the dirt trails
are not ADA-accessible; the
second half, however, is along
the Pennypack Trail, a paved
multi-use trail popular with
those using bikes, strollers,
wheelchairs, and walkers.
FACILITIES: Pennypack
Environmental Center has
restrooms, water, a picnic
area, and museum displays
on the nature and history of
the Pennypack.
BEST TIME: While the creek
flows all year, an autumn walk
gives you fall's coat of many
colors: tuliptree's yellow,
beech's orange, oak's brown,
even poison ivy's bright red.
Several meadows along the
way give you a last chance
to find butterflies and other
pollinators.
SPECIAL NOTES: Dogs are
allowed, but they must be
leashed.
SEPTA's Bus 67 stops on
Verree Road immediately
in front of the Pennypack
Environmental Center.

▲ The Pennypack
Environmental
Center houses
an interesting
collection of
Lenape artifacts.

Pennypack Creek flows more than 20 miles
through Philadelphia's Northeast, emptying into the Delaware River at another of the
walks, Pennypack on the Delaware Park (Trip
10). The creek is protected by Pennypack Park,
a 1600-acre gem that's home to 150 species of
migratory and nesting birds, not to mention
beavers, minks, and so much more. On one of
my walks, a bald eagle soared above us.

As with Wissahickon and Cobbs Creeks,
the city began setting aside this land in 1905
to protect the drinking water in Pennypack
Creek. This northern slice of the Pennypack
was also dedicated as a bird sanctuary in 1958,
and the Pennypack Environmental Center
opened in 1969.

The nature museum at the Pennypack
Environmental Center has displays, dioramas,
and artifacts, as well as an extensive collection
of Lenape artifacts found in the vicinity, including arrowheads, axe heads, and pottery shards.
If you are able to visit the park on a weekday
when the center is open, that not only allows
you to use the restroom and get oriented, but you can also visit the nature
museum, which is not open on weekends unless special programming is
happening.

"Bear Fat" Creek

Pennypack is an anglicized corruption of the Lenape *pënëpèkw*, meaning "downward-flowing water" or possibly "deep, dead water," referring to the creek's slow movement. One historian thought it meant "bear fat creek," as the water flowed about as fast as the grease the Lenape used for cooking. Early cartographers transliterated it variously as Pennishpaska, Pemipacka, Penneckpacka, and more before finally settling on Pennypack.

This walk features a maturing forest with large tuliptrees and American sycamores, not to mention a great number of beeches and walnuts. "The tallest tree measured in Philadelphia is a tuliptree located in the park," Peter Kurtz, the center's environmental education program specialist for the past 35 years, told me proudly.

The walk starts behind the Pennypack Environmental Center, at its amphitheater, where a trail heads downhill toward the creek. When this trail ends, make a quick right and then left, heading down wooden stairs. As the stairs end, turn left again, and head to a very large rock outcrop. Check out the rock's graffiti, which includes at eye level the faint formal carving "JP Verree July 4, 1872" (the letters "ree" are the easiest to find) placed there by the last member of the Verree milling family to live here (more on this soon). Behind you on the creek is the 1936 dam built not for milling, but for swimming, as the far side of the creek was once a public beach.

Now head back the way you came, pass those stone stairs you walked down, and continue on, walking the trail paralleling the creek.

▲ Pennypack Creek runs slowly through Northeast Philadelphia.

▲ Pennypack Park includes a beautiful beech forest.

The Best Beeches

You'll be walking through an exceptional beech grove, one of the handsomest beech forests in Wild Philly. Enjoy the elephantine trunks, and listen for bird song too. Both John James Audubon and Alexander Wilson birded here, coincidentally and separately, as both had ties to the community. Wilson's first indigo bunting was spotted in this park.

You'll also pass a naturalized spring on the right, with some of its stonework dating to the 1930s. Locals came here to stock up on spring water through the 1960s. A big sycamore is thriving alongside the spring.

The streamside trail is only three-quarters of a mile long. Halfway through the walk, the forest opens up to places where there is extensive jewelweed and stinging nettle, ironically growing side-by-side, as one is the antidote of the itchy other.

You'll walk over a small bridge where the trail forks. Up the right fork a short way is "Thoreau's Hut," an art installation by Ed Levine that invites you to sit in a space occupying the same footprint as the writer's famed cabin. Visit that, but return to the same trail and continue walking alongside the stream.

Pennypack Trail

You'll soon come up on Pine Road (named for the ancient pines that grew there long ago), where you'll make a left on the sidewalk to reenter the park at the picnic area. Also a parking area, this includes a section of the

Pennypack Trail, a paved multi-use trail that continues from here all the way to Pennypack on the Delaware. You may find more company on your walk, as dog-walkers, joggers, bikers, parents with strollers, and others use the trail. But at the back of the picnic area, look for a meadow with abundant wildflowers that should be attracting butterflies and other pollinators.

After the meadow diversion, head back on the paved trail and walk downstream toward Verree Road, enjoying the fall color. At the likely-closed restroom facility that once served the swimming beach, you'll find the 1936 dam we met earlier; feel free to explore here, as another meadow is tucked into this loop of the creek.

When you get to Verree Road, you'll notice that the paved trail heads under the street, continuing downstream all the way to Pennypack on the Delaware. Pop up onto the street and turn left on the road, walking along its shoulder. You'll pass the Verree House on your left, named for the family who ran a successful milling operation here for decades; in fact, this slice of Northeast Philly was once called Verreeville. The left section of the house is the oldest portion, built in 1700. The house played a key role in the Revolution, and its last miller, J. P. Verree, the rock-carver we met earlier, was both a friend of Abraham Lincoln and an abolitionist who served in Congress.

The 1687 mill, long gone, was located close to the stream and was then the second-oldest mill in Pennsylvania. Several other mills were located nearby. Like so much of Wild Philly, the once-industrialized Pennypack is returning to Lenapehoking.

As add-ons to this trip, you can walk all the way to Pennypack on the Delaware, or, in the other direction, explore the Fox Chase Farm on Pine Road at the top of the park, the very last working farm in the city.

TRIP 21 `MEDFORD, NJ`

Woodford Cedar Run Wildlife Refuge

A winter solstice walk in an evergreen-filled forest will put you in a festive mood. With beautiful views of Pine Barrens swamps and a wildlife housing area where numerous live owls, eagles, hawks, and mammals are on display, it's a holiday treat for the entire family.

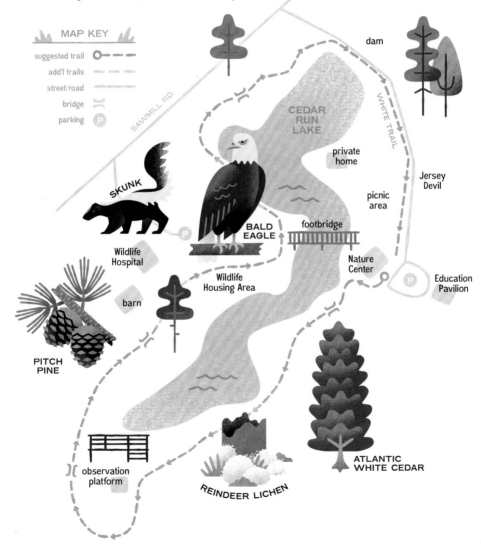

MAP KEY

suggested trail	○- - - -
add'l trails	- - -
street/road	———
bridge	)(
parking	Ⓟ

SAWMILL RD.

dam

WHITE TRAIL

CEDAR RUN LAKE

private home

Jersey Devil

picnic area

footbridge

SKUNK

BALD EAGLE

Nature Center

Ⓟ Education Pavilion

Wildlife Hospital

Wildlife Housing Area

barn

PITCH PINE

observation platform

REINDEER LICHEN

ATLANTIC WHITE CEDAR

WHERE: 4 Sawmill Road, Medford, NJ 08055

ADMISSION: Free for members and children 3 and under, $10 for adults (ages 13+), $5 for children ages 4–12; open daily from 10:00 a.m. to 4:00 p.m.

PARKING: Parking is available in the nature center's modest lot, with overflow parking nearby.

DIFFICULTY, DISTANCE, ACCESS: The recommended walk is a 1-mile hike over fairly level trails that are not ADA-accessible. The nature center, however, is accessible.

FACILITIES: There are restrooms available in the nature center, which also offers museum exhibits, live animals, a children's playroom, and gift shop. A picnic area is also available.

BEST TIME: While a walk in May or June offers mountain laurels in bloom and a July or August one presents wild blueberries ripe for picking, a December visit offers an evergreen-rich landscape with no mosquitos.

SPECIAL NOTES: Neither dogs nor bikes allowed on the trails.

There are no mass transit options here.

December 21 is typically the winter solstice, the date with the longest night and cold usually settling in. Since the dawn of time, humans have responded with holidays that bring light and cheer back into the world. Where once we lit giant bonfires, today's Hanukkah, Christmas, and Kwanzaa all revolve around light, presents, and food. Evergreens play a starring role in December, a harkening back to old beliefs that evergreens possessed a magical power that allowed them to thwart whatever demons were killing nature in winter.

So if you need a walk to sidestep the hectic nature of the holidays or crave a walk that reminds you of these holiday traditions, I've got one of the best pine-filled walks in Wild Philly: the Woodford Cedar Run Wildlife Refuge in Medford, a 171-acre preserve on the edge of the Pine Barrens. And here's a bonus reason: swamps are great mosquito habitat. In December, with no mosquitoes, the walk is much more enjoyable than during the warmer times of the year.

The Pine Barrens, which we first met in Trip 1 and will thoroughly explore in Trip 27, is a unique ecosystem centered in southern New

▼ The nature center at the Woodford Cedar Run Wildlife Refuge was formerly the Woodford home.

Jersey that features forests of pine, oak, and cedar; clean water the color of iced tea; and a diverse assemblage of plants and animals, some of which you can't find anywhere else in Wild Philly. In fact, you'll meet many oaks and pines immediately in the parking lot of the nature center, including five-needled eastern white pines and three-needled pitch pines, the latter the signature pine of the area.

The refuge opened in 1997, when the state preserved the home and property of the Woodford family to use for environmental education, and the Woodford Nature Center is a wonderful reinvention of the family's residence. Start your walk in the nature center to pay admission and enjoy its exhibits. Cedar Run also includes a Wildlife Rehabilitation Hospital and an outdoor Wildlife Housing Area with nearly sixty nonreleasable New Jersey native animals on display. Some people come just to see them, and we'll meet them halfway through our walk.

Cedar Water

▼ A trail through Cedar Run's pine forest.

This walk takes you on a 1-mile loop along the White Trail, which starts just outside the center's front door and to the right. Walk to the back of the nature center building, where the White Trail heads left. But first, walk halfway across Cedar Run Lake on the footbridge provided and take in the lovely views.

Cedar Run Lake is a classic Pine Barrens lake, with cold, clear, clean water the color of iced tea, the color due to the all-natural tannins leaching out of the trees. The lake is lined with Atlantic white cedars, the classic Pinelands swamp tree, earning the stream that was dammed here—Cedar Run—its name.

When ready, head back to start the White Trail, which offers two bonuses. First, for little ones, this is a storybook trail, with the story unfolding along the trail at thirteen different stops, the first at the trailhead. Second, for the rest of us, there is a series of signs that, when read in total, form an exceptional primer on the Pine Barrens. I highly recommend them.

You'll quickly head across a small bridge over a spring, this spot densely clustered with more Atlantic white cedars, a tree with bark that peels vertically in narrow strips.

It's a creature of the Coastal Plain, growing within a narrow band of land hugging the coast from southern Maine to Georgia and along the Gulf Coast. With a few exceptions, you will not find this growing in the Piedmont, and the tree has disappeared from Pennsylvania's slice of the Coastal Plain.

It's also a lichen-rich walk, with shield-like lichens growing on tree bark and reindeer lichen on the ground. If you have little ones, point out that this is a favorite food of Santa's reindeer (true, hence its name!).

As you wrap around Cedar Run Lake, you'll find an observation platform. Step up and see what might be there, and especially notice the smaller pines growing under the power lines ahead of you. The White Trail continues to the right, and you'll walk over several more bridges as you go.

Hallie

Halfway through your walk is the Wildlife Housing Area, where many animals are on display: barred and screech owls, red-tailed and red-shouldered hawks, a pair of very chatty crows—one an American crow and the other its cousin, a fish crow—plus a handsome peregrine falcon. Mammals are here as well, including a raccoon, skunk, and squirrels.

The largest enclosure, the one closest to the bridge, includes a bald eagles, Hallie, a magnificent bird that you can observe up close. Do read the interpretive signage here, some of which explains how each animal ended up at Cedar Run.

You've got a choice here. The bridge to the nature center where you started is just beyond the eagle cage. You can take that back or, better, continue on the White Trail for another half a mile. To find the trail, walk across the front of the private residence, and you'll quickly find the white blazes.

You'll cross another bridge and come to the driveway by which you first entered the preserve. Here, the White Trail runs along the driveway and traverses the dam built to create Cedar Run Lake. Pause on the dam, and walk over to both sides, as these are each among the best views of the walk. There's also one of the preserve's largest eastern white pines on the outflow side of the dam.

One more diversion: the Pine Barrens is the birthplace of the Jersey Devil, as every special ecosystem needs its own monster. Opposite a sign for a private residence, the Yellow Trail heads off to the left. Follow that for only a few steps to find a surprise, the devil's very own home. (I'd been looking for this for years and did not know it was here.) Your loop ends back at the nature center.

Studies show that pinene, the chemical that gives pine its characteristic smell, is calming, lowering our blood pressure. I hope your walk through a pine forest soothed you and that memories of it will light your way through the dark winter ahead. Happy holidays.

TRIP 22 — PIPERSVILLE, PA

High Rocks Vista

As the New Year starts with high expectations, consider putting yourself atop the dramatic 200-foot cliffs of High Rocks to achieve a new perspective. Surrounding Tohickon Creek, Bucks County's own Grand Canyon offers six stunning vistas along the trail.

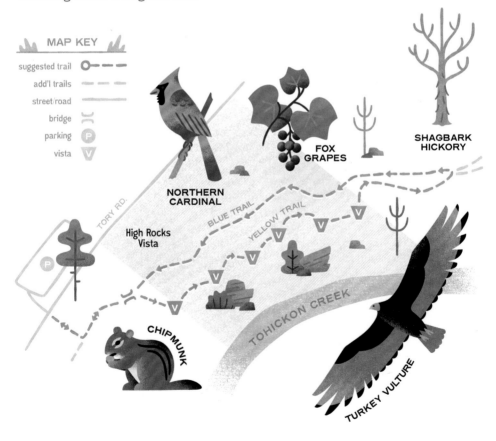

MAP KEY

suggested trail
add'l trails
street/road
bridge
parking
vista

NORTHERN CARDINAL

FOX GRAPES

SHAGBARK HICKORY

TORY RD.

High Rocks Vista

BLUE TRAIL

YELLOW TRAIL

TOHICKON CREEK

CHIPMUNK

TURKEY VULTURE

WHERE: 150 Tory Road, Pipersville, PA 18947
ADMISSION: Free; open daily from dawn to dusk.
PARKING: Ample parking is provided at the trailhead.
DIFFICULTY, DISTANCE, ACCESS: The recommended walk is a relatively easy 1.5-mile hike on trails that are rugged but not steep and along rocky trails atop cliffs. The trails are not ADA-accessible.
FACILITIES: There is no visitor center, but a portable toilet is located at the edge of the parking area.
BEST TIME: An early January walk gives you long, leafless vistas above a beautiful creek that makes an elegant oxbow curve below you. Consider returning for fall color.
SPECIAL NOTES: Bikes and dogs on leashes are welcome here.

The site is not accessible via mass transit.

My family enjoys the wonderful tradition of taking an easy nature walk on New Year's Day, an amble to get the juices flowing and to provide a respite from holiday stress. Any of the walks in this book will provide that amenity, but let's assume you'd like a New Year's walk that offers a fresh perspective on the world.

High Rocks will do that. Located in upper Bucks County, you will feel like you are standing on top of the world—because you pretty much will be. This walk takes you along a 200-foot vertical cliff above Tohickon Creek, the creek making a sinuous S-curve below you and a forest surrounding you. It's a great spot for self-reflection, for thinking about the year ahead. The hike also provides multiple selfie spots that will make all the friends in your social media feeds jealous.

While High Rocks will be found if you search for High Rocks State Park, it technically is part of the larger Ralph Stover State Park and abuts the county's Tohickon Valley Park. Donated in 1956 by famous author and Bucks County resident James Michener, High Rocks is created by two different sedimentary rocks, both Triassic in age. You can see both, especially the red argillite of the Lockatong Formation, which forms so much of the cliffs, plus the darker shales of the Brunswick Formation.

Park in the parking area on Tory Road, and read the kiosk for any updates or notes. There are park maps there as well. As the park is extensively used by rock climbers who love the challenge of scaling the cliff, you may see climbers assembling their gear here too.

Cross Tory Road to head into the trail, which goes through a mixed oak, hickory, and red maple forest. Veer toward the right, head downhill toward the creek, and walk toward the rock outcroppings. An old chain-link fence is in front of you; go to the right to where the fence ends and stand on an outcrop. There are trails from here down into a grotto, which you are welcome to explore.

Six Great Vistas

Three trails parallel the canyon rim: a higher Blue Trail marked by blue blazes, a lower Yellow Trail, and a third, not on the park's map, that hugs the chain-link fence. As you walk the well-worn fenceline trail, you'll come to a series of vistas, each better than the other, where the fence opens up to

▲ The view of Tohickon Creek from the High Rocks is magnificent.

a viewing area surrounded by older black metal fencing that protects visitors from falling.

Inhale each view, linger in each spot, notice the plants there growing around you, maybe make New Year's resolutions. Trace the route of Tohickon Creek below you as it heads toward the Delaware River.

Evergreen shrubs with small scale-like leaves grow across the canyon rim, some (the female ones) with small bluish berry-like cones eaten by many winter birds. These are eastern red junipers, dense, slow-growing shrubs, some of which seem like bonsai trees on the cliff. They are impressive plants: a West Virginia red juniper lived to be almost 1000 years old. Look for lichens, ferns, and mosses growing on the exposed rocks; sometimes one of each kind is only inches from another. I've even found dandelions toughing it out in the cracks. Poison ivy is here as well. Since the leaves are gone, be mindful of hairy-stemmed vines, a characteristic of the plant—you'll catch poison ivy by touching the vine too.

Animals of the Canyon

On one of my walks here on a windy day, I was startled to be on the edge of the canyon and looking *down* on turkey vultures soaring like black hang gliders, using the wind to hold them steady in one place. It was a cool sight. May you be this lucky.

I've also found fox scat on the trail and seen or heard woodpeckers, chickadees, cardinals, blue jays, robins, and more. Given the large number of hickories here, squirrels are a given. All of these animals are active in a winter forest.

▲ Down below, Tohickon Creek weaves through a forest of oak, hickory, and maple.

The last of the six vistas features perhaps the widest view of them all, allowing you to look downstream to where the creek curves. The fenceline trail ends here, and you'll walk uphill to turn onto the Yellow Trail. You'll soon be at a large crossroads of trails, where you'll continue to follow the yellow blazes. It soon travels across a rock face, an argillite grotto in the forest; be careful, as it may be slippery here if the trail is wet or icy.

At the three-quarters of a mile mark, you'll arrive at another junction with multiple trails converging. It's marked by a large shagbark hickory on your right, its telltale gray peeling bark a likely hibernating spot for insects or even bats. Here, turn left to head back on the Blue Trail, turning left again to follow its blazes. (Or you can continue on the Yellow Trail, which ends maybe another mile down, and turn around on the Blue Trail again.)

You'll come upon several junctions, but simply stay on the Blue Trail, which soon splits around a wonderful big oak tree. Close to the end of the walk, the trail ends at a T. Head left and cross a red bridge, where you can look down to your right to see the uptilted layers of the shale, the other rock forming the cliff.

If you make no other resolution for the New Year, resolve to keep walking in beautiful places like High Rocks. And if you'd like to extend your stay, Lake Nockamixon State Park is nearby as well—the lake is formed from Tohickon Creek—and continue exploring.

TRIP 23 ABINGTON, PA

Briar Bush Nature Center

Enjoy close-up views of squirrels and the area's many winter birds—like cardinals, titmice, dark-eyed juncos, white-throated sparrows, mourning doves, and blue jays—while sitting in a cozy cabin as they all come to the nature center's feeders. Then take a winter's stroll through a delightful slice of forest.

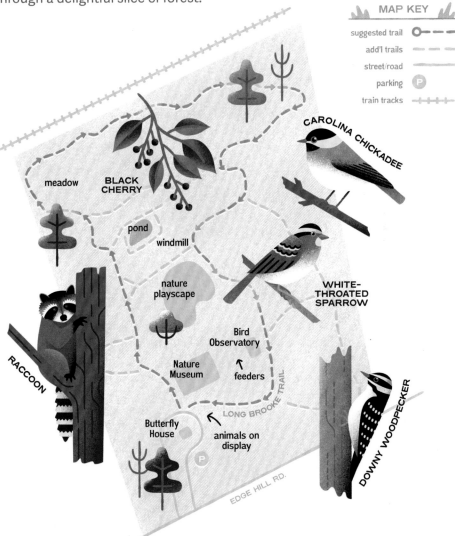

MAP KEY

suggested trail	O---
add'l trails	---
street/road	---
parking	Ⓟ
train tracks	+++++

CAROLINA CHICKADEE

meadow

BLACK CHERRY

pond

windmill

WHITE-THROATED SPARROW

nature playscape

RACCOON

Bird Observatory

Nature Museum

feeders

LONG BROOKE TRAIL

Butterfly House

animals on display

DOWNY WOODPECKER

EDGE HILL RD.

WHERE: 1212 Edge Hill Road, Abington, PA 19001

ADMISSION: Free; open from dawn to dusk; the nature museum is free to Abington residents, and admission for nonresidents is $3 per adult and $2 per child.

PARKING: Parking is available in the small lot outside the nature museum, which closes within 2 hours of sunset.

DIFFICULTY, DISTANCE, ACCESS: The recommended walk is only a half-mile long and generally flat, but there are several staircases along the way, making wheelchair access problematic.

FACILITIES: Both the nature museum and the bird observatory have water and restrooms, plus interactive exhibits for children. The nature museum includes live animals on display, plus a children's area and gift shop.

BEST TIME: While any time of year is great, a winter visit gives you great views of the diversity of Wild Philly's winter birdlife.

SPECIAL NOTES: No dogs are allowed on the trails.

For mass transit, take either the R2 Warminster Regional Rail Line or SEPTA's Bus 22 and exit at the Roslyn Station on Easton and Susquehanna Roads. Walk up the hill on Susquehanna Road, turn left on Edge Hill Road, and look for Briar Bush a few blocks up on your left.

In the winter, many of us assume that most animals have either migrated south or are hibernating, fast asleep during winter's storms. Not at all. Happily, a winter Wild Philly forest is home to a diverse array of very active animals: squirrels searching for the acorns they have stashed away, deer munching on trees and shrubs, fox and coyote prowling for mice, even red-tailed hawks flying overhead for cottontail rabbits.

▲ The nature museum at Briar Bush Nature Center has interactive exhibits and live animals on display.

Griscom Bird Observatory

At the Briar Bush Nature Center in Abington, you have a unique window—literally—into the bird life of a winter forest at its Griscom Bird Observatory. Around 1905, Everett and Florence Griscom purchased a small plot of land and built a log cabin in order to establish a bird sanctuary, likely the first in the region. The Griscoms ended up living here for more than 50 years, putting feeders up outside the cabin's windows, selling bird seed to the community, and offering bird programs to innumerable Scout groups and school children. In the early 1960s, after the couple had passed away, the neighborhood successfully convinced Abington to purchase the 12-acre property, and the Briar Bush Nature Center was born.

▲ The view from inside the Griscom Bird Observatory.

In the refurbished cabin, you can sit on benches and watch the bird show outside. Chickadees and titmice flit in and out of the feeders, nuthatches and woodpeckers cling to nearby tree trunks, and male and female cardinals visit the platform feeders or feed from the ground. Dark-eyed juncos and white-throated sparrows, a pair of northern birds that migrate to Wild Philly for the winter, are likely visitors as well. Mourning doves might join the fray, blue jays may bully their way past the others, and on rare days you might witness a Cooper's hawk grab one of these birds on a strafing run through the observatory. And, of course, acrobatic squirrels will be trying to crash the party. In addition to the birds, look for evergreen hollies growing there to give these birds winter cover.

To help in the identification, pictures and informational text line the wall below the window, describing the most common feeder visitors. Interactive exhibits in the Griscom Bird Observatory allow you to contribute to the counts and become a citizen scientist. There is also a children's niche in the observatory, where they can, for example, place birds and animals on a four-season magnetic forest mural.

Dede Long Nature Museum

When you visit Briar Bush, stop in at the Dede Long Nature Museum and ask for a trail map. The museum itself contains many interactive exhibits and a children's area too, plus a plethora of live animals like turtles, snakes, and birds.

Using the map, walk to the observatory, passing a red-tailed hawk and screech owls in their enclosures. As you turn left to get to the observatory, stop and admire the large white oak on your left as you turn—it's a beauty. The site's trails take you through a Pennsylvania forest of oak, beech, red maple, and tuliptree, among others; many key trees are labeled along the way. Depending on your interests, the center packs a lot into its 12 acres, including a storybook trail, pond, and children's nature playscape.

Of course, you can visit Briar Bush Nature Center all year, as many spring migrants stop in at the water feature outside the bird observatory; lots of brightly colored warblers and more have been spotted there. On a June walk, I witnessed my own first, a mother wood thrush feeding her nearly-grown fledgling on a trail only a few steps ahead of me. Surprisingly, the normally secretive birds didn't seem to mind my presence.

This walk is especially recommended for a snowy day. Bring a thermos of coffee and some donuts, cuddle up in the observatory like the Griscoms did last century, and keep this 100-year tradition alive by seeing how many species of birds you can find and identify.

▲ The trails at Briar Bush take you through a classic Pennsylvania forest.

Wissahickon Valley Park

Witness some of the most photogenic and most geologically interesting stony outcrops in the region, with great views of both Wissahickon Creek and its valley. Rhododendrons and hemlocks shade you much of the way, geese and ducks often swim in the creek, and the long views through a leafless forest are stunning.

WHERE: Valley Green Inn, 7 Valley Green Road, Philadelphia, PA 19128

ADMISSION: Free; open daily from dawn to dusk.

PARKING: This is a popular location, so come early to secure a coveted spot.

DIFFICULTY, DISTANCE, ACCESS: This 2-mile hike is relatively easy and flat for much of the walk, but challenging in key sections as you scamper around large rocks; portions of the trail can also be muddy and/or icy, making it not ADA-accessible. The Forbidden Drive section, however, is flat and easy for wheelchairs and strollers.

FACILITIES: There are restrooms alongside the Valley Green Inn, picnic tables nearby, and benches scattered strategically throughout the park.

BEST TIME: A winter's walk affords you long views through the forest to really see and understand the region's underlying geology.

SPECIAL NOTES: Dogs are allowed, but they must be leashed.

Although buses and trains can get you to Chestnut Hill or Roxborough, it is a bit of a hike to Valley Green Inn.

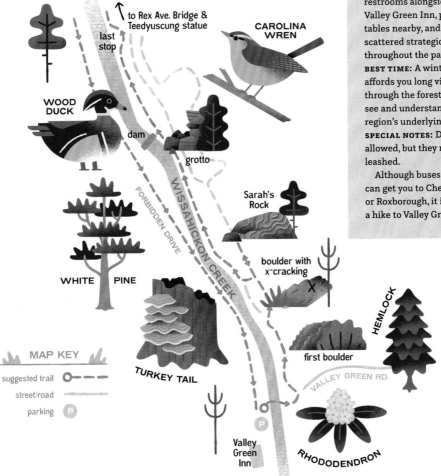

to Rex Ave. Bridge & Teedyuscung statue

last stop

CAROLINA WREN

WOOD DUCK

dam

grotto

Sarah's Rock

FORBIDDEN DRIVE

WISSAHICKON CREEK

WHITE PINE

boulder with x-cracking

HEMLOCK

first boulder

MAP KEY

suggested trail
street/road
parking

TURKEY TAIL

VALLEY GREEN RD.

Valley Green Inn

RHODODENDRON

◄ The Orange Trail through Wissahickon Valley Park features many intriguing rock outcroppings along the way.

Wissahickon Valley Park, with its Valley Green Inn and Forbidden Drive, is one of the city's most popular walking spots, crowded on any given weekend with dog walkers, hikers, runners, bikers, and even horseback riders. Frankly, it's not usually where you come to escape into nature. But the Wissahickon Valley contains some of the region's unique and most interesting geology, and this walk, along the opposite side of the creek from Forbidden Drive, is slightly off the beaten path.

Read the chapter about Wild Philly's geology before this walk. I am indebted to Sarah West, who wrote *Rediscovering the Wissahickon through Science and History* (1993), which includes this walk. These are Sarah's stops, but my text.

If you are driving to the park, use either Wise's Mill Road on the Roxborough side or Valley Green Road on the Chestnut Hill side, and walk to Valley Green Inn. As you arrive, visit the creek to see what birds may be active. While mallards and Canada geese are typically here, wood ducks—one of the region's prettiest birds—frequent this site as well.

When ready for your hike, find the Orange Trail entrance on Valley Green Road on the east (Chestnut Hill) side of the creek, uphill from the parking lots. You'll see steps leading downhill to a trail that sweeps uphill to the left, taking you back toward the creek.

The Wissahickon Formation

At a wooden shelter, the trail curves north, with rhododendrons and hemlocks around you, two plants not seen in too many other places in the region. But look at the trail underfoot as you make this curve. It is layered rock, but the layers are tilted vertically, like a cake turned on its side. The Wissahickon Formation is composed of ancient rocks that were once an island in an ancient ocean—the Iapetus, the precursor of the Atlantic—and then pushed up onto the North American plate as Africa and Europe slowly crushed into North America. The collision between plates was so prolonged and so powerful that the layers of rock, originally laid horizontally, were upended.

The large rock opposite the wooden shelter is composed of alternating bands of the Wissahickon schist this region is famous for, plus quartzite. Schist, the building block of so many of the city's homes, contains flecks of mica, both in the rock and eroded out onto the trail, and garnets, which are akin to chocolate chips in schist's cookie dough. The schist is also crenulated—wavy—which indicates the metamorphic rock, already formed under pressure, underwent pressure again as it buckled.

Just past this first stop, you'll come to a huge rock on the trail. This massive rock extends far back and uphill. As you look along its length, find the spot where a large chunk of rock seems to be missing, where a triangular slice of rock fell out. Just about halfway down the length of this rock, there is also a large X-shaped crack in its face. This is a joint in the rock, a place where compression caused the brittle rock to crack, but the rock has stayed together—one side of the crack has not moved away from the rock.

Sarah's Rock

The trail crosses a stream and forks, with the White Trail heading higher up and the Orange Trail descending to the creek. Take the White Trail for more than 500 feet and stop at another giant rock, this one beautifully composed of gray schist and wavy white lines.

▼ Wissahickon Creek is stunning as it flows through this section of Philadelphia.

This is Sarah's Rock, the one Friends of the Wissahickon trail ambassadors named after long-time geology trip leader Sarah West. Here, the metamorphic schist layers separated under pressure, and lava flowed between

them to harden into an igneous rock called pegmatite, itself composed of the white mineral feldspar. But even after the igneous intrusions hardened, the rocks again metamorphosed and these white intrusions buckled as well, forming these delightful bands.

▲ Sarah's Rock, named for Sarah West, who developed the geology walk along the Orange Trail.

It's hard to imagine the amount of time, heat, and pressure it takes to make these rocks, but they formed more than 500 million years ago, 250 million years *before* the first dinosaurs.

Head back down the White Trail toward its junction with the Orange Trail. As you get closer, you'll find walkers have created several cut-throughs to get to the Orange Trail below you. Make your way downhill on one of them, turn right on the Orange Trail, and walk north again in the direction of Sarah's Rock.

Soon you'll discover another dramatic rock, a large low section of gray rock sliced at almost a 90-degree angle—more intersecting fractures where the rock fell out. On a large slab of rock in front of this, look for the prominent lines formed by crenulations in the schist.

Next turn around and look downhill. Just before you is a large stone with the same white wavy lines you just saw at Sarah's Rock. Since the feldspar-loaded pegmatite is wavy, folding occurred after the pegmatite flowed into the rock. You'll now have to scramble up and over this rock to continue along the trail. Be careful, as footing can be challenging here—perhaps lower your center of gravity to walk more easily.

The Grotto

Another large exposure of rocks we are coming to know well—gray schist and lighter pegmatite—soon extends across the path. At the southern end, carefully examine the pegmatite, which here has noticeably larger feldspar crystals. Their larger size indicates cooler rocks that allowed the crystals time to form over a longer period and become larger.

As you walk across the face of this rock, it appears to be a large grotto with water dripping everywhere, and ferns and lichens are rich in this area. But big fractures have formed in this rock, cutting vertical slices to form the dramatic rock face. As you walk, look for a very special rock along the face, a visible band of quartzite forming two humps in the gneiss, a cursive M across the rock face. To the left, a 3-inch band of pegmatite suddenly intrudes, slicing through the quartzite band at an angle, clearly forming after the quartzite was in place. The quartzite folded over millions of years, and another mountain-building event later occurred, allowing pegmatite to intrude.

About a tenth of a mile past the grotto, one more large rock formation invites you to see schist and pegmatite. But here, notice how lichens and mosses have been growing on these rocks. Water and plants have conspired to create cracks in the rocks, allowing them to weather more and allowing solid rock to become covered over by soil. Lichens—those curious mixtures of algae and fungi—are pioneer species, the first living things to cling to rock, the first living things to begin breaking rock down to form soil.

Forbidden Drive or Teedyuscung

This completes the geology walk, but you have two choices at the moment. Walk to Rex Avenue, which offers you a bridge across Wissahickon Creek; you can take that bridge to Forbidden Drive and head back to Valley Green. Or, you can look for signs to the Teedyuscung statue and visit the monument—only after reading the section on page 37 about the statue.

There are many more trails in Wissahickon Valley Park, so return often throughout the year.

Your Street

To restore your relationship with nature, calm yourself from hectic everyday living, and even combat climate change, get to know the nature of your street and neighborhood. The health of Wild Philly depends upon a network of naturalists understanding—and advocating for—nature.

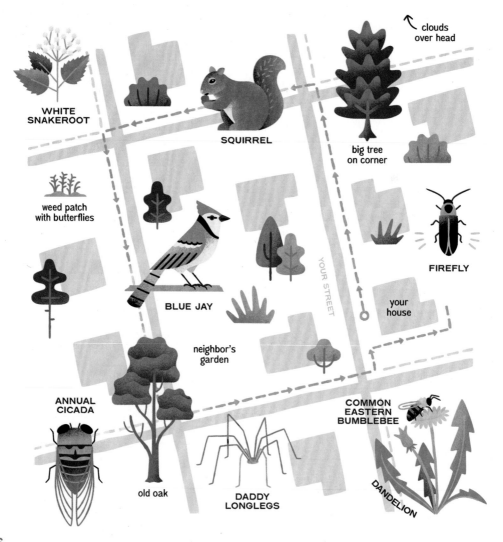

WHITE SNAKEROOT

SQUIRREL

big tree on corner

clouds over head

weed patch with butterflies

FIREFLY

BLUE JAY

YOUR STREET

your house

neighbor's garden

ANNUAL CICADA

COMMON EASTERN BUMBLEBEE

old oak

DADDY LONGLEGS

DANDELION

▲ Photographer Troy Bynum spotted this Cooper's hawk in his own yard preying on a hapless mourning dove, a surprisingly common sight among feeder-watchers.

◄ Cottontail rabbits can be found throughout the region, even in and around backyards.

I live only 2 miles from City Avenue, on a street of homes built in the 1920s. My home's foundation, like so many Philadelphia homes, is made of Wissahickon schist. But even here, in a neighborhood that has been developed for more than 100 years, nature simply abounds.

The eastern white pine towering in my neighbor's yard over my garage drops avalanches of pollen on my car, but I've heard so many birds in that one tree: cardinals and blue jays, of course, but also blackpoll warblers migrating through from the tip of South America and screech owls whinnying like horses. Squirrels have built round leafy dreys in its branches and use the power lines above my garage to tightrope-walk back and forth. They scamper around its bark like speed demons, either playing, establishing dominance, or trying to mate—I'm never sure which, but one day I'll crack the mystery.

Walking my street, I look forward to the first crocus, the first monarch, the first firefly. I've seen foxes, raccoons, opossums, and cottontail rabbits on the street as well, and a murder of crows once cruised noisily directly down my street in hot pursuit of a great horned owl. Ladybug larvae have visited me while I am reading the Sunday paper outside, and wild columbine grows out of a crack in the asphalt right up against my garage wall.

WHERE: Your neighborhood
ADMISSION: Free.
PARKING: None required.
DIFFICULTY, DISTANCE, ACCESS: The difficulty and distance of this walk is completely your choice; make it as easy or as challenging as you like.
FACILITIES: Your home base likely has all your needs taken care of.
BEST TIME: Absolutely all year long, as something is happening with the nature on your street on any given day of the year.

The Dawn Chorus

At our street's annual post-Labor Day block party one year, I witnessed uncountable numbers of nighthawks migrating south, swooping through the air while launching their characteristic "peent!" Large skeins of snow geese and Canada geese have both noisily migrated overhead, signs of the changing seasons. Red-tailed hawks searching for a rising thermal of hot air have transfixed me innumerable times. The dawn chorus of the robins frequently awakens my light-sleeper wife at the ungodly hour of 5:00 a.m. Many times I've seen bats hunting moths, their silhouettes bat-signaled against the indigo dusk sky.

Though our backyard is modest in size, our bird feeder has pulled in goldfinches and chickadees, woodpeckers adore the suet in the winter feeder, and a hummingbird or two visits our nectar feeder every day during the summer. One year, in a row of common milkweed growing against our chimney, our family reveled in the thirty monarch chrysalises attached everywhere— and we enjoyed watching many of them hatch and fly away.

There's No Place Like Home

Neither my yard nor my street is unusual. In fact, both are remarkably typical, as nature is simply everywhere. We all reside in Lenapehoking, each street a strip in the fabric of a living landscape of plants and animals. While walking Wild Philly is so important for our soul and for restoring our lost connection to the land, you don't have to venture too far afield to find nature. In fact, there's no place like home.

So pick a walk in your neighborhood that includes, say, a prominent tree or a neighbor with an especially compelling garden—on my street, our ex-pat British neighbor has an unbelievable flower garden, and I look forward to what blooms next all year. You might even head toward a vacant lot with a healthy crop of weeds. Walk that route, if not daily, then often enough to know the rhythms of nature in your neighborhood.

Studies show that time in the outdoors is beneficial, that it prolongs life. Green calms us immediately, lowering our blood pressure and slowing our pulse. When our eyes look at the fractals of tree leaves or clouds, it is calming, restorative. Pine scent is calming too, so find that nearby pine tree and breathe in a dose of medicine. You deserve an outdoor walk just for these benefits.

But combating climate change requires a nation of naturalists who know nature's schedule as well as a commuter knows the SEPTA train schedule. Wait, why is that flower blooming now, so early in the season? Wait, why is that bird here now; when it should be later? Wait, I've not heard that bird passing through in a few years. Where did it go?

Photograph a cherished flower and post it on social media or on iNaturalist—share your love of nature with your friends. Your social media app will likely let you know next year to expect that same flower, and it can begin to serve as your record of what and when you see certain special things.

▲ One of Wild
Philly's most
common birds,
the robin will nest
on just about any
street in the region.

Become an expert on the nature of your street and neighborhood by just walking and watching. Then consider sharing your knowledge with your neighbors and friends virtually and in person, and see if what you learn motivates you to do more. Who knows, you might become as crazy as me and remove all the lawn from your small front yard and turn it into a re-creation of a Philadelphia forest, mayapples growing alongside Solomon's seal and wild geraniums.

The message of this book is simple: Wild Philadelphia is there waiting for you, and all you have to do is walk. Just walk. Even if it's only outside your front door.

TRIP 26 VARIOUS SITES IN NEW JERSEY

Sex and Gluttony on Delaware Bay

Every spring, millions of horseshoe crabs haul themselves onto beaches to mate and lay eggs, a spectacle unto itself. But thousands of exhausted and emaciated migrating shorebirds have timed their northern flights to stop here and refuel on crab eggs. It's one of the country's most extraordinary natural events.

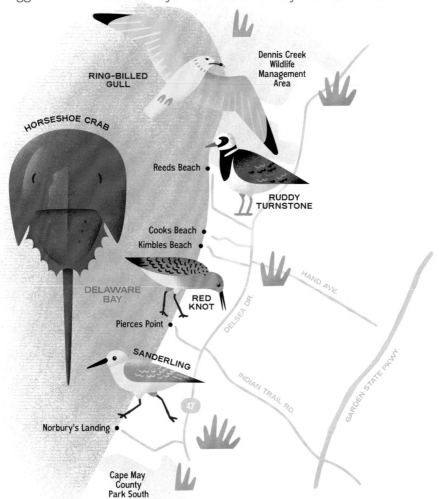

RING-BILLED GULL

Dennis Creek Wildlife Management Area

HORSESHOE CRAB

Reeds Beach

RUDDY TURNSTONE

Cooks Beach

Kimbles Beach

HAND AVE.

DELAWARE BAY

RED KNOT

DELSEA DR.

Pierces Point

SANDERLING

INDIAN TRAIL RD.

GARDEN STATE PKWY.

47

Norbury's Landing

Cape May County Park South

WHERE: Reeds Beach Road, Middle Township, NJ 08210
ADMISSION: Free.
PARKING: There is plenty of parking at Reeds Beach, though less so at the other sites noted here.
DIFFICULTY, DISTANCE, ACCESS: These are less walks than drives to a series of beaches to witness the migration and spawning event. Since the beaches are sandy, the sites are not ADA-accessible or stroller-friendly.
FACILITIES: Few, if any, facilities exist at any of these beaches.
BEST TIME: Mid-May, around Mother's Day.

▲ Horseshoe crabs mate in the surf along a Delaware Bay beach.

In mid-May, one of the country's most extraordinary natural phenomena occurs on both the Delaware and New Jersey sides of Delaware Bay. If you are into nature, it simply needs to be seen.

Horseshoe crabs, those prehistoric living fossils that have lumbered across ocean bottoms for 450 million years, haul themselves onto beaches to mate and lay eggs in the surf. Large females usually have an entourage of smaller male hangers-on. Each female lays about 80,000 eggs, each one resembling a small green BB. The crabs especially emerge at night in the full and new moons of high tides, a spectacle worth seeing in itself, as Delaware Bay has the single largest concentration of mating horseshoe crabs on the planet.

But in an extraordinary act of evolutionary synchronicity, migrating shorebirds arrive at the same time, landing on Delaware Bay beaches exhausted and emaciated from their nonstop flight over the Atlantic Ocean from South America. They're here to refuel to continue their journey to Arctic nesting grounds. To finish this remarkable trip, the famished birds need foods rich in fats.

Coincidentally, the beaches are loaded with fatty crab eggs roiling in the surf. So the shorebirds enjoy a raucous debauchery of nonstop feeding, filling up on the eggs that give them the energy they need to finish the trip.

▲ Red knots time their northward migration to fatten up on horseshoe crab eggs.

The Red Knot

The most iconic—and symbolic—of these shorebirds is the red knot, a 9-inch-long sandpiper with a terra cotta belly. The bird makes one of migration's longest runs, flying 9300 miles each spring from Tierra del Fuego at the tip of South America to nest above the Arctic Circle in the spring. For this bird, May's horseshoe crab eggs are simply essential.

Many other shorebirds join them in this feast, including other sandpiper species like dunlins and sanderlings, along with plovers, ruddy turnstones, willets, and terns—not to mention laughing, herring, and black-backed gulls.

It is a sight to behold. Arrive at low tide, and the beaches are crammed with migrating birds cheek-to-jowl in a frenzy of feeding, the cacophony of gulls impossibly loud. Arrive at nighttime high tide, and the beaches are chock-a-block with horseshoe crabs. It is a naturalist's nirvana.

Except the red knot is depressingly endangered. While horseshoe crabs have been used for fertilizer since the Lenape days, overharvesting in recent decades for industrial fertilizer, bait, and even biomedical research—the crab's blue copper-based blood is useful to researchers—has greatly depleted their numbers. With significantly fewer crabs emerging in the surf, red knot numbers have plummeted as well. If the birds leaving Delaware Bay have not gotten sufficient food, they may die on their way to the Arctic or not

▲ Reeds Beach in New Jersey is one of several Delaware Bay beaches where one can see this phenomenon.

have enough energy to reproduce. Bird experts are terrified we will lose the race of red knots that engages in this amazing migration.

While numerous beaches on both sides of Delaware Bay offer wonderful opportunities to check in on both crabs and birds, several beaches just north of Cape May offer you good views along with access to experts monitoring the situation: Reeds Beach, Cooks Beach, Kimbles Beach, Pierces Point, and Norbury's Landing. All are easily accessible off N. Delsea Drive, Route 47, the road so many Philadelphians take to Cape May.

Reeds Beach

Start at Reeds Beach, the northernmost of the five. Driving south on Route 47, turn right onto Reeds Beach Road and take this to its end, turning right on Beach Drive and taking this to the end. Park on the road, and you'll find a stone jetty going into the bay. Walk the jetty to its end, and you'll see the beach, along with signs interpreting the migration and ropes asking you not to walk any further.

These ropes are now present at all the beaches, an important effort to prevent people from disturbing the birds. If volunteer seashore stewards are present, ask where the red knots might be. They may name one of the beaches described below. One option is to head directly to that beach, or tour as many as you'd like because there's always something a little different at each. For example, bald eagles may be seen flying over, or even standing on, any of these beaches at low tide. I once spotted an anomalous turkey vulture on Cooks Beach surrounded by gulls, attracted to the dead horseshoe crabs littering the beach that got stranded as the tide went out. Not your typical Cape May shorebird!

Cooks and Kimbles

Cooks Beach is only 2 miles from Reeds Beach. Head back to Route 47, drive south, and turn right on Cooks Beach Road, which dead-ends at the beach. Kimbles Beach is the next in line, only 3 miles south of Cooks, and another right turn off Route 47. While the faded wooden street sign might be hard to read, you won't miss the large Cape May National Wildlife Refuge sign telling you to turn right on Kimbles Beach Road. The road dead-ends at the beach. These two beaches, Cooks and Kimble, offer the best views up and down the beach.

Pierces Point and Norbury's Landing

Pierces Point is only a few miles further south. Get back on Route 47, turn right, and make another right at Pierces Point Road at the King Nummy Trail Campground sign. This road curves at the shore; follow the curve to the right, past a neighborhood of beach houses, and park where the road ends at the beach. Walk to the shore.

To reach the last beach, Norbury's Landing, continue south on Route 47 for another 2 miles, turning right on Bay Shore Road, a large intersection with a traffic light. After about a mile, Bay Shore Road curves left, but drive straight on Millman Boulevard, which ends at the beach.

After visiting these sites, consider visiting one of the three New Jersey Audubon centers in operation in the area, any one of which is worth visiting: the Cape May Bird Observatory on Route 47, the Nature Center of Cape May on the ocean side of Cape May, and another observatory in Cape May Point. Ask them how you can help untangle the red knots from their plight.

TRIP 27 HAMMONTON, NJ

New Jersey Pine Barrens

This hike is at Batsto, a historic village within the massive Wharton State Forest. Here you can explore New Jersey's acclaimed Pine Barrens—the home of endless pine forests, sandy roads, cedar bogs, blueberry bushes, endangered orchids and ferns, carnivorous plants, and even the legendary Jersey Devil.

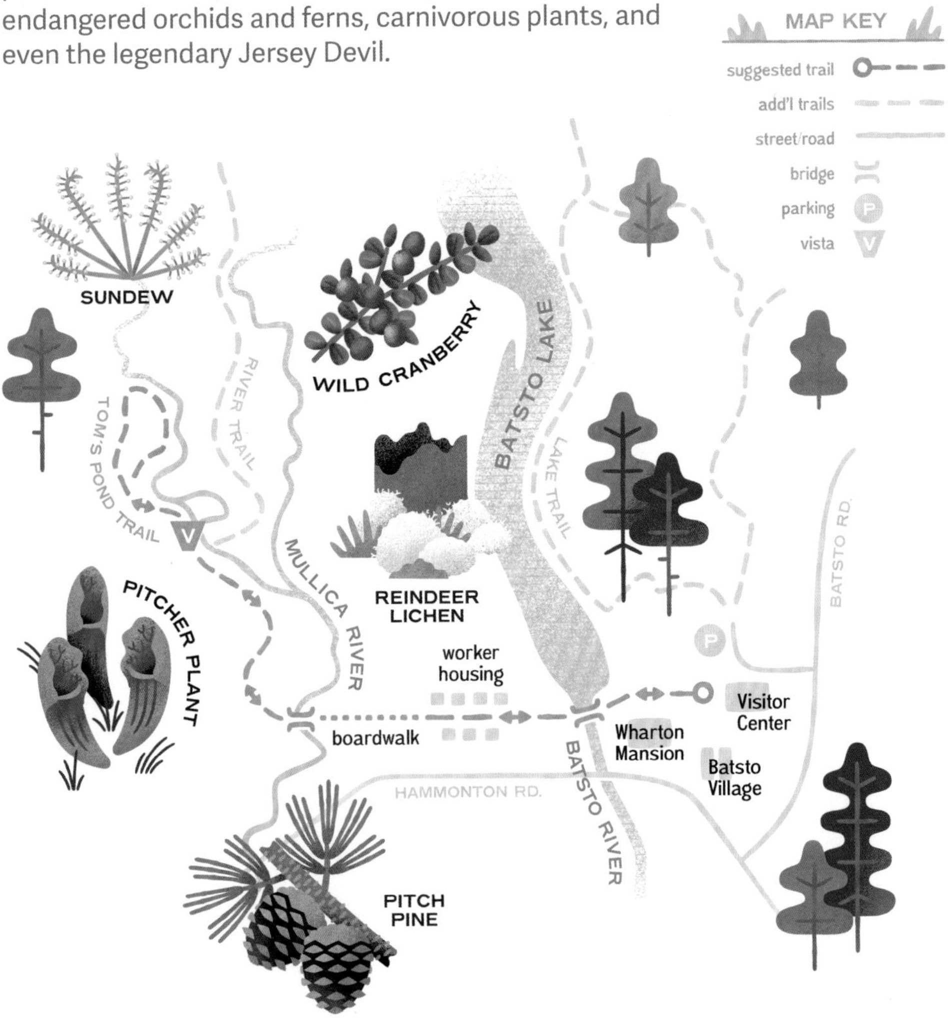

MAP KEY

suggested trail
add'l trails
street/road
bridge
parking
vista

SUNDEW

WILD CRANBERRY

RIVER TRAIL

TOM'S POND TRAIL

BATSTO LAKE

LAKE TRAIL

PITCHER PLANT

MULLICA RIVER

REINDEER LICHEN

worker housing

boardwalk

BATSTO RIVER

Wharton Mansion

Visitor Center

Batsto Village

BATSTO RD.

HAMMONTON RD.

PITCH PINE

WHERE: Batsto Village, Wharton State Forest, 31 Batsto Road, Hammonton, NJ 08037

ADMISSION: Free, but there is a parking fee on large holiday weekends; open daily from dawn to dusk.

PARKING: There is plenty of parking in the site's large parking lots.

DIFFICULTY, DISTANCE, ACCESS: The recommended walk is 2 miles, which can be shortened or lengthened as you wish. The footing is often sandy, but it's flat. Batsto Village is easily accessible for strollers and wheelchairs, though the latter might be unable to easily access all the site's buildings.

FACILITIES: Batsto Village provides restrooms, water, picnic tables, and benches with great views.

BEST TIME: While any time of year is wonderful, late spring and early summer are great for finding the carnivorous plants like pitcher plants and sundews that line cedar bogs.

SPECIAL NOTES: Dogs are allowed, but they must be leashed. Bikes are allowed as well, but the sandy soils make bike riding challenging.

▲ Batsto Village in the Pine Barrens is a museum of a once-thriving town.

Halfway between Philadelphia and the Jersey shore, the 1.1 million acres of the Pine Barrens comprise the largest remaining open space in the megalopolis that stretches between Richmond and Boston. A wildly unique ecosystem that has evolved on the long stretch of sandy soil that underlies so much of southern New Jersey, the Pine Barrens is covered in pitch pine and scrub oak, with blueberry bushes growing underneath. Pure water naturally the color of iced tea flows through its cedar swamps and bogs, the creek edges hemmed in by spongy mats of sphagnum moss and cranberry bogs. Growing from the moss are a range of orchids and carnivorous plants, like pitcher plants and sundews, plants adapted to capture and eat small insects.

While we nibbled on the edges of the Pine Barrens at Black Run Preserve (Trip 1) and Woodford Cedar Run Wildlife Refuge (Trip 21), the area is so unique that a trip to its heart is a necessity for any Wild Philly nature lover.

In the 1700s, when early colonists discovered what became known as "bog iron," iron deposits that had precipitated in the acidic groundwater, the pines suddenly became the site of numerous forges, some even producing cannonballs and musket shot for the Revolution. When better iron ore was

► The Tom's Pond Trail includes a section of boardwalk through a cedar swamp.

discovered elsewhere in the country, the furnaces fell silent. Today, ghost towns with evocative names like Martha and Ong's Hat dot the Pine Barrens. Blueberries are a hugely important crop in the area, and the bogs have made New Jersey one of the nation's most important cranberry states. In fact, the Garden State is among the top five producers of both fruits.

All of this rich human and natural history can easily be sampled from one place, Batsto Village. Founded around an iron forge in 1766, the village grew and evolved. After the Civil War, it was bought by industrialist Joseph Wharton, who purchased extensive properties in the Pinelands for his plan to provide this water to Philadelphia. But when New Jersey passed legislation forbidding the export of water to other states, thwarting Wharton's ambition, Batsto became a gentleman's farm, which the state ultimately purchased. At 122,000 acres, Wharton is the largest state forest in New Jersey.

The village includes a number of buildings you can tour, including Wharton's Italianate mansion, a Visitor Center with numerous exhibits and a gift shop, and a small nature center. The forge is gone, but it was located close to the lake that was formed when the Batsto River was dammed for hydropower.

Tom's Pond Trail

The recommended walk embraces both the history and nature of the Pine Barrens. Park at the Visitor Center, using its exhibits as your orientation and appetizer. Start your walk along the village's main street past Wharton's mansion, the lake on the Batsto River, and the village houses where workers once lived.

Leave the village on the orange-blazed Tom's Pond Trail, walking through a post-and-rail fence's gate; cross a sandy access road and follow the orange paint blazes. As you walk, notice the sandy soil and check out the pine trees—they are mostly pitch pine, their needles bundled in clusters of three.

Look for scrubby oak trees of several species around you as well. Close to the ground, you should easily find reindeer lichen, seeming like living green-blue steel wool pads. Blueberries and its cousins huckleberries and deerberries are here as well; see if you can spot those.

You'll soon walk across a boardwalk to cross the Mullica River. Look for stands of Atlantic white cedar, a tree typical of Pinelands swamps as it grows only in wetlands. Red maples and black gums are nearby, with sphagnum moss growing in and around the hummocks produced by the trees.

After the Mullica River, the trail veers gently to the right. Be mindful there is a network of unmarked trails that can easily mislead you: stay with the orange-blazed Tom's Pond Trail. About a quarter of a mile after the bridge, the yellow-blazed Mullica River Trail heads off to the right across a long bridge—do *not* go there; instead, stay on the orange-blazed trail. Only a few steps beyond this junction, you'll get the quintessential view of a Pinelands cedar bog. Welcome to Tom's Pond.

▶ The pitcher plant is one of several carnivorous plants growing in Pine Barrens bogs.

Pitcher Plants and Sundews

A sandy spot allows you to approach the pond, which is more correctly a sphagnum-covered riverside bog. Look for pitcher plants growing on the mossy mat. The plant's pitcher collects rainwater, into which the plant excretes acidic digestive juices. When an insect lands on the leaf, downward-facing hairs force it to walk downward, where it hits a slick waxy spot and slips into the water to be digested.

If you look very closely—you may have to kneel—you will find three species of another carnivorous plant, the sundew. Round-leaved, spatulate-leaved, and thread-leaved sundews are all present. See if you can find dewy secretions on this plant's leaves. Sweet-smelling, the secretions seduce insects to fly in and get stuck here. Then nearby tentacles coil around the insect and smother it, so the leaf can slowly digest it.

▶ Sundews, another carnivorous plant, grow in cedar bogs, often alongside pitcher plants.

Leaving this vista, the Tom's Pond Trail makes a circle ahead; walk the loop following the blazes, then retrace your steps back to the Visitor Center. Along the way, look for fence lizards scurrying by, towhees calling, deer jumping through the woods, and so much more.

The Pinelands even has its legend, that of the Jersey Devil. This monster was allegedly the accursed thirteenth child of an exhausted Mrs. Leeds, who asked the devil to take the boy—and he obliged. We saw the Jersey Devil's tongue-in-cheek residence at the Cedar Run Wildlife Refuge. When you walk through this forest, you know you are not in Wild Philly anymore. Instead, this is a very different, very special place. How could such a legend not arise?

If this walk whets your Pinelands whistle, the gift shop coincidentally carries numerous books on the history and ecology of the Pine Barrens, some with additional walks for you to take. Do let the pines bedevil you.

Hawk Mountain Sanctuary

Only 90 minutes from Philadelphia and world famous for both raptor observation and conservation, Hawk Mountain is one of the nation's premier spots for close-up viewing of hawks, eagles, and falcons as they soar southward on their autumnal migration. The top of the mountain also offers a 70-mile panoramic view of Penn's Woods in stunning autumn colors.

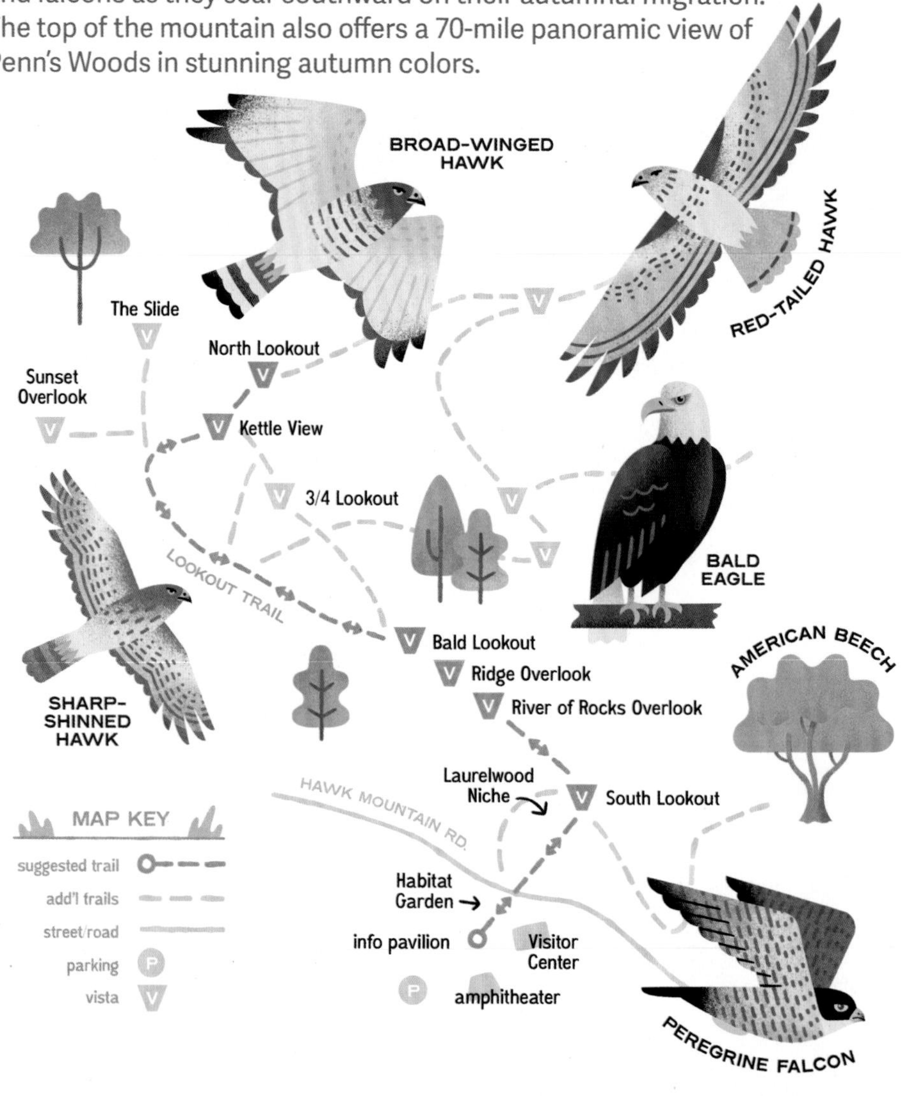

BROAD-WINGED HAWK

RED-TAILED HAWK

The Slide

North Lookout

Sunset Overlook

Kettle View

3/4 Lookout

LOOKOUT TRAIL

BALD EAGLE

AMERICAN BEECH

SHARP-SHINNED HAWK

Bald Lookout

Ridge Overlook

River of Rocks Overlook

Laurelwood Niche

South Lookout

HAWK MOUNTAIN RD.

MAP KEY

suggested trail ○----
add'l trails ----
street/road ——
parking ℗
vista Ⓥ

Habitat Garden →

info pavilion

Visitor Center

amphitheater

PEREGRINE FALCON

▲ This is just one of the many extraordinary views from the top of Hawk Mountain.

"Sharpie over Pinnacle," yelled the intern to our group, using the sharp-shinned hawk's nickname. Some fifty of us were perched on cold hard rocks on the edge of the Kittatinny Ridge, named with the Lenape word for "endless." Only a minute later, "There's a nice male kestrel coming by on the left." As she called out birds, heads whipsawed left and right.

While it was an overcast day in late October with less-than-prime hawk-watching conditions, we were treated to multiple bald eagles *and* its cousin, a golden eagle, innumerable sharp-shinned and Cooper's hawks, a harrier, an osprey, several merlins, a couple of kestrels, red-tailed hawks, cartwheeling ravens, and lots of turkey and black vultures.

This was a mediocre day by Hawk Mountain standards. For me, it was perfection.

Only 90 minutes northwest of Philadelphia, Hawk Mountain is one of the most famed birdwatching places on the planet and a must-see for any Wild Philly enthusiast. Anytime from mid-August deep into November, it is, along with Cape May Point State Park (Trip 29), the premiere place for watching migrating raptors. In mid-September, hundreds of broad-winged hawks are migrating south to the Amazon rainforest; a month later, sharp-shinned hawks are en route to Florida.

WHERE: 1700 Hawk Mountain Road, Kempton, PA 19529
ADMISSION: Members are free, $10 for adults, $7 for seniors, $5 for children ages 6–12, and free for children 5 and younger; open daily from 8:00 a.m. to 5:00 p.m.
PARKING: There is generous parking, but the lots fill up rapidly on autumn weekends, so get there early.
DIFFICULTY, DISTANCE, ACCESS: There is a very short, easy, flat walk to the South Lookout that is ADA-accessible. A 1-mile, rugged, uphill walk takes you to the second, more popular, North Lookout, but that trail is not ADA-accessible.
FACILITIES: Hawk Mountain maintains a stunning Visitor Center with restrooms, museum exhibits, a gift shop, and more. There are restrooms located near the South Lookout as well.
BEST TIME: When a cold front comes through in the fall.
SPECIAL NOTES: Neither dogs nor bikes are allowed on Hawk Mountain's trails.

Panoramic Views of Penn's Woods

Hawk Mountain, the nation's first sanctuary for birds of prey, is a private, nonprofit wildlife sanctuary supported by admission fees and membership dues. On 2600 acres abutting 9000 acres of state gameland, Hawk Mountain also offers unparalleled views of an autumn forest, the trees cloaked in stunning colors. Even without the birds, the panoramic 70-mile view is itself magnificent and worth the price of admission. Want to see Penn's Woods? Few places are better.

The sanctuary has many trails worth exploring, so check in at the Visitor Center and grab a map. For those who struggle with walking or travel in wheelchairs, South Lookout, only 175 yards from the entrance gate, is a straight and easy shot with very good views and trained educators on hand. In addition, Skyline Trail traverses the ridgeline to the nearby Appalachian Trail. But a first-time Hawk Mountain visitor should walk to the North Lookout, the mecca of hawk watching. Only 1 mile away on a wooded walk through a boulder-strewn forest, the trail ends at a series of dramatic almost-vertical steps taking you to the lookout. Kids will probably love this; grandparents perhaps not so much.

At North Lookout, the official counter sits behind a post-and-rail fence, calling out sightings; veteran birdwatchers often assemble themselves in front of the railing. Several other sanctuary staff are also there, most of them interns hired for the season. I recommend sitting as close to the counter as possible, as they will typically spot a raptor long before you might and will quickly know what it is. Eavesdropping on this inner circle is a master class in ornithology, and you should feel free to ask as many questions as you wish.

On my October visit, my brother and I spent a good 4 hours sitting here, having brought backpacks filled with food and water. You don't need to sit that long, but, while we outlasted most, there were quite a few who were there when we arrived and still there when we left. Serious birders come to Hawk Mountain.

The Cold Front

Late September and October weekends are especially crowded at the sanctuary. Hawk Mountain smartly employs many people to handle parking; simply follow their directions. If you choose to go on a weekend, arrive by 10:00 a.m. to get a better parking spot.

In addition to hawk watching, the sanctuary's trails provide great hiking, its staff offers multiple presentations, even live raptor shows, and the Visitor Center has great exhibits on hawks and the history of the sanctuary.

If you are able to visit on an off-day in the fall, I'd highly recommend it. Even better, like at Militia Hill, if a cold front moves through and the winds are from the northwest, head to Hawk Mountain immediately. On a mid-September day, you just might see the 760 broad-winged hawks spotted at the sanctuary in only one day in 2020 or the 411 sharp-shinned hawks seen a month later on that bird's big day. After only a few visits, you too will be yelling, "sharpie over Pinnacle," and all heads will swivel to the right.

TRIP 29 CAPE MAY, NJ

Cape May Point State Park

Like Hawk Mountain, this park at the tip of New Jersey is legendary among the nation's birdwatchers. Migrating raptors, songbirds, and even butterflies gather here before they make the great leap across Delaware Bay, and birdwatchers and nature lovers flock to watch them do it.

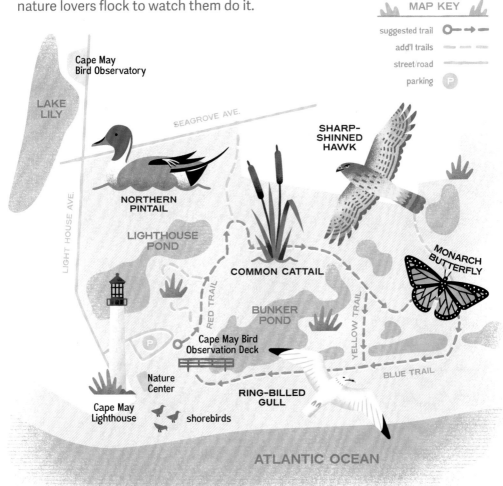

MAP KEY

suggested trail
add'l trails
street/road
parking

Cape May
Bird Observatory

LAKE
LILY

SEAGROVE AVE.

NORTHERN
PINTAIL

SHARP-
SHINNED
HAWK

LIGHT HOUSE AVE.

LIGHTHOUSE
POND

COMMON CATTAIL

MONARCH
BUTTERFLY

RED TRAIL

BUNKER
POND

YELLOW TRAIL

Cape May Bird
Observation Deck

BLUE TRAIL

Nature
Center

RING-BILLED
GULL

Cape May
Lighthouse   shorebirds

ATLANTIC OCEAN

▲ Throngs of waterfowl gather on Bunker Pond at Cape May Point.

WHERE: Light House Avenue, Cape May Point, NJ 08212

ADMISSION: Free; the parking lot's gates are open daily from 8:00 a.m. to 8:00 p.m.

PARKING: There is plenty of parking available in the large parking lot.

DIFFICULTY, DISTANCE, ACCESS: While much of this experience is observing hawks on the platform, there are hiking opportunities too. The hawk-watching platform is ADA-accessible, and there is an accessible boardwalk nature trail through a section of forests and marsh alongside the platform.

FACILITIES: While there are no facilities at the hawk-watching platform, there are restrooms in a state-operated facility across the parking lot, open from 8:00 a.m. to 8:00 p.m.

BEST TIME: Come anytime in the fall, but especially after a cold front comes through.

SPECIAL NOTES: While leashed dogs are technically allowed on the hawk-watching platform, they are not allowed on the park's trails, making it inadvisable. Bikes are not allowed on the trails as well.

Check out a map of New Jersey and notice how the state forms a V-shaped funnel, with Cape May Point sitting at the bottom of the funnel. Then imagine you were a migrating hawk flying down the Eastern Seaboard. The funnel forces you to Cape May, where the land suddenly ends and you are faced with a large expanse of sea. So you and thousands of your kin wait at Cape May Point for the right weather conditions to make the jump across Delaware Bay.

Then imagine that you are a fanatical birdwatcher living in Wild Philly. If you know it's good weather for migrating raptors, you have a tough choice—drive north to Hawk Mountain or south to Cape May Point. For any nature lover, both are required stops at some point.

So. Many. Birds.

At Cape May Point State Park, in the shadow of the historic lighthouse and at the back of a nondescript beachside parking lot, New Jersey Audubon maintains an observation deck and migratory bird count from September 1 through November 30. The site is staffed with experts, and birders flock here to watch birds make the great leap across the bay. On the third weekend

▲ The hawk-watching platform at Cape May Point abuts a saltwater marsh complex.

of October, there is even a large birding festival with an apt slogan: "So. Many. Birds."

And indeed there are. On a good day, you'll see a full complement of raptors—sharp-shinned hawks, Cooper's hawks, harriers, broad-winged hawks, ospreys, and bald eagles, among others. On October 8, 2020, more than 1400 sharp-shinned hawks and almost 1200 kestrels poured across the point. In the fall of 2020 Audubon volunteers counted more than 4000 ospreys, almost 500 bald eagles, and 700 peregrine falcons, with almost 100 of them peregrinating through on only one day, October 7. I caught a beautiful fall day there in 2019, and it was exhilarating. The raptors never stopped for many hours.

The observation deck is perched alongside Bunker Pond, part of a saltwater marsh complex. In the pond are a large and often crowded contingent of geese, swans, widgeons, teals, gadwalls, shovelers, coots, brants, egrets, and herons. And between the pond and the deck is shrubby growth that is usually bouncing with sparrows of several species plus cardinals, chickadees, titmice, migrating warblers of many kinds, orioles, mockingbirds, and more.

Monarchs: Icing on the Cake

The icing on nature's cake is that migrating monarch butterflies are also funneled to Cape May Point, and they gather here alongside the songbirds. In the bushes in front of you could be several species of warblers plus a few monarchs. I've even seen stray monarchs here in mid-November, who sadly likely did not make it to Mexico. At this crucial butterfly stopover, New Jersey Audubon also conducts a monarch census.

So at the observation platform, you never know where to look: up at the hawks, out toward the pond at the duck show, or in front of you to find the orange-crowned warbler. You'll likely suffer from a wonderful case of whip-lash after a full day at Cape May Point.

Like Hawk Mountain, park yourself near the Audubon staff and listen to them talk. When they yell "eagle," see where they point. Ask questions. Tell them your level of birding and what you would like to see. Ask them what kind of day it has been or what's been seen thus far. They'll typically have field guides for you to thumb through, a whiteboard list of their sightings, high-end binoculars for you to test drive, and sighting scopes for up-close looks at rarer birds.

When you'd like a break, there is a loop trail that leaves from near the observation deck and circles around Bunker Pond through the adjoining forest. Just beyond the adjoining pavilion, look for the sign that reads Nature Trail and take that path. While there are several colored trails, the Red Trail takes you to more birdwatching stops along the lake system, then connects back to its yellow- and blue-blazed sisters. Both the Yellow Trail and Blue Trail circle back, the latter just takes longer doing so. The Yellow Trail is an easy 1-mile loop that skirts the rear of Bunker Pond, where you can see more ducks. The last stretch parallels the beach, allowing you to pop over the dunes to grab gulls and sandpipers too.

As add-ons, the state runs a nature center at the opposite end of the parking lot from the observation deck, with exhibits on both human and natural history. The adjourning lighthouse offers tours, and the Cape May Bird Observatory is only 1 mile from here. Lastly, Sunset Beach is not far from here either: catch the sunset and buy some wave-action-smoothed quartz pebbles dubbed "Cape May diamonds" in its cheesy tourist shops.

Morning Flight

New Jersey Audubon also operates the Morning Flight songbird count at Higbee Beach, a preserved forest of several hundred acres on Delaware Bay just a few miles north of Cape May Point. There, an Audubon staffer counts birds starting at sunrise from mid-August through November 15. National Geographic calls the beach "a front-row seat to a feathered fashion show," and it is. On the last day of the count in 2020, the counter spotted 8800 birds of sixty species, including 1600 black scoters, more than 1400 each of robins and goldfinches, 900 red-winged blackbirds, and 900 northern gannets. The day before that, weather conditions were such that 27,400 birds were counted that morning, including a whopping 8400 goldfinches. Crossbills, rare in Wild Philly, were counted both days.

Staying the weekend allows you to visit both the hawk-watching and Morning Flight stations. Or perhaps visit Morning Flight early and first, and then head over to watch the raptors. Like we said: So. Many. Birds.

NATURALIST ADVISORY TEAM

Huge thanks are due to the following individuals, who provided wonderful input into both the species that define Wild Philly and the field trips that should be included in this book.

Isabella Betancourt, Curatorial Assistant, Department of Entomology, Academy of Natural Sciences of Drexel University, Philadelphia, PA

Bernard "Billy" Brown, columnist for *Grid* magazine and cohost of the "Urban Wildlife" podcast

Tony Croasdale, Environmental Education Program Specialist, Cobbs Creek Community Environmental Center, Philadelphia Parks & Recreation, Philadelphia, PA

PattiAnn Cutter, Assistant Director-Naturalist, Silver Lake Nature Center, Bristol, PA

Eduardo Duenas, Manager of School Programs, Schuylkill Center for Environmental Education, Philadelphia, PA

Mark Fallon, Director and Senior Naturalist, Briar Bush Nature Center, Abington, PA

Trish Fries, Environmental Education Program Specialist, Wissahickon Environmental Center, Philadelphia Parks & Recreation, Philadelphia, PA

Keith Russell, Program Manager, Urban Conservation, Audubon Mid-Atlantic, Philadelphia, PA

ACKNOWLEDGMENTS

In addition to the Naturalist Advisory Team, big thanks to the staff and trustees of the Schuylkill Center for Environmental Education for their support during this project. I look forward to sharing this with all of you.

Huge thanks to the many photographers whose stunning work graces these pages, especially Doug Wechsler, Willard Terry, Troy Bynum, Christian Hunold, and Chris Muller.

For the geology chapter, retired science teacher Sarah West was incredibly generous with her time in both being interviewed and giving the geology chapter a close read, all so appreciated.

Adam De Paul, a Lenape Storykeeper and Temple University instructor, was instrumental in helping me with the Lenape chapter, carefully reading and commenting on the text. In addition, Alexander R. O'Gorman, Ph.D., author of a dissertation on the Teedyuscung statue in Wissahickon Valley Park, commented on that section of the chapter. I am indebted to both.

Sandy Sorlien, an expert on the Schuylkill Navigation System, offered her expertise on the Manayunk Canal Towpath walk.

Thanks to the Entomology Department of the Academy of Natural Sciences of Drexel University for their help in selecting twenty invertebrates for the 101 species section; they were incredibly insightful in this work.

Natural Lands was extremely responsive and helpful in so many ways. Big thanks to Dan Barringer and Sean Quinn, preserve managers at the Crow's Nest and ChesLen Preserves, respectively, for their generosity of time and interest. Thanks also to Kelly Herrenkohl, Vice President for Communications and Engagement, for her advice and support.

Thanks as well to the staff and volunteers at all of the sites who commented on and corrected the trip descriptions while contributing photos of their special places.

Dr. Woodward S. "Woody" Bousquet, an expert naturalist and retired professor of environmental studies, not to mention a great friend, offered tons of insights and thoughts on the book from its inception and served as proofreader on several sections.

I am indebted to everyone at Timber Press, especially Will McKay for approaching me with the idea for *Wild Philly* and then shepherding me into the process; managing editor Mike Dempsey took the project home. Lisa Brousseau's copy editing, Sarah Milhollin's photo editing, Sarah Crumb's layout and design, and Melissa McFeeters's illustrations are all impossibly wonderful. Thank you all.

My wife, Gari, and daughters, Hannah Zoe and Molly, all great nature walkers, were so helpful for so much of the writing of this book, especially for moral support and insights.

PHOTO & ILLUSTRATION CREDITS

All illustrations by Melissa McFeeters

Alamy / Jerry Sheets, page 63
Daniel Barends, page 37
Bartram's Garden, pages 60 (right), 261–262
John Beatty, page 325
Biodiversity Heritage Library, page 50 (left)
Bowman's Hill Wildflower Preserve, pages 244–246
Briar Bush Nature Center, pages 329–330
Pete Brown and Bartram's Garden, page 260
Troy Bynum, pages 57 (top), 71, 100 (bottom right), 165, 187, 188, 203, 221, 254 (left), 269–270, 286–289, 291,
Pam Cloud, page 313
Crow's Nest Preserve, page 284
Rosalie Dutton, page 28
Fairmount Park Conservancy, page 23
Forest History Society, Durham, NC, page 43
Free Library of Philadelphia, pages 24, 60 (left)
Peter Gkonos, pages 2, 305
Jamie Graves, page 59
Mark Henninger, page 39
Dave Herasimtchuk / Freshwaters Illustrated, page 79 (right)
Holm, T. Campanius (1834), "Description of the province of New Sweden: Now called, by the English, Pennsylvania, in America." Philadelphia: M'Carty & Davis, Hathi Trust Digital Library, page 33
Winslow Homer (American, 1836–1910). Chestnutting, 1870. Wood engraving, Sheet: 11¾ × 8¾ in. (29.8 × 22.2 cm). Brooklyn Museum, Gift of Harvey Isbitts, 1998.105.157, page 44
Wes Hughes, Batsto Village, page 346
Christian Hunold, pages 7 (top row), 57 (bottom), 200, 202, 254 (right)
Alison Joyce, page 282
Arthur Klotz, page 304
Dave Lamb, page 303
Larry Niles Wildlife Restoration Partnerships, pages 341–343
Emma Lee / WHYY, page 55 (right)
The Library Company of Philadelphia, Print Department. #Log 2794.D.opp69 Landing of Penn. Dock Creek. Breton, William L., ca. 1773–1855, artist. Holden, Thomas, publisher, page 16

Library of Congress, page 17
Library of Congress, Geography and Maps Division #gm71000933. Nicole, Pierre, -1784, and John Montrésor. A survey of the city of Philadelphia and its environs shewing the...16th November. [?,1777] Map, page 19
Library of Congress, Prints & Photographs Division #HAER PA,51-PHILA,328-174 (CT). Jack E. Boucher, page 21
Bradley Maule, page 333
Melissa McCormick, Smithsonian Environmental Research Center, page 74 (bottom right)
Courtesy The Met Museum. 'Benjamin Franklin' Designed and engraved by Charles Willson Peale. Bequest of Charles Allen Munn, 1924. Accession Number: 24.90.52, page 61
Harriet Morton, page 10
Christopher Muller / BeaversMatter.org, pages 7 (bottom), 55 (left), 211–212, 219, 235, 237, 337
Fine Arts Museum of San Francisco, Gift of Mr. and Mrs. John D. Rockefeller 3rd, 1993.35.22, page 67
National Portrait Gallery, Smithsonian Institution; gift of Betty A. and Lloyd G. Schermer. #NPG.99.167.44 J. T. Bowen Lithography Company, after painting by Gustavus Hesselius, page 35
Natural Lands, page 283
Natural Lands, Mae Axelrod, pages 277, 279 (left)
Natural Lands, Sean Quinn, page 278
Natural Lands, Mark Williams, page 231
njhiking.com, page 347
Map data © OpenStreetMap contributors, page 228
"Pensilvania", 1690, by cartographer John Seller, image purchased from Barry Ruderman, Barry Lawrence Ruderman Antique Maps Inc., raremaps.com, page 15
"Philadelphia in 1702", The Miriam and Ira D. Wallach Division of Art, Prints and Photographs: Print Collection, The New York Public Library Digital Collections, page 18
Copyright Philadelphia Parks & Recreation, page 47 (right)
Philadelphia Water Department, page 75

Charles Ragucci, page 41 (top)
Rancocas Nature Center, pages 299, 301
Record Group 10, Office of the Governor, Governor Robert P. Casey, Proclamations (series #10.3), Courtesy of Pennsylvania Historical and Museum Commission, Pennsylvania State Archives, page 45
Marissa Smith, Bowman's Hill Wildflower Preserve, page 9
Smithsonian Library from the Biodiversity Heritage Library, page 65 (right)
Sandy Sorlien, pages 295–297
The State Museum of Pennsylvania, page 51
Judy Stepenaskie, page 258
Lauren Stites from Where Wild Kids Wander, page 332
Willard Terry, pages 76, 106, 114–115, 126, 127 (right), 129 (left), 130, 137 (top), 241, 293
Timber Press / Kevin McConnell, page 95
Charles Uniatowski, pages 27, 292, 334
Doug Wechsler, pages 11 (top), 49, 56, 68, 72, 99, 100 (left column and top right), 102, 104–105, 107–108, 110, 112–113, 116–120, 122–125, 127 (left), 129 (right), 132–136, 138–143, 145 (top), 147–149, 150 (bottom), 152, 154, 156, 158 (bottom left), 161–163, 168, 171–184, 188–191, 195, 197–198, 201, 204–206, 209 (bottom right), 216, 223, 225, 238, 265, 272, 315–317, 349, 355
Courtesy of The White House Historical Association. John James Audubon by John Syme, 1826, oil on canvas, page 65 (left)
wiki-Alphageekpa, page 309
Alexander Wilson, American Ornithology; or The natural history of the birds of the United States, 1808–1814, page 62
Woodford Cedar Run Wildlife Refuge, pages 320–321

Flickr
jerbirdie, pages 328, 329
Bonnie Ott, page 279 (right)
Katja Schulz, page 153
Robert Taylor, page 85 (bottom)
Nicholas A. Tonelli, page 41 (bottom)

INDEX

Betsy Brody

Naturalist **Mike Weilbacher** has directed the Schuylkill Center for Environmental Education in Philadelphia's Upper Roxborough neighborhood since 2011. An environmental educator with a passion for monarch butterflies, dragonflies, goldenrod, and trillium, Mike has more than 40 years of experience teaching through lectures, field trips, writings, and even theater and radio, his work earning him the Keystone Award from the Pennsylvania Association of Environmental Educators and the title of "Citizen Hero" from *The Philadelphia Inquirer*.

Since 1982, he has traveled the country performing a unique style of participatory environmental theater where he turns his audiences into thunderstorms, hatching tadpoles, even photosynthesizing trees. Mike has presented at nature centers, parks, schools, community festivals, churches, and museums across the country and has been a featured performer and keynote speaker at innumerable education conferences.

He's also been "Mike the All-Natural Science Guy" on WXPN-FM's children's radio show "Kid's Corner" for more than 30 years. He's written a weekly column on nature and the environment for more than 20 years, in addition to op-ed essays, book reviews, and magazine articles for local and national publications.